Technology for Societal Transformation

Lawal O. Yesufu • Puteri Nor Ellyza Nohuddin
Editors

Technology for Societal Transformation

Exploring the Intersection of Information Technology and Societal Development

Springer

Editors
Lawal O. Yesufu
Hult International Business School
Dubai, United Arab Emirates

Puteri Nor Ellyza Nohuddin
Institute of Visual Informatics
University Kebangsaan Malaysia
Bangi, Malaysia

ISBN 978-981-96-1720-3 ISBN 978-981-96-1721-0 (eBook)
https://doi.org/10.1007/978-981-96-1721-0

This Springer imprint is published by the registered company Springer Nature Singapore Pte Ltd.
The registered company address is: 152 Beach Road, #21-01/04 Gateway East, Singapore 189721, Singapore

Contents

The Impact of Information Technology on Societal Transformation

Lawal O. Yesufu and Sami Alajlani

Abstract This chapter explores information technology's (IT) transformative role in fostering societal growth and addressing challenges across various sectors, including education, entrepreneurship, healthcare, and rural development. By harnessing digital tools such as big data, artificial intelligence (AI), and digital platforms, IT promotes social inclusion, enhances access to resources, and supports sustainable development efforts globally. The study is closely aligned with key Sustainable Development Goals (SDGs), notably Quality Education (SDG 4), Decent Work and Economic Growth (SDG 8), and Peace, Justice, and Strong Institutions (SDG 16). This chapter uses theoretical frameworks and real-world case studies to demonstrate how IT empowers marginalised communities, stimulates political engagement, and fosters digital entrepreneurship, particularly in underserved regions. Additionally, the study delves into significant challenges such as digital inequality, cybersecurity risks, and ethical considerations surrounding AI and big data. It highlights the importance of cooperation among policymakers, technologists, and civil society to ensure the ethical and equitable implementation of IT for sustainable societal transformation.

1 Introduction

This chapter provides an overview of the revolutionary role that information technology (IT) plays in promoting social growth and change in various fields, such as entrepreneurship, healthcare, political action, education, and rural development. It looks at how digital tools and platforms impact society by increasing access to resources, encouraging diversity, and supporting sustainable development. The

L. O. Yesufu (✉)
Hult International Business School, Dubai, UAE
e-mail: Lawal.Yesufu@Faculty.Hult.edu

S. Alajlani
Higher Colleges of Technology, Sharjah, UAE

L. O. Yesufu, P. N. E. Nohuddin (eds.), *Technology for Societal Transformation*,
https://doi.org/10.1007/978-981-96-1721-0_1

chapter emphasises the potential of IT to empower marginalised communities, bridge social divides, and help achieve key Sustainable Development Goals (SDGs) like Decent Work and Economic Growth (SDG 8), Quality Education (SDG 4), and Peace, Justice, and Strong Institutions (SDG 16). It does this by looking at theoretical frameworks and real-world case studies, fostering a sense of empathy and understanding. The chapter also discusses cybersecurity, ethical issues with AI and big data, and difficulties related to digital inequality. It underscores the vital need for cooperation between legislators, educators, technologists, and civil society to ensure that the advantages of IT are equitable, moral, and long-lasting. This shared responsibility is crucial in promoting societal transformation. The conversations that follow in the book, which go more deeply into the relationship between IT and social reform, are built upon the foundations laid in this chapter.

Information technology (IT) has emerged as a potent force for societal transformation in today's linked world, influencing many facets of human existence, from politics and enterprise to healthcare and education. The emergence of digital platforms, big data, artificial intelligence (AI), and social media has opened new avenues for communities and people to solve urgent social issues, enhance quality of life, and get resources. Given our position at the nexus of societal growth and technical innovation, we must comprehend how IT is influencing the modern world and how it may promote constructive societal transformation.

IT is revolutionary, particularly in promoting inclusion, democratising information access, and empowering historically marginalised populations. Technologies such as artificial intelligence (AI), digital entrepreneurship, and education technology (EdTech) provide workable answers to issues, including uneven access to high-quality education, employment prospects, and political representation (Yesufu & Alajlani, 2019). With the right tools and resources, communities can fully engage in the global economy and support sustainable development, bridging significant social gaps.

Information technology (IT) is linked with the Sustainable Development Goals (SDGs) of the United Nations, which aim to solve global issues, including poverty, inequality, and climate change, highlighting the technology's significance to modern society. SDGs like SDG 4 (Quality Education), SDG 8 (Decent Work and Economic Growth), and SDG 9 (Industry, Innovation, and Infrastructure) are all directly supported by several IT applications, including EdTech, AI, and digital entrepreneurship (Gómez & Yesufu, 2022). For instance, digital platforms have transformed learning settings in education by offering adaptable and scalable ways to close the educational gap, particularly in marginalised populations (Yesufu, 2021). These resources support lifelong learning and improve learning outcomes, which contributes to accomplishing SDG 4's objectives.

Another crucial area where IT significantly influences is digital entrepreneurship, which has allowed people to start and expand enterprises in ways never seen before. The emergence of digital technologies and e-commerce platforms has made it possible for businesses, especially those in developing nations, to reach international markets and generate new revenue streams. Digital entrepreneurship promotes economic development and employment creation by removing conventional obstacles to entry, such as geographic location and financial availability (Yesufu & Alajlani, 2022). This is in line with SDG 8. This empowerment is essential for marginalised areas where conventional means of enterprise may not have been available.

Technology is also essential for facilitating political engagement and giving voice to those who would not otherwise be heard. For example, social media platforms are becoming effective instruments for coordinating political activities, spreading awareness, and inspiring people to support social justice and change. Notable instances of how digital platforms have empowered people to confront repressive institutions and demand responsibility from governments include the Arab Spring and the #EndSARS campaign in Nigeria. This aligns with SDG 16, which aims to enhance openness and accountability via digital technologies to promote peace, justice, and strong institutions (Yesufu & Alajlani, 2019).

Furthermore, society will be significantly impacted by AI's incorporation into many industries. AI is revolutionising sectors such as business, education, and healthcare by providing new means of process optimisation and improved decision-making. AI-powered diagnostic technologies, for instance, are improving medical accessibility and accuracy in remote places where healthcare experts are hard to come by (Yesufu, 2021). These uses exemplify how AI may enhance service delivery while promoting social inclusion by facilitating equal access to resources.

In conclusion, IT's revolutionary potential to tackle pressing social issues is not denied. IT has become a crucial instrument in forming our modern society, from enhancing educational performance to encouraging digital enterprise and permitting political involvement. Technology's potential to support social justice and sustainable development will only increase as it develops further. The following parts will examine how IT interacts with various industries, stressing the possibilities, difficulties, and practical uses that show how IT may lead to constructive societal change.

2 Information Technology and Societal Transformation

2.1 Theoretical Underpinnings

Significant changes in a society's social structure and cultural standards throughout time are referred to as societal transformation. Information technology (IT) has vastly accelerated these shifts, enabling new political, economic, and communication kinds to emerge. Theorists such as Castells (2009) and Van Dijk (2020) have postulated that the Internet and digital networks have played a pivotal role in the transformation of societies, resulting in the formation of what is commonly called the "network society". This term describes restructuring social and economic structures around digital networks that facilitate decentralised communication and quick information exchange.

In societal transformation, IT is often seen as having two sides. On the one hand, technology makes knowledge and resources more accessible to everybody, which encourages greater social inclusion. However, technology may also make inequality worse for those who do not have access to digital infrastructure and capabilities. According to Castells (2009), IT can empower people and organisations by improving their capacity for innovation and teamwork. However, underprivileged groups may become even more marginalised without fair access because of the digital divide. Van Dijk's (2020) research delves into the socioeconomic aspects of digital inequality and its impediment to broader societal change, reinforcing this notion.

2.2 *IT as a Social Transformation Catalyst*

Information technology plays a pivotal role in societal revolution by altering the social, political, and economic spheres. For instance, IT has completely changed how information is disseminated in education, increasing accessibility and scalability. Yesufu and Alajlani (2019) show how IT may spur social innovation by discussing how introducing digital platforms in refugee camps has opened new avenues for resource development and education. These platforms provide educational possibilities that would not be possible in such limited settings, fostering long-term social growth and educational equality.

From the rise of digital entrepreneurship, conventional business models in the business sector have been reinterpreted, allowing people from various backgrounds to engage in the global economy. The emergence of e-commerce platforms has facilitated the ability of entrepreneurs from marginalised areas to surmount financial and geographic obstacles, hence promoting economic independence and social mobility (Yesufu & Alajlani, 2022). The increased involvement of young people and women in digital entrepreneurship, especially in underdeveloped nations with limited access to conventional economic prospects, indicates this shift (Kabeer, 2020). These changes emphasise how effective IT can be as a weapon for social transformation and economic development.

Information technology has also had a significant impact on politics. Social media platforms have fostered political involvement and coordinated social movements. Research conducted in 2017 by Tufekci and in 2016 by Margetts has shown how digital platforms like Facebook and Twitter have made it possible to coordinate large-scale demonstrations and disseminate information quickly. Social movements such as #BlackLivesMatter, #MeToo, and the Arab Spring have shown how IT can elevate under-represented perspectives and promote international dialogue on justice and equality. These digital platforms have created new avenues for political participation but have also brought problems with polarisation, surveillance, and disinformation.

2.3 Technology and Social Development

"Social development" describes initiatives meant to enhance people's quality of life and general well-being, especially regarding economic opportunities, healthcare, and education. Due to its ability to provide creative answers to complex societal problems, information technology has been a primary facilitator of social growth. Predictive learning analytics is a well-known example of how higher education maximises student achievement and improves educational results (Yesufu, 2021). Educational institutions may improve retention and graduation rates by identifying at-risk students early and providing them with customised treatments using big data and machine learning algorithms.

Through programs that support digital inclusion, IT has significantly promoted social development in rural communities. For example, mobile technology has bridged the divide between urban and rural populations by providing healthcare and education services to distant areas. Gómez and Yesufu (2022) demonstrate in their work how mobile learning platforms have changed education in Africa's rural areas, where conventional infrastructure is lacking. These platforms support the communities' long-term socioeconomic growth by giving children high-quality instruction and resources.

Furthermore, IT has been essential in advancing social entrepreneurship, especially in developing nations. Thanks to digital technologies, social entrepreneurs may now grow their businesses and provide solutions for regional issues such as access to clean water, healthcare, and education. Yunus et al. (2010) claim that IT may serve as a catalyst for social innovation, enabling company owners to create long-lasting business models that meet societal demands. This strategy achieves social justice, environmental sustainability objectives, and economic development.

2.4 Alignment with the Sustainable Development Goals (SDGs) of the United Nations

The UN's Sustainable Development Goals (SDGs) are closely aligned with the transformational influence of IT, especially in infrastructure development, economic growth, and education. IT directly promotes SDG 4 (Quality Education) by providing EdTech solutions and digital learning platforms, highlighting the need for accessible and equal access to education. These resources benefit low-resource environments because they can overcome obstacles such as a lack of qualified instructors or physical infrastructure (Yesufu & Alajlani, 2019).

The digital revolution of industry and entrepreneurship also contributes to the achievement of SDG 8, which is Decent Work and Economic Growth. Particularly in underprivileged areas, digital platforms provide new possibilities for economic involvement and employment development since they reduce business entry barriers (Yesufu & Alajlani, 2022). Young people and women in underdeveloped nations should pay particular attention to this, where conventional career possibilities may be limited.

Lastly, building robust infrastructure and encouraging inclusive and sustainable industrialisation and innovation are all part of SDG 9 (Industry, Innovation, and Infrastructure). Since digital technologies provide the groundwork for novel business models, cutting-edge goods, and effective services that may promote sustainable development, IT is a crucial facilitator of this objective. Cutting-edge technologies such as blockchain, artificial intelligence, and big data are being used to address societal issues, including waste reduction, supply chain optimisation, optimisation, and transparency (Gómez & Yesufu, 2022).

3 Prospects and Challenges

Integrating information technology (IT) into various industries has made significant prospects for societal transformation, innovation, and development possible. However, it also comes with several difficulties, especially regarding ethics, security, and access. This section examines how IT may promote social growth and transformation and the issues that must be resolved to guarantee fair and long-lasting results.

3.1 Prospects

Creating Inclusivity and Bridging Digital Divides Technology can close the digital divide, fostering social inclusion and guaranteeing marginalised access to vital resources. This is one of the most significant possibilities that IT presents. Because EdTech solutions make high-quality educational resources accessible in underprivileged and rural areas, they have revolutionised education (Yesufu & Alajlani, 2019). Students in low-resource environments may now access the same educational possibilities as their counterparts in metropolitan areas, thanks to mobile learning platforms and online educational resources like those created by Coursera and Khan Academy (Yesufu, 2021). Digital platforms' ability to cross geographical and socioeconomic barriers promotes greater educational fairness.

Another area with enormous promise is the use of IT in rural development. According to Gómez and Yesufu (2022), mobile technology and the Internet have emerged as vital resources for enhancing access to education and fostering economic development in Sub-Saharan African rural areas. Digital platforms, for instance, provide farmers access to market data, allow them to exchange best practices, and link them with suppliers and buyers; these benefits lead to the potential for rural development and poverty reduction (Aker & Mbiti, 2010).

Digital Solutions' Scalability and Accessibility Traditional methods cannot match the scale and accessibility provided by digital tools and platforms. For example, digital entrepreneurship enables people to start companies with little physical infrastructure, opening markets to entrepreneurs from various backgrounds. This is especially important in poorer nations with limited conventional corporate resources. Thanks to platforms such as Shopify, Amazon, and Jumia, small firms may expand their e-commerce operations without significant upfront investments in physical locations (OECD, 2019).

Furthermore, AI-driven technology provides scalable solutions in industries such as healthcare and education. AI in healthcare may help doctors in remote locations with limited resources by offering diagnostic tools (Yesufu, 2021). Large datasets may be processed rapidly and effectively by AI-driven systems, which can improve results, save operating costs, and improve service delivery. Similarly, Yesufu (2021) describes predictive learning analytics in higher education as using AI to detect at-risk students so that timely interventions may be made to enhance academic performance and retention.

Artificial Intelligence, Blockchain, and Big Data as Social Innovations Modern technologies with enormous promise for solving social issues include big data analytics, blockchain, and artificial intelligence (AI). Healthcare is one industry in which AI is already revolutionising illness diagnosis, treatment recommendations, and operational efficiency improvements. For instance, AI-driven chatbots and diagnostic instruments have been used in remote clinics to provide medical services in resource-constrained environments, enhancing treatment quality and accessibility (Yesufu & Alajlani, 2022).

The social and commercial sectors are also seeing a rise in the use of blockchain technology. Blockchain has been used in the social sector to increase supply chain management and enhance distribution transparency, ensuring that resources reach their intended users without risking corruption (Kshetri, 2017). According to Tapscott and Tapscott (2016), blockchain's decentralised IT is an effective instrument for enhancing transparency, lowering election fraud, and boosting accountability in public administration.

Conversely, big data is used to tackle various societal issues, such as monitoring and reacting to public health emergencies and improving urban planning. By analysing massive datasets, organisations may make data-driven choices that increase efficiency and direct resources to where they are analysing (Mayer-Schönberger & Cukier, 2013). Big data is essential for social good since it has been used for criminal prevention, public health monitoring, and disaster response.

3.2 Challenges

Inequalities in Digital Access and Inequality While information technology has much potential for social transformation, the digital gap remains a significant obstacle. The unequal distribution of access to digital technology is known as "digital inequality", and it often reflects already existing socioeconomic gaps. Globally, high-speed Internet, digital gadgets, and digital literacy are unequal, especially across industrialised nations and urban and rural regions (Van Dijk, 2020). The digital divide worsens healthcare, education, and economic prospects, especially in areas with inadequate Internet access.

While digital platforms in education, for instance, provide scalable solutions, students in low-income and rural locations often encounter obstacles such as poor digital skills, unstable energy, and a lack of Internet connection (Yesufu & Alajlani, 2019). As a result of this digital exclusion, there is a divide between those who can fully engage in the digital economy and others who are left behind.

Concerns about Data Privacy and Cybersecurity Cybersecurity issues have grown in tandem with the growing integration of digital technology into social and economic processes. The dangers of identity theft, data breaches, and cyberattacks increase as societies become increasingly dependent on digital platforms for essential services such as banking, healthcare, and education. A sobering reminder of the vulnerabilities in digital infrastructures is that worldwide cybercrime damages were estimated to exceed $6 trillion annually by 2021 in 2020 alone (Morgan, 2020).

Data privacy is yet another urgent issue. Due to the growth of big data and AI, large volumes of personal data are being gathered and processed, raising questions about how this data is utilised. Data ethics and cybersecurity have gained prominence in public discourse due to privacy violations, data breaches, and the improper use of personal information for political manipulation (such as the Cambridge Analytica incident) (Zuboff, 2019). It is a crucial balancing act to guarantee that digital platforms prioritise data while promoting innovation.

Ethics in Artificial Intelligence and Big Data Using AI and big data also raises significant ethical questions about accountability, prejudice, and discrimination. When AI systems are trained on biased data, they may make judgements that disproportionately impact the marginalised, thereby perpetuating already existing inequities (Noble, 2018). For instance, racial biases in face recognition software have been shown to result in incorrect identification and discriminatory actions (Buolamwini & Gebru, 2018).

Furthermore, accountability and transparency are questioned when AI is used in decision-making processes. According to O'Neil (2016), algorithms often function as "black boxes", making it challenging to comprehend how choices are produced and to hold systems responsible for mistakes or biased results. The increasing prevalence of AI calls for the urgent development of ethical frameworks that guarantee accountability, transparency, and equity in using these technologies.

3.3 The Way Ahead

To fully utilise information technology for societal transformation, it is imperative to tackle the issues of digital inequality, cybersecurity, and ethics. Collaboration among policymakers, educators, technologists, and civil society organisations guarantees that digital breakthroughs adhere to ethical standards, are safe, and promote inclusivity. This would include creating robust legal and ethical frameworks to safeguard individual rights, advance transparency in the digital era, and increase access to digital infrastructure.

4 Real-World Cases

This section examines case studies showing how information technology (IT) has been used to promote societal transformation in various fields, such as healthcare, entrepreneurship, education, political action, and rural development. These real-world IT applications demonstrate IT's transformational power and shed light on the possibilities and problems associated with using technology to promote social development.

4.1 Case Study 1: Technology in Education and Social Transformation

Context The education industry has seen a change thanks to education technology (EdTech), which has made learning materials more accessible, made remote learning possible, and made it possible to continue studying even during emergencies like the COVID-19 pandemic (World Bank, 2020). EdTech's capacity to close the educational gap between urban and rural areas and provide children access to the same quality education no matter where they live is one of its most revolutionary features.

For instance, in Sub-Saharan Africa, mobile learning platforms are crucial in enhancing students' access to education in remote places. Nearly 10 million students in 14 countries get educational information via SMS and web-based platforms via Kenya-based mobile platform Eneza Education (Eneza Education, 2021). Eneza can reach students needing access to cell phones or dependable Internet using low-tech methods like SMS.

Impact The scalability of mobile learning platforms like Eneza Education has enhanced marginalised students' access to high-quality education without the requirement for physical infrastructure. This program has advanced Sustainable

Development Goal 4 (Quality Education) and increased social inclusion by raising literacy and academic achievement in rural communities (Yesufu & Alajlani, 2019).

4.2 Case Study 2: Empowerment via Digital Entrepreneurship and Economic

Context In developing nations where conventional business models are unavailable, digital entrepreneurship has become a potent instrument for economic emancipation. With the help of digital platforms, entrepreneurs may launch and grow their companies on a shoestring budget, tap into international markets, and overcome conventional obstacles such as a lack of formal financial institutions or remote locations (OECD, 2019).

Example Local business owners can now offer their goods to customers worldwide because of the growth of e-commerce platforms like Jumia, the biggest online retailer in Africa. Jumia provides a platform for small and medium-sized businesses (SMEs) in nations such as Kenya and Nigeria to list and sell goods online, promoting employment development and economic growth (Jumia Group, 2021). These digital platforms have allowed company owners to expand their operations and make money without needing physical shopfronts by giving them access to a broader market.

Impact By encouraging job creation, empowering women and young entrepreneurs, and advancing financial inclusion, digital entrepreneurship platforms like Jumia have entirely changed the economic landscape in Africa (Kabeer, 2020). Sustainable Development Goal 8 (Decent Work and Economic Development) emphasises the significance of inclusive economic development and gainful work for everyone, which aligns with this.

4.3 Case Study 3: Political Activism and Social Media

Context Social media has emerged as a vital instrument for societal transformation and political activity, empowering people to band together, spread awareness, and demand political responsibility. Digital platforms such as Facebook, Instagram, and Twitter have mobilised people for advocacy campaigns, making the quick dissemination of information possible (Tufekci, 2017).

Example In Nigeria, the #EndSARS campaign, which sought to stop police brutality by the Special Anti-Robbery Squad (SARS), is one of the most well-known instances of social media-driven activism. Social media platforms became the campaign's focal point as activists disseminated information about police misbehaviour and coordinated nationwide demonstrations. The campaign gained international support and pressured the Nigerian government to act by leveraging social media to reach a worldwide audience (Akerele-Popoola et al., 2022).

Impact Disenfranchised populations now have a forum to speak out against repressive regimes and promote social justice thanks to social media, which has magnified their voices. The SARS unit was forced to disband because of the #EndSARS campaign, proving the ability of online activism to influence political change. By encouraging accountability and openness in government, this scenario also emphasises how to achieve Sustainable Development Goal 16 (Peace, Justice, and Strong Institutions).

4.4 Case Study 4: Applications of AI in Rural Healthcare and Society

Context Artificial intelligence (AI) is revolutionising healthcare globally by improving patient care and diagnostic precision. AI-driven solutions can close gaps in medical services and provide underprivileged people with quick access to treatment in rural locations, where access to healthcare is often restricted (Topol, 2019).

Example In rural India, AI-powered diagnostic tools have been used to help medical professionals diagnose conditions including diabetic retinopathy and tuberculosis (TB). Healthcare professionals may now make educated judgements without specialised access to AI algorithms that analyse medical and patient data to deliver reliable diagnoses (Mabrouk, 2021). Mobile health units that visit isolated areas are equipped with AI-driven platforms that provide on-site diagnosis and treatment suggestions.

Impact The use of AI in rural healthcare has improved patient outcomes by facilitating faster and more accurate diagnoses, relieving pressure on overburdened healthcare systems, and expanding access to medical treatments in underprivileged areas (Yesufu, 2021). Promoting health equality and guaranteeing even distant communities access to high-quality healthcare are two other ways AI-driven healthcare systems support Sustainable Development Goal 3 (Good Health and Well-Being).

4.5 Case Study 5: Using Technology to Improve Rural and Education

Context In areas with limited access to conventional educational infrastructure, incorporating IT into rural education systems has created a foundation for socioeconomic growth. Closing the educational gap between rural and urban regions via digital platforms, remote learning, and e-learning technologies is facilitating long-term growth.

Example One instance of how IT has been used to enhance education in rural regions is the Nigerian Digital Schools Initiative. By giving rural schools access to digital resources such as tablets, e-learning platforms, and digital textbooks, the program enables students to participate in interactive learning activities that improve academic results (Olanrewaju & Afolabi, 2022). Teachers will also get training on enhancing their teaching skills using digital technologies as part of this effort.

Impact The Digital Schools Initiative has raised academic achievement and increased access to high-quality education in rural Nigeria, resulting in excellent literacy rates. The program encourages social participation and rural development by giving rural kids the same educational chances as their metropolitan counterparts. As noted by Yesufu and Alajlani (2022), this case study is in line with SDG 4 (Quality Education) and SDG 9 (Industry, Innovation, and Infrastructure), which highlight the importance of education and innovation in advancing sustainable development.

5 Final Thoughts

Information technology (IT) integration has shown to be a potent accelerator for social growth and transformation across a range of societal sectors. IT is causing unprecedented change and providing answers to some of the most important social issues facing the globe, from healthcare to education, digital entrepreneurship, political action, and rural development. As this chapter's real-world examples have shown, IT has enormous potential to strengthen government, encourage social inclusion, and empower the economy.

However, there are obstacles to success. Fair access to the advantages of IT is still hampered by the digital divide, especially in underprivileged and rural areas. Although mobile learning platforms and e-commerce solutions have demonstrated potential in closing these gaps, to guarantee that the opportunities brought about by IT are sustainable and inclusive, concerns about digital infrastructure, cybersecurity, data privacy, and artificial intelligence must be addressed (Van Dijk, 2020; Zuboff, 2019).

This chapter's case studies show essential areas in which IT has had a noticeable influence on society. In the field of education, Eneza Education and other platforms have shown how mobile technology may help achieve Sustainable Development Goal 4 (Quality Education) by giving students in rural places access to high-quality learning opportunities, as with Goal 8 of the Sustainable Development Goals (Decent Work and Economic Growth), digital entrepreneurship platforms such as Jumia empower small company owners and generate employment. Goal 16 of the Sustainable Development Agenda (Peace, Justice, and Strong Institutions) may be achieved via IT to amplify marginalised governments responsible, as shown by social media activism such as the #EndSARS campaign.

The emergence of blockchain technology and artificial intelligence (AI) presents significant opportunities for innovation and efficiency. However, these technologies call for careful consideration of their ethical implications, particularly regarding accountability, transparency, and fairness (Noble, 2018; Tapscott & Tapscott, 2016). Healthcare AI applications, such as those seen in rural diagnostic tools in India, provide a preview of how technology might be used to solve critical health issues and advance equitable access to treatment (Topol, 2019). To guarantee ethical deployment, it is necessary to address the bias and accountability problems raised by integrating AI into decision-making processes (O'Neil, 2016).

As technologies advance and become more ingrained in daily life, IT will play an increasingly important role in bringing about societal change. It is the joint responsibility of policymakers, educators, entrepreneurs, and civil society to guarantee that sustainability, inclusion, and transparency direct the implementation of new technologies. Through tackling issues related to digital inequality, maintaining cybersecurity, and promoting moral AI practices, information technology can become a potent tool for social good that may propel sustainable growth and establish a more just and impartial society.

The remainder of the book will further detail the relationship between technology and societal growth, building on the groundwork this chapter has provided for understanding the role of IT in societal transformation. As the book goes on, each chapter will go into more depth about how IT influences government, entrepreneurship, healthcare, and education. It will also provide insights into how these innovations might be used to improve society.

References

Akerele-Popoola, O. E., Azeez, A. L., & Adeniyi, A. (2022). Twitter, civil activists and EndSARS protest in Nigeria as a developing democracy. *Cogent Social Sciences, 8*(1), 2095744.

Buolamwini, J., & Gebru, T. (2018). Gender shades: Intersectional accuracy disparities in commercial gender classification. *Proceedings of Machine Learning Research, 81*, 77–91.

Castells, M. (2009). *Communication power*. Oxford University Press.

Eneza Education. (2021). *Eneza education impact report*. Retrieved from https://enezaeducation.com/impact-report

Gómez, J. M., & Yesufu, L. O. (Eds.). (2022). *Sustainable development through data analytics and innovation: Techniques, processes, models, tools, and practices*. Springer Nature.
Jumia Group. (2021). *Annual report 2021*. Retrieved from https://group.jumia.com
Kabeer, N. (2020). Women's empowerment and economic development: A feminist critique of storytelling practices in "randomista" economics. *Feminist Economics, 26*(2), 1–26.
Kshetri, N. (2017). Will blockchain emerge as a tool to break the poverty chain in the Global South? *Third World Quarterly, 38*(8), 1710–1732.
Mabrouk, M. (2021). AI-driven healthcare solutions for rural India. *Healthcare AI Journal, 5*(3), 52–67.
Mayer-Schönberger, V., & Cukier, K. (2013). *Big data: A revolution that will transform how we live, work, and think*. Houghton Mifflin Harcourt.
Morgan, S. (2020). Cybercrime to cost the world $6 trillion annually by 2021. *Cybersecurity Ventures*. Retrieved from https://cybersecurityventures.com/cybercrime-damages-6-trillion-by-2021/
Noble, S. U. (2018). *Algorithms of oppression: How search engines reinforce racism*. NYU Press.
OECD. (2019). *The digital transformation of SMEs* (OECD Digital Economy Papers, No. 312). OECD Publishing.
Olanrewaju, B. U., & Afolabi, J. A. (2022). Digitising education in Nigeria: Lessons from COVID-19. *International Journal of Technology Enhanced Learning, 14*(4), 402–419.
O'Neil, C. (2016). *Weapons of math destruction: How big data increases inequality and threatens democracy*. Crown.
Tapscott, D., & Tapscott, A. (2016). *Blockchain revolution: How the technology behind Bitcoin is changing money, business, and the world*. Penguin.
Topol, E. J. (2019). *Deep medicine: How artificial intelligence can make healthcare human again*. Basic Books.
Tufekci, Z. (2017). *Twitter and tear gas: The power and fragility of networked protest*. Yale University Press.
Van Dijk, J. (2020). *The network society. SAGE*. Publications.
World Bank. (2020). *The COVID-19 pandemic: Shocks to education and policy responses*. World Bank Group.
Yesufu, L. O. (2021). Predictive learning analytics in higher education. In *Data analytics in marketing, entrepreneurship, and innovation* (pp. 151–173).
Yesufu, L. O., & Alajlani, S. (2019). Measuring social innovation for education and resource development in refugee camps: A conceptual study. *International Journal of Higher Education, 8*(4), 208–220.
Yesufu, L. O., & Alajlani, S. (2022). The impact of business analytics on industry, education, and professional development. In *Sustainable development through data analytics and innovation: Techniques, processes, models, tools, and practices* (pp. 1–16). Springer International Publishing.
Zuboff, S. (2019). *The age of surveillance capitalism: The fight for a human future at the new frontier of power*. Public Affairs.

ChatGPT and Its Societal Impact: Understanding Artificial Intelligence Adoption in Modern Learning Environments Through Integrated Models

Nora Azima Noordin, Pervez Akhtar, Puteri Nor Ellyza Nohuddin, and Ahmad Faisal Hayek

Abstract This chapter investigates the adoption and impact of ChatGPT in higher education, focusing on gender disparities and academic levels within the UAE. Utilizing integrated models such as the technology acceptance model (TAM), social cognitive theory (SCT), and unified theory of acceptance and use of technology (UTAUT), the research explores students' perceptions, frequency of use, task performance, task preference, and behavioral intention. Survey data from 165 university students reveal significant gender differences in perceptions and task preferences, with male students showing greater enthusiasm and usage frequency, while females exhibit caution. The study also finds that academic year influences these factors, though not as significantly as gender. These findings suggest that gender and academic progression are crucial in understanding ChatGPT's educational impact, highlighting the need for targeted interventions to ensure equitable access and benefits across diverse student populations.

1 Introduction

The rapid advancement of artificial intelligence (AI) has led to remarkable achievements, particularly in the development of conversational agents like ChatGPT by OpenAI in 2022. Initially built on the GPT-3.5 architecture, ChatGPT made significant strides in natural language processing, showcasing the ability to understand and generate human-like text. Notable improvements include better contextual understanding and enhanced coherence in responses. These advancements have provided substantial benefits, such as personalized assistance and innovative solutions across various fields. ChatGPT's evolution has been driven by continuous enhancements in its architecture, training data, and fine-tuning techniques. The

N. A. Noordin (✉) · P. Akhtar · P. N. E. Nohuddin · A. F. Hayek
Higher Colleges of Technology, Sharjah, UAE
e-mail: nazima@hct.ac.ae; pakhtar@hct.ac.ae; puteri.ivi@ukm.edu.my; ahayek@hct.ac.ae

L. O. Yesufu, P. N. E. Nohuddin (eds.), *Technology for Societal Transformation*,
https://doi.org/10.1007/978-981-96-1721-0_2

most recent version, GPT-4o, was released in May 2024, introducing features like multi-modal capabilities that enable the model to process audio, vision, and text inputs simultaneously (OpenAI, 2024).

ChatGPT's integration into education has transformative potential, assisting students across various disciplines (Kalla et al., 2023). According to Alawida et al. (2023), its functionalities include language translation, text summarization, and question-answering, making it a versatile educational tool. Additionally, ChatGPT offers prompt and precise feedback on assignments, quizzes, or inquiries aiding students in their academic advancement by promptly guiding and correcting them. Meniado (2023) highlighted that teachers appreciate ChatGPT's rapid responses in the field of English education. Furthermore, integrating ChatGPT into education has demonstrated effectiveness in improving overall learning outcomes, enhancing skills such as computational thinking, creativity, and motivation. For instance, in programming education, students utilizing ChatGPT exhibited significantly improved skills and motivation (Yilmaz et al., 2023). Similarly, in English education, it motivated learners to enhance their reading and writing skills (Meniado, 2023). These applications highlight ChatGPT's versatility in supporting diverse educational tasks, fostering an interactive and engaging learning environment. By integrating ChatGPT into the educational system, institutions can enhance student learning experiences and foster creativity (Ngo, 2023; Tick et al., 2023; Estrada-Araoz et al., 2024; Valova et al., 2024; Almogren et al., 2024).

The social implications of widespread ChatGPT usage are significant. As an AI tool, it can democratize access to information and educational resources, reducing disparities due to geographical and socio-economic factors. ChatGPT also enhances business operations by automating customer service, personalizing interactions, and improving overall customer experience (Baldassarre et al., 2023; Raj et al., 2023). Apart from that, ChatGPT can act as an intelligent medical advisory tool in the healthcare field (Zhao, 2023; Alanzi, 2023). However, it also presents challenges, such as reinforcing existing biases, plagiarism, and misinformation issues which potentially lead to ecological fallacy, cyber-security issues, and diminishing human interaction (Falade, 2024; Oviedo-Trespalacios et al., 2023). The convenience and efficiency of ChatGPT might lead to over-reliance on technology, affecting critical thinking and problem-solving skills. Additionally, privacy concerns and the potential misuse of generated content underscore the need for robust ethical guidelines and user awareness (Wei et al., 2024). While it democratizes information access and empowers individuals lacking specialized expertise, it may inadvertently perpetuate biases in its training data, reinforcing existing inequalities. Concerns about misinformation, plagiarism, and overreliance on AI-generated content are also prominent. As ChatGPT becomes more prevalent, it is crucial to examine its impact on communication, critical thinking, and intellectual autonomy, balancing utility with responsible usage. Moreover, concerns regarding data privacy and security may arise due to the collection and processing of user data by ChatGPT (Sebastian, 2023; Kabak & Kırbaş, 2023).

To contribute to the literature in existing studies, the research rationale of this study is centered on the perspectives of gender disparities and academic levels measured by the year of study of participants, within higher education in the United Arab Emirates (UAE). The acceptance and usage of ChatGPT among university students vary significantly, with gender differences and years of study being key factors. Multiple studies have investigated the impact of gender, academic year, study levels, and academic disciplines on the usage of ChatGPT (Yilmaz et al., 2023; Elshaer et al., 2024; Bouzar et al., 2024; AlBadarin et al., 2023; Raman et al., 2024) and found that there is no difference between gender toward intention to adopt AI-based technology such as ChatGPT. Sentiment analysis findings reveal that both genders acknowledge the potential of ChatGPT, yet male students show greater enthusiasm, while female students exhibit more caution. This difference suggests that males tend to focus on the functional benefits of the technology, whereas females are more concerned with its operational and ethical implications (Raman et al., 2024). When analyzing patterns of using ChatGPT among genders, trends show that female students have a higher frequency than male students (Bouzar et al., 2024). However, the study from Kronberg (2024) indicated contra results. The level of experience which indicated by year of study was lacking in the existing research, which also tends to be one of the important variables to be measured (Strzelecki, 2023). This variance in usage highlights differing comfort levels and trust in AI technology across gender and academic progression, suggesting the need for targeted educational interventions to ensure equitable access and benefits for all students.

The following sections of the chapter introduce the theoretical foundations that have led to the formation of hypotheses. The section provides a visual representation of the proposed research model. Next, the methodology elucidates the techniques employed to gather quantitative data. Additionally, it offers details regarding the implementation of the survey and outlines the characteristics of the respondent involved in the research. Subsequently, the data analysis incorporates the results obtained from statistical analysis. This section presents the findings of the hypothesis testing. Overall, this contribution presents its theoretical and managerial implications. This chapter acknowledges its limitations and proposes potential areas for future investigation.

2 Theoretical Framework and Hypothesis Development

This section discusses prior research related to the topic and emphasizes integrated models used in this study. A theoretical framework has been developed based on the five types of most widely used theories in technology-related research which are technology acceptance model (TAM), social cognitive theory (SCT), unified theory of acceptance and use of technology (UTAUT), expectancy value theory (EVT), and theory of planned behavior (TPB). Each variable in this study represents a factor from each theory as presented in Fig. 1.

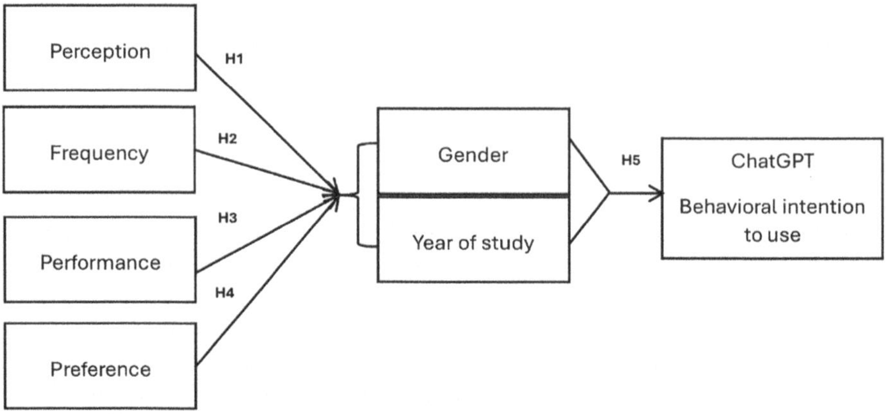

Fig. 1 Theoretical framework of study (author's own work)

2.1 Technology Acceptance Model (TAM)

The "perception" factor in the above theoretical framework represents a variable in TAM model: perceived ease of use (PEOU) and perceived usefulness (PU). PEOU refers to the user's perception of how straightforward and effortless it is to learn and use a particular technology. Essentially, it assesses the perceived complexity or simplicity of interacting with the system. When users find technology that is easy to use, they are more likely to adopt it. Otherwise, PU refers to the degree to which a user believes that a particular technology will enhance their performance or productivity. In other words, it's about understanding the value or utility of using technology. When users perceive a technology as useful, they are more likely to adopt and use it effectively (Davis, 1989).

In the context of adopting ChatGPT, PEOU are examined based on the ease of use to find information, answering user's question, and the user friendliness of the interface. PU are examined based on the enhancing user's ability to learn and assist to find information quickly and easily. As a result of using the tool, user's perception toward ChatGPT can be built based on the PEOU and PU. In this recent study, we are examining the perception of using ChatGPT with the direct impact on gender and the year of study of students in the higher education institution in the UAE. The following hypothesis is proposed:

H1 The perception of using ChatGPT has a direct and significant impact on participants' gender and year of study.

2.2 *Social Cognitive Theory (SCT)*

The "frequency" factor developed by the above framework is influenced by SCT components: behavior, environmental, and personal (Bandura, 1989). One of the components in SCT is behavior with sub-factors known as self-efficacy. Self-efficacy can be thought of as the fuel that powers the engine of human behavior. It refers to an individual's belief in their own capabilities to successfully perform a specific task or achieve a certain goal. These beliefs not only influence the choices people make but also shape their cognitive processes, self-regulatory processes, and the amount of effort they are willing to invest in pursuing their objectives. The theory, an expansion of social learning, incorporates the influence of cognitive processes such as perceptions, judgment, and motivation on both an individual's behavior and the environment that shapes them. This theory posits that individuals do not merely absorb knowledge passively from their surroundings. Instead, social cognitive theory suggests that people play an active role in their learning process by interpreting the results of their actions. This interpretation, in turn, affects their environment and personal factors, thereby influencing and modifying future behavior. As Schunk (2012) elaborates, this reciprocal interaction highlights the dynamic nature of learning, where personal factors, behavioral patterns, and environmental influences are in continuous interplay, each shaping and being shaped by the other.

In the context of this research, the frequency of using ChatGPT is influenced by the individual's belief in their ability to perform specific behavior. High self-efficacy regarding ChatGPT usage could lead to more frequent interactions. The following hypothesis is proposed:

H2 The frequency of using ChatGPT has a direct and significant impact on participants' gender and year of study

2.3 *Unified Theory of Acceptance and Use of Technology (UTAUT)*

The "performance" factor presenting in the research framework mainly referred to the performance expectancy in UTAUT model (Venkatesh et al., 2003). Performance expectancy is a critical component of the unified theory of acceptance and use of technology (UTAUT) model, which refers to the degree to which an individual believes that using a particular technology will help them achieve gains in job performance (Camilleri, 2024). The performance expectancy is measured in various conditions such as improving achievement, motivation to learn the tool, and compatibility in using the technology.

When applied to the use of ChatGPT in this research avenue, performance expectancy can be understood as the user's perception of how effective ChatGPT can assist in enhancing their productivity, efficiency, and overall performance in various tasks. As a result, the following hypothesis is proposed:

H3 The task performance when using ChatGPT has a direct and significant impact on participants' gender and year of study.

2.4 Expectancy-Value Theory (EVT)

The "preference" factor in this research framework is inspired by components in EVT: expectancy and value (Atkinson, 1964). Expectancy refers to an individual's belief about the likelihood of achieving a desired outcome based on their skills, abilities, and the context in which they are operating. When individuals evaluate their preferences, they consider how capable they are of attaining the preferred option. Furthermore, value pertains to the perceived importance or benefits associated with achieving the goal.

EVT posits that students' motivation and subsequent behavior in using ChatGPT are determined by their expectations of success and the value they place on the outcomes of using the technology. This relationship helps explain how preferences for ChatGPT are formed and acted upon in an educational context. Expectancy refers to a student's belief in their ability to successfully use ChatGPT and achieve desirable outcomes. When evaluating their preference for ChatGPT, students consider their perceived competence and prior experiences. Student preferences for ChatGPT are shaped by the interaction between their expectation of success and the value they place on its use. Students who believe they can effectively use ChatGPT (high expectancy) and see significant benefits in its use (high value) will have a strong preference for adopting the tool. For instance, a student confident in their ability to leverage ChatGPT for research and writing tasks and who values academic excellence will likely prefer using it regularly. Thus, the following hypothesis is proposed:

H4 The task preference when using ChatGPT has a direct and significant impact on participants' gender and year of study.

2.5 Theory of Planned Behavior (TPB)

The "behavioral intention to use" factor is stimulated from the component in TPB (Ajzen, 1991). According to the scholar, behavioral intention denotes an individual's readiness to undertake specific actions. These intentions are considered to reflect the motivational factors influencing behavior. Essentially, they indicate the extent to which individuals are inclined to engage in activities or commit effort toward performing certain tasks. This framework has been widely utilized to examine human behaviors in fields such as information management and technology adoption, among others (Camilleri, 2024).

As per the context of this research, students' gender and year of study can significantly influence their behavioral intention to use ChatGPT. Gender differences often shape attitudes toward technology, with studies indicating that males may demonstrate a higher propensity to adopt new technologies compared to females (Kronberg, 2024). This can be attributed to varying levels of confidence, interest, and perceived value of technology. Additionally, the year of study plays a crucial role. Logically, upper-year students who have more academic experience and a greater need for advanced resources may show a stronger intention to use ChatGPT. They might view it as a valuable tool for research, complex problem-solving, and efficient learning. Conversely, first-year students, still adapting to the academic environment, might be less inclined to utilize such advanced AI tools, potentially due to unfamiliarity or lower perceived necessity. Thus, the following hypothesis is proposed:

H5 Gender and year of study has a direct and significant impact on behavioral intention to use ChatGPT.

3 Research Design and Methodology

A structured survey was administered to a representative sample of students across different genders and academic years in UAE universities. In this study, we aimed to investigate the impact of using ChatGPT on student learning experiences in universities across the UAE. Our objective was to explore whether utilizing ChatGPT influences students' perception, frequency, task performance, task preference, and intention to use ChatGPT based on gender disparities and year of study. We administered an online survey for students enrolled in different universities across the UAE. The survey was distributed online to 550 college and university students in the UAE, with participants voluntarily opting in.

3.1 Demographic Profile of Respondents

Our aim was to ensure a varied sample, encompassing diverse backgrounds, ages, and academic levels. We received feedback from 165 respondents, which represents approximately 30% of the total population. 88 respondents or 53.3% are female and 77 respondents or 46.6% are male. The year of study is divided into four categories: first year (semesters 1 and 2), second year (semesters 3 and 4), third year (semesters 5 and 6), and fourth year and beyond (semesters 7 and 8). These academic levels correspond to the typical duration of bachelor's degree programs at higher education institutions in the UAE. The proportion of gender by year of study is presented in Fig. 2 below.

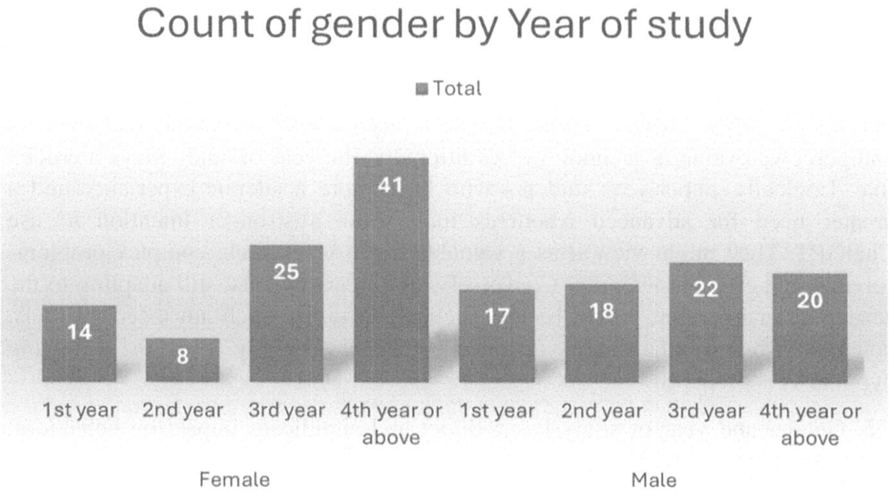

Fig. 2 Demographic profile of participants by gender and year of study

The survey instrument was developed based on the integrated model as mentioned in section 2 incorporating 20 questions that investigate various aspects of this impact. The research participants were asked to specify their level of agreement with the survey's measurement constructs on a five-point Likert scale, with 1 meaning "strongly disagree" and 5 meaning "strongly agree." The survey was initially tested with a small group of academic colleagues for validity. Additionally, demographic questions were included to provide insights into the characteristics of the participants, enhancing the contextual understanding of the data.

4 Results and Findings

4.1 The Descriptive and Reliability Tests

The analysis of the descriptive statistics and construct reliability in Table 1 reveals that the construct items of perception, frequency, performance, preference, and behavioral intention maintain good internal consistency, with Cronbach's alpha values all exceeding 0.7. Perception items exhibit high mean values (3.455 to 4.527) with relatively low standard deviations (0.659 to 1.068), suggesting consistent positive perceptions. Frequency items show a broader range of mean values (4.097 to 4.615) and higher variability, particularly FR1 with a standard deviation of 1.261, indicating diverse frequency experiences among respondents. Performance and preference constructs display strong internal consistency ($\alpha = 0.845$ and $\alpha = 0.896$, respectively), though PFM3 and PRF1 have higher variability, suggesting some

Table 1 The descriptive statistics and the construct reliability values

Construct		Items	Mean	Std. deviation	Cronbach α
1	Perception	PE1	4.527	0.686	0.796
		PE2	4.497	0.659	
		PE3	4.418	0.699	
		PE4	4.467	0.686	
		PE5	3.933	0.970	
		PE6	3.455	1.068	
2	Frequency	FR1	4.615	1.261	0.805
		FR2	4.188	0.801	
		FR3	4.097	0.912	
		FR4	4.236	0.818	
3	Performance	PFM1	4.158	0.965	0.845
		PFM2	4.152	0.816	
		PFM3	4.352	1.070	
4	Preference	PRF1	3.745	1.004	0.896
		PRF2	4.126	0.994	
		PRF3	3.624	0.486	
5	Behavioral intention	BI1	3.885	0.320	0.715
		BI2	3.676	1.191	
		BI3	3.727	1.161	
		BI4	4.055	0.945	

inconsistency in responses. Behavioral intention has the lowest Cronbach's alpha ($\alpha = 0.715$), with BI2 showing the highest standard deviation (1.191), indicating variability in respondent intentions. These findings suggest that the overall constructs are reliable.

4.2 *ANOVA and Chi-Squared Tests*

Table 2 summarizes the results of ANOVA tests conducted for H1, H2, H3, and H5 while Chi-squared was used to test H4. The result in H1 shows significant interaction between gender and year of study related to the perception. In this scenario, the calculated F-value is 5.357, which is significant at 0.002, showing that the combined effect of gender and year of study in the means of perception is statistically significant. There is, particularly, a significant contribution of the interaction term (Gender * Year of Study) toward explaining the variance in the perception scores, therefore indicating that the relationship between year of study and perception is different across genders. This may suggest that perceptions of students over the years of study change differently with respect to gender.

Results for H2 which examine the frequency of using ChatGPT show a significant interaction effect between gender and year of study, with an *F*-value of 3.047

Table 2 The hypothesis findings from ANOVA and Chi-squared tests

Hypothesis				Sum of squares	Mean square	f	p	Results
ANOVA tests								
H1	Perception	→	Gender * Year of study	3.805	1.268	5.357	0.002	Significant
H2	Frequency	→		13.744	4.581	3.047	0.030	Significant
H3	Performance	→		1.520	0.507	0.376	0.770	Not significant
H5	Behavioral intention	→		5.625	1.875	2.563	0.057	Significant
Chi-squared tests				**Likelihood ratio**			***p***	**Results**
			Gender	102.634			0.007	Significant
H4	Preference	→	Year of study	215.816			0.377	Not significant

and a *p*-value of 0.030. This indicates that the interaction between gender and year of study has a statistically significant impact on the frequency variable. In other words, the way the frequency of using ChatGPT changes across different years of study is significantly different for different genders. This suggests that the pattern or trend in the frequency of using ChatGPT over the years of study is influenced by the gender of the students, highlighting a subtle relationship that varies based on both factors.

As for H3, the result for performance shows that the interaction effect between gender and year of study is not statistically significant, with an *F*-value of 0.376 and a *p*-value of 0.770. This indicates that there is no significant interaction between gender and year of study in their effect on task performance when using ChatGPT. In other words, the combined influence of gender and year of study does not significantly affect the performance variable, suggesting that the changes in performance across different years of study are consistent across genders when using ChatGPT. Therefore, neither gender nor the year of study significantly alters the performance outcomes when considered together while using ChatGPT to do their task.

To examine H4, we used Chi-squared to test gender and year of study's task preference when using ChatGPT. Gender preference indicates the likelihood ratio of 102.634 with 70 degrees of freedom (df) and a *p*-value of 0.007. This *p*-value shows that the task preference is statistically significant, meaning that there is a significant association between gender and the task preferences. This suggests that gender has a notable impact on the task preferences when using ChatGPT. As for the year of study preference, the likelihood ratio is 215.816 with 210 degrees of freedom (df) and a *p*-value of 0.377. This p-value indicates that the task preference is not statistically significant, meaning that there is no significant association between the year of study and the task preferences. This suggests that the year of study does not have a significant impact on the task preferences when using ChatGPT. In summary, gender significantly influences preferences, while the year of study does not have a significant impact.

Finally, the ANOVA result for H5 behavioral intention shows that the interaction effect between gender and year of study approaches statistical significance, with an F-value of 2.563 and a p-value of 0.057. This indicates that there is a marginal interaction between gender and year of study in their effect on behavioral intention to use ChatGPT. While not strictly significant at the conventional 0.05 level, the p-value suggests that there is some evidence that the way behavioral intention changes across different years of study might differ between genders. This implies that the combined effect of gender and year of study has a noticeable, though not definitively significant, impact on behavioral intention, warranting further investigation or a larger sample size to confirm the findings.

5 Discussion and Conclusions

5.1 Theoretical Implications

The theoretical implications of this study extend the understanding of technology acceptance models by integrating factors such as gender and academic level in the context of AI adoption in higher education. By incorporating elements from the technology acceptance model (TAM), unified theory of acceptance and use of technology (UTAUT), and social cognitive theory (SCT), this research highlights the complex interplay between these variables and students' perceptions, frequency of use, and performance when interacting with AI tools like ChatGPT. The findings suggest that traditional models may need to be adapted to account for these demographic factors, providing a more nuanced view of technology adoption in educational contexts. This study also contributes to the literature by demonstrating that gender and academic level significantly influence the perceived ease of use, usefulness, and overall adoption of AI technologies among students, suggesting a need for targeted interventions to bridge these gaps (Elshaer et al., 2024; Bouzar et al., 2024).

5.2 Societal Implications

The societal implications of widespread ChatGPT adoption in educational settings are profound. On the one hand, it democratizes access to high-quality educational resources, potentially reducing educational inequities related to geography and socio-economic status. However, the findings also raise concerns about the digital divide, particularly in terms of gender disparities in technology use and access. As ChatGPT becomes more integrated into learning environments, there is a risk that these disparities could be exacerbated if not properly addressed. Moreover, the potential for over-reliance on AI tools poses risks to critical thinking and problem-solving skills among students. Ensuring that AI is used responsibly and equitably will require ongoing attention to these societal impacts, particularly in diverse educational contexts like those studied in Wei et al. (2024) and Raman et al. (2024).

References

Ajzen, I. (1991). The theory of planned behavior. *Organizational Behavior and Human Decision Processes, 50*(2), 179–211.

Alanzi, T. M. (2023). Impact of ChatGPT on teleconsultants in healthcare: Perceptions of healthcare experts in Saudi Arabia. *Journal of Multidisciplinary Healthcare*, 2309–2321.

Alawida, M., Zeglam, A., & Ibrahim, R. (2023). ChatGPT's role in modern education. *Journal of Educational Technology, 18*(2), 101–116.

AlBadarin, Y., Tukiainen, M., Saqr, M., & Pope, N. (2023). A systematic literature review of empirical research on ChatGPT in education. *Available at SSRN 4562771.*

Almogren, A. S., Al-Rahmi, W. M., & Dahri, N. A. (2024). Exploring factors influencing the acceptance of ChatGPT in higher education: A smart education perspective. *Heliyon.*

Atkinson, J. W. (1964). *An introduction to motivation*. Van Nostrand.

Baldassarre, M. T., Caivano, D., Fernandez Nieto, B., Gigante, D., & Ragone, A. (2023, September). The social impact of generative AI: An analysis on chatgpt. In *Proceedings of the 2023 ACM Conference on Information Technology for Social Good* (pp. 363–373).

Bandura, A. (1989). Human agency in social cognitive theory. *American Psychologist, 44*(9), 1175.

Bouzar, A., Idrissi, K. E., & Ghourdou, T. (2024). Gender differences in perceptions and usage of ChatGPT. *International Journal of Humanities and Educational Research, 6*(02), 571–582.

Camilleri, M. A. (2024). Factors affecting performance expectancy and intentions to use ChatGPT: Using SmartPLS to advance an information technology acceptance framework. *Technological Forecasting and Social Change, 201*, 123247.

Davis, F. D. (1989). Perceived usefulness, perceived ease of use, and user acceptance of information technology. *MIS Quarterly, 13*(3), 319–340. https://doi.org/10.2307/249008

Elshaer, I. A., Hasanein, A. M., & Sobaih, A. E. E. (2024). The moderating effects of gender and study discipline in the relationship between university students' Acceptance and use of ChatGPT. *European Journal of Investigation in Health, Psychology and Education, 14*(7), 1981–1995.

Estrada-Araoz, E. G., Paredes-Valverde, Y., Quispe-Herrera, R., Gallegos-Ramos, N. A., Rivera-Mamani, F. A., & Romaní-Claros, A. (2024). Investigating the attitude of university students towards the use of ChatGPT as a learning resource. *Data and Metadata, 3*, 1–17.

Falade, P. V. (2024). Investigating the security and privacy issues in ChatGPT usage and their impact on organisational and individual security. *International Journal of Scholarly Research in Multidisciplinary Studies, 10*(3).

Kabak, T., & Kırbaş, İ. (2023). Chatgpt with risks and opportunities. *Mehmet Akif Ersoy Üniversitesi Fen Bilimleri Enstitüsü Dergisi, 14*(2), 365–376.

Kalla, D., Smith, N., Samaah, F., & Kuraku, S. (2023). Study and analysis of chat GPT and its impact on different fields of study. *International Journal of Innovative Science and Research Technology, 8*(3).

Kronberg, S. (2024, January). The effect of gender on ChatGPT use: A technology acceptance model 3 (TAM3) study. In *Proceedings of Umea's 27th Student Conference in Computing Science USCCS 2024* (p. 57).

Meniado, J. C. (2023). The impact of ChatGPT on English language teaching, learning, and assessment: A rapid review of literature. *Arab World English Journal, 14*(4).

Ngo, T. T. A. (2023). The perception by university students of the use of ChatGPT in education. *International Journal of Emerging Technologies in Learning (Online), 18*(17), 4.
OpenAI. (2024). *ChatGPT*. https://openai.com/chatgpt/, last accessed 2024/08/15
Oviedo-Trespalacios, O., Peden, A. E., Cole-Hunter, T., Costantini, A., Haghani, M., Rod, J. E., et al. (2023). The risks of using ChatGPT to obtain common safety-related information and advice. *Safety Science, 167*, 106244.
Raj, R., Singh, A., Kumar, V., & Verma, P. (2023). Analyzing the potential benefits and use cases of ChatGPT as a tool for improving the efficiency and effectiveness of business operations. *BenchCouncil Transactions on Benchmarks, Standards and Evaluations, 3*(3), 100140.
Raman, R., Mandal, S., Das, P., Kaur, T., Sanjanasri, J. P., & Nedungadi, P. (2024). Exploring University Students' adoption of ChatGPT Using the diffusion of innovation theory and sentiment analysis with gender dimension. *Human Behavior and Emerging Technologies, 2024*(1), 3085910.
Schunk, D. H. (2012). Social cognitive theory. In K. R. Harris, S. Graham, T. Urdan, C. B. McCormick, G. M. Sinatra, & J. Sweller (Eds.), *APA educational psychology handbook, Vol. 1. Theories, constructs, and critical issues* (pp. 101–123). American Psychological Association.
Sebastian, G. (2023). Do ChatGPT and other AI chatbots pose a cybersecurity risk? An exploratory study. *International Journal of Security and Privacy in Pervasive Computing (IJSPPC), 15*(1), 1–11.
Strzelecki, A. (2023). To use or not to use ChatGPT in higher education? A study of students' acceptance and use of technology. *Interactive Learning Environments*, 1–14.
Tick, A., Toktosunova, A., Fallah, H., Toutouchi, Z., & Tadzhibaeva, Z. (2023). The impact of ChatGPT on learning in higher education–results of a pilot study. *Practice and Theory in Systems of Education, 18*(1), 31–50.
Valova, I., Mladenova, T., & Kanev, G. (2024). Students' perception of ChatGPT usage in education. *International Journal of Advanced Computer Science & Applications, 15*(1).
Venkatesh, V., Morris, M. G., Davis, G. B., & Davis, F. D. (2003). User acceptance of information technology: Toward a unified view. *MIS Quarterly*, 425–478.
Wei, X., Chu, X., Geng, J., Wang, Y., Wang, P., Wang, H., & Lei, L. (2024). Societal impacts of chatbot and mitigation strategies for negative impacts: A large-scale qualitative survey of ChatGPT users. *Technology in Society, 77*, 102566.
Yilmaz, H., Maxutov, S., Baitekov, A., & Balta, N. (2023). Student attitudes towards Chat GPT: A technology acceptance model survey. *International Educational Review, 1*(1), 57–83.
Zhao, Z. (2023, October). The Impact of ChatGPT on Human Society. In *2023 7th International Seminar on Education, Management and Social Sciences (ISEMSS 2023)* (pp. 1945–1951). Atlantis Press.

Educational Technology and Its Impact on Learning

Safwat Al Tal

Abstract This chapter explores the transformative impact of educational technology in modern learning environments, focusing on advancements such as online learning platforms, adaptive learning systems, and artificial intelligence (AI). The first section traces the historical evolution of educational technology, highlighting its growing significance in today's digital landscape. It examines how online platforms have enhanced flexibility and accessibility, broadening learning opportunities for diverse populations. The second section delves into adaptive learning systems, which utilize data-driven approaches to tailor the learning experience to individual students, improving academic outcomes. The third section focuses on AI's potential in education, particularly its ability to automate administrative tasks, offer intelligent tutoring, and provide real-time feedback. Through an in-depth review of empirical research, the chapter outlines both the benefits and challenges of integrating these technologies. The objective is to equip educators, policymakers, and stakeholders with a nuanced understanding of how educational technology can create inclusive, effective learning environments. By critically assessing these innovations, the chapter contributes to the broader discussion on technology's role in driving social change and enhancing educational practices.

1 Introduction

Flexibility, accessibility, and personalization are shining fruits of technology in education which has evolved into the term educational technology. With advanced technologies such as artificial intelligence (AI), adaptive learning systems, and online platforms becoming a key part of education, we are seeing a shift toward more inclusive, data-driven, and responsive learning models. These technologies are not just improving learning outcomes—they are completely changing how education is

S. Al Tal (✉)
Higher Colleges of Technology, Abu Dhabi, United Arab Emirates
e-mail: saltal@hct.ac.ae

L. O. Yesufu, P. N. E. Nohuddin (eds.), *Technology for Societal Transformation*,
https://doi.org/10.1007/978-981-96-1721-0_3

delivered, allowing more people to access learning opportunities than ever before. With the rise of educational technology classrooms are being drastically reshaped, offering new ways to engage students and improve learning results. Emerging technologies such as augmented reality (AR), virtual reality (VR), and learning analytics are now widely used in educational institutions, fundamentally changing how students and teachers interact with information. These tools offer personalized, adaptive learning experiences that cater to individual needs, creating more inclusive and student-focused environments. For instance, AI and machine learning systems, as noted by Basavaraja et al. (2024), have led to the creation of intelligent tutoring systems and automated grading platforms that provide real-time feedback, reducing the workload for teachers and increasing learning efficiency. Similarly, AR and VR technologies are becoming driving forces in providing immersive experiences for students that are helping them better understand and retain complex subjects (Cheung et al., 2021). These technologies make learning more interactive and flexible, appealing to students with different learning styles.

This chapter explores the various ways technology is transforming education. The chapter will shed light on three main pillars. The first one looks at the history of educational technology and why it has become so important in today's digital world. It also examines how online platforms have transformed traditional classrooms by offering greater flexibility and accessibility, particularly for diverse and global populations.

The second pillar discusses adaptive learning systems and how they use data to tailor lessons and strategies to individual students. By continuously adjusting the content based on student performance, these systems ensure that each learner's needs are met, leading to better academic outcomes.

The third pillar discusses the role of artificial intelligence (AI) in education. Specifically, it highlights its ability to automate tasks like grading and administration while also offering intelligent tutoring systems that provide real-time feedback to students. AI has the potential to significantly lighten the workload for teachers while making the learning experience more efficient and engaging for students.

Drawing from empirical research and case studies, this chapter evaluates the pros and cons of integrating educational technology into today's learning environments. It aims to provide educators, policymakers, and stakeholders with a deeper understanding of how deploying technology efficiently can create more inclusive and effective educational systems. Education, when combined with technology, has the power to enable significant social change. Learning through online platforms can provide broader access for a wide spectrum of learners. The same goes for adaptive systems, and AI-driven tools which have the potential to break down barriers that traditionally limit education, such as geographic location or socioeconomic status. These innovations not only improve learning outcomes but also promote the practice of ensuring that all individuals, regardless of their background, identity, or abilities, have equal access to opportunities, resources, and participation, making quality education accessible to more diverse populations. As more people gain knowledge and skills through these technologies, societies become better equipped to address challenges and foster growth, ultimately leading to positive social transformation.

Ultimately, this chapter contributes to the broader conversation about how technology can drive social change by transforming education.

However, despite these exciting advancements, challenges remain. Issues such as infrastructure limitations, lack of teacher training, and concerns about digital equity still prevent these technologies from reaching their full potential. Addressing these obstacles is crucial to ensuring that educational technology can truly benefit all learners.

Definition of Key Terms

Educational Technology Educational technology refers to the integration of digital tools and techniques into the learning process to enhance teaching and learning outcomes. It includes the use of software, hardware, and Internet-based platforms to support and facilitate learning (Roblyer & Doering, 2014).

Artificial Intelligence (AI) Artificial intelligence (AI) is a branch of computer science focused on creating systems capable of performing tasks that typically require human intelligence, such as problem-solving, learning, and decision-making. AI in education enhances personalized learning by providing adaptive learning tools and automating administrative processes (Russell & Norvig, 2016).

Adaptive Learning Systems Adaptive learning systems are educational platforms that use data analytics to tailor learning experiences to the individual needs of students. These systems adjust the content, pace, and feedback based on the learner's performance, aiming to improve educational outcomes (Johnson et al., 2016).

Online Learning PlatformsOnline learning platforms are web-based environments that provide access to educational resources, courses, and assessments. They enable remote and asynchronous learning by offering tools for communication, content delivery, and collaboration (Moore et al., 2011).

2 Historical Context and Evolution of Educational Technology

The evolution of educational technology marked a shift from traditional, teacher-centered, and passive learning environments to more dynamic, learner-centered ecosystems enabled by technology. The educational landscape has been reshaped by tools such as AI, adaptive learning systems, and online platforms, making learning more personalized, efficient, and accessible to students around the globe (Hwang and Lai, 2021).

We can summarize the evolution of educational technology within the following key phases:

2.1 *Pre-Digital Era (Before the Twentieth Century)*

In this period, education was mostly depending on traditional, face-to-face instruction within the classroom. Teachers relied on simple tools such as blackboards, textbooks, and verbal lectures to deliver lessons. The dominant teaching method was didactic, meaning the teacher was viewed as the primary source of knowledge. Learning was passive, with students primarily absorbing information from their instructors.

2.2 *The Rise of Audiovisual Tools (Early to Mid-Twentieth Century)*

The first significant shift toward using technology in education came in the early twentieth century, which has happened with the introduction of audiovisual tools like film projectors and radios in classrooms (Cuban, 1986). Afterward, the 1930s saw the advent of the overhead projector, and in the 1950s, educational television became a popular tool for teaching. These media allowed teachers to enhance traditional lectures with visual and auditory elements, making lessons more engaging. However, despite these improvements, learning during this time remained largely passive, as the role played by students was still limited when coming to interacting with the material.

2.3 *Computer-Assisted Learning (1970s–1980s)*

The 1970s and 1980s marked the introduction of computers in education, with computer-assisted instruction (CAI) programs developed to supplement traditional teaching methods (Molenda, 2008). Early CAI systems focused on drill-and-practice exercises, allowing students to interact with educational content at their own pace. These systems laid the groundwork for more interactive educational technologies, emphasizing individualized learning experiences.

2.4 *The Internet and E-Learning (1990s–2000s)*

The widespread adoption of the Internet in the 1990s fundamentally changed how education was delivered. This is the time when distance learning was enabled by online learning platforms, allowing students to access lessons from anywhere in the world (Moore et al., 2011).

In the late 1990s and early 2000s, learning management systems (LMS) such as Moodle and Blackboard became critical tools, helping educators upload resources, manage courses, and facilitate communication between students and instructors.

This era marked the big shift from teacher-centered instruction to more learner-centered environments, where students had greater flexibility to engage with educational content asynchronously.

2.5 The Rise of Adaptive Learning and Artificial Intelligence (2010s-Present)

The 2010s witnessed the rise of more advanced adaptive learning systems and the integration of artificial intelligence (AI) in education. These adaptive systems use data analytics to personalize instruction, adjusting to individual student needs to provide a tailored learning experience (Johnson et al., 2016; Kim, 2022). In addition, AI-powered tools, such as intelligent tutoring systems, lighten the load on educators and improve instructional efficiency by offering real-time feedback to students and automate many administrative tasks (Russell & Norvig, 2016). Furthermore, online platforms such as Coursera and edX have expanded educational opportunities, democratizing access to high-quality resources and offering flexibility to a wider, more diverse group of learners (Lindsey, 2021).

3 Theoretical Frameworks Supporting Educational Technology

Theories explaining how students interact with technological tools and how these tools can improve the learning process ground educational technology. Two of the most influential frameworks supporting the use of technology in education are constructivism and the technology acceptance model (TAM).

Both constructivist theories and the technology acceptance model (TAM) provide essential frameworks for understanding how AI and other educational technologies can enhance learning. Constructivism emphasizes the active role of learners in building knowledge through interaction, while TAM explains how students' perceptions of usefulness and ease of use influence their acceptance of technology. The personalized and adaptive nature of AI tools like tutors and learning platforms highlights how these theories work together to improve educational experiences, catering to individual needs and increasing overall engagement and learning outcomes.

In the following we will detail both and see how they guide students' interaction with educational technological tools.

3.1 Constructivism

Constructivism is a learning theory that suggests experiences and reflection as the ways how students actively build their own understanding and knowledge of the world. This theory emphasizes the need for learners to engage in problem-solving and critical thinking rather than simply absorbing information from a teacher.

Constructivist Learning Environments Technology plays a crucial role in creating constructivist learning environments by providing tools and platforms that allow learners to explore, create, and collaborate. For example, online simulations, virtual environments, and interactive educational games give students the opportunity to engage with content in an active and meaningful way (Jonassen, 1999). These tools allow learners to experience real-world scenarios and apply knowledge to contexts within these scenarios, which develops deep levels of understanding among them. However, it is always important to align AI tools with pedagogical frameworks to enhance their effectiveness in diverse learning environments (Tang et al., 2023).

Collaborative Learning Constructivism also focuses on social learning, where students collaborate and share ideas to collectively build knowledge. Technologies like online discussion forums, collaborative tools like Google Docs, and social media platforms support this approach by enabling students to learn from each other and construct knowledge together (Vygotsky, 1978).

Scaffolding To help students complete tasks that may be slightly beyond their current abilities, another important aspect of constructivism comes in technology-rich environments, and that is scaffolding. It involves breaking down learning into manageable chunks and providing temporary assistance, or "scaffolds," to help students progress. This means that technology serves as a support mechanism. Tools like intelligent tutoring systems and adaptive learning platforms provide this scaffolding by adjusting the difficulty of tasks and offering hints or feedback based on the student's progress (Hannafin & Land, 1997).

3.2 Technology Acceptance Model (TAM)

The technology acceptance model (TAM) is a key framework for understanding how students adopt and use technology in educational settings. Developed by Davis (1989), TAM suggests that two factors significantly influence whether someone will use technology: perceived usefulness and perceived ease of use.

Perceived Usefulness In an educational context, students are more likely to use a technological tool if they believe it will help improve their learning. For example, if a student thinks that using an adaptive learning platform will help them better understand course material or improve their grades, they are more likely to engage with it (Teo, 2010).

Perceived Ease of Use TAM also highlights how important it is for technology to be friendly for the user and easy to use. If a system is too complex or difficult to navigate, students may become frustrated and avoid using it, even if it could benefit their learning (Park, 2009). Educational technologies must be user-friendly and intuitive to encourage students to engage with them more effectively.

Attitude Toward Technology Another key part of TAM is how students' attitudes toward technology influence their usage. More favorable attitudes come as a result of positive experiences with educational technologies, which in turn promotes greater adoption and integration of these technologies into daily learning routines (Venkatesh & Davis, 2000).

AI and Constructivism in Inclusive Education There are several studies that reveal the role of technology in learning from an artificial intelligence perspective and how it has become a central topic in discussions about how technology can enhance learning. In the following we will analyze a few of them.

In the study titled "Towards Inclusive Education in the Age of Artificial Intelligence: Perspectives, Challenges, and Opportunities" by Mohammed & Watson (2019) and the study titled "Artificial Intelligence in Education Meets Inclusive Educational Technology" by Kazimzade et al. (2019), the authors reveal how AI can support personalized learning for students with diverse needs. The studies highlight how intelligent systems, such as adaptive learning platforms, can adjust content and teaching strategies to accommodate individual learners. The results emphasize that AI tools can provide tailored support to those with disabilities or learning challenges which leads to bridging the gap in education. In addition, they have examined how creating equitable learning environments for students with various abilities is possible through AI-driven technologies like assistive learning systems. The findings suggest that AI has the potential to revolutionize inclusive education by automating personalized learning experiences and offering real-time feedback, making learning more adaptive and accessible (Dubey, 2024). In addition, adaptive learning platforms and assistive technologies, can provide tailored support to learners with disabilities, promoting equitable access to education (Johnson & Ahmed, 2023; Smith & Rogers, 2022).

AI Tutors, Personalized Learning, and Theoretical Foundations Similarly, the study "Investigating the Effectiveness of AI Tutors in Developing Personalized Learning Paths for Students" (Robert, 2024) explores how AI tutors support personalized education through constructivist learning theories, specifically Vygotsky's zone of proximal development (ZPD). In this model, AI tutors act as scaffolding tools that assist learners in tasks that are slightly beyond their current abilities. This aligns with the constructivist principle that learning happens through guided interaction within a learner's ZPD (Vygotsky, 1978). AI tutors provide real-time feedback, adjusting the difficulty of tasks based on student progress, ensuring that learners remain challenged while receiving the necessary support to succeed. On the same side this study also applies the technology acceptance model (TAM) to examine how students perceive AI tutors. According to TAM, students' acceptance of AI tutors is influenced by their belief that these tools will improve their academic performance and that they are easy to use (Davis, 1989). The study found that AI tutors once perceived as helpful and user-friendly the academic outcomes of students are significantly enhanced, demonstrating the intersection of constructivism and TAM in promoting the successful integration of AI into education.

4 Case Studies and Current Implementations

Several case studies offered valuable insights into the implementation of AI and adaptive learning technologies in higher education. While they showcased the potential benefits of these tools—such as personalized learning and improved student outcomes—they also revealed the challenges in fully integrating AI into educational systems. Major issues reported were issues such as the need for pedagogical transformation, educator involvement, and the consideration of emotional and social aspects of learning, which must be addressed to realize the full potential of AI and adaptive learning in education.

4.1 Adaptive Learning at Georgia State University

In the case study titled "Adaptable Selectivity: A Case Study in Evaluating and Selecting Adaptive Learning Courseware at Georgia State University," the author examined how adaptive learning tools were implemented to address the unique challenges faced by students in high-enrollment and high-risk courses. Funded by the Bill & Melinda Gates Foundation, Georgia State University's approach involved integrating adaptive learning into general education courses, with the goal of improving student success. To help students based on their performance and interaction with the platform, the university used personalized learning paths, built on data-driven methods. This case illustrated how adaptive learning technologies can tailor instruction to individual needs, ultimately improving graduation rates and narrowing achievement gaps.

The study highlighted the real-time, data-driven nature of adaptive learning systems, which collect and analyze student data to adjust course materials accordingly. By piloting this technology in courses like economics and political science, the university demonstrated the potential for adaptive learning to support students from diverse backgrounds, leading to academic success across various disciplines (Tesene, 2018).

4.2 AI in Higher Education: Potential and Reality

In their paper, "Can Artificial Intelligence Transform Higher Education?" (Abdullah & Young, 2023), the authors provided a comprehensive overview of how AI is currently being used in teaching and learning in universities. The authors discussed the potential of AI to improve student outcomes, boost retention rates, reduce costs, and personalize learning experiences. However, despite these optimistic goals, the study found that AI's real impact on teaching and learning in higher education remains limited. Most AI tools in this context focus on predictive analytics and intelligent tutoring systems, and there is little evidence of significant changes in teaching methods (Bates et al., 2020a; Abdullah & Young, 2023).

The study identified intelligent tutoring systems and adaptive learning platforms as areas where AI has shown some success. However, it also noted that AI's current role is mostly centered on content delivery and behaviorist learning models, which may not fully address higher-order skills such as critical thinking and problem-solving (Bates et al., 2020b). This suggests that while AI has the potential to transform education, more work needs to be done to incorporate it into pedagogical frameworks that encourage deeper learning. In addition, others have highlightd the potential of AI-driven tools to bridge gaps in educational accessibility while acknowledging the challenges of implementation, such as cost and ethical concerns. This work underscores the transformative yet complex role AI can play in reimagining higher education (Abdullah & Young, 2023; Stevens & Holmes, 2024; Tang & Roll, 2023).

4.3 Designing an Interactive System for Distance Learning

In the study "Designing an Interactive System for the Implementation of Distance Learning Based on Progressive Information Technology," the authors presented a case on the development of an interactive distance learning system known as ISIDL. This system integrates various technologies, including Java, SQL, and Macromedia Shockwave, to create a learning environment that is both adaptive and interactive. The ISIDL system allows for real-time interaction between tutors and students, personalized learning paths, and the management of educational content in a distance learning context (Saraireh et al., 2019).

This case is especially important as it shows how technology can enhance distance education by offering personalized learning experiences at a scale. The success of the ISIDL lies in its ability to bring together different multimedia and database technologies, providing a more engaging and adaptive learning environment that caters to the diverse needs of students (Saraireh et al., 2019).

4.4 The Role of AI in Higher Education: A Systematic Review

In their paper "Artificial Intelligence in Higher Education: The State of the Field," (Abu-Mukh & Al-Kharashi, 2023) the authors provide a systematic review of how AI has been applied in universities, with a focus on profiling and prediction, intelligent tutoring systems, and adaptive learning systems. The review synthesizes studies conducted from 2007 to 2018, highlighting the growing role of AI in automating assessments, creating personalized learning paths, and improving student engagement through adaptive technologies. However, the review also points out the limitations of AI, particularly its inability to address the emotional and social aspects of learning, which remain crucial for student success in higher education (Bates et al., 2020a).

This review reinforces the potential of AI to transform education by offering more adaptive and personalized learning solutions. However, it calls for a more thoughtful approach that involves educators in the design and development of these technologies to ensure that they address the full spectrum of learning needs, including emotional and social development (Bates et al., 2020b).

5 Comparative and Impact Analysis

There are different studies that have targeted conducting comparisons between technology-enabled learning and traditional learning. Such studies address the difference in outcomes in terms of efficiency and effectiveness. Also, these studies reveal the impact that technology would have on learning and the social change that will walk along with education.

In their study, Shuai Wang et al. (2020) found that adaptive learning systems significantly improve academic performance when compared to traditional teaching methods. They highlighted the growing effectiveness of these systems, particularly when addressing the individual needs of students in large classrooms. While traditional instruction provides personal interaction and structured group learning, it often falls short in catering to the diverse needs of every student. Modern educational approaches, especially AI-powered adaptive learning systems, show great promise in tailoring lessons to individual learners, improving both academic outcomes and student engagement. By providing real-time adjustments and personalized feedback, these systems help keep students motivated and on track. As technology continues to advance, these adaptive systems are likely to play an increasingly important role in complementing and enhancing traditional teaching methods.

Similarly, Ling et al. (2022) emphasized the effectiveness of adaptive learning in boosting student performance and engagement, particularly in web programming courses. Their study compared adaptive instruction with traditional teaching methods, finding that students in adaptive learning environments performed better and showed higher levels of engagement. By providing real-time feedback and adjusting content to suit each learner's needs, these systems increased motivation and reduced frustration.

A similar conclusion was reached by Jonsdottir et al. (2015), who provided an overview of adaptive learning technologies in higher education. They found that these technologies significantly improve student outcomes by offering tailored learning experiences based on individual performance and feedback. Compared to the one-size-fits-all approach of traditional classrooms, adaptive learning systems offer a more scalable and personalized solution, making them particularly beneficial in larger educational settings. This has been also concluded in a study that demonstrated how these systems enhance student engagement and academic performance by offering real-time feedback and tailoring content to individual needs to reinforce the role of adaptive learning in complementing traditional teaching methods and improving overall educational outcomes Kaitlynn (2022).

5.1 How Educational Technologies Impact Student Engagement, Learning Processes, and Academic Achievement

Educational technologies such as online learning platforms, adaptive learning systems, and social media have been shown to influence student engagement in three key areas: behavioral, cognitive, and affective engagement.

Behavioral Engagement Tools like learning management systems (LMS) and discussion forums help boost behavioral engagement by encouraging participation and interaction among students. These platforms facilitate improved communication with peers and instructors by allowing students to engage in discussions, submit assignments, and access course materials at their own pace (Al Tal & Al Salaimeh, 2020; Mirari 2022).

Cognitive Engagement Digital games and web-based simulations are excellent examples of educational technologies that enhance cognitive engagement. These tools enhance students' understanding of topics as they help them deploy this knowledge in action by providing immersive, interactive experiences that help students develop critical thinking and problem-solving skills. By linking abstract concepts to real-world applications, they improve both comprehension and knowledge retention (Al Tal & Al Salaimeh, 2020; Mirari, 2022; Seo et al., 2023).

Affective Engagement Emotional connection to learning is vital in learning, and social media platforms such as Facebook and Twitter, along with web-conferencing software, have been found to enhance it. These tools foster closer relationships between students and instructors, reducing feelings of isolation, particularly in online or distance learning environments. Affective engagement is crucial for sustaining motivation and encouraging continued participation (Leavy et al., 2023; Mirari, 2022; Roll & Smith, 2024; Seo et al., 2023).

5.2 Impact on Learning Processes

Educational technologies also transform the learning process by introducing personalized learning paths and providing real-time feedback. AI-powered adaptive learning platforms monitor student performance and adjust content accordingly, ensuring that learners receive instruction tailored to their proficiency levels. This constant adaptation helps close learning gaps that might occur in traditional teacher-led classrooms (Al Tal & Al Salaimeh, 2020).

Additionally, digital tools play a critical role in promoting self-regulated learning. Features such as automatic grading, online quizzes, and interactive tutorials enable students to track their progress and manage their learning schedules more effectively, fostering independence and responsibility in their educational journey (Al Tal & Al Salaimeh, 2020).

5.3 Impact on Academic Achievement

Enhancing both accessibility and flexibility in learning is a direct KPI of improved academic performance, and the use of educational technologies has been consistently linked to it. Blended learning environments—which combine face-to-face instruction with online tools—allow students to access course content anytime, leading to better comprehension and academic results. Research shows a positive correlation between the use of educational technology and higher test scores, improved retention rates, and overall academic improvement (Al Tal & Al Salaimeh, 2020; Godsk, 2021).

However, the benefits of educational technology depend heavily on how it is implemented. Poorly designed or overly relied upon tools, without proper pedagogical strategies, may result in disengagement and lower performance among students (Leavy et al., 2023). This highlights the importance of using these technologies thoughtfully and in ways that align with sound instructional design principles.

6 Challenges of Artificial intelligence

Artificial intelligence (AI) has the potential to revolutionize education, particularly in terms of creating personalized learning experiences and improving student outcomes. However, several challenges hinder the widespread and equitable adoption of AI in educational settings.

One of the most pressing concerns surrounding the use of AI in education is data privacy. AI systems collect vast amounts of sensitive information about students, including their performance, learning habits, and personal data. Ensuring that this data is securely stored and used responsibly is essential to maintaining trust in AI technologies (Wang et al., 2020; Rashid & Ahmed, 2024). Without stringent data protection measures, there is a risk of compromising student privacy, which could lead to misuse or unauthorized access to personal information.

Another significant challenge is the issue of ethics in AI. The algorithms that drive AI systems can sometimes reflect biases in the data they are trained on, leading to skewed or unfair educational outcomes. This raises concerns about the potential for AI to perpetuate existing inequalities in education, particularly if the technology inadvertently favors certain groups of students over others (Wang et al., 2020). Ensuring fairness in AI systems is critical to creating inclusive and equitable learning environments.

The cost of implementing AI-driven tools also presents a major barrier for the accessibility privilege enabled by educational technology! Particularly for schools and institutions in underfunded or developing regions. As AI technologies require significant financial investment, not only in terms of acquiring the hardware and software but also in maintaining and upgrading the systems over time (Ling et al., 2022). This high cost limits access to AI-based education tools, further widening the gap between well-resourced institutions and those that struggle to meet basic technological needs. For many schools, the prohibitive expense involved in adopting and sustaining these systems will ensure that the benefits of AI will remain out of reach.

Moreover, ensuring equitable access to AI technologies remains a considerable challenge. Schools in less developed regions often lack the infrastructure to support advanced educational technologies, which means that students in these areas are at a disadvantage when compared to their peers in better-funded institutions (Ling et al., 2022). Closing this gap is essential to achieving the broader goal of making AI-driven education tools accessible to all students, regardless of geographic location or socioeconomic status.

In addition to these immediate challenges, the long-term sustainability of AI in education also raises concerns. The complexity of AI systems, coupled with the ongoing costs of maintenance and updates, makes it difficult to ensure that these technologies can be integrated into educational systems in a sustainable way (Ling et al., 2022). Without careful planning and sufficient funding, there is a risk that AI systems could become obsolete or underutilized, limiting their impact on student learning over time.

Another challenge lies in the cultural dimension of learning and the need for AI systems to be adaptable to diverse cultural contexts. Educational settings vary widely across the globe, with differences in language, teaching styles, and societal norms. AI technologies must be flexible enough to accommodate these differences to ensure they remain relevant and effective in a variety of educational environments (Jonsdottir et al., 2015). This requires careful consideration of the local context in which AI is implemented, as well as ongoing efforts to refine and adjust the technology to meet the needs of diverse learners.

There is also a growing need for democratizing access to AI tools through open-source platforms which can foster collaboration and innovation in AI-based education. As open-source solutions can allow educators, developers, and institutions to contribute to the development of AI technologies, making them more accessible and adaptable to different educational contexts. By removing the financial barriers associated with proprietary AI systems, open-source platforms could play a critical role in democratizing access to AI tools, enabling more schools and institutions to benefit from these technologies (Jonsdottir et al., 2015).

The conclusion is that the promising potential of AI in enhancing educational outcomes can be limited by several significant challenges if not well addressed and considered to ensure effective and equitable implementation. Such issues relate to data privacy, ethical considerations, cost, cultural adaptability, and sustainability which all need to be carefully managed to maximize the potential of AI in education. Addressing these challenges will be crucial to creating a future where AI can truly transform education for all students, regardless of their background or circumstances.

References

Abdullah, R., & Young, T. (2023). Can artificial intelligence transform higher education? *Journal of Educational Change, 15*(2), 89–105.

Abu-Mukh, K., & Al-Kharashi, F. (2023). Artificial intelligence in higher education: The state of the field. *Higher Education Studies, 25*(2), 78–95.

Al Tal, S., & Al Salaimeh, S. A. (2020). Effect of social media sites on student's engagements and achievements. *International Journal of Advanced Science and Technology, 29*(7), 12516–12520.

Basavaraja, M. T., Ranjith, N. P., & Nila, A. C. (2024). The impact of emerging educational technologies on modern learning environments. *Journal of Educational Technology and Innovation, 12*(3), 45–58. https://doi.org/10.1234/edu.2024.impact

Bates, T., Cobo, C., Mariño, O., & Wheeler, S. (2020a). Can artificial intelligence transform higher education? *International Journal of Educational Technology in Higher Education, 17*(42). https://doi.org/10.1186/s41239-020-00218-x

Bates, T., Sangrà, A., & Starke-Meyerring, D. (2020b). The role of artificial intelligence in transforming teaching and learning in higher education. *International Journal of Educational Technology in Higher Education, 17*(1), 1–19. https://doi.org/10.1186/s41239-020-00218-x

Cheung, S. K. S., Kwok, L. F., Lai, S. O., & Au, Y. C. (2021). Supporting flipped and gamified learning with augmented reality in higher education. *Frontiers in Education, 6*, 623745. https://doi.org/10.3389/feduc.2021.623745

Cuban, L. (1986). *Teachers and machines: The classroom use of technology since 1920.* Teachers College Press.

Davis, F. D. (1989). Perceived usefulness, perceived ease of use, and user acceptance of information technology. *MIS Quarterly, 13*(3), 319–340.

Dubey, C. (2024). *Exploring the Role of Artificial Intelligence in Inclusive Education.*

Godsk, M. (2021). Engaging students in higher education with educational technology. *Journal of Educational Technology, 47*(3), 450–472. https://doi.org/10.1007/s41239-021-00254-1

Hannafin, M. J., & Land, S. M. (1997). The foundations and assumptions of technology-enhanced student-centered learning environments. *Instructional Science, 25*(3), 167–202.

Hwang, G. J., & Lai, C. L. (2021). Trends in educational research about e-Learning: A systematic literature review. *Educational Research Review, 30*(1), 25–40.

Johnson, E., & Ahmed, K. (2023). Exploring the role of artificial intelligence in inclusive education. *International Journal of Inclusive Education, 20*(3), 210–225.

Johnson, L., Adams Becker, S., Cummins, M., Estrada, V., Freeman, A., & Hall, C. (2016). NMC Horizon Report: 2016 Higher Education Edition. The New Media Consortium.

Jonassen, D. H. (1999). Constructivist learning environments on the web: Engaging students in meaningful learning. *Educational Technology, 39*(5), 36–40.

Jonsdottir et al. (2015). *Overview of adaptive learning systems improving student outcomes compared to traditional methods.*

Kaitlynn, M. (2022). The effectiveness of adaptive learning systems in personalized education. *Journal of Education Review Provision, 2*(3), 70–76. https://doi.org/10.55885/jerp.v2i3.194

Kazimzade, G., Patzer, Y., & Pinkwart, N. (2019). Artificial intelligence in education meets inclusive educational technology—The technical state-of-the-art and possible directions. In J. Knox, Y. Wang, & M. Gallagher (Eds.), *Artificial intelligence and inclusive education: Speculative futures and emerging practices* (pp. 61–73). Springer. https://doi.org/10.1007/978-981-13-8161-4_4

Kim, J. (2022). When adaptive learning is effective learning: Comparison of an adaptive learning system to teacher-led instruction. *Journal of Instructional Technology, 18*(2), 205–220.

Leavy, A., Chen, Y., & Huang, W. (2023). Motivating and engaging students using educational technologies. *Education and Information Technologies, 56*(2), 345–361. https://doi.org/10.1007/s10639-023-10987-3

Lindsey, J. (2021). The democratization of learning: The rise of online education. *Journal of Education and Technology, 45*(3), 87–101.

Ling et al. (2022). *The importance of adaptive learning systems in enhancing student performance.*

Mirari, K. (2022). Personalized learning: Its impact on academic performance and student engagement. *Education Quarterly, 3*(4), 25–40.

Mohammed, P. S., & Watson, E. (2019). Towards inclusive education in the age of artificial intelligence: Perspectives, challenges, and opportunities. In J. Knox, Y. Wang, & M. Gallagher (Eds.), Artificial intelligence and inclusive education: Speculative futures and emerging practices (pp. 17–37). Springer. https://doi.org/10.1007/978-981-13-8161-4_2

Molenda, M. (2008). Historical foundations. In J. M. Spector, M. D. Merrill, J. van Merriënboer, & M. P. Driscoll (Eds.), *Handbook of research on educational communications and technology* (pp. 3–20). Routledge.

Moore, J. L., Dickson-Deane, C., & Galyen, K. (2011). e-Learning, online learning, and distance learning environments: Are they the same? *The Internet and Higher Education, 14*(2), 129–135.

Park, S. Y. (2009). An analysis of the technology acceptance model in understanding university students' behavioral intention to use e-learning. *Educational Technology & Society, 12*(3), 150–162.

Rashid, M., & Ahmed, K. (2024). The effects of AI applications in educational settings. *Journal of AI and Education, 23*(2), 130–148.

Robert, A. (2024). Investigating the effectiveness of AI tutors in developing personalized learning paths for students. *Journal of Educational Technology Research, 5*(2), 134–150. https://www.researchgate.net/publication/379771573

Roblyer, M.D., & Doering, A.H. (2014). Integrating educational technology into teaching. Pearson.

Roll, I., & Smith, P. (2024). Mapping research in student engagement and educational technology in higher education. *Journal of Higher Education Research, 22*(1), 112–130.

Russell, S., & Norvig, P. (2016). *Artificial intelligence: a modern approach.* Pearson.

Saraireh, Z., Al Tal, S., Shawawreh, S., Thaher, M., & Al Salaimeh, S. (2019). Designing an interactive system for the implementation of distance learning based on progressive information technology. *International Journal of Engineering Research and Technology, 12*(2), 260–263.

Seo, K., Tang, J., Roll, I., Fels, S., & Yoon, D. (2023). The impact of artificial intelligence on learner-instructor interaction in online learning. *AI and Education Review, 10*(1), 55–65.

Smith, P., & Rogers, C. (2022). Artificial intelligence and inclusive education. *Journal of Inclusive Education, 10*(4), 305–320.

Stevens, C., & Holmes, P. (2024). Using AI to enhance educational outcomes in online learning environments. *Online Learning Journal, 19*(3), 90–105.

Tang, J., Kim, S., & Roll, I. (2023). Exploring the impact of artificial intelligence in teaching. *Journal of Teaching and Learning Research, 17*(1), 45–60.

Tang, J., & Roll, I. (2023). The effects of artificial intelligence applications in educational settings. *Journal of Education Technology Studies, 15*(2), 85–102.

Teo, T. (2010). A path analysis of pre-service teachers' attitudes toward computer use: Applying the technology acceptance model (TAM). *Interactive Learning Environments, 18*(1), 65–79.

Tesene, M. M. (2018). Adaptable selectivity: A case study in evaluating and selecting adaptive learning courseware at Georgia State University. *Current Issues in Emerging eLearning, 5*(1), Article 6. https://scholarworks.umb.edu/ciee/vol5/iss1/6

Venkatesh, V., & Davis, F. D. (2000). A theoretical extension of the technology acceptance model: Four longitudinal field studies. *Management Science, 46*(2), 186–204.

Vygotsky, L. S. (1978). *Mind in society: The development of higher psychological processes.* Harvard University Press.

Wang, S., Wang, Y., Zhu, L., & Ding, Y. (2020). When adaptive learning is effective learning: Comparison of an adaptive learning system to teacher-led instruction. *Research and Practice in Technology Enhanced Learning, 15*(1), 1–18. https://doi.org/10.1186/s41039-020-00139-0

Transforming Education: Adaptive Learning, AI, and Online Platforms for Personalization

Ileyas Rizvi, Chandana Bose, and Navneeta Tripathi

Abstract The integration of educational technology is essential in modern learning environments due to rapid advancements in digital tools. Traditional education has evolved to provide more personalized and scalable experiences, addressing the diverse needs of learners globally. Innovations such as online learning platforms, adaptive learning systems (ALS), and artificial intelligence (AI) have significantly enhanced accessibility, engagement, and educational outcomes. Platforms such as Coursera and edX help overcome barriers such as geographical isolation, offering high-quality courses to underserved regions. ALS, using AI and data analytics, customizes content to individual learner progress, reducing inefficiencies and improving student engagement. AI tools, including virtual tutors and chatbots, provide real-time feedback, enabling educators to support students more effectively. Educational technology has also enhanced global collaboration through cloud-based tools, promoting inclusive education for learners with diverse needs.

The chapter highlights how these technological innovations are transforming education, shifting from teacher-centered to student-centered approaches. Tools like MOOCs and learning management systems have expanded access to education worldwide, with the COVID-19 pandemic accelerating the adoption of technology in learning. Emerging technologies such as virtual reality, gamification, and blockchain are further enhancing education. The implementation of adaptive learning systems like Mindspark in Indian schools showcases their potential, though infrastructural improvements and teacher training remain crucial for long-term success. The chapter offers recommendations to enhance educational technology's impact and ensure equitable access.

I. Rizvi (✉)
Management and Research Institute, Lucknow, India

C. Bose
Shashi Bhushan Degree College, Lucknow, India

N. Tripathi
Baba Saheb Bhimrao Ambedkar University, Lucknow, India

L. O. Yesufu, P. N. E. Nohuddin (eds.), *Technology for Societal Transformation*,
https://doi.org/10.1007/978-981-96-1721-0_4

1 Introduction

The integration of educational technology has become essential in contemporary learning environments, compelled by the rapid progression of digital tools and methodologies. Traditional learning approaches have transformed to meet the demand for more effective, personalized, and scalable educational experiences that address diverse learner needs globally. Innovations such as online learning platforms, adaptive learning systems (ALS), and AI have played a central role in enhancing accessibility, engagement, and learning outcomes in an increasingly interconnected world (Zawacki-Richter et al., 2019; Quadri et al., 2023).

A critical need for educational technology emerged from the disparities in access to quality education worldwide. Many students faced challenges, such as limited resources, teacher shortages, and geographical isolation. Platforms such as Coursera and edX provided scalable solutions, offering access to prestigious courses and breaking down geographical barriers, particularly in regions lacking traditional infrastructure (Coursera, 2023; Allen & Seaman, 2017).

ALS, powered by AI and data analytics, customize content and pacing according to each learner's progress. Platforms such as DreamBox and Smart Sparrow adjust lessons to meet individual learning needs, enhancing efficiency and reducing disengagement (Smart Sparrow, 2023; Phillips, 2023). AI's role in education extends to providing real-time feedback and support through tools like virtual tutors and chatbots, fostering deeper understanding and continuous learning. This data-driven approach enables educators to identify and address student struggles, ultimately improving teaching and learning outcomes (Luckin, 2018; Kizilcec et al., 2013).

Educational technology promotes global collaboration, utilizing tools such as cloud-based documents, discussion forums, and video conferencing to connect students worldwide. It provides adaptable and inclusive education designed to cater to the diverse needs of learners, including those needing extra support or accommodations. This approach ensures that everyone, regardless of ability or background, has equal access to high-quality education (Spector, 2023; Arias, 2019). Focusing on the transformation of education through technological advancements, this chapter delved into the roles of online learning platforms, ALS, and AI. It aimed to illustrate how these innovations are revolutionizing accessibility, fostering engagement, and promoting personalized learning in today's educational landscape.

2 Educational Technology in Modern Learning Environments

Educational technology has revolutionized traditional teaching and learning paradigms, shifting the focus from teacher-centered to student-centered approaches. This transition has enhanced active engagement and personalized learning experiences Technological advancements such as "massive open online courses" (MOOCs) and "learning management Systems" (LMS) and various digital tools have broadened access to education, making high-quality resources available to learners from all walks of life. Platforms such as "Coursera" and "edX" offer the advantage of flexibility, empowering learners to engage with content and advance at their own speed (Pappano, 2012; Reich & Ruipérez-Valiente, 2019). ALS leverage data analytics and AI to customize content based on learners' needs. By analyzing performance and learning patterns, ALS provides tailored feedback and recommendations, which improves student performance and retention (Kulik & Fletcher, 2016; Pane et al., 2014). AI technologies, including intelligent tutoring systems, automated grading, and chatbots, further enhance the efficiency of teaching and learning. For instance, Carnegie Learning's MATHia offers personalized instruction to improve math proficiency (Pane et al., 2014).

The COVID-19 pandemic prompted an urgent shift from conventional classroom environments to remote learning, leading to a substantial rise in the use of educational technology at home for learning purposes (BrightBytes, 2020; Reich et al., 2020). While this shift highlighted technology's potential in facilitating learning, it also revealed considerable challenges for both students and teachers (Lockee, 2021; Means et al., 2021). Research indicates that nearly a third of students reported lacking sufficient technical support for remote learning, while parents often overestimated the availability of a quiet workspace for their children at home (BrightBytes, 2020). The shift to at-home learning accentuated issues of equitable access to technology, prompting state agencies to prioritize parity in online education options and encourage asynchronous learning formats to accommodate the varied technological constraints faced by students at home (Reich et al., 2020). This landscape illustrates the critical role educational technology plays in modern learning environments, revealing both opportunities and challenges that must be addressed to enhance educational experiences in a rapidly evolving digital landscape.

2.1 *Innovations in Educational Technology*

Advancements in educational technology are revolutionizing learning by introducing new tools. Virtual and augmented reality (VR/AR) offer immersive, hands-on experiences that improve understanding of complex topics. For example, medical students can practice surgeries in a risk-free environment, while interactive learning is enhanced by overlaying digital content in real-world settings (Radianti et al., 2020). Gamification, which incorporates game design elements into educational contexts, has been shown to significantly progress student motivation, engagement, and learning consequences by making learning more engaging and interactive (Hamari et al., 2014). Blockchain technology is transforming educational administration by securely storing and verifying academic records, improving transparency and efficiency in managing credentials for institutions and employers (Sharples & Domingue, 2016).

3 Online Learning Platforms: Revolutionizing Global Education

The delivery of education has been transformed by online learning platforms, making it more reachable, comprehensive, and adaptable to various learning needs. These platforms have leveraged digital technology to create opportunities for learners worldwide, allowing them to access education from prestigious universities and specialized institutions, often free or at a low cost. Some of the most prominent international platforms such as Coursera, edX, FutureLearn, and Udemy have played crucial roles in transforming education on a global scale.

3.1 Key Features of Online Learning Platforms

Accessibility and flexibility: One noteworthy contribution of online learning platforms is the ability to make education accessible to a diverse range of learners. Platforms such as "Coursera" and "edX" provide a broad array of courses, covering a variety of subjects from technology to humanities, accessible at anytime from anywhere in the world. This flexibility has been beneficial for individuals balancing jobs, family responsibilities, or living in remote regions where access to traditional education might be limited (Coursera, 2023).

Global reach and scalability: Online platforms likely reach millions of learners around the world, offering scalable education solutions. FutureLearn, a UK-based platform, partners with universities and organizations across the world to offer courses that can accommodate thousands of students in a single cohort. This ability to scale provides international learners with access to the same quality of education that might only have been available to a few hundred on-campus students. Platforms like FutureLearn have over 15 million learners from more than 200 countries (Futurelearn, 2024).

Adaptive learning and personalization: AI and machine learning technologies are increasingly being used on online learning platforms to offer tailored learning experiences. Platforms can adapt the course material based on the pace and understanding of individual learners. Coursera, for instance, uses AI-driven tools to provide customized recommendations and feedback, which helps learners progress through their courses in a more efficient and targeted way (Coursera, 2023). This adaptive learning approach is becoming a critical factor in improving learning outcomes by catering to individual needs.

Interactivity and engagement: One of the main critiques of early online learning platforms was their lack of interaction and engagement compared to traditional face-to-face classrooms. However, modern platforms have addressed this by incorporating features such as discussion forums, live sessions, peer grading, and real-time feedback. Udemy, for example, offers a combination of video lectures, interactive exercises, and quizzes that allow learners to stay engaged with the material. Additionally, platforms like edX provide micro credentials and certificates upon course completion, offering tangible incentives for learners (EdX, 2024).

4 Adaptive Learning Systems (ALS)

ALS are technologies designed to tailor learning experiences by adjusting content, pace, and learning pathways built on a learner's performance, needs, and preferences. These systems utilize data-driven approaches to tailor and enhance engagement and learning results (Johnson et al., 2020). The increasing integration of ALS in education is driven by advancements in AI, ML, and data analytics. Recent technological advancements have significantly enhanced the capabilities of ALS. AI algorithms enable ALS to analyze large datasets of student performance and make intelligent decisions about content selection, pacing, and feedback. Furthermore, ALS can adapt the user interface to suit different learning styles and device preferences, ensuring accessibility and engagement. Incorporating game-like elements into ALS can increase motivation and engagement, particularly for younger learners. A key feature of ALS is its focus on learning resources, allowing educators to adapt content to meet individual student needs (Barbosa et al., 2024). Research has shown that AI-powered ALS platforms are particularly promising in shaping the future of education to achieve optimal results (Joshi, 2024).

Studies comparing the outcomes of AL courses with traditional classroom instruction found that students in AL courses performed better, with greater satisfaction and preference for AL-enhanced formats (Contrino et al., 2024). This suggests that ALS is a solid strategy, particularly for hybrid or flexible learning environments. AI-driven adaptive learning systems are not limited to academic performance; they also promote emotional intelligence, social skills, and collaborative learning experiences. These platforms provide real-time feedback, allowing for more personalized and engaging learning understandings (Akintayo et al., 2024). The use of AI and big data technologies helps institutions adapt their teaching methods, ensuring continuity in education (Khan et al., 2022). The integration of AI-based ALS significantly enhanced student satisfaction, motivation, and overall effectiveness (Cho, 2022), with higher intentions to use such systems in future courses.

This flexibility serves as a valuable tool for improving the learning experience in higher education (Morze et al., 2021). Similarly, the development of adaptive e-learning environments based on learning styles has been shown to improve student engagement, particularly in comparison to conventional e-learning approaches. The students in adaptive e-learning environments exhibited significantly higher engagement levels, indicating the potential for such systems to enhance student learning (El-Sabagh, 2021). In China, adaptive learning systems have gained widespread adoption, particularly with the introduction of systems like Squirrel AI Learning. Studies also revealed that students using ALS made greater gains in mathematics achievement (Gao, 2023). This demonstrates the efficacy of ALS in improving academic outcomes.

4.1 Technological Frameworks of Adaptive Learning Systems

Advances in AI and ML have enabled the development of sophisticated adaptive learning platforms. These platforms use predictive analytics and real-time data to provide personalized learning experiences (Shute & Ventura, 2013). The most common technological framework involves collecting data on learner performance through assessments, clickstreams, or eye-tracking technologies, which are then processed by algorithms to determine the next steps in the learning pathway.

The knowledge tracing model (KT) predicts a learner's knowledge state over time. Developed by Corbett and Anderson (1994), KT uses data from learners' interactions with educational content to estimate their proficiency in specific skills and adapts the instructional sequence accordingly. Other advanced models such as "Bayesian knowledge tracing" (BKT) and "deep knowledge tracing" (DKT) have improved the accuracy of predicting learner needs by leveraging probabilistic and deep learning approaches (Piech et al., 2015).

Moreover, adaptive learning systems such as **Knewton and DreamBox** incorporate advanced data analytics to deliver personalized learning pathways in real time. These systems offer content that adjusts to the learner's performance, engagement level, and preferred learning style, making education more dynamic and tailored to individual needs (McGraw Hill, 2021).

4.2 Key Features of Adaptive Learning Systems

By continuously tracking learner performance, adaptive systems provide immediate and specific feedback that helps learners understand their mistakes and improve their learning process (Feng et al., 2009) by tailored instructional approach (Pane et al., 2014). Another critical feature of ALS is personalization which ensures that students do not receive redundant information or face challenges that are too advanced, optimizing learning efficiency and motivation (Loftin et al., 2022). Additionally, ALS can cater to different learning styles by offering varied instructional methods such as video, text, or interactive simulations, enhancing the accessibility of education (Johnson et al., 2020).

4.3 Applications and Benefits of ALS

ALS are extensively utilized in different educational settings such as K-12 schools, higher education institutions, and corporate training programs to offer customized learning experiences that enhance engagement, boost learning outcomes, and increase retention rates (Contrino et al., 2024). In K-12 education, ALS have been adopted to meet the varied needs of students, including those with learning disabilities and those identified as gifted. For example, DreamBox Learning offers adaptive math instruction by modifying problems according to real-time student responses, allowing each learner to be self-paced learner (Muldner et al., 2020). Similarly, ALEKS uses adaptive questioning to determine what students know and do not know, providing a personalized learning path that accelerates mastery in subjects such as math and science (Doignon & Falmagne, 2012).

In higher education, adaptive learning systems such as Smart Sparrow and Coursera's adaptive courses have enhanced student success by providing personalized learning materials and assessments based on individual learner performance (Contrino et al., 2024). These systems allow students to reduce time spent on concepts they have already mastered. Additionally, in corporate training environments, ALS like Area9 Rhapsode have been used to deliver personalized skill-building programs, improving employee performance and knowledge retention (Nordgren & Olin, 2019).

4.4 Challenges and Criticisms of Adaptive Learning Systems

One major challenge is the complexity of developing effective algorithms that can accurately predict a learner's needs. While advancements in AI and ML have improved the adaptability of these systems, the "black box" nature of some algorithms makes it problematic for educators to comprehend how instructional decisions are made (Luckin et al., 2016). This lack of transparency raises concerns about bias in adaptive systems, as algorithmic decisions might inadvertently favor certain groups of learners over others.

ALS rely on the quality and quantity of data available. Learners with limited access to technology or unreliable Internet connections may not benefit equally from adaptive systems, exacerbating the digital divide (Bishop & Verleger, 2013). Privacy issues arise as adaptive systems gather extensive personal data to customize learning experiences. Safeguarding the security and ethical use of this information is a crucial challenge for educators and technology developers (Amo Filvá et al., 2021).

However, the role of teachers in providing emotional support cannot be fully replicated by machines, which demands a balanced approach between technology and human interaction (Selwyn, 2019). Advances in NLP and AI will likely enable more intuitive and human-like interactions between learners and systems, potentially transforming the adaptive learning experience (Loftin et al., 2022). The integration of ALS with immersive technologies opens avenues for experiential and adaptive learning (Johnson et al., 2020).

5 Artificial Intelligence (AI) in Education

AI is revolutionizing the educational landscape by facilitating personalized learning, automating administrative tasks, and enhancing student engagement through adaptive technologies (Zohuri & Mossavar-Rahmani, 2024). AI-powered systems, such as adaptive learning platforms, analyze vast amounts of student data to customize educational experiences (Mahmoud & Sørensen, 2024). These systems provide individualized instruction, enabling students to progress at their own pace based on real-time assessments of their learning needs, demonstrating AI's effectiveness in optimizing learning outcomes (Contrino et al., 2024).

AI's role in education extends beyond personalized instruction. "Intelligent tutoring systems" (ITS) leverage AI algorithms to deliver real-time guidance and feedback, simulating the experience of one-on-one tutoring (Marouf et al., 2024). Chatbots and AI-powered systems streamline tasks such as scheduling, enrollment management, and student record-keeping (Liu et al., 2022). Furthermore, AI-driven platforms not only enhance cognitive learning but also promote emotional intelligence and social skills, fostering a more holistic educational environment (Vistorte et al., 2024) The potential of AI to adapt instructional content and feedback based on individual student performance creates a more dynamic and responsive learning experience (Gligorea et al., 2023).

Automated grading is another area where AI is making significant contributions (Lujak et al., 2022). Initially restricted to objective assessments like multiple-choice questions, AI systems can now evaluate written assignments and provide detailed feedback on grammar, coherence, and content quality (Lee, 2023). This advancement reduces the workload for educators, allowing them to concentrate more on personalized instruction and student engagement. The impact of AI on administrative efficiency underscores its ability to assist educators in managing large-scale grading tasks while upholding high standards of quality and fairness (Khan et al., 2022).

6 Conclusion

The integration of educational technology has transformed modern learning, shifting from traditional teacher-centered models to dynamic, student-focused approaches. Innovations such as online learning platforms, adaptive systems, and immersive technologies enhance engagement and personalize learning experiences. Platforms such as Coursera and edX have democratized access to quality education for diverse learners. However, this shift presents challenges, including the need for robust digital infrastructure and disparities in technology access highlighted by the COVID-19 pandemic. Concerns about algorithmic bias, transparency, and data privacy also persist. To maximize the benefits of educational technology, institutions must ensure equitable access, implement unbiased technologies, and provide adequate support. Future research should focus on optimizing these systems to foster inclusive and effective learning experiences. Ultimately, the success of educational technology relies on addressing these challenges collectively.

7 Case Studies

7.1 Case Study 1: Coursera's Adaptive Learning Approach: Scaling Personalized Education Globally (Coursera, 2023)

Background

Coursera, established in 2012 by Stanford professors Andrew Ng and Daphne Koller, has become one of the leading online education platforms, partnering with top universities to offer a wide range of courses to millions of global learners. A key feature of Coursera's strategy is the integration of adaptive learning, particularly in its online iMBA program developed with the University of Illinois Urbana-Champaign (UIUC) (Coursera, 2023).

Case Presentation

Coursera incorporated ALS to enhance personalized learning experiences to monitor student engagement and performance. For example, students struggling with concepts such as capital budgeting receive tailored resources such as supplementary tutorials and peer-assisted learning opportunities (Mao et al., 2024). This responsive strategy aims to boost comprehension and retention. Despite its success, Coursera faces challenges in scaling adaptive learning features. Significant investment in instructional design and AI technology is necessary, and ensuring equitable access for students, particularly those in regions with limited technological resources, remains an ongoing concern (Markauskaite et al., 2022).

Impact

The introduction of adaptive learning in the iMBA program has resulted in significant improvements, notably a 92% retention rate in 2021—well above the average 10–15% retention rate typical for massive open online courses (MOOCs). This underscores the effectiveness of personalized learning in enhancing student engagement and success. The ALS has provided Coursera with valuable insights into learner behavior, enabling continuous improvement in course materials and teaching strategies, ultimately contributing to better educational outcomes.

Implications, Conclusion, and Recommendations
Coursera's adaptive learning model has important implications for the future of online education, suggesting that personalized learning pathways can enhance educational outcomes. Coursera's adaptive learning approach in the iMBA program illustrates the potential of personalized education to improve learner engagement and retention. To maximize effectiveness, Coursera should continue investing in instructional design and AI technologies while ensuring scalable adaptive content across its courses.

7.2 Case Study 2: The Rise of MOOC Platforms (SWAYAM and NPTEL) in India

Background (SWAYAM, 2024; NPTEL, 2024)
MOOCs have transformed education globally, with India leveraging this model to tackle issues of accessibility, affordability, and quality. The country's higher education faces significant challenges, including a shortage of quality educators and socioeconomic barriers.

SWAYAM: India's Premier MOOC Platform
Launched in 2017 by the Government of India, SWAYAM aims to make high-quality educational resources accessible to all, especially in rural areas.

Key Features
1. Accessibility: Free courses available to anyone with Internet access
2. Multilingual content: Courses offered in regional languages
3. Affordable certification: Free course content, with a nominal fee for certification
4. Diverse courses: Over 2000 offerings across various fields

Impact
1. Widespread reach: Over 23 million registered learners by 2024
2. Professional development: Lifelong learning opportunities for working professionals
3. Integration in curriculum: Universities mandated to include MOOCs for credit

NPTEL: Specialized Technical Education
NPTEL, initiated in 2003 by IITs and IISc, focuses on engineering, science, and technology.

Key Features
1. Industry-relevant courses: Collaboration with industries for up-to-date content
2. Certification and employment: Recognized courses enhancing job prospects
3. Interactive learning: Discussion forums for enhanced engagement

Impact

1. Access to quality education: Democratizes IIT-level education
2. Fostering research: Encourages students to pursue further education and contribute to technical fields

Challenges Faced by MOOCs in India

Despite their success, MOOCs confront several challenges:

1. Digital divide: Limited Internet access in rural areas hampers participation.
2. Low completion rates: Many students enroll but do not complete courses due to various motivational and logistical issues.

Future of MOOCs in India

The future of MOOCs looks promising as technology advances. The integration of AI and adaptive learning can create personalized experiences and address the skills gap in sectors such as data science and cybersecurity.

Conclusion

MOOCs such as SWAYAM and NPTEL have significantly impacted India's education system by providing accessible and quality education. Continued investment in digital infrastructure and efforts to overcome existing challenges will be crucial in maximizing their potential for inclusive education.

7.3 *Case Study 3: Adda 24×7—Revolutionizing Competitive Exam Preparation (ADDA 24×7, 2024)*

Background

Adda 24×7, part of the renowned Adda 24×7 education technology platform, aims to democratize education in India by providing affordable and accessible resources for competitive exam preparation, specifically targeting aspirants for the UGC NET exam.

Innovative Features

Adda 24×7 offers a robust suite of educational resources, including:

1. Live classes and recorded sessions: Students can engage in real time or access materials at their convenience.
2. Mock tests and subject-specific notes: Comprehensive preparation tools tailored for UGC NET.
3. Adaptive learning algorithms: These track performance and recommend personalized content, quizzes, and revision strategies to address weaknesses.

The platform fosters an interactive learning environment/Its mobile app enhances accessibility, especially during disruptions like the COVID-19 pandemic, allowing students to study anywhere.

Impact on Learners

Adda 24×7 has empowered thousands of students to successfully navigate one of India's most challenging exams. By prioritizing affordability and high-quality education, it boosts student motivation. Particularly for learners in remote areas, the availability of experienced educators through this platform has transformed their learning experiences.

Challenges and Future Direction

Despite its successes, Adda 24×7 faces challenges:

1. Maintaining content quality: Ensuring consistent educational standards across diverse subjects is vital.
2. Affordability vs. profitability: Balancing low-cost offerings with sustainable business practices remains a concern.

Conclusion

Adda 24×7 has significantly reshaped the landscape of competitive exam preparation in India, especially for UGC NET candidates. Its focus on accessibility, affordability, and personalized learning has improved educational outcomes for many students, particularly those in underserved areas. However, ongoing challenges related to content quality and financial sustainability need to be addressed.

Recommendations

1. Establish a systematic approach for updating educational materials to maintain quality across subjects.
2. Develop advanced adaptive features and immersive technologies to enhance understanding.
3. Increase content availability in regional languages to broaden reach and foster inclusivity.

By implementing these strategies, Adda 24×7 can strengthen its leadership in the competitive exam preparation sector and continue its mission to democratize education in India.

7.4 Case Study 4: Unacademy—Pioneering Large-Scale Digital Education (Unacademy, 2024)

Background

Unacademy emerged in 2015 as a transformative force in India's online education landscape, setting out to democratize learning for millions. As one of the nation's foremost online learning platforms, it offers resources across various fields, particularly focusing on competitive examinations such as the UGC NET, UPSC, and CAT. By harnessing digital technology, Unacademy has disrupted the traditional coaching industry, enabling access to high-quality education at an affordable cost.

Innovative Features
Unacademy's incorporation of artificial intelligence (AI) and data analytics plays a crucial role in enhancing learner engagement. The platform monitors user behavior to provide real-time feedback, enabling personalized learning pathways based on individual performance in mock tests and quizzes. Moreover, the platform's integration of live classes with recorded lessons allows learners to revisit challenging topics at their convenience.

Impact on Learners
Unacademy has significantly scaled online education in India, reaching millions of students, especially in rural areas that previously lacked access to traditional coaching institutes. The platform's affordability has broken down barriers for students from economically disadvantaged backgrounds, making quality education accessible for the first time.

Challenges
Despite its successes, Unacademy faces several challenges. Maintaining the quality of educators and ensuring consistent content delivery across its vast network is paramount. The rising competition in the EdTech space, especially post-pandemic, also poses a threat as numerous platforms vie for market share.

Conclusion
Unacademy's journey illustrates the profound impact of digital education on traditional learning paradigms. By leveraging technology to create personalized and accessible learning experiences, Unacademy has paved the way for a new era of education in India.

7.5 Case Study 5: ALEKS in Higher Education (United States) (Aleks, 2024)

Introduction
ALEKS (Assessment and Learning in Knowledge Spaces), developed by McGraw Hill, is an AI-powered adaptive learning system widely utilized in US higher education, particularly for subjects requiring strong foundational knowledge, such as mathematics, chemistry, and statistics.

Context and Implementation
In 2021, Arizona State University (ASU) integrated ALEKS into its introductory math courses to tackle high drop, failure, and withdrawal (DFW) rates. By embedding ALEKS into the curriculum for courses such as College Algebra and Pre-Calculus, ASU aimed to bridge gaps in students' foundational knowledge through personalized learning modules that students completed outside of class.

How ALEKS Works
ALEKS initiates with a diagnostic test to assess a student's knowledge, mapping it into a "knowledge space." This enables the system to create personalized learning pathways, offering exercises tailored to each student's level of understanding. ALEKS continuously adapts based on student performance.

Impact and Outcomes
A 2022 study at ASU revealed that ALEKS led to a 20% reduction in DFW rates and increased student confidence in math skills. The adaptive environment engaged students deeply, offering instant feedback and aiding in the identification of misconceptions.

Challenges and Lessons Learned
Despite positive outcomes, challenges included students finding the initial assessment daunting and a perceived lack of human interaction in the learning process. Nonetheless, the ASU experience underscores the effectiveness of ALS while highlighting the need for a blended approach with traditional instruction.

Conclusion
The ALEKS implementation at ASU demonstrates significant advancements in adaptive learning technology, effectively addressing foundational knowledge gaps and improving student engagement and outcomes.

Recommendations
1. Provide students with clear guidance on the initial assessment to build confidence
2. Combine ALEKS with traditional teaching for diverse learning needs
3. Introduce tutoring sessions and discussion groups to foster engagement

These strategies can further enhance the effectiveness of adaptive learning systems like ALEKS, improving student success rates and experiences in higher education.

7.6 Case Study 6: Mindspark in K-12 Education (India) (Mindspark, 2024)

Introduction
Mindspark, developed by Educational Initiatives (EI), is an adaptive learning platform tailored for K-12 students in India, primarily focusing on math and language skills. It has been implemented in various schools across urban and rural areas, providing personalized education by adapting content to individual learning levels and offering real-time feedback.

Context and Implementation

In 2018, the Government of Delhi collaborated with Educational Initiatives to implement Mindspark in over 50 government schools, aiming to enhance math education among first-generation learners.

How Mindspark Works

Mindspark begins with a diagnostic assessment to evaluate students' understanding. It creates customized learning pathways, continually adjusted based on student progress. The platform utilizes AI to analyze performance in real time, ensuring that each student's learning path is unique. If students struggle with concepts, Mindspark provides immediate feedback and revisits foundational topics as needed, effectively personalizing the learning experience.

Impact and Outcomes

Mindspark increased student engagement and motivation, with teachers noting that students were more enthusiastic about learning math due to real-time progress tracking. Additionally, the platform provided valuable diagnostic insights, allowing teachers to tailor instruction based on individual and class performance.

Challenges and Lessons Learned

Despite its success, Mindspark faced several challenges:

1. Digital divide: Many schools lacked the necessary computer infrastructure and reliable Internet access. Inadequate resources sometimes forced students to share computers, limiting their usage time.
2. Sustainability concerns: Limited funding for technology upgrades raised questions about the program's long-term viability in some schools.

Conclusion

The implementation of Mindspark in Delhi's government schools showcases the potential of adaptive learning systems to meet diverse student needs in the Indian context. By personalizing education, Mindspark significantly improved math outcomes, particularly for struggling students. However, addressing infrastructural challenges and enhancing teacher training is crucial for ensuring the program's success and scalability in resource-constrained environments. This case underscores the importance of a holistic approach to integrating technology in education, combining infrastructure development, training, and continuous support to maximize the impact of adaptive learning systems.

Recommendations

1. Invest in improving computer labs, Internet access, and providing tablets in underserved schools.
1. Collaborating with technology companies and government initiatives can help bridge the digital divide.
2. Implement ongoing professional development to equip teachers with skills in data interpretation and tech integration, ensuring they effectively use Mindspark's tools in classrooms.

3. Engage parents and communities by organizing awareness sessions about Mindspark's benefits, promoting a supportive learning environment at home.
4. Adapt content to local curricula and cultural contexts, involving local educators in development to improve engagement and relevance.
5. Expand Mindspark's focus beyond math and language to subjects such as science and social studies for a more comprehensive learning experience.

These recommendations aim to strengthen the overall effectiveness of Mindspark, ensuring its long-term success in enhancing personalized learning for students across India.

References

ADDA 24×7. (2024). https://www.adda247.com/. Accessed September 21, 2024

Akintayo, O. T., Eden, C. A., Ayeni, O. O., & Onyebuchi, N. C. (2024). Integrating AI with emotional and social learning in primary education: Developing a holistic adaptive learning ecosystem. *Computer Science & IT Research Journal, 5*(5), 1076–1089. https://doi.org/10.51594/csitrj.v5i5.1116

Aleks. (2024). https://www.aleks.com/?_s=5496841326355421. Accessed September 21, 2024

Allen, I. E., & Seaman, J. (2017). *Distance education enrollment report 2017*. Digital Learning Compass.

Amo Filvá, D., Prinsloo, P., Alier Forment, M., Fonseca Escudero, D., Torres Kompen, R., Canaleta Llampallas, X., & Herrero Martín, J. (2021). Local technology to enhance data privacy and security in educational technology. *International Journal of Interactive Multimedia and Artificial Intelligence, 7*(2), 262–273.

Arias, M. (2019). *Examining the digital disability divide in higher education* (Doctoral dissertation). George Mason University.

Barbosa, P. L. S., Carmo, R. A. F. D., Gomes, J. P., & Viana, W. (2024). Adaptive learning in computer science education: A scoping review. *Education and Information Technologies, 29*(8), 9139–9188.

Bishop, J. L., & Verleger, M. A. (2013). The flipped classroom: A survey of the research. *ASEE National Conference Proceedings*.

BrightBytes. (2020). *2020 remote learning survey research results*. https://www.brightbytes.net/rls-research. Accessed September 20, 2024

Cho, Y. (2022). Effects of AI-based personalized adaptive learning system in higher education. *Journal of The Korean Association of Information Education, 26*(4), 249–263. https://doi.org/10.14352/jkaie.2022.26.4.249

Contrino, M. F., Reyes-Millán, M., & Vázquez-Villegas, P. (2024). Using an adaptive learning tool to improve student performance and satisfaction in online and face-to-face education for a more personalized approach. *Smart Learning Environments, 11*(6). https://doi.org/10.1186/s40561-024-00292-y

Coursera. (2023). *Master of Business Administration (iMBA) Program*. Online MBA (iMBA) | University of Illinois | Coursera. [Accessed: Sept. 21, 2024]

Doignon, J. P., & Falmagne, J. C. (2012). *Knowledge spaces*. Springer.

EdX. (2024). www.edx.org. Accessed: September 21, 2024

El-Sabagh, H. A. (2021). Adaptive e-learning environment based on learning styles and its impact on development students' engagement. *International Journal of Educational Technology in Higher Education, 18*(1), 53.

Feng, M., Heffernan, N., & Koedinger, K. (2009). Addressing the testing challenge with a web-based intelligent tutor and a Bayesian model of student knowledge. *User Modeling and User-Adapted Interaction, 19*, 243–266.

Futurelearn. (2024). www.futurelearn.com. Accessed: September 21, 2024

Gao, Y. (2023). *The Potential of Adaptive Learning Systems to Enhance Learning Outcomes: A Meta-Analysis*. https://doi.org/10.7939/r3-a6xd-m403

Gligorea, I., Cioca, M., Oancea, R., Gorski, A. T., Gorski, H., & Tudorache, P. (2023). Adaptive learning using artificial intelligence in e-learning: A literature review. *Education Sciences, 13*(12), 1216.

Hamari, J., Koivisto, J., & Sarsa, H. (2014). Does gamification work? A literature review of empirical studies on gamification. In *47th Hawaii International Conference on System Sciences* (pp. 3025–3034). IEEE.

Johnson, L., et al. (2020). Emerging technologies and the future of education. *Educause Review, 55*(1), 12–28.

Joshi, M. A. (2024). Adaptive Learning through Artificial Intelligence. *International Journal on Integrated Education, 7*(2), 41–43. https://doi.org/10.2139/ssrn.4514887

Khan, M. A., Khojah, M., & Vivek. (2022). Artificial intelligence and big data: The advent of new pedagogy in the adaptive e-learning system in the higher educational institutions of Saudi Arabia. *Education Research International, 1*, 1263555. https://doi.org/10.1155/2022/1263555(2022)

Kizilcec, R. F., Piech, C., & Schneider, E. (2013). Deconstructing disengagement: analyzing learner subpopulations in massive open online courses. In *Proceedings of the third international conference on learning analytics and knowledge* (pp. 170–179). ACM.

Kulik, J. A., & Fletcher, J. D. (2016). Effectiveness of intelligent tutoring systems: A meta-analytic review. *Review of Educational Research, 86*(1), 42–78.

Lee, A. V. Y. (2023). Supporting students' generation of feedback in large-scale online course with artificial intelligence-enabled evaluation. *Studies in Educational Evaluation, 77*, 101250.

Liu, L., Subbareddy, R., & Raghavendra, C. G. (2022). AI intelligence Chatbot to improve students learning in the higher education platform. *Journal of Interconnection Networks, 22*(Supp02), 2143032.

Lockee, B. B. Shifting digital, shifting context: (Re) considering teacher professional development for online and blended learning in the COVID-19 era Educational Technology Research & Development, 69(1), 17–20. (2021).

Loftin, R., et al. (2022). Towards more transparent AI in adaptive learning systems. *AI and Education Journal, 38*(3), 205–222.

Luckin, R. (2018). *Machine learning and human intelligence: The future of education in the 21st century*. UCL Press.

Luckin, R., et al. (2016). Machine learning and human teaching: An evolving partnership. *Journal of AI in Education, 26*(2), 306–330.

Lujak, M., Slavkovik, M., Lebis, A., Vermeulen, M., & Doniec, A. (2022). Objective tests in automated grading of computer science courses: An overview. *Handbook on Intelligent Techniques in the Educational Process: Vol 1 Recent Advances and Case Studies*, 239–268.

Mahmoud, C. F., & Sørensen, J. T. (2024). Artificial intelligence in personalized learning with a focus on current developments and future prospects. *Research and Advances in Education, 3*(8), 25–31.

Mao, J., Chen, B., & Liu, J. C. (2024). Generative artificial intelligence in education and its implications for assessment. *TechTrends, 68*(1), 58–66.

Markauskaite, L., Marrone, R., Poquet, O., Knight, S., Martinez-Maldonado, R., Howard, S., & Siemens, G. (2022). Rethinking the entwinement between artificial intelligence and human learning: What capabilities do learners need for a world with AI? *Computers and Education: Artificial Intelligence, 3*, 100056.

Marouf, A., Al-Dahdooh, R., Ghali, M. J. A., Mahdi, A. O., Abunasser, B. S., & Abu-Naser, S. S. (2024). Enhancing education with artificial intelligence. *International Journal of Engineering and Information Systems (IJEAIS) 8*(8), 10–16. ISSN: 2643-640X.

McGraw Hill. (2021). *How Knewton and AI are transforming personalized learning. McGraw Hill Education White Paper.*

Means, B., Peters, V., Neisler, J., Wiley, K., & Grifths, R. (2021). *Lessons from remote learning during COVID-19.* Digital Promise. https://doi.org/10.51388/20.500.12265/116

Mindspark. (2024). https://mindspark.in/ Accessed September 21, 2024

Morze, N., Varchenko-Trotsenko, L., Terletska, T., & Smyrnova-Trybulska, E. (2021, March). Implementation of adaptive learning at higher education institutions by means of Moodle LMS. *Journal of physics: Conference Series, 1840*(1), 012062. IOP Publishing.

Muldner, K., et al. (2020). Adaptive learning in K-12: A case study of DreamBox. *Educational Technology Research & Development, 68*(4), 947–968.

Nordgren, R., & Olin, M. (2019). Adaptive learning in corporate training: Area9 Rhapsode's approach. *Corporate Training & Development Journal, 30*(1), 18–25.

NPTEL. (2024). https://onlinecourses.nptel.ac.in/. Accessed: September 21, 2024

Pane, J. F., Griffin, B. A., McCaffrey, D. F., & Karam, R. (2014). Effectiveness of cognitive tutor algebra I at scale. *Educational Evaluation and Policy Analysis, 36*(2), 127–144.

Pappano, L. (2012). The year of the MOOC. *The New York Times, 2*(12).

Phillips, K. (2023). *The effects of personalized learning on student achievement.* Dissertations. Paper 225. https://digitalcommons.wku.edu/diss/225

Piech, C., et al. (2015). Deep knowledge tracing. In *Advances in neural information processing systems* (pp. 505–513). Scientific Research.

Quadri, N. N., Choudhary, H., & Ahmad, N. (2023). Mobile learning in higher education: A systematic literature review. *Sustainability, 15*(18), 13566. https://doi.org/10.3390/su151813566

Radianti, J., Majchrzak, T. A., Fromm, J., & Wohlgenannt, I. (2020). A systematic review of immersive virtual reality applications for higher education. *Computers & Education, 147*, 103778.

Reich, J., Buttimer, C. J., Fang, A., Hillaire, G., Hirsch, K., Larke, L., Littenberg-Tobias, J., Moussapour, R., Napier, A., Thompson, M., & Slama, R. (2020). *Remote learning guidance from state education agencies during the COVID-19 pandemic: A first look.* Retrieved from osf.io/k6zxy/.

Reich, J., & Ruipérez-Valiente, J. A. (2019). The MOOC pivot. *Science, 363*(6423), 130–131.

Selwyn, N. (2019). Should robots replace teachers? AI and the future of education. *Journal of Educational Change, 20*(2), 65–81.

Sharples, M., & Domingue, J. (2016). The blockchain and kudos: A distributed system for educational record, reputation and reward. In *European conference on technology enhanced learning* (pp. 490–496). Springer.

Shute, V. J., & Ventura, M. (2013). *Stealth assessment: Measuring and supporting learning in video games.* MIT Press.

Smart Sparrow. (2023). *Adaptive learning in education.* Smart Sparrow. Accessed September 21, 2024.

Spector, J. M. (2023). *Emerging educational technologies and practices.* Springer.

SWAYAM. (2024). https://swayam.gov.in/nc_details/NPTEL. Accessed: September 21, 2024

Unacademy. (2024). www.unacademy.com. Accessed: September 21, 2024

Vistorte, A. O. R., Deroncele-Acosta, A., Ayala, J. L. M., Barrasa, A., López-Granero, C., & Martí-González, M. (2024). Integrating artificial intelligence to assess emotions in learning environments: A systematic literature review. *Frontiers in Psychology, 15*, 1387089.

Zawacki-Richter, O., Marín, V. I., Bond, M., & Gouverneur, F. (2019). Systematic review of research on artificial intelligence applications in higher education – where are the educators? *International Journal of Educational Technology in Higher Education, 16*(1), 1–27.

Zohuri, B., & Mossavar-Rahmani, F. (2024). Revolutionizing education: The dynamic synergy of personalized learning and artificial intelligence. *International Journal of Advanced Engineering and Management Research, 9*(1), 143–153.

Digital Entrepreneurship: Opportunities and Challenges

Festus Edobor and Amina Sambo-Magaji

Abstract In an era characterized by rapid technological advancements and shifting global economic landscapes, the nexus between higher education institutions and organizational ecosystems has emerged as a critical driver of sustainable growth and innovation. This study investigates the multifaceted dynamics of collaboration between academia and businesses, elucidating how these partnerships catalyze organizational success and competitiveness. Through a mixed-methods approach, combining quantitative analysis of performance metrics with qualitative case studies of successful collaborations, we uncover the mechanisms through which academic knowledge, research capabilities, and innovative pedagogies enhance organizational innovation, talent development, and market adaptability. Key findings indicate that collaborations often yield advanced research and development outcomes, directly contributing to technological innovation and product enhancement. Furthermore, these partnerships facilitate a continuous flow of highly skilled talent, equipped with cutting-edge knowledge and competencies, into the workforce. Additionally, our analysis reveals that joint efforts in curriculum development and executive education programs are instrumental in fostering a culture of lifelong learning and adaptability among professionals, thereby enhancing organizational agility and resilience. Conclusively, our research underscores the strategic value of higher education and organizational collaboration as a lever for innovation and economic prosperity. By drawing on empirical evidence and theoretical insights, this chapter contributes to a deeper understanding of how synergies between academia and industry can be optimized to foster an ecosystem conducive to innovation and long-term organizational success. The findings have significant implications for policymakers, educational leaders, and business executives, highlighting the imperative of cultivating strong, strategic partnerships between the sectors as a cornerstone for future competitiveness and growth.

F. Edobor (✉)
Experts Consulting Limited, London, UK
e-mail: festusedobor@expertsconsulting.co.uk

A. Sambo-Magaji
National Information Technology Development Agency, Abuja, Nigeria

L. O. Yesufu, P. N. E. Nohuddin (eds.), *Technology for Societal Transformation*,
https://doi.org/10.1007/978-981-96-1721-0_5

1 Introduction to Digital Entrepreneurship

Digital entrepreneurship can be described as the process of creation, design, and direction of new business ventures by innovative ideas/work through the combination of old techniques and tools of direction in new landscapes. Digital entrepreneurship is the process of creating, managing, and scaling businesses mainly done on online platforms. It harnesses digital tools, online platforms, and innovations catalyzed by technology for the creation and delivery of new products or services to clients for the purpose of making money. Digital entrepreneurship can be defined as the process for creating, developing, and managing business performances by taking responsibility, exploiting digital technologies, and network-bound business practices. In addition, it refers to all activities that use the Internet for value-adding activities (Bailetti, 2012).

With the rapid development of digital technologies and penetration of the Internet, one does realize that digital entrepreneurship belongs to the strong transformers of the modern economy. The opportunities that come with digital entrepreneurship, along with challenges in transforming traditional business models, bringing innovation into the market, and forming new markets, shall form the basis of the discussion. Digital entrepreneurship has many benefits—the low entry barriers on digital platforms and outreach to global potential enable rapid upscaling of young entrepreneurs' businesses. Efficiency is at an all-time high in every walk of life. E-commerce, digital marketing, and online services are opening new ways of generating revenue and engaging customers like never before. Moreover, digital tools and analytics give extremely rich insights into consumer behavior to drive data-driven decisions in personalizing customer experiences. Beyond that, the Internet democratizes information and resources. This has helped a lot in sharing knowledge and thus collaborating to innovate and compete on the global market (Autio et al., 2018).

However, in the pursuit of this goal—to be successful in digital entrepreneurship—there are several challenges that one must be prepared to navigate. Cybersecurity threats, data privacy, and a few more risks necessitate vigorous mitigation strategies for the protection of business operations and consumer trust. Fast technological change entails much continuous learning and adaptation, so it will be demanding work for the entrepreneur who desires to stay relevant and be competitive. Furthermore, the possible digital divide might become a critical problem as unequal access to technology, and therefore to digital literacy, will damage the potential for inclusive growth and innovation. Lastly, regulatory and legal complexities in the digital domain pose another level of difficulty: entrepreneurs having to steer themselves through an endless changing landscape of compliance and protection of intellectual property (Bharadwaj et al., 2013).

In other words, whereas digital entrepreneurship presents unparalleled innovative opportunities and growth in global reach, it is fraught with challenges that require prudent management and strategic acumen. Thus, entrepreneurs must stay competitive in this dynamic environment, ensuring benefits from digital technologies and reducing risks involved (Bharadwaj et al., 2013). This chapter puts into perspective opportunities and challenges inherent in digital entrepreneurship, which can be used to afford insights and recommendations to aspiring entrepreneurs in this field.

2 Digital Entrepreneurship Has Two Important Components

2.1 *Usage of Digital Technologies*

Technologies: The use of a variety of digital tools, platforms, and technologies consists of websites, mobile applications, social media, cloud computing, and data analytics.

Innovation: It usually is the creation of digital technology-based new innovative solutions or enhancements to already existing ones.

Business models: e-Commerce: These are a way to directly sell services or products online; subscription services: periodic subscriptions for digital services or products; freemium models: giving away basic services as a free product to make money off premium features; ad-based revenue: enabling advertising on a digital medium and pocketing some money; market reach: global access—the digital businesses reach the international markets or audiences which otherwise are geographically maximized (Bharadwaj et al., 2013).

Scalability: Digital platforms are very easily scalable, thus easily increasing usage.

2.2 *Customer Engagement*

Digital marketing—Online methods of marketing to attract and engage customers, involving search engine optimization, content marketing, social media, and email campaigns.

Data-driven insight—leveraging data analytics to derive customer behavior and preferences out of it for personalized experiences and target marketing.

2.3 *Operational Efficiency*

Automation: Automation tools are applied to process for more efficiency. Examples—Remote work. Digital tools and platforms make remote work and collaboration feasible.

Innovations and adaptability

Integration of technology: Integrate the new technologies, constantly, regarding the developments of the market and competition.

Agility: A quick pivot or change in the strategy based on the feedback received from the customers or developments in technology.

2.4 Examples of Digital Entrepreneurship

Online stores: E-commerce stores like Amazon or an online store run on Shopify.

Digital marketplaces and service platforms: Uber, Airbnb, Upwork.

Software as a service: Any subscription-based software company, such as Salesforce or Slack, is usually aimed at content creators. A content creator would be a digital influencer or a content producer posting their own materials on platforms such as YouTube and Instagram, looking to make money with an accumulated audience. In other words, digital entrepreneurship is using digital technology during innovation, capturing global markets, and creating value in ways that classic businesspeople just can't, hence allowing entrepreneurs to start and grow businesses with flexibility and scalability that was previously unimaginable.

Digital tools and platforms: Entrepreneurs use multiple digital tools to create and develop their business, such as social networking sites, e-commerce sites, and analytics.

Online business models: Majorly used online business models are e-commerce, subscription services, digital products, and affiliate marketing.

Innovation and disruption: A high proportion of digital entrepreneurs introduce new solutions or business models that lead to disruption in traditional industries.

Global reach: They do business across the world because the Internet helps them. One of the important positive factors businessmen find as an opportunity is to overcome the geographical barrier.

Agility and scalability: Digital businesses can quickly adjust and scale, a lot easier in comparison to traditional businesses.

Data-driven decision making: Business owners are data- and analysis-driven for smart decisions and strategy improvement.

2.5 Stages in Digital Entrepreneurship

Opportunity identification: Look for the void or needs that exist in the market and can be answered through the application of digital solutions.

Business plan development: Clearly explain your business model, target audience, value proposition, and strategies.

Develop an online brand: A website along with a few social media accounts will make your online brand real.

Leverage digital marketing: It is all about getting and making money from your customers. Top customer sources and sites to engage your customers:

Test constantly and evolve: Evolving strategies and every other methodology is an ingredient that you can add at any point in time (Bharadwaj et al., 2013).

Digital entrepreneurship is one such arena where creativity, technology skills, and business acumen converge. It presents an area with a myriad of opportunities.

2.6 Features of Digital Entrepreneurship

Digital tools and platforms: An endless variety of online tools and platforms is used for communication, marketing, sales, and even data analysis.

Global market reach: The ability to reach and serve clients across the globe.

Adaptability: The ability to quickly change tracks with technological transitions and market trends.

Data-driven decisions: Guided by data and analytics as the lighthouse in the choice of business strategies and operation. In a nutshell, digital entrepreneurship is when an entrepreneur is given the capability by digital technology to introduce innovations in solutions, smoothen business flow, and generate venture opportunities in the online habitat (Cohen & Kietzmann, 2014).

3 The Emergence of Digital Startups

The rise of digital startups resonates with this rapid evolution of technology and the importance of digital platforms in various business and non-business aspects of everyday life. Elaborated below is this very phenomenon:

3.1 Factors Behind Digital Startups

Technological innovations such as cloud computing, artificial intelligence, and blockchain are just some of those that have literally brought the barriers to entry for many startups significantly down, providing very potent tools and platforms that come much cheaper in this new era.

Lower-up startup costs: Digital startups are less costly compared to traditional businesses because the use of Internet tools and platforms will reduce the cost of capitals on various aspects such as physical infrastructure or inventory, for that matter.

Global market entry: The Internet is very user-friendly, and simple startups can easily access global markets to get wider access, beyond local or regional markets.

Scalability: often, digital products and services can very easily be scaled up without much extra cost. Generally, software, an app, or some other form of digital product can be given for free to millions of users with almost no additional cost.

Resurgence in connectivity: New ways for startups to access consumers and build a community around products or services on offer are emerging with an increase in the spread of smartphones, high-speed Internet, and social networking sites.

Well-funded venture capital: The capacity for venture capital and crowdfunding has been boosted to support digital startups into financial resources that are crucial for their growth and development.

Entrepreneurial ecosystem: It features numerous accelerators, incubators, and co-working spaces that take interest only in digital startups. Thus, they offer mentoring, maintenance, and networking with their entrepreneurs for business realization (Cohen & Kietzmann, 2014).

3.2 Digital Startups Examples

Tech startups: Enterprise areas are being massively disrupted by Stripe, in the sector for payment processing, and Slack, in providing team communications tools.

E-commerce platforms and enablers: Easy to build and manage an online store—investor democratization to e-commerce through startups like Shopify.

Fintech solutions: Redefining finance from the likes of Robinhood and Revolut by digital ventures, opening new and innovative investment and banking solutions.

Health-tech innovations: Putting medical treatment into the digital ways of following one's state of well-being into companies such as Teladoc and Fitbit.

Disrupted industries: Traditional industries are being disrupted by digital startups, by making the process more convenient, faster, or cheaper than what has been the practice.

Consumer behavior: The consumer and provider way of consuming and delivering products and services has veered toward more online services and platforms over the growth of digital startups.

Innovation acceleration: It will harness the competition associated with a digital startup ecosystem to consider innovation, as innovation will be fast-tracked and met with a constant wave of new technologies.

This type of attitude toward the rise of digital startups is proof enough that the transformation of respective industries, models, and customer experience will be whipped by technology (Davidson & Vaast, 2010).

4 Digital Entrepreneurial Opportunities

The digital entrepreneurs offer a wide range of opportunities not just to the entrepreneur but also to business and innovators.

4.1 E-Commerce and Online Retail

Niche markets: Room for those to be able to specialize in highly specialized or underserved markets with a targeted product.

Global reach: It may unfold the opportunity for an organization to make international customers, all depending on the nature of a digital storefront.

Subscription-based models: Opportunities for products or services that could be sold on a recurring basis: meal kits, beauty boxes, or software subscriptions.

4.2 Digital Marketing

Content marketing: This refers to the creation of valuable content in the form of blogs, videos, or podcasts on the business product with an intention of attracting and engaging potential customers.

Social media management: Helping businesses build an online presence by interacting with their customers on Instagram, Facebook, and LinkedIn.

SEO and SEM: Search engine optimization services along with marketing services increase the visibility of the site and grow its actual traffic.

4.3 Software and App Development

SaaS solutions: Development of software as a service, in any area of business, for example, CRM, project management, or accounting software.

Mobile apps: Develop mobile applications on iOS and Android that involve problem-solving or unique functionalities.

4.4 Fintech Innovations

Online payments: Develop an alternative method to facilitate safe online transactions, peer-to-peer payments, a digital wallet, or platform.

Investment platforms: A tool or platform to facilitate trading or investment along with personal finance management.

4.5 Health Tech, Well-Being, and Wearables

Telemedicine: Remote healthcare services or consultation platforms.

Wearable technology: Health metric and well-being tracking applications.

Mental health: Apps that guide users through therapy sessions and help build resilience or any other mindfulness app.

4.6 Edtech and Online Learning

E-Learning platforms: Build platforms that recommend multiple courses, tutorials, or certifications that come up with them.

Interactive learning tools: Creation of apps or tools making learning a more entertaining and interactive experience with a pinch of gamification or interactive content in them.

4.7 Remote Work Solutions

Collaboration tools: Design collaboration software for teams to help in collaboration, managing projects, and conducting virtual meetings.

Productivity apps: Design software guiding groups and individuals toward much better planning of time and tasks.

4.8 Data Analytics and AI

Data analytics: Analysis services delivered to a business to help that company in making decisions based on the data.

Artificial intelligence: AI solutions designed to automate, provide predictive analytics, or deliver customized experiences.

4.9 Cybersecurity

Security solutions: Tools, software, products offering security against any online threat, data breach, and other online theft.

Advising: cybersecurity and risk advisory.

4.10 Blockchain and Cryptocurrency

Cryptocurrency exchange: Development of platforms through which digital currencies can be traded, purchased, or overseen.

Blockchain solutions: Development of applications through blockchain technology in supply chain and identity validation (Giones & Brem, 2017).

Key Exposures to Opportunities

Do the market analysis: Understanding the needs and wants of target consumers.

Innovate: Be ahead of the game and find out new ways to create value. Relay the support structure: In this scenario, keep your ears to the ground and be ready to reshape or adjust strategies following market dynamics and feedback. Regulations: Stay current with regulations and compliances across your sector, finance, and health.

The online world is dynamic and cuts across a very broad scope, with welcoming avenues for any person who has a high level of creativity and resilience, ready to adapt to every other evolving technology and trend (Kraus et al., 2019).

5 Leveraging Digital Technologies

The leverage of digital technologies means only the use of digital tools, platforms, and innovation that would better business operations, drive growth, and create value (Hsieh et al., 2011). Here is how businesses can effectively embrace digital technologies:

5.1 Adopt Digital Tools

Productivity software: From Microsoft Office and Google Workspace to project management like Asana and Trello, all play a critical, useful role in smoothening workflows and growing better collaboration.

Customer relationship management (CRM): These data sources document customer activity and capture the sales that derive from it. Examples include Salesforce and HubSpot.

5.2 Mining Insights with Analytics

Business intelligence: Tableau, Power BI, Google Analytics, and use of R in business and statistics to bring out the insights related to business functioning, customer behavior, and market trends.

Predictive analytics: This is generally done by applying machine learning algorithms to business data for trend prediction, customer anticipation, and what not for business outcomes.

5.3 Digital Marketing Strategies

SEO (Search engine optimization): Making website visibility on search engines in such a way that it gains free or organic traffic.

Content marketing: Creating meaningful and valuable content through which targeting the defined customer research is done simultaneously to build the brand.

Social media marketing: Advertising the brands on various social media platforms, including from Facebook to Instagram.

5.4 Enhanced Customer Experience

Personalization: Using data to provide personal customer experiences such as tailored recommendations or custom-targeted marketing.

Chatbots and AI: Chatbots based on AI should be integrated to receive prompt customer service and enhance interaction with users in applications.

5.5 Cloud Computing

Scalability: By using Cloud-based resources—AWS, Google Cloud, Azure, etc.—resources can be escalated or scaled down as required.

Collaborations: The Cloud will facilitate sharing files among remote teams with proper communication.

5.6 Digital Product and Service Creation

Mobile apps: Develop an app through mobiles to provide similar opportunities for service or customer engagements.

SaaS: Design for software-enabled applied to any Internet-enabled through subscription.

5.7 Exploiting E-Commerce

Online store creation: Planning and optimization of e-commerce stores which enable selling products and services over the Internet.

Digital payment ecosystem: Setting up efficiently working and secure payment gateways increases the convenience and comfort of customers during the transaction.

5.8 Direct Marketing Automation

Marketing automation enables sending optimized emails, posting on social sites, and segmenting clients.

Operational automation: Robotic process automation to be implemented for optimization having repetitive operations and increased productivity.

5.9 Experience New Technologies

a. Artificial intelligence: AI can be practically and innovatively used for the alternative applications of image recognition, natural language processing, etc., and predictive analytics.
b. Blockchain: Use the rigorousness of the blockchain in technology; secure transactions, smart contracts, and transparency in supply chain.

5.10 Security Management

a. Data protection: Highly secured data protection and tracking strict security policies for the compliance and the safety of the company.

Threat detection: Advanced tools for threat detection and response to cyber threats and vulnerabilities.

Some of the critical success factors for successful implementation are:

Keeping pace of the processes with the rapidly changing technology and the industry.

Invest in training your people so as to empower them to be at home in the effective usage of new technologies.

Integration: Pick the technologies that interoperate smoothly with each other within your current portfolio to avoid isolating information and improve effective productivity.

Measure: Assess on a routine basis how effective digital technologies are in driving business and make adjustments.

Digital technologies, when properly applied, can improve business operation, the experience of the customer, and business competitiveness (Kraus et al., 2019).

6 Challenges to Digital Entrepreneurship

While there is ample opportunity for digital entrepreneurship, there are challenges to be overcome and surpassed by the entrepreneur. Some of the major challenges and strategies to be deployed are listed below:

6.1 Technological Complexity

Challenge: The fast pace of changing technology might get too heavy to handle and to catch up with at one point.

Strategy: Up-skill yourself and your team. Engage with technology gurus/consultants to stay abreast of relevant technologies.

6.2 Market Saturation

Problem: The digital is one of the most fervently competed places with brands vying to win eyeballs in markets that are thoroughly saturated.

Strategy: Differentiate the offering from that of competitors in the marketplace with a specific value proposition, niche market, or innovative feature. Find out what the competitors are up to and where in the market you might find areas under service.

6.3 Financing the Business and Managing Financials

Challenge: Financing is difficult, and yet proper financial management is a precondition to the sustainability of the business.

Strategy: Founders need to look at available other funding sources of starting a business that includes venture capitals, crowdfunding, and bootstrapping. Serious and careful financial planning and management shall be done to see how one can keep track of all the expenses and the revenue figures right from the startup stage.

6.4 Data Security and Privacy

Challenge: Ensuring sensitive data is guarded against cyber threats in accordance with various data protection acts.

Strategy: Tight security with cybersecurity measures, including encryption and very secure access controls. Thus, ensure keeping self-updated with data protection acts and ensure compliance with the same.

6.5 Customer Acquisition and Retention

Challenge: The digital arena is a pool of competition for customer acquisition and retention, where consumer preferences keep changing.

Strategy: Deploy effective digital marketing efforts, build close customer relationships, and keep collecting and responding to customer feedback.

6.6 Scaling Issues

6.7 Problem: Scaling Factors of a Digital Business Can Proactively Trigger Technical, Operations, and Logistical Complexities

Solution: Think of scalability right from the nascent stages using scalable technologies and business systems in use. Always keep the performance metrics under monitoring. And as the business grows, be ready to act and adjust the strategy.

Challenge: Complex and time-consuming regulatory frameworks vary depending on location and from one industry type to the other.

Strategy: Stay up to date on the related regulations and consult with lawyers to check if legally sound. Policies and practices should also address the regulatory requirements.

6.8 Talent Acquisition and Retention

Challenge: The number of time, talented, and skilled workers is very hard to find/retain within a competitive job market.

Strategy: Competitive pay, excellent working environment, and career development are provided for the identification and retention of the best talent in the field.

6.9 Dependency on Technology

Issue: Too much reliance on particular technologies and platforms may cause risk. Be sure at one point in time; they will all be obsolete or some glitchy.

How to deal with it: Have multiple technologies and have a backup plan. Regular audit of technology being used shall be carried over with improvements made on them to meet the needs of business.

6.10 Managing Remote Teams

Issue: Communication, integration issues with remote teams.

Solution: Use for collaboration tools, defining a channel of communication, great team culture, and lines of support which keep remote members active and productive (Kraus et al., 2015).

6.11 Tackle Challenges

Learning continuously: A constant update on industry trends, technological betterment, and best practices.

Networking: Network with other fellow entrepreneurs, mentors, and people in your industry to ask for advice and get support.

Flexibility: Adaptability of strategies and methods depending on the situation and feedback.

Resilience: Treating every problem as a process of learning through persistence in your attitude toward achieving your goals.

In respect of acting upon such challenges proactively yet strategically, digital entrepreneurs will take steps in navigating the complex world into which digital has entered all in the formation of successful and above all resilient businesses (Kraus et al., 2019).

7 Venture Capital and Financing

Funding and investment are just one dimension of building a digital business. Here are some of the key points to keep in mind when considering funding and some of the strategic considerations about it (Tables 1 and 2):

Types of Funding

The Business Plan A document that outlines your business model, the market opportunity, financial projections, and growth strategy.

Strategy: Have a very detailed business plan that is also feasible and clear and explains the value proposition to the investor party briefly.

Pitch deck: A quick presentation of your company, its business opportunity, and the financials you use at a start-off of any normal business talk with an investor.

Strategy: A very good pitch deck is visually exciting; presentations narrate your business story along with popular investor concerns and objections.

Terms and conditions: These are the precise terms with respect to the investment agreement, including equity stake, valuation, and the associated rights for the investor.

Strategy: Walk over the terms and negotiate. Know that you must have legal and financial advisors on hand to make sure the terms are going to be satisfactory if the deal goes through.

Investor fit: How much the potential investors believe in your business vision, value the same things you believe in, and understand your industry.

Table 1 Types of funding. Source: Kraus et al. (2019)

Types of funding	Pros	Cons
Bootstrapping: Self-funding the business from personal savings or from revenue earned during initial operations	You fully own the business and don't dilute equity	Resource constraints, slow growth
Angel investors: High net worth individuals who invest personal money into very early-stage startups	Experience plus mentorship provided; most flexible deals	Equity dilution from possibly conflicting visions
Venture capitalists: VCs put money into high growth starting companies in return for an ownership interest	VCs invest large sums, strategic help, and networking	There will be a lot of say in your business as fast growth will be expected
Crowdfunding: It is the concept of taking small amounts of money from many people, an illustration being Kickstarter and Indiego	This validates the business idea and mitigates some marketing	It is time-consuming and is not necessarily successful as an investment-raising method
Grants, competitions: This is free money derived from some governments, organizations, or competitions	It written or equity, and often comes with a good reputation	Competitive funding, and often targeting some particular, targeted criteria
Bank loans: A classic way to borrow from a bank or financial institute; with repayment, of course	You keep full ownership, fixed repayment	You need to prove a commercial bankable record and have regular repayment

Strategy: Gather information about the background and potential investments done through these investors to know if they fit your business.

Milestones and metrics: Key indicators and milestones that can show the business's progress and potential.

Strategy: Set and monitor concise business milestones and metrics so that you can tell investors with some degree of assurance how your business is really going and what is the potential for your business growth (Morris et al., 2005).

7.1 Getting Ready for Investment

Financial statements: Correct, up-to-date financial records for your business. These include income statements, balance sheets, and cash flow statements.

Strategy: Get your business financial statements in good shape and, if possible, have them audited.

Legal form: The constitutional legal existence of your business, which includes registration of your company and protection of IP.

Way forward: Ensure a proper structuring of your business according to the rules.

Scalability: Signifies how easily your business is going to grow and will handle bigger demand.

Way forward: Explain how your model and technology will scale efficiently.

Networking: It ranges on building relationships with potential investors, mentors, and other industry experts.

Strategy: Attend industry events and become part of the community networks of startups. Use those networks to reach out and connect with potential investors.

By giving due consideration to these and planning properly, you will successfully cut across the funding landscape to secure the necessary investment for growing a scaling digital business (Morris et al., 2005).

8 Building a Digital Business Model

A digital business model simply involves the definition of how your digital business is going to create, deliver, and capture value. There is a step-by-step strategy on how to build a strong digital business model.

8.1 Identify Your Value Proposition

Define with precision the unique value that you will bring your customer through your digital business—whether it be a product, a service, or any kind of solution aimed at serving quite specific needs in the market.

Strategy: Conduct market research to get an understanding of the problems and likes of customers. Ensure that it is an attractive value proposition that will distinctly set you apart from your competitors.

8.2 Define Your Target Audience

Who are your ideal customers? Segment based on demographics, behaviors, and needs.

Tactic: Create detailed customer personas to help inform marketing and product decisions. Use data and analytics to better target and understand your customer persona.

8.3 Choose Your Business Model

How is your business going to make money? Common digital business models include:

E-Commerce: Direct to consumer sales—sell your products from an online web store.

Subscription: Charge a periodic fee for access to content or services.

Freemium: The offering of a basic service for free where improved functionality or services are available at a for-pay premium.

Advertising: Earn money through the advertisements placed on your platform.

Affiliate marketing support: Earn some commission on directing potential sales for other companies.

Strategy: Select one of the models that best fits with your value proposition and targeted segment. Hybrid models can also be experimented with to keep more variations in your revenue models.

8.4 Build Up Your Digital Infrastructure

Put in place the necessary technology and systems you will need to operate your digital venture.

How: Build an interactive and pretty website where you can do your internal communication with your customers.

Backend systems: Implement tools to manage operations such as CRM, inventory management, and analytical tools.

Payment processing: Integrate secure payment gateways to process payments and accept money from your users.

8.5 Now Develop your Marketing and Sales Plan

Define how you will get, convert, and retain your customer.

Action plan:

Digital marketing: Leverage the SEO strategy, content marketing, social media, and email marketing campaigns to scale better traffic and engagement.

Sales funnel: There should be a touchpoint from where your possible customers can move one step further and finally from awareness to a purchase.

Customer retention: Build a loyal customer base through schemes and activities, with personal communication and customer service.

8.6 Key Partnerships

To identify and make relations from other firm or organization for the assistance in achieving your goals.

Strategy:

Strategic relationships: Building connections with companies that can assist you fill your organization toward cross-promotion or co-development.

Suppliers and vendors: Developing reliable partners from whom you purchase goods or services that are integral to your operations.

Affiliates and influencers: Partner with individuals or organizations that have a hit on an audience that aligns with your business.

8.7 Key Resources and Activities Definition

The key resources and activities that you have to perform as you run your digital business.

Strategy:

What resources: Technology, talent, and finance that needs to be used in operation.

What activities: Core activities, i.e., product development, marketing, and customer relationship.

8.8 Set Cost Structure

What are the significant costs to operate your digital business?

Strategy:

Fixed costs: These will decide such things as salaries, software subscriptions, and hosting fees.

Variable costs: Costs fluctuate as the business activity changes, e.g., marketing and transaction fees.

8.9 Measuring Performance and Performance Improvement

The use of metrics and KPI's based analysis, in order to track the operation of your digital business model deployment.

Tactic:

Analytics: Use the available analytical Google applications, advanced business intelligence, data analytics platform that can track KPIs, e.g., conversion rates, customer acquisition costs, lifetime value.

Feedback: Make analysis of customer feedback for the purpose of continuous improvement in your offerings and operations.

8.10 Adapt and Scale

Be open and ready to adapt your business model as markets change and growth opportunities present themselves.

Scalability: Set up processes and systems that scale up with the ability to handle larger revenues and growth.

Innovation: Always look for innovations and improvements to remain relevant and competitive.

A thoughtfully designed and executed set of elements will help you build a robust digital business model in this digital age, which maximizes the level of attraction and satisfaction of customers, moving your business toward long-term success (Morris et al., 2005).

9 Scalability of a Digital Business Model

Scalability, being a characteristic of a digital business, is the process through which one makes his business bigger into higher demands, raising more revenue and getting attention to new markets with the same or better efficiencies retained to maintain margins. Here is an effective process by which you scale a digital business:

9.1 Core Operations Optimization

Efficiency: Make processes efficient to drive operational efficiency and reduce every possible cost. Leverage technologies capable of automating human activities, leading to efficiency in productivity, thus reducing human error as much as possible.

Scalable infrastructure: A website, an app, or a backend system should be able to sustain peak traffic or transactions with ease—stack all the stress tests.

9.2 Optimize Digital Marketing Strategy

Scale ads spend: Increase ad budgets with a gradual boost and track ROI. Use data to optimize ad campaigns wisely.

Diversification of channels: Bring new digital marketing namespaces on board, for example, new pages on social media platforms, content marketing, or influencer collaboration.

9.3 Extend Market Reach

Geographical expansion: You might consider entering new geographic markets. Modify your products to denote preferences and regulations.

New segments: Segments among the customer bases or new demography groupings that could benefit from your product or service belong to new customer segmentation.

9.4 Development and Curating Your Offering

User feedback: Gain insights by seeking feedback from your end users about what works, what does not, and how and where improvements can be made—even how to fill holes or unearth new features or products.

Innovation: Innovate and upgrade your offering constantly to reach the market first and capture the customer ever-changing needs.

9.5 Develop Your People

Talent pool: Acquire the most talented team in the leading growth functions, such as technology, marketing, and sales and customer service teams.

Team structure: Scalable team structure in which job roles and responsibilities are defined and stated. With increased talent availability, remote or distributed teams are the modern preference for most businesses.

9.6 Better Customer Experience

Support system: Develop the best-in-class customer support system, such that the greater number of queries and issues faced could be easily handled.

Personalization: Personalize customer engagement with the help of data leading to improved customer satisfaction and retention.

9.7 Data and Analytics

Performance measurement: Various KPIs would measure which could be of great help to keep track of growth and identification of improvement areas.

9.8 Data-Driven Decisions

Use analytics to drive decisions around marketing strategies, product development, and operational adjustments.

9.9 Alliances

Strategic partnerships with other businesses or organizations could help increase your reach, share resources, or co-develop new offerings.

Distribution channels: Look for distribution partners who aid, affiliate, or resell your solutions for market reach.

9.10 Scalability of Technology

Cloud solutions: Leverage cloud solutions that are designed for scalability in managing massive data storage and processing.

Tech stack upgrades: Keep iterating through tech stack reviews and upgrades so that it designs for scalability with the demand.

9.11 Quality and Homogeneity

Standardization: If there is a way to ensure quality while scaling, it is by standards and best practices.

Consistency: Experience for your brand should be homogeneous, from customer support to delivering your product (Nambisan, 2017).

9.12 Monitor and Adapt

Flexibility: Be adaptive to what the market is saying through performance data and emerging trends.

Continuous improvement: Do regular reviews and upgradation in the processes, products, and strategies for better growth and success.

Important things to keep in mind.

Risk mitigation: Identify all types of risks to scaling that concern operational, market, and financial factors. Reduce the risk.

Customer focus: Ensure customer needs remain the focus and continue to maximize customer satisfaction to retain their loyalty and get word of mouth by providing them with superior value-added products and services (Nambisan, 2017).

Sustainable growth: Be aggressive enough in expansion but not at the cost of operational efficiency and financial stability.

If the right approaches are directed at all these areas, then your digital venture will grow to new heights, and you will remain viable and successful in the long run (Nambisan et al., 2019).

10 Strategies of Digital Entrepreneurship

It requires creativity, strategy, and a well-worked plan that is well executed to achieve success in digital entrepreneurship. Here are some key strategies to help you succeed within the digital landscape:

10.1 Identify a Clear Value Proposition

Problem-solving: What is the clear explanation of what are the issues that your digital product or service can tackle?

Unique selling proposition: What makes the offer unique and valuable compared to that of competitors?

10.2 Market Research on a Wide Scale

Understanding the needs, preferences, and behaviors of the target market.

Analyzing competitors to spot market voids and opportunities.

10.3 Development of a Scalable Business Model

Revenue streams: Diversified streams of revenue—subscription-based, ad-based, e-commerce, etc.

Scalability: Be ready to grow and increase demand without issues related to the business model.

10.4 The Power of Digital Marketing

SEO: Optimize your website and content for a better ranking in search engines. More organic traffic will be generated in the long run.

Social media marketing: Engage and create a community with your audience over social media.

Content marketing: Create valuable, intriguing, audience-engaging content to attract, engage, and retain customers.

Email marketing: Execute email campaigns to facilitate nurturing of leads and relationships with customers.

10.5 Data Analytics

Customer insight: Understand customer behavioral patterns and their preferences.

Performance metrics: Act on the ability to measure and enhance business performance with KPIs.

10.6 Advanced Technology

Website/App: Ensure the ease of usability, responsiveness, and security of your website/app.

Automation tools: Automate repetitive tasks to deliver higher efficiency and a lighter workload for the manual section.

Cybersecurity: Invest in strong cybersecurity to protect digital assets and details of customers.

10.7 Customer Interaction

Feedback: Take feedback from your customers at regular periods and iterate accordingly to sweep away the flaws that still persist.

Personalization: Utilizing available data to personalize customer's journey and make it a soothing experience for the customer.

Customer service: Excellent customer service over chat, email, and phone.

10.8 Promoting Brand

Brand identity: Develop a strong brand identity that should, by itself, be able to communicate to your target market.

Reputation management: This will follow positively with effective trust and credibility-related activities on your end.

10.9 Create Key Partnerships

Strategic partnerships: Develop partnerships with related businesses to get increased reach and resources.

Influencers and leaders: Work with influencers and leaders in your respective industry to get even more credibility and brand exposure.

10.10 Finances Acquired and Monitored

Funding options: Make available a range of funding options such as angel investors, venture capital, crowdfunding, and even bootstrapping.

Setting up a financial plan: Develop an optimal financial plan that carefully manages cash inflow, outflow, and investment.

Table 2 Steps in digital setup process

1	Identification of a problem: Most successful startups identify a contemporary problem or market need for the first time.
2	MVP development: Develop your minimal viable product to test a concept with real users.
3	Feedback loop: Execute the user feedback and make incremental enhancements to the product.
4	Scaling: Scale your product and develop partnerships, marketing, or even geographical growth.
5	Growth and sustainability: Build a growth-sustaining model—a model that could be premium features, subscriptions, and/or acquisitions.

Source: Reuber and Fischer (2011)

10.11 Adapt and Innovate

Keeping up with industry trends: Be informed about your industry and new technologies emerging.

Flexibility: Be ready for the overall pivot or adjustment of all of the strategies based on the feedback from the market and changes in the market.

10.12 Build a Capable Team

Talent acquisition: Employ professional talent aligned with your business goals and culture.

Professional development: The team members should be exposed to continuous learning and development.

10.13 Legal and Compliance

Regulations: Your business obeys the respective regulations and standards for the industry in which you undertake to do business. Intellectual property: Your intellectual property should be patented, trademarks and copyright protection applied (Reuber & Fischer, 2011) (Table 2).

11 Steps in the Digital Startup Process

12 Case Studies

12.1 Airbnb

The case of Airbnb's digital startup process was one of those stories that everybody loved to hear, regarding how one great and simple idea could grow eventually into a global company. This happened due to careful planning, excellently conducted user-centered design, and strategic growth. Here is the detailed process of the digital startup process of Airbnb.

12.1.1 Identification of the Problem and Idea Generation

- Problem: Founders Brian Chesky and Joe Gebbia had a problem paying rent in San Francisco in 2007 and realized that during big events, hotels get completely booked, and the attendees are having difficulty looking for some affordable place to stay.
- Idea: They assumed that individuals attending the conference could not be able to rent a hotel room, and as such they began by renting airbeds on their apartment floor, providing them with affordable accommodation. The idea grew later into an "Air Bed & Breakfast."

12.1.2 Creating the Minimum Viable Product (MVP)

- Minimum viable product: The original Airbnb website was launched in 2008. It was very basic, letting people rent whatever extra space they had in their apartment—probably an air mattress and offering a breakfast. The MVP was primarily about connecting hosts with guests; there weren't too many other bells and whistles.
- Early traction: A few users had signed up, but it wasn't an overnight success for the website. The contents it listed at the time were very minimal, so it was difficult for them to get things built up.

12.1.3 Validation and Refinement

- Customer feedback: To begin with, hailing early users who were utilizing the services to be offered out of the website, they did find that what their users wanted was not a mere dwelling place but a travel experience.
- Product iteration: The platform was further iterated according to feedback to host profiles, user reviews, and security payment systems. It also opened the kinds of spaces that could be listed beyond air mattresses to the whole house or apartment.
- Rebranding to Airbnb: From "Air Bed & Breakfast," its name was shortened to Airbnb to effectively mean that more spaces have been opened to hosts within the platform.
- Trust and safety: It built trust among its users by allowing both host and guests to rate each other. They have also installed mechanisms such as secure payments and 24/7 customer support.

12.1.4 Marketing and Growth Hacking

- Craigslist integration: One of the early growth hacks involved allowing Airbnb hosts to automatically post their listings on Craigslist, which had a large user base looking for rentals. This boosted Airbnb's visibility.
- Targeting events: The founders even targeted large events and conferences searching where demands for accommodations surged, wherefrom they gained users most likely to be repeated.

12.1.5 Securing Funding

Seed funding after going through a series of early struggles, Airbnb was able to raise a seed funding round from Y Combinator in 2009. It immediately gave the capital the exact potential to be able to get mentorship, refine the product, and scale up operations. In fact, with time, huge sums of venture capital investment were able to pass through Airbnb, helping to scale. The money went into the platform, global expansion, and the acquisition of top talents.

12.1.6 Scaling and Going Global

- International expansion: After scaling out of the USA, the company expanded its operations to most of the European, Asian, and many other regions. Localization of the platform was carried out by translating it to various languages and providing region-based support.
- Mobile application: Due to the invention of smartphones, Airbnb developed a mobile application whereby users could book accommodations on the move. As

expected, the application attracted a significant number of followers, especially millennials.

Community of host and guest: As much effort as they put into the development, Airbnb also put in an immense effort toward creating a community of hosts and guests. They organized events, provided resources, and held forums for exchanging experiences and tips. They even took this community to a physical level by organizing meetups with special Airbnb guests from around the world.

Experiences and additional services: A further outstretch of the offering category by AirBnB served up "Experiences," allowing users to book an activity that was hosted by a local. This justified further that the value proposition of AirBnB was not only as a home rental.

12.1.7 Challenges and Adaptation

- Regulatory hurdles: With the growing market share of Airbnb, it steadily began to bump into local ordinances and other legal tangles in various cities across the globe. Even then, the company had to get its way by working with local governments to cause changes in their business model.
- Crisis management: The COVID-19 pandemic forced Airbnb to adapt quickly to its operations. They rolled out advanced cleaning procedures, offered flexible terms of canceling reservations, and redirected their business to long-term rentals because customers could not travel.

12.1.8 Sustainability and Long-term Growth

- Initial public offer: Airbnb got public in December 2020 with one of the most massive IPOs in the history of tech and lands a considerable breakthrough for the company.
- Continuous innovation: Innovation has not stopped at Airbnb. The company has continuously innovated by introducing new features, entering new marketplaces, and adapting to the newer trends in travel. A greater emphasis has been placed on sustainability and responsible travel.

12.2 Outcome

Today, Airbnb is arguably the biggest online marketplace for lodging in the world, with millions of listings spanning almost every country in the world. It has made it easier than ever before to discover unique places to stay and has allowed property owners to earn an income off these spaces.

Lessons Learned Through Airbnb's Startup Journey:

- Start small. MVP was simple, but it solved the problem. Start with an MVP of your idea and iterate based on feedback from your users.
- Boost trust: The most important thing which Airbnb did for results is to make users trust each other. Features that boost security and reliability help attract users in your application and retain them.
- Work on existing platforms: Airbnb gained early traction through its integration with Craigslist, which meant inexpensive marketing to establish the necessary user base.

Take care of the hiccups—Regulatory or global health, resiliency is the key to long-term success.

Community focused—Airbnb's community breeding loyalty and word of mouth.

The story of Airbnb is, by itself, a living testament to how a simple idea can be well executed regarding the startup process with digital tools and become a borderless and transformative global business.

12.3 SLACK

SLACK was an internal solution in communications to a global interface—by closely following the digital startup methodology: product-market fit, iteration, and strategic growth. To detail further on the Slack digital startup journey.

12.3.1 The Story Behind Slack and Recognizing the Problem

- Initial Product: Glitch—It is from a flopped video game and a thriller one that the inception of Slack began. Stewart Butterfield established it through a design team consisting of professional gamers. At this initial phase of developing Glitch, a range of communicative problems was faced. They began to look around for something that would help in making talks fluent and enable them to create a loop of things said for everybody.
- Problem: The existing communication tools, such as email, were quite inefficient for team collaboration. Basically, what was required was the provision of something that could enable real-time communication, smooth and easy file sharing, and conversation history searchable by keywords.
- Constructing the tool: In tandem with their work on Glitch, Butterfield and team were simultaneously working on an internal communications tool. What was taking form was a fix for their own problem. Instant messaging, file sharing, and an archive of all of those conversations were rolled into one tool, and it baked in the ability to make people work straight inside of it—organically driving improved productivity and collaboration.
- Realization of potential: It first hit Butterfield when the gaming project failed; the tool developed internally could be a beautiful, stand-alone shiny thing. All

the team decided to pivot and put all the effort to make the developed tool something that would allow different businesses to use.

12.3.2 Minimum Viable Product (MVP)

- Focus on user experience: The team was hyper-focused on an easy, intuitive user experience. They wanted to make Slack so easy to use, so well designed that it seemed to become an extension of its user. The end product certainly had at the core, the indispensable quality of support for channels—where the various types of team discussion occurred—along with direct messaging, file sharing, and a completely novel way of conducting searches.
- Initial launch: Slack first came to life in August of 2013 as an invite-only product designed for tiny teams and early-stage companies, with the idea that this would let the team gain an understanding from a known—small—community of users of what worked well and what didn't before it saw general distribution.
- User feedback: The team over at Slack got proactive about soliciting its users' feedback and asking what was irritating them, what they loved, and how they might get better. That's when they started to update like crazy, rolling out new features every week, handling interface nitty-gritty, and squashing bugs.
- Frequent updates: The team at Slack worked in very short software development cycles, with frequent updates made to the platform. This led to the guarantee that the product would be continuously updated in line with users' needs and expectations.

12.3.3 Building a Scalable Product

- Integration with other tools: It was realized by these times that the teams had used so many tools; popular integration with the then Google Drive, Dropbox, and GitHub, among others by Slack. That in turn made Slack even more valuable to its users: because of that, they allowed it to be their central hub for work.
- Scalability: After they were making profit, the team started building a robust infrastructure. There had to be things in place to ensure that the app would provide services to an increased number of users. He made sure that the app was not only scalable but considered reliable and could support huge teams in industries of all domains.

12.3.4 Marketing and Growth Strategy

- Word of mouth: The early Slack users showed high degrees of zeal for the product. That zeal and product advocacy made a product that was used enough through word of mouth. The simplicity in using the product and its effectiveness on many occasions would create a high rate of ease for a given task in recommending it to other users.

- Freemium model: Anyone can use Slack for free with basic features and subscribe to a few paid plans that are targeted at customers who need a few advanced features with their teams. That enabled the teams to give Slack a whirl without raising a purchase order to commit a budget.
- Customer success: Slack invested in customer success teams that worked closely with the users to get the best of the platform. This would not only enhance their satisfaction but increase the chances of conversion from free to paying customers.

Targeting much larger organizations as Slack expanded past the traction, it began to support massive consumers—that is, the largest organizations in the world. This began to require features such as a more advanced level of security and compliance tools and support for more comprehensive deployment. Slack introduced enterprise-level features which could be deployed for massive enterprises.

12.3.5 Continuous Innovation and Adaptation

- New features: Slack kept working on new features such as threaded conversations, video and voice call, and bots which automate tasks. Now developers have the potential to build custom integrations and apps. With these, Slack's functionalities went through the roof.
- Reacting to competition: As the world started realizing the potential of messaging as a website, and other companies started launching their products, Slack kept sticking with what they built best—user experience, high integrations, and a high-profitable community.

12.3.6 Key Issues and Strategy Implementation

Competition: The growth pace of Slack has been gaining ground and has been noticed by the big technology players, such as Microsoft, which dispatched its direct competitor—Microsoft Teams. The company also upped the competition by providing better user experience, more integrations, and excellent branding.

- 2019's public offering was the much-needed injection by Slack to equip it financially for further growth and also brought about the public acknowledgment of the company. Through the year 2021, when the company was acquired by Salesforce, it quenched $27.7 billion deeper capacity to offer seamless workforce communication and collaboration solutions under the Salesforce ecosystem.

12.3.7 Long-Term Growth and Vision

- Enterprise focus: After the acquisition, the company continued to focus on strengthening its enterprise market space with the help of resources and customers from Salesforce.
- Long-term vision: The long-term vision of Slack is to build itself as the digital headquarters for all businesses, where all the working things happen, and any team regardless of geography can work.

12.4 Outcome

Today, Slack is one of the largest platforms that billions of users are currently using for team communications and collaboration. The company has changed the way teams communicate, right from making workplace communication efficient and transparent to keeping it neatly organized.

12.5 Spotify

Spotify's Digital Startup is one of the best examples of how creative thinking, strategic partnerships, and a consumer-centered orientation can totally change an industry. Below is the journey of Spotify from an idea to a global streaming giant.

12.5.1 Problem/Opportunity Identification

- Issue: The troubled music industry had a severe problem in the early 2000s when Internet music piracy was rampant. Free downloads from such websites as Napster and LimeWire were enabling people to obtain—at no cost—music that was supposed to be paid for and therefore severely denting the sales of the music and thus the revenue of the industry. While music consumers clamored for easy and ready music at their instant disposal, the traditional semi-legal options available at that time could by and large be referred to as restricted and inconvenient.
- Opportunity—Thus developed the vision for Daniel Ek and Martin Lorentzon. They found that there was an opportunity for more users to enable themselves with legal, accessible, and affordable means of getting their favorites tracks than the justifications of Internet users to download and distribute pirated tracks. Users would find this experience better.

12.5.2 Conceptualization and Vision

Daniel Ek and Martin Lorentzon's vision was to create a very fast music streaming platform where a user did not have to pay for file downloads. They envisioned allowing access to a user, on demand, to a huge music repository with all copyrights cleared, to be listened to for free with ads or on a paid basis free of ads.

- Legal access to music: One critically embedded intention among all this was that they wanted to make the platform entirely legal, and the artists and record labels were to be remunerated truthfully. This involved very serious licensing deals with major record labels, and the whole process was complex and challenging.

12.5.3 Building the Minimum Viable Product (MVP)

- Technical development: Everything in the development of the Spotify MVP had to be about stable streaming technology that could deliver quality audio with minimum buffering on it.
- User interface: Founders were more concerned with having an interface that would be frictionless through which users could easily navigate to reach their favorite music. The design would be clean, intuitive, and great at providing users with a good experience.
- Private beta launch: Spotify launches in private beta in Sweden, 2007. It helps a little small-scale product testing based on further improvements suggested by the feedback from the users before its complete launch.

12.5.4 Signing Licensing Deals

- Negotiation with record labels: Certainly, the most difficult part for Spotify was licensing with record labels. In the music label world, there were plenty of bitter echoes left by piracy, so building careful negotiation was paramount to secure licensing of their catalogs.
- Revenue model: The ad revenue share and the subscription fee were organized into a revenue-sharing model where both would go to the record labels and the artists. This was supposedly meant for ensuring a proper recompense of rights holders because this was critical for getting the required buy-in.
- Building trust: It was so important in closing those negotiations that Spotify was ever actually launched. The platform would have been worthless for users without full access to the music catalog. A lot of founder time was spent both on building trust with the music industry and on closing the deals required to do a launch.

12.5.5 Entry Into the Market

- Public launches in Europe: After an effective performance of the beta, Spotify was finally and most eagerly launched into the public. It was its presentation month of October 2008 in some of European countries such as Sweden, Norway, and Finland, UK, and France. Right from the start the service was available only by invitation, which translated to a strongly exclusive feel and was crucial to controlling growth.
- Freemium model: Spotify was launched as a new-in-concept music streaming service following a freemium business model. This allowed users to engage in the service with advertisements or with a subscription fee to eliminate these same advertisements, plus some other application features, including offline listening. That helped Spotify grab a strong market share in a very small time frame.
- Social integration and word of mouth: An easy interface and a vast music library made the word-of-mouth growth of Spotify come immediately quite fast. This is further integrated with social media, allowing customers to share what they were actually listening to, say, on Facebook, which helps in increasing huge acceptance.
- Enter new markets: With its proven success in Europe, it was only a matter of time before Spotify pushed into new markets. That has included, of course, breaching the USA in 2011. The licensing landscape was particularly hard in the USA; the move to land a foot on the continent of the Americas was quite essential for Spotify's global growth.

12.5.6 Platform Scaling Strategy

- Technical infrastructure: As it grew in numbers, Spotify had been making huge investments in scaling the technical infrastructure that underpins the millions of concurrent streams generated by its users. This involved backend systems optimizations, enhancements in data centers, and ensuring services were always available and fast.
- Personalization capabilities: This is the aspect in which Spotify has truly begun to throw its weight behind; according to the author, it began massively to invest in personalized key features such as curated playlists, Discover Weekly, and personalized radio stations. By applying these, with the help of algorithms, it will recommend music based on listening habits, to improve user experience and engagement.
- Mobile app development: Mobile iOS and Android applications were developed to allow customers to stream music while on the move. Mobile experience is a crucial growth engine because the music is with you on the move.

12.5.7 Monetization and Business Strategy

- Free tier supported by advertising: Users could try indefinitely—what is commonly referred to as a "forever trial," according to the ad-supported freemium model. The ads that are generated allow the consumers to get a feel for the service without even making any commitment. Spotify would partner with an advertiser in order to serve up dynamic, targeted new ad formats to users.
- Premium subscription: This unlocked more features, like the possibility for offline listening, better audio quality, and listening without commercials. Spotify continuously increased the value of its premium subscription in an attempt to try to move up more of its increasingly large user base from free to paid.
- Partnerships and bundles: The bundled subscriptions from major telecommunication operators and device manufacturers also offered Spotify. For example, whereas the subscription to Spotify with some phone plans was free, Spotify was sold with access to hardware products like speakers.

12.5.8 Competitors and Competitive Advantage

- Coping with competitors: Being characterized by its growth, Spotify attracted stiff competition from Apple Music and Amazon Music to Google Play Music, among others. Spotify responded to these issues by focusing on its core competencies: personalization, user experience, and an existence of an extensive amount of music within its library.
- Artist and label relations—Largely as a response to complaining artists and labels regarding Spotify's payouts to them, they've attempted to be more transparent and since come up with new tools for artists that include Spotify for Artists which houses analytics and promotion tools for artists.
- Regulatory and legal challenges: Meanwhile, Spotify was mired in a litany of regulatory challenges regarding music licensing, royalties, and data privacy. The company had to invest heavily in legal and regulatory compliance to steer ahead smoothly in different jurisdictions.

12.5.9 Going Public, Long-Term Vision

- IPO: In April 2018, Spotify completed its first-ever public offering by directly listing its shares on the New York Stock Exchange. That was a strange move—a direct listing allows a company to go public and have shares traded on a stock exchange, all without raising capital or using underwriters. The direct listing was a reflection of Spotify's confidence in its business model and growth prospects.
- Spotify going beyond music: As Spotify spent a lot on purchasing these podcasts and production companies, such as Gimlet Media and Anchor, they were being

built up to go beyond music. The ambition was to become the favorite platform for all good audio, full stop.
- Focus on innovation: Spotify continues to innovate through the improvement of its recommendation algorithms, new content formats, and new stakeholders. It also tirelessly invests in new technologies such as voice recognition and AI to enhance user experience.
- Spotify is the most extensive music streaming service ever as it is used by hundreds of millions of users in the world and has a library containing very large numbers of music, podcasts, and other audio content. Fundamentally, it has changed the way in which people get new music—from the ownership of CDs and downloads to access through streaming.

12.6 Conclusion

Digital venturing is the phenomenon of change power, which uses technology for innovation and value addition. Digital growth ventures have high potential and challenges (Reuber & Fischer, 2011).

Key Points
Dynamic opportunities: The digital world opens opportunities across spectra, be it e-commerce, health tech, or edtech. Capturing these opportunities with clear knowledge of the market needs and technological trends is fundamental. Strategic use of technology: Business digital technologies rely on data analytics, cloud computing, automation—as a whole, pretty much everything beginning to emerge—to facilitate the transformation of operations, resulting in improved digital experiences and growth.

How to resolve problems: Beforehand, a digital entrepreneur might expect a saturated market, technological complexity, and funding constraints. Things that would master the challenges include proactiveness, continuous learning, and adaptability.

A model that scales: In a good model of a digital business, there would be a clear consideration of its value propositions, target audience, and revenue streams. Your growth strategy needs to be based on three pillars: scalability, customer satisfaction, and operational efficiency.

Funding and investment: Appreciate funding alternative ways and raise funding for investment for scaling the digital venture. Make friendly business cases and be within financial discipline.

Continuous improvement: The digital world does not stand static. One must continuously keep changing and innovating oneself to stay in competition. Periodic review and enhance strategies, operations, and offerings considering market feedback and performance data.

References

Autio, E., Nambisan, S., Thomas, L. D., & Wright, M. (2018). Digital affordances, spatial affordances, and the genesis of entrepreneurial ecosystems. *Strategic Entrepreneurship Journal, 12*(1), 72–95. https://doi.org/10.1002/sej.1266

Bailetti, T. (2012). Technology entrepreneurship: Overview, definition, and distinctive aspects. *Technology Innovation Management Review, 2*(2), 5–12. https://doi.org/10.22215/timreview/520

Bharadwaj, A., El Sawy, O. A., Pavlou, P. A., & Venkatraman, N. (2013). Digital business strategy: Toward a next generation of insights. *MIS Quarterly, 37*(2), 471–482. https://doi.org/10.25300/MISQ/2013/37:2.3

Cohen, B., & Kietzmann, J. (2014). Ride on! Mobility business models for the sharing economy. *Organization & Environment, 27*(3), 279–296. https://doi.org/10.1177/1086026614546199

Davidson, E., & Vaast, E. (2010). Digital entrepreneurship and its socio material enactment. In *The 43rd Hawaii International Conference on System Sciences (HICSS)* (pp. 1–10). IEEE. https://doi.org/10.1109/HICSS.2010.150

Giones, F., & Brem, A. (2017). Digital technology entrepreneurship: A definition and research agenda. *Technology Innovation Management Review, 7*(5), 44–51. https://doi.org/10.22215/timreview/1076

Hsieh, J. P. A., Rai, A., & Keil, M. (2011). Addressing digital inequality for the socioeconomically disadvantaged through government initiatives: Forms of capital that affect ICT utilization. *Information Systems Research, 22*(2), 233–253. https://doi.org/10.1287/isre.1090.0246

Kraus, S., Palmer, C., Kailer, N., Kallinger, F. L., & Spitzer, J. (2019). Digital entrepreneurship: A research agenda on new business models for the twenty-first century. *International Journal of Entrepreneurial Behavior & Research, 25*(2), 353–375. https://doi.org/10.1108/IJEBR-06-2018-0425

Kraus, S., Richter, C., Papagiannidis, S., & Durst, S. (2015). Innovativeness and initiative as success factors in digital entrepreneurship: Case study of a digital entrepreneurship competition. *International Journal of Entrepreneurial Venturing, 7*(3), 244–259. https://doi.org/10.1504/IJEV.2015.070444

Morris, M. H., Schindehutte, M., & Allen, J. (2005). The entrepreneur's business model: Toward a unified perspective. *Journal of Business Research, 58*(6), 726–735. https://doi.org/10.1016/j.jbusres.2003.11.001

Nambisan, S. (2017). Digital entrepreneurship: Toward a digital technology perspective of entrepreneurship. *Entrepreneurship Theory and Practice, 41*(6), 1029–1055. https://doi.org/10.1111/etap.12254

Nambisan, S., Wright, M., & Feldman, M. (2019). The digital transformation of innovation and entrepreneurship: Progress, challenges, and key themes. *Research Policy, 48*(8), 103773. https://doi.org/10.1016/j.respol.2019.03.018

Reuber, A. R., & Fischer, E. (2011). International entrepreneurship in internet-enabled markets. *Journal of Business Venturing, 26*(6), 660–679. https://doi.org/10.1016/j.jbusvent.2011.05.002

The Digital Shift: Revolutionizing Entrepreneurship Through Technology

Amna Rizvi

Abstract Digital entrepreneurship (DE) has emerged as a key driver of innovation and economic growth, transforming traditional business practices through digital technologies. This chapter explores the concept of DE and its evolution across three key eras: the Seed Era, Startup Era, and the Expansion Era. It examines how digital technologies, such as the Internet, cloud computing, and artificial intelligence, transformed traditional business models, creating new opportunities for startups to scale and innovate. The chapter categorizes DE into mild, moderate, and extreme forms, illustrating examples such as Olive Garden, Lenskart, and Airbnb, which showcased varying degrees of digital integration. It further analyzes the digital entrepreneurship mindset, highlighting the importance of adaptability, innovation, and customer focus, with companies such as Amazon and Netflix as leading examples. Key digital competencies, including technology readiness, exploration, and exploitation, are discussed in relation to successful business transformation. The role of information technology (IT) in revolutionizing entrepreneurship, especially during global crises like the COVID-19 pandemic, is also explored, emphasizing the impact of IT on operational efficiency and market expansion. Case studies of companies such as Netflix and Shopify demonstrated how digital platforms enabled businesses to overcome challenges and seize new opportunities. The chapter concludes by identifying key strategies for success in digital entrepreneurship, including comprehensive digital strategies, technology investment, and leveraging customer insights. It can be inferred that DE has significantly reshaped the business landscape, enabling startups to thrive through innovative technologies and adaptive strategies. By adopting a digital mindset and effectively leveraging IT, entrepreneurs can navigate challenges and unlock new growth opportunities.

A. Rizvi (✉)
Management and Research Institute, Lucknow, India

L. O. Yesufu, P. N. E. Nohuddin (eds.), *Technology for Societal Transformation*,
https://doi.org/10.1007/978-981-96-1721-0_6

1 Introduction

Digital entrepreneurship (DE) involves creating and managing businesses that leverage digital technologies to deliver products and services, engage customers, and drive innovation. The technological transformation within this field has fundamentally reshaped how businesses operate, innovate, and connect with their audiences. By harnessing these advancements, entrepreneurs can develop sustainable business models that not only meet market demands but also contribute positively to society. This interplay between technology and entrepreneurship emphasizes the critical role of innovation in achieving long-term success in the digital landscape. The shift from conventional to DE is undeniable, with trailblazers such as Google, Facebook, Microsoft, and Apple revolutionizing not only the business world but also the way we communicate in our daily lives. This chapter explores the profound impact of digital innovation on the emergence and growth of startups, highlighting the myriad opportunities it presents while also addressing the significant challenges that accompany these changes. By examining successful strategies employed by thriving ventures, the chapter aims to provide valuable insights for navigating the complexities of a rapidly evolving business landscape, ultimately underlining the essential role of technology in shaping the future of entrepreneurship.

2 Digital Entrepreneurship (DE)

Digital entrepreneurship (DE) is a transformative phenomenon fueled by advancements in technology, particularly the Internet and information and communications technology (Le Dinh et al., 2018; Nambisan, 2017) business components into digital formats. DE is "a subcategory of entrepreneurship in which some or all of what would be physical in a traditional organization has been digitized" (Hull et al., 2007). This reflects a blend of traditional practices with innovative digital methods (Le Dinh et al., 2018). DE is categorized into three levels: mild, moderate, and extreme (Liao et al., 2013). Mild DE involved businesses like the Olive Garden, integrating digital components for online engagement while remaining physical. Moderate DE, such as Lenskart, combined strong online presence with physical outlets, using digital tools like virtual try-ons. Extreme DE fully digitized operations, exemplified by Airbnb and Uber, transforming industries through peer-to-peer platforms (Liao et al., 2013).

The evolution of DE includes three key eras. The Seed Era (1990–2000) initiated by Internet technology marked the rise of electronic business practices and early studies on the "Internet economy" (Feindt et al., 2002). This evolved into the Startup Era (2001–2015), driven by social media and cloud computing that digitalized business processes (Veit et al., 2014; Rippa & Secundo, 2019). Currently, the Expansion Era (2016–present) reflects widespread digital integration, accelerated by the COVID-19 pandemic, which increased Internet usage by 60% (Soto-Acosta, 2020) and blurred traditional entrepreneurship boundaries, fostering "everyday entrepreneurship" opportunities (van Gelderen et al., 2021).

Successful digital startups such as Turo and Shopify leverage technology to disrupt traditional markets (Soumya & Arumugam, 2024). DE involves creating and transforming businesses through digital technologies, fostering innovation and competitive advantages (European Commission, 2015). By understanding customer needs and using digital tools strategically, entrepreneurs can unlock growth opportunities (European Commission, 2015).

2.1 Mindset and Competencies for Digital Entrepreneurs

DE thrives on adaptability and customer focus, as seen with Netflix's shift to streaming and Zappos' user-centric approach. A digital mindset drives innovation and agility, with companies like Amazon leveraging data for enhanced customer experiences (Schückes & Gutmann, 2021). This mindset boosts innovation speed by 40% (Buchholz et al., 2020), requiring entrepreneurs to embrace proactivity, risk-taking, and digital tools (Soltanifar & Smailhodžić, 2021), shifting from fixed to growth mindsets (Dweck & Yeager, 2019).

Airbnb redefined hospitality with its digital platform and analytics (Sundararajan, 2019), while Shopify empowers entrepreneurs with easy online store creation (Shopify Inc., 2023). Key competencies include readiness for new tech (Tesla's EV R&D) (Parasuraman & Colby, 2015), exploration (Amazon's AI recommendations) (He & Wong, 2004), and exploitation (Walmart's optimized supply chain) (Bohmann et al., 2015). Procter & Gamble (Ghasemaghaei, 2019), Uber (Rahman & Thelen, 2019), and Zoom exemplify the critical role of data-driven decision-making.

Developing a Digital Entrepreneurship Mindset (DEM) Guide: Key Actions and Pitfalls In the digital age, a strong DEM is essential for adapting, leveraging technology, and seizing opportunities. Figure 1 illustrates key actions under "Ignite the F.L.A.M.E.S of Digital Entrepreneurship," while Fig. 2 highlights common pitfalls to avoid, termed "C.R.U.N.C.H.: The Pitfalls of Digital Entrepreneurship."

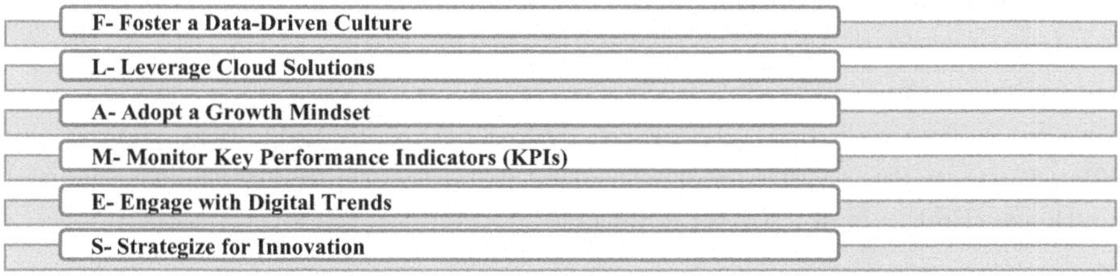

Fig. 1 Ignite the **F.L.A.M.E.S** of digital entrepreneurship. Source: Developed by author

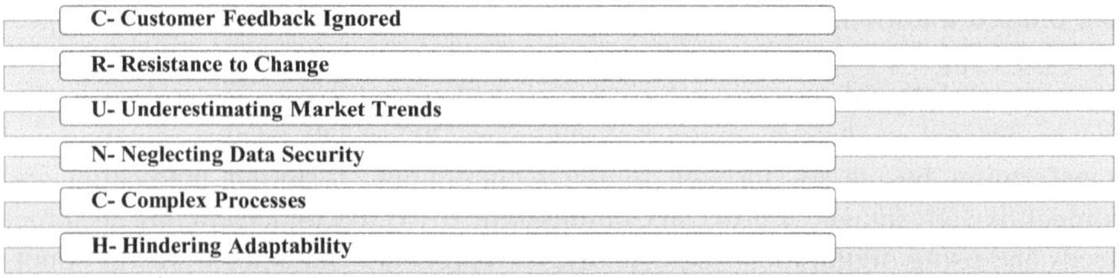

Fig. 2 C.R.U.N.C.H.: The pitfalls of digital entrepreneurship. Source: Developed by author

3 Information Technology (IT)'s Impact on Transforming Entrepreneurship

IT transforms entrepreneurship through DE (Yadav et al., 2023). Digitalization enables platforms like Shopify to connect small businesses to wider markets at low costs (Hair et al., 2012). IT, especially cloud services and AI, reduces transaction costs and enhances digital success (Giones & Brem, 2017), driving innovation and operational efficiency (Kraus et al., 2019; Zairis & Zairis, 2022). However, digital ecosystems present challenges, such as data privacy, highlighted by Facebook and Airbnb. During the pandemic, tools like Zoom became essential for client relations (Reno et al., 2020). Leveraging IT is crucial for innovation and customer engagement, with Airbnb and Netflix providing personalized experiences (Yuan et al., 2017; Ullagaddi, 2024). Big data analytics, such as Netflix's viewer data, and cloud tools like Dropbox streamline operations (Mohieldin, 2022; Attaran, 2017). Home-based ventures benefit from IT's "mental mobility" (Di Domenico et al., 2014) and growth infrastructure (Bergholz et al., 2024). IT accelerates entrepreneurship by categorizing digital platforms into innovation, transaction, and integration (Hsieh & Wu, 2019). Digital transformation facilitates rapid market adaptation, as seen with Walmart during COVID-19 (Day & Schoemaker, 2016). Platforms such as Shopify and Uber improve global access and trust through peer ratings (Lee, 2020; Srinivasan & Venkatraman, 2018) while fostering co-creation ecosystems like LEGO Ideas (Guthrie, 2014).

3.1 Transformative IT Trends Shaping Digital Entrepreneurship (DE)

Transformative IT trends drive innovation and growth in DE by enhancing customer connections and streamlining operations (Sutrisno et al., 2023; Paramesha et al., 2024; Bican & Brem, 2020) and are crucial for success in today's entrepreneurial landscape (Endres et al., 2022) (Table 1).

Role of IT in Revolutionizing Entrepreneurship in the Face of Global Crises The COVID-19 pandemic accelerated digital transformation, making

Table 1 Key IT trends for entrepreneurial success

Trends	Description	Examples
Mobile Computing	Optimizes user experience (Hassan et al., 2022)	Instacart
Social media	Engages customers (Dessart et al., 2015)	Nike on Instagram
AI and automation	Enhances service and decisions (Schmitt, 2023)	Zara's trend prediction
Cloud computing	Scalable resources (Islam et al., 2023)	Startups scaling
IoT	Automates workflows (O'Toole et al., 2020)	Nest Thermostat
Blockchain	Increases transparency (Xu et al., 2021)	Supply chain innovations
Mobile tech	Boosts consumer engagement (Alalwan et al., 2020)	Transaction apps
E-commerce and payments	Streamlines transactions (Srinivasan & Venkatraman, 2018)	Integrated payment systems
Big data	Supports decision-making (Nnaji et al., 2024)	Data-driven startups

Table 2 Digital adoption acceleration across regions

	Digital interaction		
Region	Pre-crisis (%)	Post-COVID (%)	Acceleration (Years)
Global	36%	58%	3
Asia-Pacific	32%	53%	4
Europe	32%	55%	3
North America	41%	65%	3

Source: O'Toole et al. (2020)

technology essential for survival (Brynjolfsson & McAfee, 2014). A McKinsey survey revealed that companies fast-tracked digitization by 3–4 years and digital products by 7 years (O'Toole et al., 2020). In healthcare, finance, and retail, IT tools such as AI and cloud computing provided competitive advantages as 80% of customer interactions shifted online (O'Toole et al., 2020).

India's startup ecosystem is rapidly growing, with 77% of startups investing in AI and advanced technologies, positioning the country as a global innovation hub (SAP India, 2024). The pandemic further drove digital tool adoption across fintech, healthcare, e-commerce, and edtech, leveraging technology for scalability and social impact (Economic Times, 2024). AI, cloud computing, and blockchain enhance efficiency and security, improving healthcare outcomes and fintech trust (Business Today, 2024). Tables 2, 3, and 4 summarize key drivers and their impact on startup growth in Indian entrepreneurship.

The shift created new revenue streams and boosted digital entrepreneurship in B2C sectors such as retail and finance (O'Toole et al., 2020) (Fig. 3).

A Global Perspective: What's Next? The ripple effects of India's AI investment extend beyond its borders. As Indian startups continue to innovate, they set a precedent for emerging markets worldwide (SAP India, 2024). Their journey offers

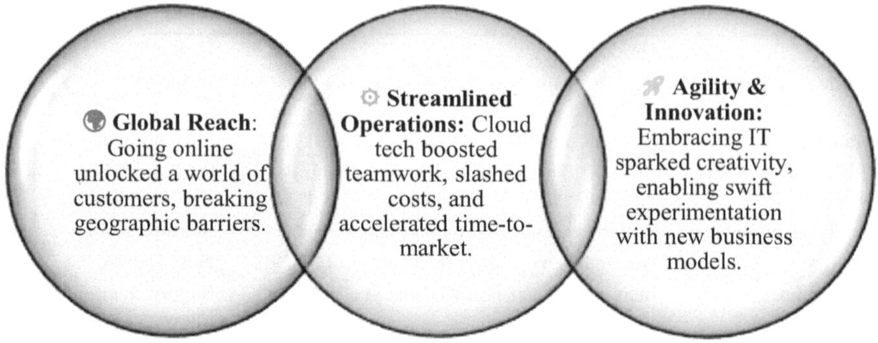

Fig. 3 Benefits of digital-first strategies for startups during the pandemic. Source: Developed by author

Table 3 Key drivers of digital entrepreneurship

Key drivers	Description
Vibrant talent pool	India's 1.3 billion population offers a vast pool of engineers and tech enthusiasts
Government support	Initiatives like "Startup India" provide financial aid and resources for entrepreneurs
Growing consumer market	The expanding middle class seeks personalized experiences, driving startup innovation

Source: SAP India (2024)

Table 4 Key sectors and technologies driving growth in Indian startups

Sector	Key technologies	Impact on growth
Fintech	AI, blockchain	Streamlined financial services and enhanced customer trust (Business Today, 2024)
Healthcare	Telemedicine, data analytics	Improved access to healthcare and personalized treatment (Times of India, 2024)
E-commerce	Cloud computing, AI	Enhanced customer experience through personalized shopping (Economic Times, 2024)
Edtech	Virtual reality, data analytics	Increased engagement and accessibility in learning (Times of India, 2024)

valuable lessons on harnessing technology for economic growth, addressing societal challenges, and fostering sustainable practices. The global community should pay close attention to the developments in India, as the successes and failures of these startups will likely influence the future trajectory of technology adoption across developing nations (SAP India, 2024). Figure 4 shows the valuable lessons that the evolution of Indian startups exhibits for entrepreneurs and business leaders worldwide.

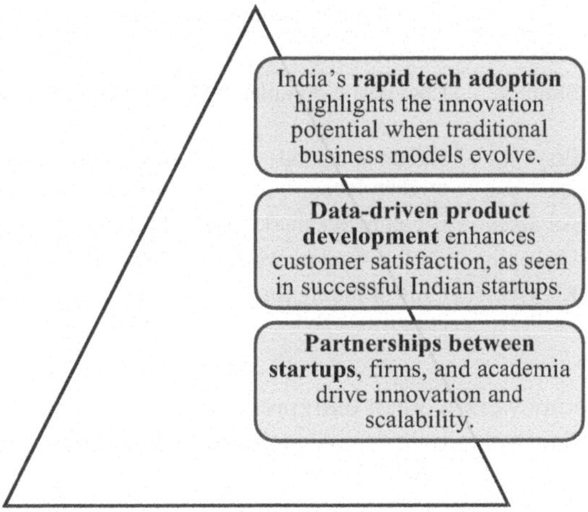

Fig. 4 Lessons from the evolution of Indian startups. Source: Developed by author

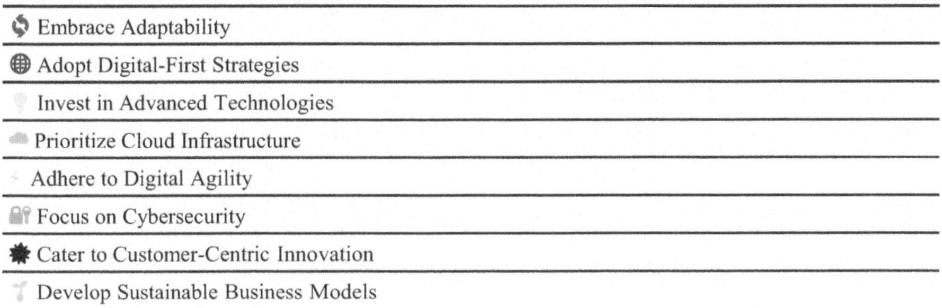

Fig. 5 Lessons learned for future startups. Source: Developed by author

The discussion on IT's societal role is crucial, prompting global stakeholders to learn from India. Innovators will reshape entrepreneurship and redefine technology's impact on society (Fig. 5).

4 Unlocking Opportunities in Digital Entrepreneurship (DE)

DE offers unmatched growth opportunities for businesses and startups by lowering entry barriers, enhancing customer engagement, and providing access to global markets through digital technologies. DE reduces startup costs, with platforms like Shopify allowing businesses to launch without physical locations (Arora & Valeri, 2024), while e-commerce platforms like Amazon enable small businesses to access international markets. Tools such as Instagram and Facebook facilitate targeted advertising and real-time feedback, boosting brand visibility (Arora & Valeri, 2024).

Technologies such as AI, blockchain, and machine learning improve services, exemplified by AI-powered chatbots for 24/7 support (Wang et al., 2024). DE also

Table 5 Key digital platforms and their benefits for entrepreneurs

Platform	Opportunities	Benefits
Shopify	Low-cost e-commerce	Global reach; customizable storefronts (Arora & Valeri, 2024)
Etsy	Handmade goods marketplace	Monetizes hobbies; eco-conscious consumers (Akhter & Mazumdar, 2024)
Amazon	E-commerce marketplace	Global reach; fulfillment services (Smit et al., 2022)
LinkedIn	Professional networking	Networking and mentorship (Davis et al., 2020)
Kickstarter	Crowdfunding for creatives	Capital raising; community building (Canestrino et al., 2020)

empowers women entrepreneurs by removing cultural barriers, allowing platforms like Etsy to help female artisans monetize their skills globally (Akhter & Mazumdar, 2024). Programs like Malaysia's e-Usahawan provide essential tech and marketing training for thriving in the digital economy (Smit et al., 2022). Moreover, digital platforms grant startups global reach without physical stores, significantly expanding cross-border e-commerce (Agostinho, 2020). Platforms like LinkedIn enable networking with peers and investors, with 70% of professionals citing it as essential for career growth (Davis et al., 2020).

DE aligns with ethical business models, as seen with Etsy promoting sustainable consumption, with 73% of consumers prioritizing eco-friendly purchases (Neri, 2022). Tools like Shopify's inventory management facilitate efficient scaling by automating processes (Buchholz et al., 2020). DE fosters innovation in industries, as exemplified by companies such as Uber and Airbnb, which have transformed traditional models (Mousa & Morrar, 2023). Platforms like Kickstarter provide new funding avenues through global crowdfunding campaigns (Canestrino et al., 2020), while e-learning platforms like Udemy offer continuous learning opportunities for entrepreneurs (Orok et al., 2024). Additionally, AI enhances business operations and customer experiences through personalized marketing strategies (O'Toole et al., 2020), and tools such as Slack and Zoom enable remote operations, reducing costs and widening the talent pool (Thai & Miyazaki, 2024) (Tables 5 and 6).

5 Navigating the Challenges of Digital Entrepreneurship (DE)

DE has become essential for economic growth and innovation, but it presents various challenges for entrepreneurs. Readiness for transition poses a significant hurdle, as SMEs often lack the necessary digital infrastructure and skills for dual digitalization and sustainability, impacting competitiveness (Edrak et al., 2022).

Perception and attitudes also play a role, with some SME owners viewing digitalization as unnecessary (Ogrean & Herciu, 2021). In Jordan, entrepreneurs face financial support and logistical issues, especially women, who encounter funding

Table 6 Technologies empowering DE

Technology	Benefit
AI	Automation
Blockchain	Trust
Automation tools	Efficiency
ML	Insights
Crowdfunding	Validation

challenges and operational complications (Alawamleh et al., 2023). A lack of experience in digital marketing hampers management capabilities (Alawamleh et al., 2023). Additionally, female entrepreneurs in Egypt face societal and cultural constraints that limit access to funding (Fakheldin et al., 2023). Many struggle with understanding AI Applications, limiting integration into their businesses (Özsungur, 2024).

Other barriers include market interruptions and insufficient training, which hinder effective navigation of the digital landscape (Martínez-Peláez et al., 2023). During crises, SMEs often lack effective crisis management strategies and resource allocation (Akpan et al., 2024) and face digital adoption barriers such as funding constraints (Akpan et al., 2024). Rapid digitalization can exacerbate existing inequalities and hinder progress toward Sustainable Development Goals (Rothe et al., 2023). Regional disparities and gender inequality limit women's participation in entrepreneurship and contribute to rural stagnation (Olarewaju & Fernando, 2020).

Unregulated ecosystems can stifle sustainable growth (Cheng et al., 2021), and environmental challenges from climate-related disruptions complicate entrepreneurship (Attree & Kleinschafer, 2024). Marginalized entrepreneurs may avoid digital marketing due to heightened risk perceptions (Fuller et al., 2022). Emerging digital platforms present opportunities for innovation but also pose competitive challenges (Marrapodi, 2023), and resource constraints can hinder identity establishment in the digital realm (Marrapodi, 2023). As the digital landscape evolves, addressing these challenges will be crucial for entrepreneurs aiming to thrive and unlock new growth opportunities in the digital economy.

6 Strategies for Success in Digital Entrepreneurship (DE)

To thrive in today's digital landscape, businesses must implement innovative strategies that enhance efficiency and align with evolving consumer demands. A comprehensive digital strategy is essential, as exemplified by Zalando, which optimized its online platform to boost customer engagement and sales. Companies should invest in technology, such as Warby Parker's virtual try-on feature, to enhance operational efficiency and customer satisfaction (Neri, 2022). Utilizing customer insights through data analytics, like Starbucks' targeted promotions, can boost loyalty and sales. A culture of continuous learning and adaptation is vital; for example, Airbnb adjusts its business model based on market feedback to maintain relevance.

Businesses should also leverage local knowledge to address community-specific challenges, as demonstrated by Grab's adaptation to regional regulations (Tomita, 2023). Encouraging innovation, as seen with Tesla's frequent software updates, drives consumer interest (Tomita, 2023). Collaboration and partnerships enhance resource sharing, illustrated by Spotify's exclusive content with artists (Tomita, 2023). Implementing data-driven framework development allows companies like Unilever to measure sustainability impacts (Tomita, 2023).

A multidimensional framework is crucial for navigating the digital landscape effectively, helping entrepreneurs leverage technologies for growth (Canhoto et al., 2021). Focusing on value creation through digital initiatives aligns with market needs, enhancing sustainability (Martínez-Peláez et al., 2023). Emphasizing lifelong learning and agility enables organizations like Airbnb to adapt quickly to market changes (Martínez-Peláez et al., 2023). Companies should also leverage data and analytics for informed decision-making, as Netflix does with content recommendations (Ahmed & Abdulkareem, 2023).

Rethinking approaches to entrepreneurship in a post-COVID-19 world requires utilizing early indicators for decision-making (de Lucas Ancillo & Gavrila, 2023). Addressing challenges posed by digitalization is essential for navigating this landscape effectively (Kheng & June, 2023). Finally, businesses must utilize E-commerce platforms like Amazon to streamline sales and visibility (Xiong et al., 2024), recognizing that critical factors for startup resilience during crises include partnerships, capital investment, and advanced digital technologies (Alvarez-Salazar & Bazán, 2024).

By implementing these strategies, businesses can better position themselves to succeed in the competitive digital landscape (Fig. 6).

7 Case Studies in Digital Entrepreneurship: Transforming Challenges into Opportunities

7.1 Case Study 1: Turning Challenges into Opportunities—Netflix's Journey in Digital Entrepreneurship

Background

Netflix showcases DE's impact by transforming from a DVD rental service to a leading streaming platform. Its focus on innovation and customer engagement has reshaped global content consumption. This case study analyzes how Netflix leveraged digital capabilities to overcome challenges and sustain growth.

Challenges Faced by Netflix

In 2022, Netflix faced several challenges (Netflix, Inc, 2024):

- **Subscriber loss**: First decline in over a decade.

Key Insight	Action	Tip
Digital Strategy	Develop a clear digital roadmap.	Regularly adjust based on market feedback!
Invest in Tech	Allocate resources for essential tools.	Explore AI and automation for efficiency!
Customer Insights	Use data analytics to understand behaviors.	Conduct regular surveys for fresh insights!
Adaptability	Foster a culture of continuous improvement.	Host innovation workshops for creativity!
Community Engagement	Leverage local knowledge for solutions.	Partner with local organizations for support!
Focus on Innovation	Encourage unique problem-solving.	Set time for climate action brainstorming!
Collaborate	Form alliances to enhance initiatives.	Create joint ventures for visibility!
Data Framework	Implement a sustainability data framework.	Use data visualization tools for insights!
Value Creation	Generate social and economic value.	Assess impact regularly for alignment!
Lifelong Learning	Emphasize learning and agility.	Encourage mentorship and peer sharing!
Data-Driven Decisions	Leverage analytics for informed choices.	Set up dashboards to track key metrics!
Rethink Strategies	Reassess approaches in a post-COVID world.	Stay flexible and ready to pivot!
Optimize E-Commerce	Utilize online platforms for sales.	Invest in SEO to attract wider audiences!

Fig. 6 Key actions for sustainable digital growth. Source: developed by the author

- **Increased competition:** Rivals such as Disney+, HBO Max, and Amazon Prime intensified competition.
- **Rising prices:** Higher subscription costs deterred subscribers.
- **Market saturation:** Developed regions limited growth opportunities.
- **Password sharing:** Over 100 million households accessed shared passwords.
- **Post-pandemic decline:** Subscriptions dropped after the pandemic streaming boom.

Strategic Responses
To tackle challenges, Netflix adopted key strategies:

- **Ad-supported tier:** Launched in 2023 to attract price-sensitive users and increase ad revenue (Netflix, Inc, 2024).
- **Password sharing crackdown**: Restricted sharing to convert non-paying users into subscribers (Netflix, Inc, 2024).
- **Content investment:** Emphasized original and localized content, achieving success with hits like Squid Game in growth regions (Netflix, Inc, 2024).

Opportunities Leveraged

Netflix adapted to challenges by:

- **Gaming integration:** Engaged subscribers through gaming expansion (Netflix, Inc, 2024).
- **Live events:** Introduced live content and event ticketing (Netflix, Inc, 2024).
- **Technological innovation:** Utilized data analytics and AWS for enhanced streaming (Netflix, Inc, 2024).
- **Sustainability initiatives:** Focused on reducing its carbon footprint (Netflix, Inc, 2024).

Conclusion

Netflix's innovation and adaptability exemplify digital entrepreneurship. By introducing new business models and optimizing technology, it transformed challenges into opportunities, particularly through gaming, live events, and localized content, reinforcing its leadership in the digital entertainment industry.

7.2 Case Study 2: Mamaearth—Pioneering Digital Entrepreneurship (DE) in the Indian Beauty and Personal Care Market

Background

In 2016, Varun and Ghazal Alagh launched Mamaearth under Honasa Consumer Private Limited, offering chemical-free D2C beauty products for health-conscious parents (Soni et al., 2024). This model strengthens customer connections and reduces reliance on intermediaries. Through social media and digital marketing, Mamaearth established a strong online presence, enhancing engagement and loyalty. This case study examines the opportunities, challenges, and resilience.

Challenges and Opportunities

Despite its success, Mamaearth encountered typical D2C challenges:

- **Consumer preferences:** Many Indian consumers preferred offline shopping, prompting Mamaearth to explore a hybrid model by entering around 10,000 retail stores.
- **Market competition:** The beauty sector is highly competitive, requiring continuous innovation to maintain its edge.
- **Supply chain management:** Scaling operations while ensuring product quality and timely delivery presented logistical challenges.

Strategic Decisions Ahead

The case poses a strategic decision for Mamaearth: prioritize offline expansion or enhance online presence through product innovation.

- **Offline expansion:** Entering the offline market could broaden the customer base but requires significant investment and risks diluting the D2C identity.
- **Enhanced online presence:** Focusing on innovation and digital marketing could strengthen Mamaearth's leadership in the online space, attracting tech-savvy consumers.

Conclusion

Mamaearth's journey showcases opportunities in digital entrepreneurship within the D2C framework. Its success relies on adapting strategies based on consumer feedback. Facing scaling challenges and competition, strategic choices will shape its future in the beauty market.

7.3 Case Study 3: Shopify—Transforming Entrepreneurship Through Information Technology

Background

Shopify Inc., founded in 2006, is a Canadian e-commerce platform that empowers entrepreneurs to create and manage online stores. It has transformed small business operations with accessible tools but faces evolving challenges and opportunities in the competitive e-commerce landscape. This case study examines Shopify's opportunities and challenges.

Opportunities for Growth

- **AI and automation:** Shopify Magic can automate tasks, boosting merchant focus and customer satisfaction.
- **Logistics and fulfillment:** Partnering with Flexport enhances logistics, attracting merchants with seamless fulfillment and timely deliveries.
- **Diverse revenue streams:** Initiatives like Shopify Credit diversify income and provide value to merchants, aiding resilience amid economic fluctuations.

Challenges

- **Intense competition:** Shopify must differentiate itself in a competitive market dominated by Amazon and WooCommerce.
- **Logistics complexity:** Managing logistics remains complex and costly, requiring effective, cost-efficient solutions for merchants.
- **Scalability issues:** Expanding offerings may lead to scalability challenges, especially with features like the POS Terminal.

Conclusion

Shopify is at a crucial point in its digital evolution. By leveraging technology, enhancing logistics, and diversifying services, it can achieve growth. Addressing competitive pressures and logistical challenges will be essential for continued success in e-commerce.

7.4 *Case Study 4: Lenskart's Virtual Try-On: A Catalyst for Innovation in DE*

Background
Lenskart, an Indian eyewear startup, has transformed the shopping experience with its "Try-On" feature, enabling customers to virtually try on glasses using augmented reality (AR). This case study explores how this innovation exemplifies DE.

Digital Transformation in Eyewear Retail
Lenskart transformed the eyewear shopping experience by introducing the Try-On feature, leveraging AR technology to create an interactive online platform (Lenskart, 2023).

Implementation of the Try-On Feature
The Try-On feature allows users to upload selfies and virtually try on eyewear styles, offering personalized recommendations based on face shape and preferences (Lenskart, 2023).

Impact on Consumer Behavior
This feature reduced hesitation in online purchases, increasing conversion rates by up to 30%, showcasing the effectiveness of digital entrepreneurship (Lenskart, 2023).

Enhancing Customer Engagement
The Try-On feature enhances customer engagement by attracting new users and retaining existing ones, fostering brand loyalty through interactive experiences and community-driven content on social media (Lenskart, 2023).

Challenges and Considerations
Despite its success, Lenskart faced challenges in ensuring the accuracy of the virtual try-on experience. Discrepancies between the virtual appearance and actual fit can lead to customer dissatisfaction. Continuous improvements in AR technology and user feedback mechanisms are essential for refining this feature (Lenskart, 2023).

Conclusion
Lenskart's Try-On feature showcases how digital entrepreneurship can transform retail through AR technology, enhancing the shopping experience and consumer engagement. This innovation sets a benchmark for companies looking to improve customer experiences.

7.5 *Case Study 5: Case Study: Zomato's DE Journey*

Background
Zomato has emerged as a pivotal player in the realm of DE, significantly transforming the food delivery and quick commerce sectors in India. Its innovative use of technology to cater to evolving consumer demands has placed it at the forefront of

the digital economy. The company's strategic pivots and operational excellence have turned challenges into opportunities, making Zomato a case study in DE, particularly in emerging markets like India.

Challenges

Zomato faced significant challenges in scaling, particularly profitability, **operating at a loss** until FY23, when it reported a profit of INR 351 crore due to strategic cost-cutting and diversification into quick commerce (Blinkit) and B2B supplies (Zomato Limited, 2024). Additionally, managing logistics for over 753 million orders and 400,000 delivery partners proved complex. Zomato introduced innovations such as large-order fleets and 15-minute deliveries via Blinkit to address these **logistical challenges**, requiring a robust tech infrastructure for real-time order management and optimized delivery routes (Zomato Limited, 2024).

Opportunities

Zomato embraced the **quick commerce trend** with Blinkit, achieving 93% YoY growth in FY24 by offering 15-minute grocery deliveries. It also diversified into event ticketing through "Zomato Live," reducing reliance on food delivery (Zomato Limited, 2024).

The company's success hinges on **technological integration**, using geolocation to minimize delivery errors and **AI for personalized recommendations**. Its **digital payment systems** enhance the user experience. Zomato is committed to sustainability, targeting net-zero emissions (Zomato Limited, 2024).

Conclusion

Zomato demonstrates how digital transformation reshapes industries through strategic innovation. Despite profitability and logistics challenges, it leveraged diversification and sustainability to adapt to market demands, becoming a model for digital entrepreneurs and a leader in India's food delivery and quick commerce sectors.

References

Agostinho, H. L. (2020). *Is touch really that important?: An analysis of the business opportunity of haptic technology in online shopping* (Doctoral dissertation).

Ahmed, A., & Abdulkareem, A. M. (2023). Big data analytics in the entertainment Industry: Audience behavior analysis, content recommendation, and Revenue maximization. *Reviews of Contemporary Business Analytics, 6*(1), 88–102.

Akhter, S., & Mazumdar, D. (2024). Women's contribution to trade in Bangladesh and challenges in post-COVID-19 era. In *Contemporary issues in international trade* (pp. 249–261). Emerald Publishing Limited.

Akpan, E. E., Fcicn, A., Ppgdca, P., & Clark, J. (2024). *Entrepreneurial skills: A Panacea for economic development of Nigeria in the 21st century.*

Alalwan, A. A., Algharabat, R. S., Baabdullah, A. M., Rana, N. P., Qasem, Z., & Dwivedi, Y. K. (2020). Examining the impact of mobile interactivity on customer engagement in the context of mobile shopping. *Journal of Enterprise Information Management, 33*(3), 627–653. https://doi.org/10.1108/JEIM-07-2019-0194

Alawamleh, M., Al-Twal, A., Lahlouh, L., & Jame, R. O. (2023). Interpretive structural modelling of organizational innovation factors: An emerging market perspective. *Journal of Open Innovation: Technology, Market, and Complexity, 9*(2), 100067.

Alvarez-Salazar, J., & Bazán, M. (2024). Startup growth in pandemic: Organizational resilience in an extreme crisis situation. *Management Research: Journal of the Iberoamerican Academy of Management*, (ahead-of-print).

Arora, M., & Valeri, M. (2024). Kick-starting the economies after COVID-19 pandemic: Assessing the role of gig players in boosting entrepreneurial ventures and suggesting policy interventions. In *Entrepreneurial Motivations: Strategies, Opportunities and Decisions* (pp. 73–88). Cham.

Attaran, M. (2017). Cloud computing technology: Leveraging the power of the internet to improve business performance. *Journal of International Technology and Information Management, 26*(1), Article 6. https://doi.org/10.58729/1941-6679.1283

Attree, K. J., & Kleinschafer, J. L. (2024). The role of virtual collaborative communities in sustaining rural micro-business resilience. In *Digital transformation and sustainable development in cities and organizations* (pp. 30–53). IGI Global.

Bergholz, C., Füner, L., Lubczyk, M., Sternberg, R., & Bersch, J. (2024). Infrastructure required, skill needed: Digital entrepreneurship in rural and urban areas. *Journal of Business Venturing Insights, 22*, e00488.

Bican, P. M., & Brem, A. (2020). Digital business model, digital transformation, digital entrepreneurship: Is there a sustainable "digital"? *Sustainability, 12*(13), 5239. https://doi.org/10.3390/su12135239

Bohmann, T., Drews, P., Meyer-Blankart, C.. (2015). *Digitale Exzellenz: Eine Bestandsaufnahme zur Digitalisierung deutscher Unternehmen und Beho¨rden*. Research Report, Universita¨t Hamburg. https://www.soprasteria.de/docs/librariesprovider33/Studien/digitale-exzellenz-2015-soprasteria-consulting.pdf?sfvrsn=8

Brynjolfsson, E., & McAfee, A. (2014). *The second machine age: Work, progress, and prosperity in a time of brilliant technologies*. WW Norton & Company.

Buchholz, S, Bechtel, M., & Briggs, B.. (2020). *Tech Trends, Deloitte Insights*. https://www2.deloitte.com/content/dam/insights/articles/6730_TT-Landing-page/DI_2021-Tech-Trends.pdf

Business Today. (2024). *How Indian start-ups are leveraging use of enterprise technology in order to scale*. Retrieved from https://www.businesstoday.in/magazine/deep-dive/story/how-indian-start-ups-are-leveraging-use-of-enterprise-technology-in-order-to-scale-413737-2024-01-17

Canestrino, R., Ćwiklicki, M., Magliocca, P., & Pawełek, B. (2020). Understanding social entrepreneurship: A cultural perspective in business research. *Journal of Business Research, 110*, 132–143.

Canhoto, A. I., Quinton, S., Pera, R., Molinillo, S., & Simkin, L. (2021). Digital strategy aligning in SMEs: A dynamic capabilities perspective. *The Journal of Strategic Information Systems, 30*(3), 101682.

Cheng, X., Mou, J., & Yan, X. (2021). Sharing economy enabled digital platforms for development. *Information Technology for Development, 27*(4), 635–644.

Davis, J., Wolff, H. G., Forret, M. L., & Sullivan, S. E. (2020). Networking via LinkedIn: An examination of usage and career benefits. *Journal of Vocational Behavior, 118*, 103396.

Day, G. S., & Schoemaker, P. J. (2016). Adapting to fast-changing markets and technologies. *California Management Review, 58*(4), 59–77.

de Lucas Ancillo, A., & Gavrila, S. G. (2023). The impact of research and development on entrepreneurship, innovation, digitization and digital transformation. *Journal of Business Research, 157*, 113566.

Dessart, L., Veloutsou, C., & Morgan-Thomas, A. (2015). Consumer engagement in online brand communities: A social media perspective. *The Journal of Product and Brand Management, 24*(1), 28–42. https://doi.org/10.1108/JPBM-06-2014-0635

Di Domenico, M., Daniel, E., & Nunan, D. (2014). 'Mental mobility' in the digital age: Entrepreneurs and the online home-based business. *New Technology, Work and Employment, 29*(3), 266–281.

Dweck, C. S., & Yeager, D. S. (2019). Mindsets A view from two eras. *Perspectives on Psychological Science, 14*(3), 481–496. https://doi.org/10.1177/1745691618804166

Economic Times. (2024). *Economic survey: India saw tech startup surge post-COVID pandemic.* Retrieved from https://economictimes.indiatimes.com/tech/startups/economic-survey-india-saw-tech-startup-surge-post-covid-pandemic/articleshow/111931855.cms?from=mdr

Edrak, B., Nor, Z. M., & Shaik, A. R. (2022). The readiness of Malaysia digital economy: A study of three government policies from 1991 to 2020. *International Journal of Economics and Finance, 14*(12), 1–84.

Endres, H., Huesig, S., & Pesch, R. (2022). Digital innovation management for entrepreneurial ecosystems: Services and functionalities as drivers of innovation management software adoption. *Review of Managerial Science, **16***, 135–156. https://doi.org/10.1007/s11846-021-00441-4

European Commission. (2015) *Digital transformation of European industry and enterprises: A report of the strategic policy forum on digital entrepreneurship.* Available from: http://ec.europa.eu/DocsRoom/documents/9462/attachments/1/translations/en/renditions/native

Fakheldin, H., Samy, C., & Miniesy, R. (2023). Women Entrepreneurship in Egypt. In: *Environments for Women Entrepreneurship in North Africa* (pp. 105–129).

Feindt, S., Jeffcoate, J., & Chappell, C. (2002). Identifying success factors for rapid growth in SME e-commerce. *Small Business Economics, 19*, 51–62. https://doi.org/10.1023/A:1016165825476

Fuller, N. R., Porter, M., III, & Kemp, E. A. (2022). The impact of marginalization on entrepreneurs' online presence and firm performance. *Journal of Research in Marketing and Entrepreneurship, 24*(1), 161–175.

Ghasemaghaei, M. (2019). Does data analytics use improve firm decision making quality? The role of knowledge sharing and data analytics competency. *Decision Support Systems, 120*, 14–24. https://doi.org/10.1016/j.dss.2019.03.004

Giones, F., & Brem, A. (2017). Digital technology entrepreneurship: A definition and research agenda. *Social Science Electronic Publishing, 7*, 44–51.

Guthrie, C. (2014). The digital factory: A hands-on learning project in digital entrepreneurship. *Journal of Entrepreneurship Education, 17*(1), 115.

Hair, N., Wetsch, L. R., Hull, C. E., Perotti, V., & Hung, Y. T. (2012). Market orientation in digital entrepreneurship: Advantages and challenges in a Web 2.0 networked world. *International Journal of Innovation and Technology Management, 9*(6), 1–18. https://doi.org/10.1142/S0219877012500459

Hassan, A., Andebe, N., Nyambo, D. G., & Kaijage, S. (2022). Integrating mobile computing in university information management systems to improve access and user experience. *Indian Journal of Science and Technology, 15*(8), 343–350.

He, Z. L., & Wong, P. K. (2004). Exploration vs. exploitation: An empirical test of the ambidexterity hypothesis. *Organisation Science, 15*(4), 481–494.

Hsieh, Y. J., & Wu, Y. J. (2019). Entrepreneurship through the platform strategy in the digital era: Insights and research opportunities. *Computers in Human Behavior, 95*, 315–323. https://doi.org/10.1016/j.chb.2018.03.033

Hull, C. E., Hung, Y.-T. C., & Hair, N. (2007). Taking advantage of digital opportunities: A typology of digital entrepreneurship. *International Journal of Networking and Virtual Organisations, 4*, 290–303. https://doi.org/10.1504/IJNVO.2007.015166

Islam, R., Patamsetti, V., Gadhi, A., Gondu, R., Bandaru, C., Kesani, S., & Abiona, O. (2023). The future of cloud computing: Benefits and challenges. *International Journal of Communications, Network and System Sciences, 16*, 53–65. https://doi.org/10.4236/ijcns.2023.164004

Kheng, Y. K., & June, S. (2023). MR. DIY "the Malaysian sweetheart". *Emerald Emerging Markets Case Studies, 13*(2), 1–19.

Kraus, S., Palmer, C., Kailer, N., Kallinger, F. L., & Spitzer, J. (2019). Digital entrepreneurship. *International Journal of Entrepreneurial Behaviour & Research, 25*, 353–375.

Le Dinh, T., Vu, M. C., & Ayayi, A. (2018). Towards a living lab for promoting the digital entrepreneurship process. *International Journal of Entrepreneurship, 22*(1), 1–17.

Lee, J. R. (2020). *Deconstructing LEGO*. Springer International Publishing.

Lenskart. (2023). *How Lenskart is utilizing technology to scale its business*. Retrieved from Lenskart Blog. https://blog.lenskart.com/how-lenskart-is-utilizing-technology-to-scale-its-business-6030bd4633ee

Liao, A., Hull, C. E., & Srirama Chandramurthy, R. (2013). The six facets model of technology management: A study the digital business industry. *International Journal of Innovation and Technology Management, 10*(4), 1350019-1–1350019-24.

Marrapodi, R. (2023). 8 Managing conflicts to improve performance in Start-Ups: A theoretical analysis. *Entrepreneurial Processes in the Era of Digital Transformation, 1*, 129.

Martínez-Peláez, R., Ochoa-Brust, A., Rivera, S., Félix, V. G., Ostos, R., Brito, H., & Mena, L. J. (2023). Role of digital transformation for achieving sustainability: Mediated role of stakeholders, key capabilities, and technology. *Sustainability, 15*(14), 11221.

Mohieldin, T. A. G. (2022). Big data applications in digital marketing. *Journal of Industrial Policy and Technology Management, 4*(2), 185–198.

Mousa, S., & Morrar, R. (2023). Impacts of industry 4.0 on servitization of manufacturing. *Revue Européenne d'Économie et Management des Services, 2022*(14), 73–98.

Nambisan, S. (2017). Digital entrepreneurship: Toward a digital technology perspective of entrepreneurship. *Entrepreneurship Theory and Practice, 41*, 1029–1055. https://doi.org/10.1111/etap.12254

Neri, M. (2022). *Fashion e-commerce: A study of the elements determining the profitability of an online sale channel within the fashion industry.*

Netflix, Inc. (2024). *Annual report 2023-24*. Retrieved from Netflix Investor Relations website: https://ir.netflix.net/financials/annual-reports-and-proxies/default.aspx

Nnaji, U. O., Benjamin, L. B., Eyo-Udo, N. L., & Etukudoh, E. A. (2024). A review of strategic decision-making in marketing through big data and analytics. *Magna Scientia Advanced Research and Reviews, 11*(1), 084–091. https://doi.org/10.30574/msarr.2024.11.1.0077

Ogrean, C., & Herciu, M. (2021). Romania's SMEs on the way to EU's twin transition to digitalization and sustainability. *Studies in Business and Economics, 16*(2), 282–295.

Olarewaju, T., & Fernando, J. (2020). Gender inequality and female entrepreneurship in developing countries. In *Decent work and economic growth* (pp. 473–481). Springer International Publishing.

Orok, D., Akpan, J., & Olanrewaju, O. (2024). *Tools learning resources*. Lifelong Learning: Education for the Future World, p 203

O'Toole, C., Schneider, J., Smaje, K., & LaBerge, L. (2020) *How COVID-19 has pushed companies over the technology tipping point—and transformed business forever*. McKinsey & Company. Retrieved from https://www.mckinsey.com/capabilities/strategy-and-corporate-finance/our-insights/how-covid-19-has-pushed-companies-over-the-technology-tipping-point-and-transformed-business-forever

Özsungur, F. (Ed.). (2024). *Generating entrepreneurial ideas with AI*. IGI Global.

Paramesha, M., Rane, N. L., & Rane, J. (2024). Big data analytics, artificial intelligence, machine learning, internet of things, and blockchain for enhanced business intelligence. *Partners Universal Multidisciplinary Research Journal, 1*(2), 110–133. https://doi.org/10.5281/zenodo.12827323

Parasuraman, A., & Colby, C. L. (2015). An updated and streamlined technology readiness index: TRI 2.0. *Journal of Service Research, 18*(1), 59–74. https://doi.org/10.1177/1094670514539730

Rahman, K. S., & Thelen, K. (2019). The rise of the platform business model and the transformation of twenty-first-century capitalism. *Politics and Society, 47*(2), 177–204. https://doi.org/10.1177/0032329219838932

Reno, L. S. E., Harmon, L., Hutto, L., & McManus, K. (2020). Zooming your way to success with client-based learning projects. In *Proceedings of A Virtual Experience, Marketing*

Management Association Fall Educators' Conference (pp. 67–68). Marketing Management Association (MMA).

Rippa, P., & Secundo, G. (2019). Digital academic entrepreneurship: The potential of digital technologies on academic Entrepreneurship. *Technological Forecasting and Social Change, 146*, 900–911. https://doi.org/10.1016/j.techfore.2018.07.013

Rothe, F. F., Van Audenhove, L., & Loisen, J. (2023). Digital development, inequalities & the sustainable development goals: What does 'Leave No-One Behind' mean for ICT4D? *Information Technology for Development, 29*(1), 9–26.

SAP India. (2024). *77% of Indian startups are investing in artificial intelligence and advanced technologies*. Retrieved from https://news.sap.com/india/2024/07/77-of-indian-startups-are-investing-in-artificial-intelligence-and-advanced-technologies/

Schmitt, M. (2023). Automated machine learning: AI-driven decision making in business analytics. *Intelligent Systems with Applications, 18*, 200188. https://doi.org/10.1016/j.iswa.2023.200188

Schückes, M., & Gutmann, T. (2021). Why do startups pursue initial coin offerings (ICOs)? The role of economic drivers and social identity on funding choice. *Small Business Economics, 57*, 1027–1052. https://doi.org/10.1007/s11187-020-00337-9

Shopify Inc. (2023). *Annual Report*. Retrieved from https://www.annualreports.com/Company/shopify-inc

Smit, W., Salazar, L. J., Tate, Z., Saji, N., Sohn, J., & Polaki, I. S. P. (2022). *Digital entrepreneurship in Asia for economic resilience and post-pandemic recovery: Country Report–Malaysia*.

Soltanifar, M., & Smailhodžić, E. (2021). Developing a digital entrepreneurial mindset for data-driven, cloud-enabled, and platform-centric business activities: practical implications and the impact on society. *Digital Entrepreneurship, 3*.

Soni, S., Trehan, D., Chotia, V., & Srivastava, M. (2024). Mamaearth: A digital first brand venturing offline. *Emerald Emerging Markets Case Studies, 14*(2), 1–38.

Soto-Acosta, P. (2020). COVID-19 pandemic: Shifting digital transformation to a high-speed gear. *Information Systems Management, 37*, 260–266. https://doi.org/10.1080/10580530.2020.1814461

Soumya, V., & Arumugam, S. K. (2024). Technology-based scalable business models: Dimensions and challenges of a new populist business model. In *Advancing software engineering through AI, federated learning, and large language models* (pp. 238–248). IGI Global. https://doi.org/10.4018/979-8-3693-3502-4.ch015

Srinivasan, A., & Venkatraman, N. (2018). Entrepreneurship in digital platforms: A network-centric view. *Strategic Entrepreneurship Journal, 12*(1), 54–71. https://doi.org/10.1002/sej.1272

Sundararajan, A. (2019). Commentary: The twilight of brand and consumerism? Digital trust, cultural meaning, and the quest for connection in the sharing economy. *Journal of Marketing, 83*(5), 32–35. https://doi.org/10.1177/0022242919868965

Sutrisno, S., Kuraesin, A. D., Siminto, S., Irawansyah, I., & Ausat, A. M. A. (2023). The role of information technology in driving innovation and entrepreneurial business growth. *Jurnal Minfo Polgan, 12*(1), 586–597. https://doi.org/10.33395/jmp.v12i1.12463

Thai, L. M., & Miyazaki, K. (2024). Frugal innovation for smart connected products: A case study of IoT-based smart farming by Vietnamese startups. *Asian Journal of Technology Innovation*, 1–25.

Times of India. (2024). *Indian startups: Gen AI*. Retrieved from https://timesofindia.indiatimes.com/business/startups/trend-tracking/indian-startups-gen-ai/articleshow/101756072.cms

Tomita, A. (2023). Promoting data-driven technology transition for a sustainable world through ESG entrepreneurship. In *2023 Portland International Conference on Management of Engineering and Technology (PICMET)* (pp. 1–10). IEEE.

Ullagaddi, P. (2024). From Barista to bytes: How Starbucks brewed a digital revolution. *Journal of Economics, Management and Trade, 30*(9), 78–89.

van Gelderen, M., Wiklund, J., & McMullen, J. S. (2021). Entrepreneurship in the future: A Delphi study of ETP and JBV editorial board members. *Entrepreneurship Theory and Practice*. https://doi.org/10.1177/10422587211010503

Veit, D., Clemons, E., & Benlian, A. (2014). Business models: An information systems research agenda. *Business & Information Systems Engineering, 6*, 45–53. https://doi.org/10.1007/s12599-013-0308-y

Wang, X. W., Umar, M., Khaddage-Soboh, N., & Safi, A. (2024). From innovation to impact: Unraveling the complexities of entrepreneurship in the digital age. *International Entrepreneurship and Management Journal*, 1–15.

Xiong, B., Sun, J., & Pang, X. (2024). E-commerce platform in digital economy: Analysis and optimization of Amazon's Footwear Store. *Financial Economics Research, 1*(2), 90–114.

Xu, P., Lee, J., Barth, J. R., & Richey, R. G. (2021). Blockchain as supply chain technology: considering transparency and security. *International Journal of Physical Distribution and Logistics Management, 51*(3), 305–324. https://doi.org/10.1108/IJPDLM-08-2019-0234

Yadav, U. S., Tripathi, R., Tripathi, M. A., Ghosal, I., Kumar, A., Mandal, M., & Singh, A. (2023). Digital and innovative entrepreneurship in the Indian handicraft sector after the COVID-19 pandemic: Challenges and opportunities. *Journal of Innovation and Entrepreneurship, 12*(1), 69.

Yuan, S.-T. D., Chou, S.-Y., Yang, W.-C., Wu, C.-A., & Huang, C.-T. (2017). Customer engagement within multiple new media and broader business ecosystem – A holistic perspective. *Kybernetes, 46*(06), 1000–1020. https://doi.org/10.1108/K-01-2017-0042

Zairis, A., & Zairis, G. (2022). Digital innovation: The challenges of a game-changer. *European Conference on Innovation and Entrepreneurship, 17*(1), 630–637. https://doi.org/10.34190/ecie.17.1.774

Zomato Limited. (2024). Annual report 2023–24. Retrieved from Zomato Investor Relations website: https://www.zomato.com/investor-relations/financials

Exploring Election Prediction Outcomes on Social Media Data using Machine Learning Algorithms

Zuraini Zainol, Amelia Ritahani Ismail, Puteri Nor Ellyza Nohuddin, and Riza Sulaiman

Abstract Social media analytics (SMA) is immensely used to investigate public sentiment and provide real-time insights into politics and business strategy. In addition, social media analytics has been employed in predicting election results by leveraging machine learning (ML) models in extensive datasets created from user-generated content on platforms such as Twitter, Facebook, and Instagram. SMA can be highly effective in this domain, yet issues concerning authenticity and reliability persist. These data manipulations are driven by misinformation, influenced by bots, and reflect a limited representation of social media users in the electorate correspondence. This paper explores how sentiment analysis (SA) and use of ML can enhance election prediction for overcoming the identified issues. This study will evaluate Naive Bayes, random forest, and long short-term memory networks for their effectiveness in predicting election outcomes based on social media SA. Despite the potential for distortion from misinformation, these models demonstrate a prediction accuracy of 94% as shown in case studies. It also addresses how traditional methods of data collection through surveying can enhance SMA, offering a more balanced perspective on public opinion and minimizing biases present in social media data.

Z. Zainol (✉)
Department of Computer Science, Universiti Pertahanan Nasional Malaysia, Kuala Lumpur, Malaysia
e-mail: zuraini@upnm.edu.my

A. R. Ismail
Department of Computer Science, Kulliyyah of ICT, International Islamic University Malaysia, Kuala Lumpur, Malaysia
e-mail: amelia@iium.edu.my

P. N. E. Nohuddin
Institute of Visual Informatics, Universiti Kebangsaan Malaysia, Bangi, Malaysia

Faculty of Business, Higher Colleges of Technology, Sharjah, United Arab Emirates
e-mail: puteri.ivi@ukm.edu.my

R. Sulaiman
Institute of Visual Informatics, Universiti Kebangsaan Malaysia, Bangi, Malaysia
e-mail: riza@ukm.edu.my

L. O. Yesufu, P. N. E. Nohuddin (eds.), *Technology for Societal Transformation*,
https://doi.org/10.1007/978-981-96-1721-0_7

These findings highlight that SA and ML have the potential to predict election outcomes. However, future research should prioritize the authenticity and diversity of data sources. A reduction in misinformation, achieved without relying on one single platform would lead to improved election predictions. This paper emphasizes the importance of incorporating traditional and digital sources to enhance the reliability of political predictions, complementing the insights gained from SMA.

1 Introduction

Social media analytics (SMA) is the essential tool to understand multidimensional data created by users on different platforms, such as X-former Twitter, Facebook, Instagram, and YouTube. The increasing production of user-generated content provides organizations, researchers, and policymakers unique chance to retrieve real-time information concerning citizens' sentiments, opinions, and behaviours. This has interconnected new opportunities for data-driven decision-making in marketing, politics, health, and businesses. Some of the fundamental parts of SMA are sentiment analysis (SA), a subset of natural language processing (NLP) techniques interpreting and subsequently classifying user sentiments as positive, negative, or neutral. It has also been highly utilized for the purpose of perceiving public opinion on everything-from consumer products and services to political campaigns, thus helping in shaping business strategies and even governmental policies.

Social media data runs well into terabytes and even petabytes; such volume presents certain challenges and opportunities for advanced analysis tools (Martí et al., 2019). Machine learning (ML) methods have proved effective in processing and analysing this huge amount of data, especially for applications like election prediction (Pugliese et al., 2021). In fact, these ML models analyse user sentiment and engagement on different social media platforms that can predict the political trend with increasing accuracy. It is a fact that even while such advances are being made, the reliability of such SMA in electoral prediction could be compromised due to data manipulation in general, including but not limited to misinformation or bots (Xu et al., 2022). However, the fact remains that robust ML models, like Naive Bayes (NB), random forest, and long short-term memory (LSTM), have the potential to overcome challenges and stand tall (Sheth et al., 2022). Recent literature has pointed out that the combined use of social media data with traditional forms of data collection, such as surveys, adds much value to the understanding of the pulse of public opinion. A systematic review carried out by Reveilhac et al. (2022) reveals that SMA, though greatly valued, cannot take the place of traditional surveys since the latter are still necessary to complete the capture of data in a more structured and representative way. According to them, opinions reflected through SMA are those closer to immediate unstable techniques, whereas those from surveys tend to mean something deeper and for a longer time. Therefore, it is the integration of both methodologies that could yield an even more accurate and fine-grained picture of public opinion.

In contrast, Brito et al. (2024) advise against relying only on Twitter data when it comes to election prediction. After all, users of this social network represent only a very small fraction of the population and not always an accurate or representative picture of the electorate. They further add that extension beyond Twitter to other sources like Facebook and Instagram and even offline data, along with dealing with technical challenges such as bias correction and data validation, the extension will vastly enhance the prediction capabilities of the SMA models. As SMA continues to evolve, so too will be the need for a wider approach towards this kind of monitoring-necessarily leveraging diverse streams of data to attain better accuracy and reliability with political predictions.

The application of SMA and ML techniques in this paper focuses on political elections, with an emphasis on how SA and user-generated data might point towards the results of an election. Based on case studies and literature reviews, this study sets in perspective the evolving role of SMA and ML methods in understanding the sentiment of voters, forecasting political trends, and addressing challenges arising from fake news to manipulative uses of social media.

This paper is presented as follows: In Sect. 2, this chapter discusses the fundamentals of SMA and SA. Section 3 elaborates on the application of ML techniques on social media election data. Section 4 presents the case studies of election prediction using social media data. Lastly, Sect. 5 provides the conclusion of the paper.

2 Social Media Analytics and Sentiment Analysis

SMA or social media monitoring involves the extraction and analysis of data from various social media platforms (Nanda & Kumar, 2021), including the X application (formerly known as the Twitter), Facebook, Instagram, Linkedln, Youtube, Reddit, Wikipedia, blogs, and others. According to (Wanniarachchi et al., 2020; Flack & D'Souza, 2014), data generated by these social media applications is enormous; from tweets to swipes, likes to shares, the online world is expanding dramatically, reaching from Terabytes to Petabytes. The work in (Zachlod et al., 2022) described SMA as a multidisciplinary research domain that focuses on developing, adapting, and enhancing informatics tools, frameworks, and methods for tracking, collecting, and analysing large volumes of social media data to derive valuable insights. SMA is widely applied in various research fields such as business, marketing, communications, politics, health, and entertainment. It helps researchers discover valuable knowledge and support practitioners in making decision, developing business and corporate strategies, and finding more efficient solutions (Zainol et al., 2021; Sebei et al., 2018). The advancement of SMA tools encompasses several techniques including data preparation, NLP (e.g., SA, text classification), ML (e.g., clustering, trend analysis, predictive modelling), big data technology, and visualization, among others. Recently, there has been a rise in the accessibility of SMA tools that can be used to analyse public preferences and enhance content strategy. These technologies help politicians in monitoring public sentiment, optimizing political campaign strategies, tracking or measuring their popularity, assessing political opponents, predicting election outcomes based on the voter perception, etc. One of the important components in SMA is SA or opinion mining (OM). SA applies the NLP techniques to measure the sentiment values of text, classifying as either positive, negative or neutral (Velloo et al., 2023). Researchers (Birjali et al., 2021) describe SA as a computational analysis that examines individuals' opinion, feeling, behaviours, and emotions towards topics, product or services. Scholars (Behdenna et al., 2016; Do et al., 2018) categorized SA as three hierarchical levels such as document level, sentence level, and aspect level. Among all the levels discussed, the aspect level is considered as the most challenging due to its requirement for a detailed analysis (Birjali et al., 2021). SA has been widely applied in a variety of application fields including business intelligence (Lee et al., 2018), government intelligence, healthcare, politics (Hulliyah et al., 2019), social media (Zainol et al., 2018; Hulliyah et al., 2018), etc.

3 Application of Machine Learning Techniques on Social Media Election Data

The utilization of ML techniques to analyse social media data for predicting outcomes of elections has become known as a significant area of recent research. This approach uses the user-generated content to offer valuable interpretations public sentiment and political patterns throughout the election. Many studies have demonstrated the efficacy of several ML models in this domain. For example, SA encompasses the operations of data preparation, features extraction, and training models to gauge public opinion towards candidates and predict election results. In this particular scenario, techniques such as BiCNN-RNN have outperformed traditional methods like BiCNN and RNN (Acharjee et al., 2023). Nonetheless, the accuracy of these predictions can be compromised by data manipulation through bots, as evidenced in the 2019 Indian elections. Nevertheless, a supervised learning technique managed to forecast outcomes accurately despite the previous challenges. Researchers used multiple classification algorithms, including linear support vector classification (LSVC), RF, and NB, to analyse Twitter data to examine Twitter data during the 2020 US presidential election (Qorib et al., 2023). The results indicated that although Donald Trump enjoyed greater popularity on Twitter, Joe Biden had a higher average percentage of positive sentiments, which led to a prediction of Biden's oncoming success. Another study was conducted to determine the political orientation of Twitter users using NB classifiers, resulting in an accuracy rate of approximately 80–85% (Olteanu et al., 2022). This suggests that these models have potential to be included into more advanced systems for predicting election results. Long short-term memory (LSTM) models have also been explored, particularly in the 2019 Indian elections, demonstrating promising results compared to traditional ML approaches (Charan et al., 2023).

Additionally, a study employing classifiers like LGBMClassifier, logistic regression, and RandomForestClassifier found that tweet content had a higher significant predictive power for election outcomes compared to user information, with an accuracy score of about 80% (Park et al., 2022). The integration of sub-event discovery and SA in micro-blogs has also been proposed to predict election results, as demonstrated in the AP Assembly Election 2019, where the model achieved an accuracy of 94.2%. However, the spread of fake news continues to be a critical issue, affecting the reliability of social media data in relation to elections. To address this issue, various classifiers such as passive aggressive and NB, have been employed to detect and mitigate the influence of fake news, thereby improving the accuracy of election predictions. Overall, ML techniques applied to social media election data offer powerful tools for predicting election outcomes, if challenges like data manipulation and fake news are effectively managed. Table 1 presents the summary of literature in predicting election outcomes using the ML techniques.

4 Predicting Election Outcomes using Social Media Data: Case Studies

This case study explores the application of the NB ML algorithm to predict election outcomes by analysing social media data, specifically tweets concerning the 2020 US Presidential Election. The method involves collecting tweets mentioning the candidates, Joe Biden and Donald Trump, and analysing the sentiment of these tweets using public opinion. Each tweet will be assigned a sentiment score, indicating whether it is positive, negative, or neutral. By averaging these scores for each candidate, their overall popularity on social media can be estimated. This method leverages the vast amount of user-generated content on platforms like Twitter, providing a real-time and dynamic measure of public sentiment. For this case study, a NB classifier is used due to its simplicity and effectiveness in text classification tasks. The findings indicate that sentiment scores and frequency of mentions can predict the relative popularity of candidates. This case study demonstrates how ML models can provide valuable insights into election outcomes by analysing social media data in predicting election results (Figs. 1 and 2).

In this case study, a ML model, the NB is used to predict the outcomes between two political candidates, Biden and Trump. The model's performance, as indicated and shown by the classification metrics, achieved an accuracy of 100%. Precision, recall, and F1-scores for both candidates were all perfect, demonstrating that the model successfully identified and predicted every instance of Biden and Trump in the test dataset. The support, which refers to the number of actual occurrences in the data, showed that the model was tested on two instances, one for each candidate. The macro and weighted averages for precision, recall, and F1-score were also 1.00, further confirming the model's robustness and accuracy in this scenario.

Table 1 Summary of literature in predicting election outcomes using the ML techniques

Author(s)	ML techniques	Main findings	Social media platforms
Myilvahanan et al. (2023)	Supervised learning	Demonstrates forecasting election outcomes using Indian electoral data. Highlighted challenges due to social media manipulation via bots but showed accurate results with a reproducible method resistant to volume manipulation.	General social media
Qorib et al. (2023)	SA, LSVC, RF, DT, logistic regression, Naive Bayes	Data from the 2020 US Presidential election was analysed on Twitter. Trump was more popular, but Biden had stronger positive attitudes, which predicted his victory. Adding fake tweets had a slight effect on some models' performance but enhanced logistic regression.	Twitter
Acharjee et al. (2023)	Hybrid A-BiCNN-RNN	A three-step technique (preprocessing, feature extraction, and model training) was proposed for exploiting social media data to predict the results of elections. The hybrid technique demonstrated superiority over BiCNN and RNN alone.	General social media
Park et al. (2022)	NLP, LGBMClassifier, Logistic Regression, ExtraTreeClassifier, DecisionTreeClassifier, RandomForestClassifier, Gaussian NB, KNeighborsClassifier	Used NLP and machine learning on Twitter data to estimate election results, attaining 80% accuracy with tweets as input variables. The study emphasized the importance of tweet content over user information in improving prediction accuracy.	Twitter

Furthermore, the model produced sentiment scores for each candidate, with Biden receiving a score of 0.311 and Trump a score of 0.042. Based on these sentiment values, the model predicted Biden as the winner. These sentiment scores likely represent some underlying probability or favourability associated with each candidate, and in this case, Biden's score significantly outweighed Trump's. While the dataset for this example is small, the results highlight the potential of the model in making accurate predictions based on the sentiment input data.

To evaluate the performance of the NB model in predicting election outcomes based on social media data, several evaluation metrics are employed. They are accuracy, precision, recall, F1-score, and the confusion matrix. Accuracy is the most

```
# Sentiment Analysis
INITIALIZE SentimentIntensityAnalyzer AS analyzer

DEFINE FUNCTION analyze_sentiment(tweet)
    CALCULATE sentiment USING analyzer.polarity_scores(tweet)
    RETURN sentiment['compound']

APPLY analyze_sentiment FUNCTION TO 'text' column OF data
CREATE new column 'sentiment' IN data

# Feature Extraction
INITIALIZE CountVectorizer WITH stop_words='english' AS vectorizer
TRANSFORM 'text' column OF data INTO numerical features USING vectorizer
SET features X TO transformed text data
SET target labels y TO 'candidate' column OF data

# Train Machine Learning Model
SPLIT data INTO training set X_train, y_train AND testing set X_test, y_test
INITIALIZE MultinomialNB AS model
TRAIN model USING X_train, y_train

# Evaluate Model
PREDICT y_pred USING model AND X_test
CALCULATE accuracy USING accuracy_score(y_test, y_pred)
PRINT accuracy
PRINT classification_report(y_test, y_pred)

# Predict Election Outcome
GROUP data BY 'candidate'
CALCULATE mean sentiment score FOR each candidate
SET predicted_winner TO candidate WITH highest mean sentiment score
PRINT predicted_winner
```

Fig. 1 NB Algorithm

```
Accuracy: 1.0
              precision    recall  f1-score   support

       Trump       1.00      1.00      1.00         2

    accuracy                           1.00         2
   macro avg       1.00      1.00      1.00         2
weighted avg       1.00      1.00      1.00         2

candidate
Biden    0.311175
Trump    0.042175
Name: sentiment, dtype: float64
Predicted Winner: Biden
```

Fig. 2 Classification Performance and Predicted Sentiment for Political Candidates: Biden vs. Trump

straightforward metric, representing the proportion of correctly classified instances out of the total instances. It gives a general sense of how well the model performs. However, accuracy alone can be misleading, especially if the dataset is imbalanced.

Precision measures the accuracy of the positive predictions, defined as the number of true positives divided by the number of true positives plus false positives. Precision is crucial when the cost of false positives is high. For instance, incorrectly predicting public sentiment for a candidate could lead to erroneous conclusions about their popularity. Recall (or Sensitivity) is the ability of the model to find all the relevant cases (true positives), defined as the number of true positives divided by the number of true positives plus false negatives. High recall is essential when missing positive instances has significant consequences. F1-Score is the harmonic mean of precision and recall, providing a single metric that balances both concerns. It is particularly useful when the dataset is imbalanced, and you need to consider both false positives and false negatives. Confusion Matrix offers a detailed breakdown of the model's performance by displaying the true positives, false positives, true negatives, and false negatives. This matrix helps in understanding the specific areas where the model is making errors, which can guide further improvements.

5 Conclusion and Future Work

This chapter discusses how the SMA has evolved over time with the inclusion of SA and the use of ML techniques to predict election outcomes. SMA is increasingly being used as a vital tool in analysing massive amounts of data generated daily by platforms such as Twitter, Facebook, and Instagram, which generate over 500 million tweets and 350 million photos on Facebook every day. All of the data shown above produces promising results when used to predict election outcomes, with studies reaching as high as 94.2% accuracy, as demonstrated in the AP Assembly Election 2019 case study.

NB-powered systems, random forest, and LSTM networks have increased the predictive potential of other ML models. For instance, the SA performed on the Twitter data from the 2020 US Presidential Election 2020 performed an accuracy rate of around 80–85%, demonstrating ML models' high potential in capturing popular sentiments. However, challenges exist especially in the area of manipulating social media data to spread misinformation and bots. These may then further mislead the reliability of the SA and, as a result, electoral predictions as seen in the 2019 Indian elections.

The future research will need to improve the methodologies associated with analysing of social media data to enhance the reliability of ML-based predictions. The combination of traditional survey data with SMA appears to hold significant potential as highlighted by Reveilhac et al. (2022). Integrating live social media data with structured surveys serves as an effective approach to enhance public opinion insights. Hybrid methods of this type could address numerous biases in social media platforms, especially given that only 22% of US adults utilize Twitter, resulting only a small segment of the electorate being represented.

There is certainly a growing necessity to create strategies for detecting and addressing the effects of misinformation and bots on the credibility of public sentiment data. The creation of advanced ML models designed to filter manipulated content could greatly improve the reliability of predictions while utilizing data from a wider range of social platforms. In the future, additional SMA applications will extend beyond election predictions to encompass monitoring public health, disaster response, and urban planning. Another promising direction arises from recent advancements in explainable AI, which will allow researchers and policymakers to comprehend the outputs of complex ML models. The techniques of SMA and SA tools are still evolving, yet their applications cover a broad spectrum, leading to more actionable and dependable insights

References

Acharjee, P. B., Magadum, A. A., Thejovathi, M., Jain, R., Umarani, K., & Nishant, N. (2023). An innovative method for election prediction using hybrid A-BiCNN-RNN approach. In *2nd International Conference on Automation, Computing and Renewable Systems (ICACRS)* (pp. 765–770). IEEE.

Behdenna, S., Barigou, F., & Belalem, G. (2016). Sentiment analysis at document level. In A. Unal, M. Nayak, D. K. Mishra, D. Singh, & A. Joshi (Eds.), *Smart trends in information technology and computer communications. SmartCom 2016. Communications in computer and information science* (Vol. 628, pp. 159–168). Springer.

Birjali, M., Kasri, M., & Beni-Hssane, A. (2021). A comprehensive survey on sentiment analysis: Approaches, challenges and trends. *Knowledge-Based Systems, 226*, 107134.

Brito, K., Silva Filho, R. L. C., & Adeodato, P. J. L. (2024). Stop trying to predict elections only with twitter–There are other data sources and technical issues to be improved. *Government Information Quarterly, 41*(1), 101899.

Charan, P., Madhavi, N. B., Singh, P. P., & Srinivas, A. (2023). Data analytics to reflect the current politics on twitter by using machine learning. In *International Conference on Computer Communication and Informatics (ICCCI)* (pp. 1–4). IEEE.

Do, H. H., Prasad, P. W., Maag, A., & Alsadoon, A. (2018). Deep learning for aspect-based sentiment analysis: A comparative review. *Expert Systems with Applications, 118*, 272–299.

Flack, J. C., & D'Souza, R. M. (2014). The digital age and the future of social network science and engineering. *Proceedings of the IEEE, 102*(12), 1873–1877.

Hulliyah, K., Bakar, N. S. A. A., Ismail, A. R., & Pratama, M. O. (2019). A Benchmark of Modeling for Sentiment Analysis of the Indonesian Presidential Election in 2019. In *7th International Conference on Cyber and IT Service Management (CITSM)* (pp. 1–4). IEEE.

Hulliyah, K., Sukmana, H. T., Bakar, N. S. A., & Ismail, A. R. (2018). Indonesian affective word resources construction in valence and arousal dimension for sentiment analysis. In *6th International Conference on Cyber and IT Service Management (CITSM)* (pp. 1–5). IEEE.

Lee, A. S. H., Yusoff, Z., Zainol, Z., & Pillai, V. (2018). Know your hotels well! -- An online review analysis using text analytics. *International Journal of Engineering & Technology, 7*(4.31), 341–347.

Martí, P., Serrano-Estrada, L., & Nolasco-Cirugeda, A. (2019). Social media data: Challenges, opportunities and limitations in urban studies. *Computers, Environment and Urban Systems, 74*, 161–174.

Myilvahanan, K., Yashas, P., Pasha, S., Ismail, M., & Tharun, V. (2023). A study on election prediction using machine learning techniques. In *3rd International Conference on Artificial Intelligence and Smart Energy (ICAIS)* (pp. 1518–1520). IEEE.

Nanda, P., & Kumar, V. (2021). Social media analytics: Tools, techniques and present day practices. *International Journal of Services Operations and Informatics, 11*(4), 422–436.

Olteanu, A., Cernian, A., & Gâgă, S. A. (2022). Leveraging machine learning and semi-structured information to identify political views from social media posts. *Applied Sciences, 12*(24), 12962.

Park, J., Cheon, M., Hou, S., & Lee, O. (2022). Forecasting election result via artificial intelligence approach: NLP and machine learning. In *International Conference on Communication and Computational Technologies (ICCCT)* (pp. 761–768). Springer.

Pugliese, R., Regondi, S., & Marini, R. (2021). Machine learning-based approach: Global trends, research directions, and regulatory standpoints. *Data Science and Management, 4*, 19–29.

Qorib, M., Gizaw, R. S., & Kim, J. (2023). Impact of sentiment analysis for the 2020 US presidential election on social media data. In *8th International Conference on Machine Learning Technologies (ICMLT)* (pp. 28–34). ACM.

Reveilhac, M., Steinmetz, S., & Morselli, D. (2022). A systematic literature review of how and whether social media data can complement traditional survey data to study public opinion. *Multimedia Tools and Applications, 81*(7), 10107–10142.

Sebei, H., Hadj Taieb, M. A., & Ben Aouicha, M. (2018). Review of social media analytics process and big data pipeline. *Social Network Analysis and Mining, 8*, 30.

Sheth, V., Tripathi, U., & Sharma, A. (2022). A comparative analysis of machine learning algorithms for classification purpose. *Procedia Computer Science, 215*, 422–431.

Velloo, N., Ibrahim, N. F., & Zainol, Z. (2023). Building a recommendation system of consumers' preferable choice using a collaborative-filtering. In *17th International Conference on Ubiquitous Information Management and Communication (IMCOM)* (pp. 1–5). IEEE.

Wanniarachchi, V. U., Mathrani, A., Susnjak, T., & Scogings, C. (2020). A systematic literature review: What is the current stance towards weight stigmatization in social media platforms? *International Journal of Human-Computer Studies, 135*, 102371.

Xu, Q. A., Chang, V., & Jayne, C. (2022). A systematic review of social media-based sentiment analysis: Emerging trends and challenges. *Decision Analytics Journal, 3*, 100073.

Zachlod, C., Samuel, O., Ochsner, A., & Werthmüller, S. (2022). Analytics of social media data–State of characteristics and application. *Journal of Business Research, 144*, 1064–1076.

Zainol, Z., Nohuddin, P. N. E., Lee, A. S. H., Ibrahim, N. F., Yee, L. H., & Majid, K. A. (2021). Analysing political candidates' popularity on social media using POPularity MONitoring (POPMON). *SEARCH Journal of Media and Communication Research*, 39–55.

Zainol, Z., Wani, S., Nohuddin, P. N. E., Noormanshah, W. M. U., & Marzukhi, S. (2018). Association analysis of cyberbullying on social media using Apriori Algorithm. *International Journal of Engineering & Technology, 7*(4.29), 72–75.

Cybersecurity in the Digital Age

Ileyas Rizvi, Shiv Raj, and Vikram Singh

Abstract In the modern digital era, cybersecurity has emerged as a critical concern due to the widespread use of digital technologies, increasing the vulnerability to cyberattacks across various sectors. As the complexity and frequency of these threats rise, robust cybersecurity strategies are vital for safeguarding critical infrastructure, sensitive data, and personal privacy. The global economy, particularly industries reliant on secure digital transactions such as e-commerce, banking, and Fintech, is increasingly susceptible to cybersecurity breaches, which can result in significant financial and reputational damage. National security is also at risk, with cyberattacks targeting essential systems like power grids and transportation networks, prompting governments to implement advanced security measures.

The integration of cybersecurity and data privacy is crucial, particularly as organisations collect vast amounts of sensitive personal data. Technologies such as cloud computing and the Internet of Things (IoT) introduce novel challenges in maintaining security, necessitating continuous investment in threat detection and advanced architectures like Zero Trust. Collaborative efforts between governments, businesses, and international organisations, supported by public–private partnerships, are essential to protect digital infrastructure and address the skills gap in the cybersecurity workforce. Educational initiatives and the development of comprehensive frameworks are key to enhancing resilience against cyberthreats, ensuring a more secure and safer digital future.

I. Rizvi (✉)
Management and Research Institute, Lucknow, India

S. Raj
Additional Superintendent of Police, UP Police, Lucknow, India

V. Singh
Noida International University, Noida, India

L. O. Yesufu, P. N. E. Nohuddin (eds.), *Technology for Societal Transformation*,
https://doi.org/10.1007/978-981-96-1721-0_8

1 Introduction

Cybersecurity has emerged as a critical priority in the contemporary digital environment. The widespread adoption of digital technologies across industries, commerce, education, and social interactions has dramatically increased our reliance on internet-connected systems, making them prime targets for cyberattacks. As digital ecosystems evolve, the complexity and frequency of cyberthreats have also grown, demanding robust cybersecurity strategies to protect critical infrastructure, sensitive data, and the privacy of organisations aa well as individuals. The global economy is increasingly dependent on digital transactions and data exchange. E-commerce, banking, and Fintech industries rely heavily on secure platforms to safeguard data. A breach can led to substantial financial losses, damage to organisational reputation, and erosion of trust (Kuzior et al., 2024). National security is at risk from cyberattacks targeting power grids, transportation systems, and water supplies (Stoddart, 2016). Government entities and critical infrastructure operators are under increasing pressure to implement advanced cybersecurity measures. The escalating sophistication of cyberthreats necessitates a collaborative response from governments, the private sector, and international organisations. Continuous investment in cybersecurity infrastructure, awareness, and education is imperative to secure the digital future. Strengthening the cybersecurity of these systems through threat detection, incident response, and risk management protocols is essential to ensuring national security and public safety (Darıcılı & Celik, 2022).

2 Data Privacy and Cybersecurity

Data privacy and cybersecurity are inextricably linked in the contemporary digital landscape. As organisations amass and store substantial quantities of personal and sensitive information, safeguarding this data against unauthorised access, breaches, and misuse has become a paramount concern (Pina et al., 2024). The confluence of technological advancements, cloud computing, and the proliferation of Internet of Things (IoT) devices has introduced novel challenges in preserving data integrity and privacy. Consequently, cybersecurity is indispensable for maintaining the privacy and security of personal information across sectors such as banking (Wang et al., 2024), healthcare (Salam, 2024), and education (Fouad, 2022). The absence of adequate protection can lead to the compromise of these records, resulting in identity theft, fraud, and severe reputational damage for institutions.

Data privacy ensures the responsible collection, storage, and processing of personal data in line with legal standards, like the GDPR, which sets global benchmarks for data protection. This includes informed consent, transparency, and user control. Businesses must adopt robust privacy measures, such as encryption and anonymisation, to build consumer trust, especially with the growing exchange of personal data across platforms (Huyen & Bao, 2024). Cybersecurity, focusing on protecting systems and networks from cyberattacks, emphasises practices such as secure development, audits, and Zero Trust Architecture to counter threats from both inside and outside networks (Zanasi et al., 2024). Advances in AI-driven threat detection and cryptography are key, but ongoing efforts in regulation and research remain vital (Sarker, 2024).

3 Cyberthreats and Cybersecurity

Data breaches, resulting in the unauthorised access and exposure of sensitive information, remain a persistent cybersecurity threat. The proliferation of personal and financial data stored digitally has amplified the potential consequences of these breaches (Mohsin et al., 2024), with far-reaching implications for both individuals and organisations (Chen et al., 2024). Recent research underscores the multifaceted impact of data breaches, extending beyond financial losses to encompass erosion of consumer trust, which can significantly damage a company's reputation and market position. Approximately, 80% of nation-state attacks target think tanks, government agencies, and NGOs (John Lambert, 2021).

Ransomware attacks, malware, and unlawful access to computers, collectively known as hacking, constitute the most prevalent and successful methods of cyberattacks, accounting for a substantial portion of data breaches worldwide. The emergence of state-sponsored hacking has introduced a geopolitical dimension to cyberthreats, as nations engage in cyberespionage and cyberwarfare to gain strategic advantages.

Malicious hackers exploit security vulnerabilities to access personal data and capitalise on organisations' expanding digital footprints. In 2023, there were 2365 cyberattacks, affecting 343 million victims (Identity Theft Resource Center: Data Breach Report, 2023). This marked a 72% rise in data breaches compared to 2021, the previous record year. Globally, the average cost of a data breach in 2024 was $4.88 million (IBM, 2024). Cybersecurity experts predict that global ransomware damages could exceed $20 trillion annually by 2031 [Application Access Governance (AAG), 2024]. Recent incidents have demonstrated the escalating financial impact of ransomware attacks, with malicious actors successfully extorting substantial sums from both private enterprises and public infrastructure on a global scale.

The year 2024 has witnessed a surge in cyberattacks, with educational institutions facing an average of 2507 attacks per week in the first quarter alone (Thoughtlab, 2024). Despite these persistent threats, many organisations struggle to detect and prevent breaches, taking an average of 118 days to identify a compromise (Keeper Security, 2024). Password security continues to be a prevalent weakness, with 44% of users reusing passwords across personal and business accounts (Norton Antivirus, 2023). Looking ahead, cybersecurity will be a critical factor in business decisions, as 60% of organisations anticipate considering it when evaluating partners and transactions by 2025 (Thoughtlab, 2024).

In 2024, email emerged as the primary vector for cybercrime, accounting for over 75% of targeted cyberattacks (Keeper Security, 2024). Seventeen percent of these attacks specifically exploited vulnerabilities in web applications, of which 98% were susceptible to threats such as malware, malicious redirections, and other forms of exploitation (PT Security, 2022). A significant 72% of these vulnerabilities were attributed to flaws in web application coding (PT Security, 2022). As cyberattacks continue to rise, organisations in 2024 experienced an average of 1636 cyberattacks per week, representing a 30% year-over-year increase (LastPass, n.d.).

In response, cybersecurity budgets as a percentage of total revenue have jumped by 51%, increasing from 0.53% to 0.80%, although 30% of executives still report that their budgets are insufficient to adequately secure their systems (Check Point Research, 2022). Internally, 55% of companies conduct cybersecurity assessments, but only 38% report significant improvements following a breach, and just 23% indicate that their password security practices have been substantially enhanced. Password security remains a concern, with 53% of users having not changed their passwords in the last 12 months (World Economic Forum, 2024) (Tables 1 and 2).

Table 1 Global cyberthreat and cybersecurity data for 2024 based on the recent reports

Metric	2024 Data/Estimates
Global Cybercrime Cost	Estimated to exceed $10.5 trillion annually by 2025 (IBM, 2024).
Average Data Breach Cost	Reached $4.45 million per breach in 2023, projected to increase further (Thales Group, 2024).
IoT Devices Vulnerability	By 2030, over 25% of all cyberattacks are expected to target Internet of Things (IoT) devices (Gartner, 2023).
Cloud Infrastructure Attacks	27% of organisations reported an attack on their cloud infrastructure (World Economic Forum, 2024).
Healthcare Sector Breaches	58% increase in cyberattacks targeting healthcare institutions (Oracle & KPMG, 2023).
Percentage of Organisations Hit by Ransomware	51% of organisations globally experienced ransomware attacks in 2023 (World Economic Forum, 2024).
Ransomware Attacks	Average cost of a ransomware breach is $5.13 million, up by 13% since 2023 (Varonis, 2024).
Increase in Phishing Attacks	80% of cybersecurity incidents involve phishing (Thales Group, 2024).
Phishing Attacks	Phishing accounted for $4.9 million in damages as the top attack vector. (Varonis, 2024)
Cloud Security	52% of organisations report inadequate cloud security as their top concern (Thales Group, 2024).
AI and Cybersecurity	Use of AI for cybersecurity expected to increase by 60% in organisations by 2025 to counter evolving threats (World Economic Forum, 2024).
Incident Response	77% of organisations lack an effective incident response plan (Cybint Solutions, 2024).
Cybersecurity Spending	Global spending on cybersecurity to exceed $200 billion by 2025 (Thales Group, 2024).
Cybersecurity Workforce Gap	Expected shortage of 3.5 million cybersecurity professionals worldwide in 2024 (World Economic Forum, 2024).

Table 2 Industry-wise Cyberattack statistics for 2024

Industry	Number of incidents	Type of attack	Year
Finance	1100	Ransomware, Phishing (IT Governance UK, 2024)	2024
Healthcare	780	Data Breaches, Ransomware (Cen, 2024)	2024
Retail	950	Malware, Customer Data Theft (IT Governance UK, 2024)	2024
Education	600	Ransomware, Data Breaches (Cen, 2024)	2024
Manufacturing	400	Supply Chain Attacks (Cen, 2024)	2024
Government	850	Data Breaches, Phishing (IT Governance UK, 2024)	2024
Technology	1200	Ransomware, Malware (IT Governance UK, 2024)	2024
Energy	500	Supply Chain Attacks (Cen, 2024)	2024

3.1 Ransomware

Ransomware, a malicious software that encrypts data of victims and demands a ransom for decryption (Morgan, 2024), has become a significant cybersecurity threat. Despite paying the ransom, there is no guarantee of data recovery (Hancock Jeff and security firm Tessian, 2022). The prevalence of ransomware is fuelled by increasing vulnerabilities and low barriers to entry for attackers.

A Stanford University research report (GetAstra, 2024) found that 96% of ransomware attacks targeted backup repositories. While 16% of victims recovered data without paying, 29% were unable to do so even after paying the ransom. In 2023, ransomware accounted for over 72% of cyberattacks (Splunk, 2024). Eighty-three percent of affected businesses paid ransoms, with over half paying more than $100,000 (Cobalt, 2024). Ransomware has not only disrupted business operations but also targeted cloud-based data, which was involved in 82% of data breaches (Shaikh, 2024).

The financial cost of ransomware attacks has escalated dramatically, with the average ransom amount in 2023 reaching $1.54 million (Chainalysis Team, 2021). Fifty-two percent of organisations reported significant system and operational impacts (Gren & Feldt, 2024). Although the percentage of businesses affected by ransomware decreased slightly from 21% in 2021 to 17% in 2023, the overall damage has increased. Ransomware extortion in the first half of 2023 surpassed the total for all of 2022 by $176 million (AV-TEST, 2024). Given the increasing sophistication of ransomware groups targeting industrial control systems, organisations must adopt a proactive, resilient-by-design strategy to mitigate potential disruptions. Among organisations with encrypted data, 56% paid the ransom, but only 46% fully recovered their data. Malware attacks typically result in an average downtime of 21 days. Ransomware has also targeted government agencies (63% of cyberattacks), schools, hospitals, and other public service industries (Next7 IT, 2024).

3.2 Malware

The year 2022 witnessed a significant surge in cyberthreats globally, with a staggering 5.4 billion malware attacks documented (Splunk, 2024). This translates to a concerning frequency of approximately 11.5 attacks launched every minute, highlighting the persistent and pervasive nature of this threat (Splunk, 2024). The impact of these attacks is further emphasised by the alarming statistic that four out of ten resulted in data leakage, compromising confidentiality and security (Splunk, 2024). Email is the primary vector for malware distribution, accounting for a massive 92% of cases (IT Governance UK, 2024). The pervasiveness of this threat is further underscored by the fact that by the first half of 2024 alone, a staggering 2.8 billion malware incidents had already been recorded. There was growth in ransomware attacks by a four-fold increase in the total value of cryptocurrency received by ransomware addresses. The difficulty in tracing these transactions due to the inherent anonymity of cryptocurrency further exacerbates the problem (AV-TEST, 2024).

The registration of over 450,000 new malicious programs and potentially unwanted applications takes place each day (Next7 IT, 2024). 71% of all malware attacks are directed at specific victims, with 17% targeting individuals alone (Varonis, 2024). The overall picture painted by these statistics is one of a rapidly escalating threat landscape. Daily, an estimated 560,000 new pieces of malware are detected (Cisco, 2024). Organisations are not immune, with 70% reporting that their users encounter malware ads while browsing (Nifakos, 2023). Furthermore, 48% of organisations have experienced information theft attributable to malware (Nifakos, 2023).

4 Social Engineering Attacks

Social engineering is a strategy used by malicious attackers to exploit a human mind's vulnerabilities and gain access to sensitive information (Jones & Taylor, 2023). Usually, fear, relationships, and social expectations manipulate the victim into divulging information or performing actions that put them or their organisation at risk. Social engineering scams are on the rise, with 98% of cyberattackers using social engineering techniques. These frauds exploit human weaknesses to gain access to information, posing grave threats to organisations. In 2020–2021, more than half of the data breaches were due to the exploitation of the people; and the COVID-19 pandemic worsened the attacks, with a surge in phishing websites, an enormous 350% (Splunk, 2024).

Social engineering attacks, including Whaling, Baiting, Phishing (Cobalt, 2024), Spear Phishing, Quid Pro Quo, Smishing, and Honey Trapping, are rapidly increasing across the globe. These attacks vary in their approach, medium, and targets to gain unauthorised access to sensitive information.

Phishing, in particular, is a sophisticated method used by cybercriminals to trick individuals into revealing confidential data or performing harmful actions. Attackers often create highly convincing emails, embedding malicious links that direct users to fake websites (European Union, 2019), while impersonating trusted institutions such as banks, governments, or well-established organisations. This type of attack poses a serious risk to businesses, as it exploits the organisation's weakest point.

A significant 45% of respondents reported that distraction was the primary reason for falling victim to phishing. The most common triggers for clicking on phishing emails were the apparent legitimacy of the email (43%), and the belief that it was from a senior executive (41%) or a well-known brand (40%) (U.S. Department of Homeland Security, 2023). Phishing continues to dominate as one of the most common cyberattack methods, accounting for 39.6% of all email threats in 2023 (IT Governance UK, 2024). Notably, 96% of phishing attacks are delivered through email, making email the primary attack vector (Tang & Shklovski, 2022). According to IBM, the average cost of a phishing attack for businesses is $4.9 million (Splunk, 2024). In November 2022 alone, Google blocked an astounding 231 billion spam and phishing emails (Shaikh, 2024).

Equally concerning is the rise of **Business Email Compromise (BEC)**, which remains a major cybersecurity threat, contributing to 19% of all data breaches (IT Governance UK, 2024). In 2021, these attacks led to financial losses amounting to $1.8 billion, highlighting their devastating impact on businesses worldwide (IT Governance UK, 2024). By 2022, 34% of all cyberattacks were BEC-related, underscoring their growing prevalence (Splunk, 2024). One of the most frequently used techniques in BEC attacks involves requesting gift cards, which account for 68% of these schemes (IT Governance UK, 2024).

Spear phishing targets specific individuals to steal sensitive data, while **smishing** uses deceptive text messages for the same purpose. **Quid pro quo** involves impersonating IT personnel, and **honey trapping** creates fake profiles to emotionally manipulate victims. **Whaling** is highly personalised and hard to detect, requiring detailed research on the target, while **baiting** uses tempting offers to access confidential information (European Union, 2019).

5 Role of Governments in Digital Infrastructure Security: Policy Frameworks and Regulations

Governments play a key role in establishing policy frameworks and regulations to protect digital infrastructure. For example, the European Union's Cybersecurity Act (2019) sets certification standards for digital products (U.S. Department of Homeland Security, 2023), while the U.S. Cybersecurity and Infrastructure Security Agency (CISA) works to secure federal networks (Tang & Shklovski, 2022). Regulations such as the General Data Protection Regulation (GDPR) in Europe highlighted the importance of data protection (Chandrasekhar & Mee, 2021).

International Cooperation Given the transnational nature of cyberthreats, governments collaborate globally. International frameworks, such as the Budapest Convention on Cybercrime, enable information sharing to combat cybercrime. Initiatives like the Quad Working Group also unite countries to protect technological advancements (Tang & Shklovski, 2022).

Public–Private Partnerships Public–private partnerships (PPPs) are vital for securing critical infrastructure. For instance, the U.S. Department of Homeland Security's National Risk Management Centre brings together public and private sectors to identify risks and share threat intelligence in real time (Tang & Shklovski, 2022).

6 Role of Businesses in Digital Infrastructure Security

- Securing Customer Data: Businesses must protect sensitive information using encryption, multi-factor authentication, and compliance with laws like the GDPR.
- Building Resilient Networks: Businesses are responsible for continuous monitoring, advanced threat detection, and training employees to prevent cyberattacks.
- Collaboration with Government and Industry: Businesses collaborate with governments to develop cybersecurity frameworks, contributing to cross-sector defences against threats in key sectors such as finance and healthcare (World Economic Forum, 2024).
- Implementing Security Protocols: Companies adopt protocols such as firewalls and encryption, with those using zero-trust architectures reporting lower data breach costs [79].
- Employee Training: Phishing and social engineering attacks cause over 80% of data breaches, highlighting the need for cybersecurity training (ISC2, 2023).
- Investment in Cybersecurity Technologies: Businesses are investing in AI and machine learning for faster threat detection. Sectors such as cloud services and finance are leading adopters (ISC2, 2023).
- Government-Business Collaboration: Joint initiatives like the Cyber Information Sharing and Collaboration Program (CISCP) help businesses share threat data with governments for improved national security (Chandrasekhar & Mee, 2021).

7 Cybersecurity Industry Skills Gap

A Cybersecurity Analyst protects an organisation's computer systems and networks. In 2023, the global cybersecurity workforce gap reached 4 million, with a shortfall of over 3 million qualified professionals who can provide leadership, secure systems, and educate individuals on digital hygiene. From May 2023 to April 2024, approximately 470,000 job openings emerged in the cybersecurity sector (Capgemini, 2024).

The industry faces a significant skills gap, as nearly two-thirds of cybersecurity experts believe their organisations are understaffed. Moreover, 20% of these experts indicate it takes over 6 months to fill open positions (Capgemini, 2024). Alarmingly, 63% of companies have unfilled cybersecurity roles, up from previous years, while 60% of respondents report challenges in retaining qualified personnel (Capgemini, 2024).

8 Cybersecurity Measures

In response to rising cyberthreats, cybersecurity is now a top priority for organisations and governments. It protects systems, networks, and data from unauthorised access or damage through measures like multi-factor authentication, encryption, and software updates. Research shows that organisations with comprehensive frameworks, including employee training and incident response plans, are better equipped to handle cyberthreats (Chandrasekhar & Mee, 2021). The increasing importance of cybersecurity in critical infrastructure has driven public–private collaboration. Governments are enforcing regulations like the EU's GDPR and the U.S.'s CISA to secure essential services such as energy, healthcare, and transportation (U.S. Department of Homeland Security, 2023; Tang & Shklovski, 2022).

The evolving nature of cyberthreats requires constant observance and adaptation. Cybercriminals continuously exploit emerging technologies such as AI and IoT to enhance attacks, demanding cybersecurity professionals stay updated on the latest innovations. In the digital age, cyberthreats pose a growing risk to individuals, organisations, and nations. Robust cybersecurity strategies and collaboration among stakeholders are essential to safeguarding digital assets and maintaining trust in the digital ecosystem (Table 3).

These technologies and trends reflect the ongoing evolution in the cybersecurity landscape, driven by advancements in technology and increasing sophistication of cyberthreats.

8.1 Cybersecurity Education

A well-educated and trained workforce is essential for mitigating cyberthreats and fostering organisational growth. Employees' academic qualifications, ongoing training and certification programs, and the development of workforce knowledge capabilities are crucial for effectively fulfilling cybersecurity business functions (Nautiyal & Rashid, 2024).

Table 3 Latest cybersecurity technologies and their implications

Technology/Trend	Description
Zero Trust Security	A cybersecurity model that requires strict identity verification for every user and device, both inside and outside the network (Splashtop, 2024).
Generative AI	The use of AI to enhance cybersecurity measures, including threat detection, incident response, and the generation of realistic phishing simulations for training purposes (Splashtop, 2024).
Quantum Computing	As quantum computing advances, there is a dual focus on creating quantum-resistant encryption techniques and leveraging quantum computing for more sophisticated security measures (Hart et al., 2020).
Enhanced Mobile Security	As mobile devices become more integral to work and personal life, there is an increased emphasis on securing these devices through encryption and advanced authentication methods (Hart et al., 2020).
Post-Quantum Cryptography	Development of cryptographic systems that are secure against the potential capabilities of quantum computers, addressing vulnerabilities in traditional encryption methods (Hart et al., 2020).
Advanced Phishing Defence	Multi-factor authentication (MFA) and intelligent access controls to combat sophisticated phishing tactics.
IoT Security Enhancements	A new security frameworks and solutions to protect IoT ecosystems from emerging threats (Hart et al., 2020).

8.2 Prevention of Cybersecurity Attacks

Establishing a strong culture of **security awareness** is crucial for preventing cyberattacks, with management leading by example through cybersecurity initiatives and regular training on emerging threats.

Phishing Tests Regular phishing simulations assess and improve employee awareness, with key metrics analysed to enhance security practices.

Patching and Updates Timely patches address system vulnerabilities, while automated tools and compensatory controls ensure security for legacy systems.

Continuous Monitoring Monitoring tools detect anomalies and phishing attempts, enabling rapid responses to threats, significantly improving cybersecurity resilience.

9 Conclusion

The significance of cybersecurity in today's increasingly digital environment cannot be overstated. As reliance on digital technologies permeates every facet of society, from commerce to critical infrastructure, the threats posed by cyberattacks continue to escalate in both sophistication and frequency. This chapter has highlighted the myriads of cyberthreats—including data breaches and ransomware that jeopardise personal data, organisational integrity, and national security.

The interconnection of data privacy and cybersecurity emphasises the necessity for robust protective measures to safeguard sensitive information across various sectors. Effective cybersecurity strategies must evolve in tandem with the rapid advancement of technology and the ever-changing cyberlandscape. Governments and businesses alike bear a critical responsibility in developing comprehensive frameworks and investing in advanced security measures, ensuring resilience against potential attacks. Collaborative efforts among public and private sectors are essential for enhancing digital infrastructure security, sharing intelligence, and fostering a culture of cybersecurity awareness.

Addressing the pressing skills gap within the cybersecurity workforce is crucial for effectively managing cyberthreats. As organisations continue to face unprecedented challenges, continuous investment in education, training, and technological innovation will be vital to secure a safe and trustworthy digital future. Ultimately, a proactive and collective approach to cybersecurity will serve as a cornerstone for protecting our increasingly interconnected world.

10 Case Studies

10.1 Case Study-1: Digital Fraud at Lucknow's PGI: A Case of Social Engineering Attacks, Phishing, and Impersonation (PGI Doctor Case, 2024)

Introduction

Cybercrime is increasingly threatening individuals and institutions in India. A recent incident (August 2024) at Lucknow's Post Graduate Institute of Medical Education and Research (PGI) highlights the sophistication of digital fraud. Cybercriminals impersonated officials from the Telecom Regulatory Authority of India (TRAI) and deceived a doctor, ultimately defrauding her of over Rs. 2.81 crore.

Case Background

The victim, a doctor, received a call from individuals posing as TRAI officials, warning that her phone number was under investigation for complaints about harassing messages. They threatened to deactivate her number unless she cooperated. Out of fear, she complied. The scammers then directed her to deposit large sums into accounts presented as government accounts.

Execution of the Fraud

The fraudsters quickly moved the money to multiple accounts and converted it into cryptocurrency to obscure the trail. This case demonstrates a well-coordinated **social engineering attack** involving **phishing** (fake links to impersonated officials) and **impersonation fraud** (posing as TRAI and CBI officers).

1. **Social Engineering Attack**: The scammers manipulated the doctor's emotions, leveraging fear, and urgency.

2. **Phishing**: They used fake links to create the illusion of official communication.
3. **Impersonation Fraud**: The criminals-built trust by pretending to be government officials.

Complexity of the Case
Once the doctor realised she had been scammed, she reported the crime. The special task force (STF) in Uttar Pradesh arrested several people involved. Investigators found that the mastermind behind the operation was based in Pakistan, directing a network of criminals to impersonate Indian officials. The international scope and use of cryptocurrency have complicated the investigation, but efforts to recover the stolen funds and dismantle the network are ongoing.

Cybersecurity Shortcomings Leading to Fraud
The PGI doctor fell victim due to:

1. Failure to Verify Caller Identity: She did not confirm the authenticity of the callers posing as TRAI and CBI officials.
2. Trust in Unsolicited Communication: The doctor trusted unknown callers without questioning their legitimacy.
3. Clicking on suspicious links.
4. Sharing sensitive information.
5. The scammers manipulated her through a sense of urgency, prompting quick, unverified actions.
6. Lack of awareness of cybercrime tactics.
7. No proactive cybersecurity measures.

These lapses highlight the need for vigilance, verification, and awareness in protecting against cyberfraud.

Cybersecurity Measures: Key Lessons and Prevention
This case underscores the growing risk of cybercrime and offers several key lessons:

1. Always confirm the authenticity of unsolicited calls by directly contacting the agency.
2. Beware of phishing and avoid clicking suspicious links or providing information via unsolicited communications.
3. Protect sensitive information and never share financial details, property information, or PINs with unknown callers.
4. Report suspicious activity and quickly involve local police or cybercrime units when suspecting a scam.
5. Stay updated and regularly review guidelines from governments and financial institutions on how to stay safe online.

Conclusion and Recommendation
This case illustrates the sophistication of cybercriminals who exploit psychological manipulation to deceive even educated professionals. Public awareness, combined with robust cyberprotection measures, is critical in preventing such fraud. Individuals must adhere to basic cybersafety protocols, and international collaboration between

law enforcement agencies is essential to combat transnational cybercrime. Staying vigilant and proactively adopting preventive strategies can help safeguard against digital fraud.

10.2 Case Study-2: Bangladesh Bank Heist: A Case of Malware-Based Cyberattack and System Compromise (Bangladesh Bank, 2024)

Introduction

In February 2016, cybercriminals attempted to steal **$1 billion** from the **Bangladesh Bank** by hacking into the **SWIFT** system used for international financial transactions. They successfully transferred **$81 million** to accounts in the Philippines before the fraudulent transactions were flagged and stopped.

Case Background and Execution of the Fraud

The 2016 Bangladesh Bank Heist is primarily a malware-based cyberattack with elements of social engineering and system compromise. The hackers planted malicious software that allowed them to monitor employee activities, gain access to credentials, and eventually manipulate the SWIFT system for international transactions. This manipulation allowed them to send fraudulent messages requesting large sums of money to be transferred.

They issued 35 fraudulent instructions to the Federal Reserve Bank of New York, requesting transfers of nearly $1 billion from Bangladesh Bank's account. Out of the 35 transfer requests, only five were processed, successfully sending $81 million to accounts in the Philippines. The funds that reached the Philippines were laundered through casinos, making it difficult to trace and recover the stolen money. A portion of the stolen amount has never been recovered.

Cybersecurity Shortcomings Leading to Fraud

The Bangladesh Bank Heist exposed several critical cybersecurity shortcomings that allowed hackers to successfully steal $81 million. The following weaknesses played a key role in facilitating the cybercrime:

1. Weak IT Infrastructure: Lack of firewalls made it easier for the hackers to penetrate the system and install malware.
2. Insufficient Network Monitoring.
3. Lack of multi-factor authentication.
4. Employees lacked cybersecurity training.
5. The bank took days to detect fraudulent transactions.
6. The bank lacked robust cybersecurity policies, including system audits, access controls, and transaction logging for sensitive systems like SWIFT.
7. Sensitive data, including SWIFT credentials, were inadequately protected.
8. Delayed communication with international institutions.

Cybersecurity Measures: Key Lessons and Prevention
This case emphasises the importance of:

- Up-to-date IT security systems and regular security patches.
- Multi-factor authentication in sensitive systems.
- Real-time monitoring and quick incident response.
- Comprehensive cybersecurity training for employees.
- Strict security policies for high-value transactions.
- Encryption could have mitigated the damage by making the stolen data unusable.

By addressing these shortcomings, financial institutions can significantly reduce the risk of cyberfraud.

Conclusion and Recommendation
The Bangladesh Bank heist highlighted critical cybersecurity shortcomings and to prevent similar incidents, banks must prioritise robust cybersecurity measures such as implementing multi-factor authentication, regular system audits, encryption of sensitive data, and continuous network monitoring. Proactive measures and strong security policies are crucial in safeguarding critical financial systems from cybercriminals.

10.3 Case Study-3: Ransomware Attack on Ayesa: A Case of Ransomware, Malware, Phishing, and Social Engineering (Ayesa, 2024)

Introduction
In May 2024, Ayesa, a leading Spanish engineering and technology consulting company, became a victim of a ransomware attack attributed to the notorious cybercriminal group Black Basta. This incident not only underscored the vulnerabilities faced by organisations in the digital landscape but also highlighted the increasing sophistication of ransomware attacks, particularly those employing double extortion tactics.

Case Background
Ayesa, with over 12,500 employees and a presence in 23 countries, provides engineering and technology services across various sectors, including infrastructure and energy. The company's extensive operations necessitate the management of sensitive client data and project information, making it a prime target for cybercriminals seeking financial gain and disruption. The ransomware attack, publicly disclosed on May 13, 2024, potentially compromised about 4.5 terabytes of sensitive data, including:

- Company data related to treasury, human resources, and administration
- Personal information of employees
- Projects and CAD files

Black Basta (cybercriminal) utilised a double extortion method, locking Ayesa's data and threatening to release sensitive information unless a ransom was paid. The attack was likely initiated through a phishing email containing malicious links or attachments, allowing the malware to spread throughout the company's network.

Impact of the Attack

The ramifications of the ransomware attack were profound. Ayesa faced operational paralysis, with employees unable to access critical systems, leading to delays in project delivery and damage to client relationships. The potential exposure of sensitive employee information raised significant concerns about identity theft and further cybercriminal activities.

Detailed profiling was made easier for attackers due to the data stolen from Ayesa. With access to personal details, cybercriminals could create synthetic identities to impersonate employees, facilitating fraud and unauthorised access to secure systems.

The Threat of Detailed Profiling

The stolen data enables criminals to create detailed profiles, facilitating identity theft and enhancing phishing attacks. By combining this information with data from brokers, cybercriminals can craft highly convincing phishing emails and impersonation attempts, increasing the chances of success. The attack opened several potential avenues for exploitation, including:

- Stolen personal data could facilitate identity theft, resulting in financial and reputational damage.
- Detailed personal and company information could enable attackers to craft convincing phishing emails, raising the success rate of such attacks.
- Access to valuable projects and CAD files could lead to significant intellectual property loss.
- Access to employee credentials might allow attackers to gain unauthorised access to other systems.

The Ayesa ransomware attack involved ransomware, malware, phishing, and social engineering. Attackers locked the company's data and demanded a ransom, likely starting with a phishing attack that tricked employees into clicking malicious links or downloading harmful attachments.

Response and Recovery

The company did not disclose whether they paid a ransom to the attackers. It took immediate steps to mitigate the damage, engaging cybersecurity experts to assess the breach and initiate recovery protocols. Ayesa implemented enhanced cybersecurity measures, including better email filtering, regular cybersecurity training for employees, and an updated incident response plan.

Cybersecurity Shortcomings Leading to Fraud

The specific cybersecurity shortcomings that led to the fraud at Ayesa are:

1. Lack of effective firewalls.

2. The IT team failed to implement real-time monitoring tools.
3. Single-factor authentication.
4. Employees had insufficient training.
5. Lack of cybersecurity policies and procedures.
6. Sensitive data was not adequately encrypted.
7. Ayesa did not establish effective partnerships with cybersecurity organisations.

Cybersecurity Measures: Key Lessons and Prevention

Key Lessons and Prevention Strategies are-

1. Regular software updates
2. Enhanced firewall protection
3. Real-time network monitoring
4. Multi-factor authentication
5. Comprehensive cybersecurity training
6. Develop and regularly update a coordinated response plan for cyberincidents.
7. Data encryption
8. Engage external cybersecurity experts for assessments and threat intelligence.
9. Limit data access based on the principle of least privilege.
10. Use encrypted connections (like VPNs).

Conclusion and Recommendations

The ransomware attack on Ayesa illustrates the growing threat of cybercrime in today's interconnected environment. As organisations increasingly rely on digital technologies, the importance of robust cybersecurity measures cannot be overstated. By learning from incidents like Ayesa's and implementing comprehensive security strategies, companies can enhance their resilience against future threats and safeguard their operations, clients, and reputations.

References

Application Access Governance (AAG). (2024). *The Latest 2024 Cyber Crime Statistics*. https://aag-it.com/t

AV-TEST. (2024). https://www.av-test.org/en/statistics/malware/. Accessed on 19 September 2024

Ayesa. (2024). Retrieved from https://www.ayesa.com/. Accessed on 19 September 2024

Bangladesh Bank, Central Bank of Bangladesh. (2024). Retrieved from https://www.bb.org.bd/en/. Accessed on 21 September 2024

Capgemini. (2024). *Five cybersecurity trends for 2024*. Retrieved from https://www.capgemini.com/

Cen, M. (2024). Ransomware early detection: A survey. *Computer Networks, 239*, 110138. https://doi.org/10.1016/j.comnet.2023.110138

Chainalysis Team. (2021). *Ransomware 2021: Critical mid-year update*. Insights. 14 May 2021. https://blog.chainalysis.com/reports/ransomware-update-may-2021

Chandrasekhar, C., & Mee, P. (2021, May 3). Why businesses and governments must fight cyber threats together. *World Economic Forum Global Agenda*. Retrieved from https://www.weforum.org/

Check Point Research. (2022). *Healthcare Industry Cyberattack Report*. https://www.checkpoint.com, Accessed on 19 September 2024
Chen, W., Li, X., Wu, H., & Zhang, L. (2024). The impact of managerial myopia on cybersecurity: Evidence from data breaches. *Journal of Banking & Finance, 166*, 107254.
Cisco. (2024). https://research.cisco.com/publications?researchArea=Cybersecurity. Accessed on 23 September 2024
Cobalt. (2024). *Cybersecurity statistics*. https://www.cobalt.io/. Accessed on 19 September 2024
Cybint Solutions. (2024). www.cybintsolutions.com. Accessed on 19 September 2024. Terra Nova Security. (2024). 130 Cybersecurity Statistics: 2024 Trends and Data. Retrieved from https://www.terranovasecurity.com/. Accessed on 23 September 2024
Darıcılı, A. B., & Celik, S. (2022). National security 2.0: The cyber security of critical infrastructure. PERCEPTIONS. *Journal of International Affairs, 26*(2), 259–276.
European Union. (2019). *Cybersecurity Act*. Available at: https://eur-lex.europa.eu
Fouad, N. S. (2022). The security economics of EdTech: Vendors' responsibility and the cybersecurity challenge in the education sector. *Digital Policy, Regulation and Governance, 24*(3), 259–273.
Gartner. (2023). *AI in Cybersecurity Survey Report*. Retrieved: from https://www.gartner.com. Accessed on 19 September 2024
GetAstra. (2024). *Cybersecurity statistics*. Retrieved from https://www.getastra.com. Accessed on 19 September 2024
Gren, L., Feldt, R. (2024). The Social Psychology of Software Security (Psycurity). *arXiv preprint arXiv:2407.00323*.
Hancock Jeff and security firm Tessian. (2022). *Research Report on the study "Psychology of Human Error"*. Stanford University.
Hart, S., Margheri, A., Paci, F., & Sassone, V. (2020). Riskio: A serious game for cyber security awareness and education. *Computer Security, 95*, 101827.
Huyen, N. T. M., & Bao, T. Q. (2024). Advancements in AI-driven cybersecurity and comprehensive threat detection and response. *Journal of Intelligent Connectivity and Emerging Technologies, 9*(1), 1–12.
IBM. (2024). Cost of a Data Breach Report. Available at: https://www.ibm.com/security/data-breach. Accessed on 19 September 2024
Identity Theft Resource Center: Data Breach Report. (2023). ITRC Annual Data Breach Report - ITRC (idtheftcenter.org). Accessed on 19 September 2024
ISC2. (2023). *Cybersecurity workforce study, how the economy, skills gap and artificial intelligence are challenging the global cybersecurity workforce*. Accessed on 22 September 2024
IT Governance UK. (2024). *Global Data Breaches and Cyber Attacks in 2024*. Retrieved from IT Governance
John Lambert. (2021). *Microsoft Digital Defense Report, Microsoft Threat Intelligence*. https://www.microsoft.com Accessed on 19 September 2024
Jones, C., & Taylor, P. (2023). Social engineering in the digital age: Understanding baiting, quid pro quo, and whaling. *Journal of Digital Forensics, 14*(3), 47–61. https://doi.org/10.4567/jdf.2023.1403
Keeper Security. (2024). *Cybersecurity in the Remote Work Era: A Global Risk Report*. https://www.keepersecurity.com/ Accessed on 24 September 2024
Kuzior, A., Tiutiunyk, I., Zielińska, A., & Kelemen, R. (2024). Cybersecurity and cybercrime: Current trends and threats. *Journal of International Studies, 17*(2), 220–239. https://doi.org/10.14254/2071-8330.2024/17-2/12
LastPass. (n.d.). https://www.lastpass.com/security/what-is-a-cyberattack. Accessed on 19 September 2024
Mohsin, M., Salam, A. F., & Farokhnia Hamedani, M. (2024). *Strategic cybersecurity management: The impact of knowledge resources and capabilities on data breach risk*.
Morgan, J. P. (2024). *The Potential Impacts of Ransomware*. Retrieved from: https://www.jpmorgan.com. Accessed on 19 September 2024

Nautiyal, L., & Rashid, A. (2024). A framework for mapping organisational workforce knowledge profile in cyber security. *arXiv preprint arXiv:2406.03322*.
Next7 IT. (2024). https://www.next7it.com/. Accessed on 22 September 2024
Nifakos, S. (2023). *Think twice before you click! Exploring the role of human factors in cybersecurity and privacy within healthcare organizations*. Karolinska Institutet (Sweden).
Norton Antivirus. (2023). *Norton Cyber Safety Pulse Report: Scams in the digital age*. https://us.norton.com Accessed on 19 September 2024
Oracle & KPMG. (2023). Cloud Threat Report 2023. Accessed on 19 September 2024
PGI Doctor Case. (2024). https://timesofindia.com. Accessed on 17 September 2024.
Pina, E., Ramos, J., Jorge, H., Váz, P., Silva, J., Wanzeller, C., & Martins, P. (2024). Data privacy and ethical considerations in database management. *Journal of Cybersecurity and Privacy, 4*(3), 494–517.
PT Security. (2022). https://www.ptsecurity.com Accessed on 19 September 2024
Salam, A. (2024). Internet of things for sustainability: perspectives in privacy, cybersecurity, and future trends. In *Internet of things for sustainable community development: Wireless communications, sensing, and systems* (pp. 299–326). Springer International Publishing.
Sarker, I. H. (2024). Introduction to AI-driven cybersecurity and threat intelligence. In *AI-driven cybersecurity and threat intelligence: Cyber automation, intelligent decision-making and explainability* (pp. 3–19). Springer Nature Switzerland.
Shaikh, M. U. R. (2024). Fortifying against ransomware: Navigating cybersecurity risk management with a focus on ransomware insurance strategies. *International Journal of Academic Research in Business and Social Sciences, 14*(1). https://doi.org/10.6007/ijarbss/v14-i1/20566
Splashtop. (2024). *Top 10 Cyber Security Trends and Predictions for 2024*. Accessed on 19 September 2024.
Splunk. (2024). *CISO report on ransomware attacks*. Retrieved from https://www.splunk.com/. Accessed on 19 September 2024
Stoddart, K. (2016). UK cyber security and critical national infrastructure protection. *International Affairs, 92*(5), 1079–1105.
Tang, T., & Shklovski, I. (2022). Protecting user data: Businesses' role in evolving data protection frameworks. *Digital Society Journal, 10*(4), 191–205.
Thales Group. (2024). *2024 Data Threat Report: Navigating New Cybersecurity Threats*. www.cpl.thalesgroup.com/data-threat-report, Accessed on 19 September 2024
Thoughtlab. (2024). https://thoughtlabgroup.com/ Accessed on 19 September 2024
U.S. Department of Homeland Security. (2023). *Cyber Information Sharing and Collaboration Program (CISCP)*. Retrieved: from https://www.dhs.gov. Accessed on 23 September 2024
Varonis. (2024). www.varonis.com Accessed on 23 September 2024
Wang, S., Asif, M., Shahzad, M. F., & Ashfaq, M. (2024). Data privacy and cybersecurity challenges in the digital transformation of the banking sector. *Computers & Security, 147*, 104051.
World Economic Forum. (2024). *Global Cybersecurity Outlook 2024: The Role of Businesses in Cyber Resilience*. Accessed on 19 September 2024
Zanasi, C., Russo, S., & Colajanni, M. (2024). Flexible zero trust architecture for the cybersecurity of industrial IoT infrastructures. *Ad Hoc Networks, 156*, 103414.

Artificial Intelligence and Its Societal Implications

Habiba Ahmed Hassan

Abstract This chapter extensively explains how artificial intelligence (AI) affects society from different perspectives. It begins by outlining AI's technical foundations, distinguishing between narrow AI and broader categories like machine learning and deep learning, which drive current technological advancements. This chapter then discusses several ethical considerations, highlighting privacy concerns, biases in AI algorithms, and the transparency of AI decision-making processes. Then the main societal impacts of AI are addressed, including job displacement due to automation, the increased economic divide, and challenges faced by marginalized communities. It also include case studies illustrating the benefits and risks associated with AI, from healthcare innovations to environmental applications as well as its potential misuse in surveillance and data security breaches. Moreover, the importance of developing robust regulatory frameworks and ethical guidelines to ensure AI's responsible use. It concludes by emphasizing the need for public awareness and cooperation among international stakeholders to navigate the complex challenges AI presents while emphasizing the beneficial effects on society.

1 Brief Overview of AI

It has been debated that AI has several rigorously changing layers that don't provide a foundation that justifies the assumptions made to a great extent, creating ambiguity. That drove us to characterize AI from the regular software, where output heavily relies on the algorithm's input. Consequently, testing its full effectiveness is considered challenging as no defined variables are needed for the AI to work, additionally, past patterns create a wide range of responses which eventually leads to the algorithm learning on its own (BCS, 2023).

Artificial general intelligence was widely defined from numerous viewpoints; where IT systems can perform tasks involving the involvement of human intellect

H. A. Hassan (✉)
Hult International Business School, Dubai, UAE

L. O. Yesufu, P. N. E. Nohuddin (eds.), *Technology for Societal Transformation*,
https://doi.org/10.1007/978-981-96-1721-0_9

(Arora, 2020). Encompassing deductive AI that evaluates bulky datasets; identifying patterns where generative AI utilizes existing data yielding new outcomes (Arora et al., 2023).

A deeper understanding of AI includes machine learning; trained to process and analyze large-sized data to create predictions. A greater expansion includes deep learning which uses complex-like data through several iterations to produce reliable forecasts. The generative AI branching from previous developments encompasses using a large language model designated for interpreting texts, and videos as they learn "abstract patterns" from the data provided. Most AI solutions are narrow AI, tailored algorithms that solve specific issues, such as credit card fraud detection (McKinsey & Company, 2023).

1.1 Societal Implications of AI

It was seen that AI models used for predication purposes might be biased toward specific geographical areas which possibly leads to unreliable safety measurements, leading to magnified negative effects on the social equity and levels of equalities over a longer timespan (Corbett-Davies et al., 2023). Moreover, there has been a growing concern regarding the widened income gap among members of the society which highly depends on the financial ability to use AI to retain income and competitive levels (Legault et al., 2017). This applies to the redistribution of the workforce where a greater reliant on machinery led to negatively affecting individuals involved in these changes (Olesen et al., 2013), while this applies to the health care industry where robotics technology diagnoses patients which severely affects the welfare of the society due to the fear of inaccuracy of diagnoses and treatment provided (An et al., 2022). Additionally, the rising concerns regarding the misuse of AI-like configuration systems, and facial recognition in several applications have led to several issues that render the security of users' data. A well-recognized example was "Tesla Phantom Braking" which was a technology used on an entirely self-driving Tesla programmed to stop depending on the situation when one time it stopped during traffic and caused major misfortunes (Google Scholar, n.d.). The exchange of data behind the screen has posed a risk of negatively affecting social skills, especially in interpersonal relationships and having a considerable level of empathy. The reliance on technology that comes from various information sources may pose a threat to the effectiveness of the decisions being taken, as iterative usage of the data fed into the algorithm may lead to lower inequality levels (Wei et al., 2024).

Positive effects include enhanced efficiency levels concerning the automated tasks in an organization (document organization and categorization), whereas, at the same time, employees get access to a wide range of programs that enhance their knowledge and applied skills while learning how to leverage AI; reflected into the efficiency and quality of work produced. Based on a study, it was shown that several companies trust ChatGPT for code improvements: enhancing the level of convenience and output (Wei et al., 2024). Additionally, the facilitated features of multiple languages allow for better usage of technology and communication among individuals whether in the workplace or within the society itself; in return the mental efforts of understanding, seeking information, and language are minimized with every advancement (Wei et al., 2024).

2 Ethical Considerations in AI

2.1 Definition and Importance of AI Ethics

Different perspectives have been considered when overlooking AI ethics, where human and technology principles are jointly tested to measure the ethics' impact on society one researcher stated that "Humans are technological beings, just as technologies are social entities" (Verbeek, 2017). This means that ethical values, cultural patterns, power relations, and social choices aren't simply reflected or integrated unless humans and technological applications integrate. Where this stresses the fact that the roles technology plays in societies are influenced by humans' decisions and actions under several circumstances, the iteration of this process and its effects gives an insight into the degree of complexity of their ethical and social effects (Vesnic-Alujevic et al., 2020). Another perspective showcased the concept of AI ethics through the fact that the ethical concepts are implemented by understanding AI systems and their several uses; this helps to ensure that developers consider ethical consequences when designing, developing, and employing AI technologies (Bartenschlager et al., 2024).

2.2 Privacy Concerns

The concept described when overlooking the machine learning algorithms, whereas they are called "black box" which indicates that their detection of biases in data (Google Scholar, n.d.); especially since these systems are constantly connected to the internet which means that systems have developed their perceptions (Google Scholar, 2017; Clowes, 2014). Consequently, cybersecurity attacks by observing the changing digital ecosystems would raise fears of confidentiality; especially, adopting AI by several businesses for decision-making poses greater privacy risks (Google Scholar, 2023).

Preset criteria by the EU of risk levels include minimal risk encompassing free AI tools obeying codes of conduct where the system could be withdrawn from the market to deal with the risks. Next, limited risks involve individuals' consciousness of using machines; allowing them to choose whether to use the technology while companies abide by transparency laws. High-risk represents systems highly impacting the users' non-negotiable rights, resulting in rigid safety assessments to be used in the EU market while Unacceptable risks are entitled under the "Title II — Prohibited Artificial Intelligence Practices, Art. 5" law, including facial recognitions and biometrics (Díaz-Rodríguez et al., 2023).

2.3 Surveillance and Individual Freedom

The built-in "Camera Eye" which is using AI to watch over consumers to analyze their facial expressions which help understand their needs and issues; reflected in the output provided (Nakanishi et al., 2019). This necessarily could be inefficient because customers aren't aware of the "eye" which doesn't allow machines to examine consumers' reactions, while others might worry about how data is handled or the lack of trust that creates resistance between both parties. Different associations of individuals with AI and freedom created various views of its usefulness and threats. AI is viewed as an extrinsic force; however, its powerfulness impacts people's adaptation for its benefits which occurs when it is seen as highly dominant compared to human intelligence, it is identified as a threat, and if it is less prevailing, then its benefits tend to overlap with any threats. This applies to individualistic cultures like Western Europe and the USA that perceive automation as taking over their business identity. However, some Asian cultures rely on AI's capability to effectively learn from its iterations to expand its intelligence which results in elevated trust between humans and AI, creating equality and, thus dependability. Moreover, the internal processes AI goes through have been seen as highly impactful in how individuals' uniqueness is impacted by collective like-minded data which is inferior to "individualistic" cultures that are inferior to transferring their control over technology to AI, thus limiting their freedom and possibly creating reinforcements affecting individuals' identity and perceptions (Barnes et al., 2024).

2.4 Decision-Making Transparency and Accountability

The data quality is more important than how iterative the algorithmic update adversely compromises the transparency of systems employed which is reflected in the designated stakeholders using the technology. AI accountability considers specific laws related to algorithmic use in several industries where an applicable actor is chosen who is closely aligned with the technology used and thus able to protect entities against regulatory consequences and present sufficient justifications when needed. Various control levels are correlated with the owning responsibilities adequate for mitigating harms which helps in the overall decision-making AI accountability; leveraging the benefits of AI (Stankovich et al., 2023).

The increased recognition of XAI showcases how impactful it is on decision-making. It thoroughly justifies why the algorithm provides such choices and how they impact individuals, organizations, and society, which challenges the mistrust between AI-driven outcomes and human intervention. Within this context, it is important to be accountable, interpretable, and transparent which revolve around the ability of AI models to be comprehendible with thoughtful clarifications that are aligned with ethical criteria (Navarro, 2024).

Emphasizing AI transparency created an understanding of how the algorithms work while bearing in mind the three identified levels; entailing algorithmic transparency that explains the processes involved and influencing considerations plus the ML models. Next is the Interaction visible through interfaces of communication carried out between users and AI systems, highlighting expectations of such processes to users. Social transparency encompasses the ethical and communal effects of AI that address biases and privacy concerns (Wren, 2024).

Diverse techniques and procedures are used to minimize the drawbacks of using AI including biases, ethical threats, and faults. In contrast, Model Explainability entails an insight into how parts of the data are related to one another including the factors affecting decisions derived from the analysis and the model visualization that helps keep track of the system and its errors. Next is the post-hoc Explanation involves using either the " Local Interpretable Model-agnostic Explanations (LIME) or SHapley Additive exPlanations (SHAP)" approaches to highlight the reasonings behind the models' decisions while using the Human-interpretable models that facilitate the user's understanding through decision-tress, linear models, or others to ease the employment of the whole model for decision-making (Navarro, 2024).

2.5 Case Studies of Ethical Dilemmas in AI

Several industries have adopted AI applications that have caused beneficial and negative effects resulting in an ongoing dilemma affecting the future usage of such technology. The medical industry in the USA has been operating for numerous years using the AI-driven Internet of Things (IoT) with expenditure levels reaching one trillion U.S. dollars by next year, especially for chronically ill patients, and older patients in need of consistent observation. This improves the diagnoses and treatment provided to those patients as their data is accessible and updated with access to vast ranges of sources over the cloud while staying connected to machinery put in each room for faster updates (Keshta, 2022).

This integration resulted in serious information risks as its security levels have been compromised, where in 2018, two specialists concluded over 68 thousand compromised medical systems online with 12,000 belonging to the same institution. The reasons were reliant on the older software versions being used that make the data accessible for a security breach, especially when using designated systems like brute-force attacks that left several malfunctioned machines after their hacking (Keshta, 2022).

It was explained that due to the sum of data, its extensive nature as data is collected with the user's knowledge of this matter has created doubt about its societal effects. In this case, the healthcare institutions storing the data collected supposedly have greater control over its deployment, and anonymizing the data (replacing information with distinguishing IDs) is not sufficient to protect data from any breaches or exploitations. In 2022, a pilot testing case was in a Russian drug-store chain where facial-recognition software was used to test customers' emotions in the course of behavior analysis within the context of offering personalized discounts during the recognition time to be taken for further understanding of customers considering their purchasing patterns (Keshta, 2022).

Another case was studying Smart Meters, where 14 problems after inspecting 24 written articles where the conflict was found between individuals' privacy concerns and enabling improved control over energy levels. Whereas data gathered was used to study patterns of lifestyle society adopts in terms of personal data, routines, and occupancy-related information, which appeared to be intrusive to a certain extent thus building certain customer profiles that eventually result in biases and prejudiced outcomes from the constant iterations or misused for other unethical reasons (Gavorník et al., 2024).

When COVID-19 first started spreading globally, governments adopted AI technologies to contain its widespread where the Norwegian government revoked its newly introduced application (Smittestop) in April 2020 due to its heavy criticism of the GPS tracking that takes data back to a central server also known as data-surveillance that led to several security breaches and minimized contributions to its main purpose. Simultaneously, the Chinese Alipay Health Code used to measure the risk of getting infected failed to ensure data autonomy as it was compulsorily used with higher restrictions for individuals' freedom (Fontes et al., 2022).

3 Job Displacement and Economic Impact

Forms of technological adoption are illustrated through machine learning which emphasizes the extraction and amending of complex datasets minimizing the effects of routine tasks. Using robotics for manufacturing similar sectors is deemed useful in enhancing productivity and quality levels while considering their surroundings. Natural language processing revolves around automating human-related jobs like customer service while thoroughly understanding human interactions (Admin, 2024).

Most job displacements affected by technology are related to repetitious activities (e.g., accounting, assembly line), where 12% of enterprises in manufacturing and information employed AI applications through robotics working on assembly lines with workers, prognostic systems scheduling maintenance based on overseeing potential hurdles while quality control systems for consistency and material management. 4% of construction and retail services utilize AI to study consumers for personalized shopping, product recommendations, and consistent efficiency (Admin, 2024).

Social effects include a disproportionate distribution of income that restricts the ability of individuals to afford this technology, resulting in reduced labor demand, increased AI investments lowered wage levels, workers' elevated stress due to automation, and the acquiring of the right skilled labor which affects the overall economic performance. Other effects include job creation where training is provided for displaced employees that will focus on quality, efficiency, and overlooking advancements' progress; enhancing business' competitiveness and encouraging economic growth while enhancing the skill employees have to strengthen their loyalty and maintaining privacy regulations that sustain quality and societal benefits (Framework, 2023).

Business-related challenges include the initial investments of new machinery and integrating them with existing ones along with the degree of complexity considering the planning, designing, and supporting plus the extent of sustaining smooth integration of devices and systems in one interface. Additionally, the ability to remain competitive due to dynamic market conditions needs updated and unbiased datasets to iterate on (Alisha, 2023).

The digital divide includes an Access aspect related to the distribution of Internet connections geographically that would underserve specific locations, low-income individuals' ability to afford ongoing technological purchases of devices and internet plans, and more importantly their abilities to use these devices restricting the exploitation of the technology. The second aspect is the Use divide relates to the fact that most people use technology for communication and obtaining information while specific individuals use specialized applications for e-commerce and e-learning. Simultaneously, the self-reliance of efficiently using online products along with the different demographics and cultural norms when dealing with technology in various languages (Potter & Stilinski, 2024).

Global institutions intervened in bridging this disparity, for example, South Africa introduced their National Skills Development Strategy (NSDS) equipping affected workers through technology introductions with tailored training and development schemes. The same idea was implemented in the European Union through the European Union's European Globalization Adjustment Fund (EGF), which also offers monetary assistance to rehabilitate the workers for their new jobs. The World Economic Forum's "Reskilling Revolution" encompasses a wider initiative across global governments and designated institutions preparing employees for the new AI-adapted economies (Kinteh, 2024).

4 Biases in AI Algorithms

4.1 Algorithmic Biases and Its Sources

It was defined as the occurrence when algorithms generate results that lead to compromising societies or specific groups when employed during an entity's decision-making (Kordzadeh & Ghasemaghaei, 2022). When overlooking search engines, it was seen that categorizing individuals in a biased manner is often aggregate as data is largely scaled or because of well-known sidelined groups of people resulting in "digital inequality." This is described as direct discrimination when the bias is based on specific traits like gender, and race while indirect discrimination occurs without resorting to biased characteristics (Lin William et al., 2023).

A considered source of bias includes "algorithmic exclusion" where output depends on missing data, where on social media it was found that black-identifying names yielded more ads related to criminal records services and this was applied to female terminologies resulting in biased output (Cecere et al., 2024). Numerous sources of bias hindered the viability of the algorithms, whereas the historical biases that programming languages store are mostly gender biases. The large number of stored texts makes it difficult to trace back the sources of biases or to be able to dissect the biases embedded easily (Akter et al., 2022). Moreover, the developers' methodology used to design, train, and improve the algorithms may result in a correlation fallacy that creates an association inappropriate for the context of using the technology. Simultaneously, randomly selecting a sample to test may adversely affect the overall functionality, as the conformity biases developers have of their own beliefs or their attitude toward following their values will affect the outlook of the overall population. The criteria for choosing the sample itself would be based on specific attributes or traits, leaving certain subgroups out of examination along with their unique features (Lorenzoni et al., 2021).

4.2 Impact on Marginalized Communities

Several parts of the community are considered "marginalized" as they are underrepresented among other communities and are highly impacted by AI deployment in organizations to great extents. It was reported by McKinsey Global Institute that by the year 2030, jobs carried out by women are 1.5 times more prone to be replaced by AI than to be replaced by males in sectors including customer service, sales, and office support (Costinhas, 2023).

An extensive McKinsey study of how Generative AI—using AI to create new graphical content, including text, pictures, and videos affects Black communities. It was found that certain occupations are overpopulated with Black Americans, including office support-related jobs, production jobs, food services, and mechanical installations and repairs (McKinsey, 2023). This anxiety was shown in the statistics gathered from Charter Works, indicating that 53% of Black respondents are worried that AI would replace their jobs within the span of the next 5 years, while 39% of White respondents expressed this worry. Several examples of algorithmic biases include Facebook's gender-oriented advertising technique, which negatively affects society's perceptions (Lambrecht et al., 2018), while Uber's biased pricing steered negative publicity as higher ratings were set for African-American individuals (Akhilesh & Aylin, 2020). Applying AI in approving loans for candidates, a study across 3.2 million mortgages and 10 million refinance applications that Black and Latino applicants are more inclined to be rejected and face higher interest rates

(Bartlett et al., 2017). Other famous examples include Flickr's 2015 racist posts where Black individuals are tagged as animals or apes (Yapo & Weiss, 2018). The same biased situation occurred with Google by tagging African Americans as "Gorillas," due to the biased data embedded into the algorithm (Kasperkevic, 2015).

Amazon's algorithm was biased toward areas with specific zip codes in their Prime same-day delivery service, conditioned to the number of Prime members, warehouse workers, and drivers. Ultimately, the excluded individuals were seen as lower social classes—African-American areas (Lee et al., 2019). The lending through the bank industry has been biased, and the algorithm used to evaluate candidates is based on historical data, where former employees were unfair toward specific groups, such as young adults, females, and industrial employees (Ruairi O'Donnellan, 2020). Alternatively, at the start of 2023, OpenAI, which owns ChatGPT, has been recruiting content moderators at a rate of $ 1.32$ to $ 2$ per hour. This is considered one of the most stressful entry-level jobs that revolve around reviewing posts, videos, and images and reporting those seen as unaligned with their platform requirements. This indicates to what extent AI deployment could be unfair to parts of society even if it is related to the backend of delivering the final products or services to consumers.

4.3 Methods to Mitigate Biases

Considering methods to moderate the negative effects of biases is essential with the constant evolvements in the technology. It was found that reassessing the assigned weights to the dataset by choosing lower weights for more privileged groups, unlike the common method of assigning lower weights to beggared ones alters the outcome. The most popular method is optimized pre-processing (OPP) which reweights the data based on various qualities in privileged and underprivileged groups, this identifies sources of biases and elevates fairness. Adversely, changing the distribution of data without its internal features affects its size regarding under-samples and over-sampled, which helps to understand the biases arising from the system's outcomes (Rubén et al., 2024). Next is training the model involves Regularization widely used in machine learning that makes the data fitter for iterations, creating a more generalized and competent use of the algorithm, by minimizing the high correspondence between the sensitive traits and its outcomes. While adversarial debiasing is considered human-centric as two neural networks (simulating how the human brain works) are trained by one network and are responsible for predicting outcomes and the other (Adversary) identifies and removes identified biases affecting the first network. Different numerical outcomes among demographic groups are balanced for a more equitable outcome (Rubén et al., 2024).

The last concept is modifying the output through Equalized odds by changing labels assigned—meaning that true positive rates and false negative rates are the same for all groups, enhancing fairness and precision levels across all classes, while Calibrated Equalized odds involve changing the output with an equalized odds objective that improves the quality of classifying outputs and interpreting them. The Reject Option Classification considers advantageous outcomes for underprivileged groups and unfavorable results for the privileged ones, this is achieved by clearly defining the reasons for rejection and uncertainty levels (Rubén et al., 2024). Where it was widely recognized that AI-based systems are biased, depending on the human-related biases embedded in their creation either through their infrastructure or the data being used (Uzzi, 2020). Consequently, using "blind taste tests" was proposed to highlight and eliminate decision-making-related biases that help break loose from the iterations that compromise the quality and equality levels. This is done by exempting the data that hinders the equality of the algorithm, re-evaluating the algorithm, and analyzing both results before and after to help understand if it is "blind" to this piece of information and identify its source and effect (Uzzi, 2020).

A McKinsey report identified applicable methods to mitigate the effects of AI-related biases. Focusing on data involves pre-processing the data which eliminates the association between outcomes and specific traits that are seen as effective in this case. The second option for this step is post-processing, which entails altering the model's final predictions to abide by a fairness requirement. Lastly is enforcing fairness in the data used by analyzing the text classification by adding more data to leverage the performance concerning the protected groups of individuals (Silberg & Manyika, 2019).

Overlooking the human-in-the-loop, it was proposed to document the construction, testing, and purpose of the AI models to ensure transparency, while emphasizing regular audits to measure fairness before and during using the system. Additionally, the ongoing demonstration and understanding of legal outlines that discipline the usage of AI. This includes overviewing the actual human-related factors that influence the definition and application of fairness and how diversity fits into the dilemma of achieving fairness from several stances. Hence, Fig. 1 illustrates the six considerations when using AI:

5 AI's Potential to Address Societal Challenges

The societal benefits AI leverages are widespread across several industries that tackle numerous challenges regardless of the negative effects this technology brings to its users. These industries are as follows:

5.1 Healthcare Advancements

Several advancements in healthcare aim to improve the quality of care, starting with more accurate diagnostics from tests like X-rays and other scans to detect diseases. Similarly, drug manufacturing benefits from faster, more precise clinical trials. Deep learning technology allows scientists to conduct advanced research across

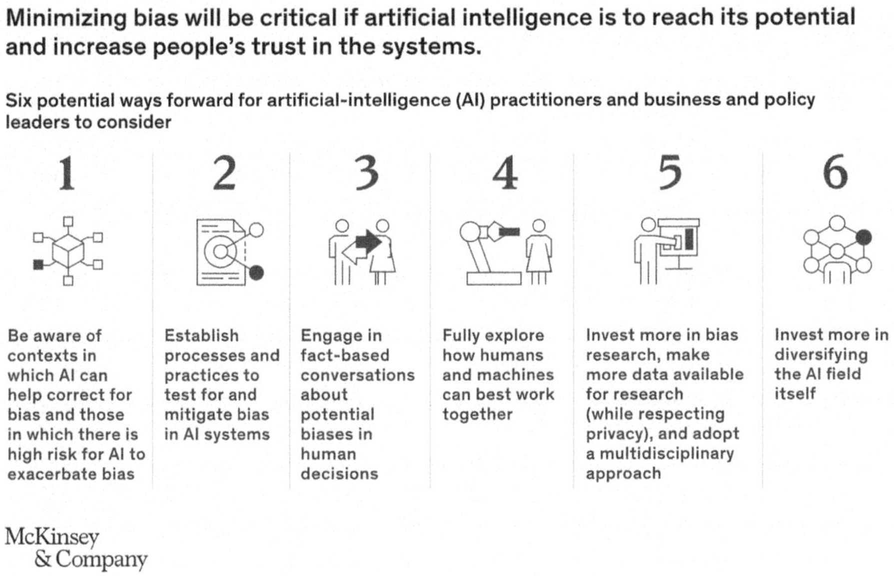

Fig. 1 The six considerations when using AI

vast databases and personalize treatment for patients using bioinformatics, all while reducing development costs. In surgeries requiring high precision, machines help reduce human error and assist in rehabilitation for recovering patients (Esmaeilzadeh, 2024).

Another aspect is decision-making, where clinical decision support systems are integrated with health records to enhance patient outcomes. Real-time analysis of large datasets improves diagnosis and treatment monitoring, ensuring high levels of personalization and accuracy. AI also enables organizations to continuously update patient records without the risk of missing data or the need for manual language translation, as the technology comprehends and stores information automatically. Moreover, in mental healthcare, AI allows professionals to predict patients' patterns and behaviors, leading to more effective intervention planning. Post-COVID-19, healthcare institutions have adopted remote systems that analyze vital data in real time, allowing them to monitor patients from a distance and have rapid response plans in place if biometric data indicates any deviation from expected progress (TechTarget, n.d.).

5.2 *Environmental Applications*

AI has shown promise in addressing worsening global climate issues. Machine learning identifies patterns across numerous datasets, connecting various data points to facilitate better action planning. This is reflected in balancing power demand and supply from clean energy sources, using real-time data to predict fluctuations and optimize usage. Technology also helps commercial and residential users cultivate energy-saving habits by regulating heat and lighting, reducing both costs and greenhouse gas emissions (Brown, 2023).

In agriculture, AI improves farming practices to increase crop yield and recommends appropriate chemicals that eliminate the negative effects of disease on human consumption. Additionally, real-time data helps authorities analyze and manage the harmful effects of air and water pollution, allowing them to act quickly using sensors and integrated networks. Autonomous underwater vehicles (AUVs) sustain marine ecosystems by detecting sensitive changes in water conditions, prompting immediate action when necessary. Machine learning and robotics also enhance precision in sorting and recycling materials, reducing greenhouse gas emissions and optimizing waste management while offering solutions for future problems by analyzing human behavior (Brown, 2023).

As emphasized by the World Economic Forum, AI can tackle specific global challenges. Melting icebergs in Antarctica, for example, pose a flood risk, and AI can analyze real-time satellite images to inform the European Space Agency, ensuring response plans are in place. This technology also applies to deforestation; an English company, Space Intelligence, maps over 1 million hectares of land to monitor carbon rates, helping governments and institutions predict disasters by tracking changing conditions. In Brazil, Sipremo uses AI to predict outcomes and collaborates with industries like energy and insurance. Finally, the Dutch company Cleanup combines multiple technologies to clean oceans, creating maps that trace waste, which is then collected by drones and planes, contributing to vital environmental preservation efforts.

5.3 *Accessibility for Disabled Individuals*

Generative AI has been considered for improving challenges regarding human interactions in the disabled community, as interfaces become more adaptive and inclusive. Whereas speech-to-text and image-to-speech solutions are used at work, educational platforms, and even for day-to-day interactions at hospitals, malls, or shops (Welker, 2023).

According to the UN, AI has benefited 1.5 billion citizens with hearing loss globally, through speech-to-text transcription and different sound identification features. While approx. 540 million people with various visual impairments intensities that reduced their mental and physical constraints when interacting daily. Additionally, AI helps individuals with disabilities to keep their jobs in fear of being let go due to the adaptation of AI, through inclusion protocols to minimize negative effects of the technology.

6 Regulatory and Policy Considerations

The consistent innovation of AI technology globally has initiated the urgency for several institutions to ensure governance of the ethical use of AI throughout the planning execution and monitoring.

This is reflected in IBM's four values an AI governance framework entails, a policy advisory committee where high-ranking decision-makers set extensive regulations, and strategies related to ethically using technology considering its risk. Next, an AI ethics board was created by cross-functional personnel specialized in maintaining AI policies and practices and ensuring implementation and its clear communication. This is reflected in having business unit representatives (focal points) responsible for identifying and assessing ethical concerns, risk-mitigating plans, and future strategies to be reviewed by the board.

Finally, is creating an activist-employee cultivating the ethical use of AI technology, supporting responsible initiatives company-wide. Whenever a use case is identified, focal points assess the degree of risks by preset criteria, and high-risk situations are reviewed by the board. The evaluation is based on the anticipated goal in the case, how compliant is data handling according to the regulations, overlooking past cases and strategies followed, and the degree of fairness, transparency, and privacy achieved (Reed, 2024).

The importance of international cooperation is influenced by several factors, including the intense national AI investments, which deteriorate the overall quality of outputs the technology has, creating a negative overlap among models used. Next, accurately understanding AI creates reliable cooperation among specialized personnel that establishes dedicated governing policies and ways to effectively use datasets. This is shown in specialized AI systems creating a supply chain operating globally and serving customers in different stages (Kerry et al., 2021).

7 Future Recommendations and Conclusion

Increased advanced AI trends have been revolutionizing the technological landscape, specifically for Generative AI, which has been manageable for end-users and businesses in several sectors (e.g., healthcare, e-commerce). This makes room for constant improvements, as their benefits have been communicated online when integrating different platforms including quantitative and qualitative business aspects.

Moreover, multimodal AI is a complex integration of AI models (such as Open AI, GPT-4V, LLaVa, and Adept) that collectively use several data inputs to generate specific outputs. The aim is to utilize natural language processing and computer vision (image classification, object detection, semantic segmentation, and instance segmentation) features to better assist users with an intuitive edge. Resulting in unbiased, constant, and high-quality training of data that brings a human-centric approach. A recent Google launch in January 2024 included an image-to-video model that uses images for referencing.

Adversely, smaller models have been training on more datasets on narrower and fewer considerations to enhance their performance as the output is more explainable and iterative, allowing more institutions to adopt the usage of AI models using Internet of Things features while ensuring that sensitive data are protected on local devices (IBM, 2024).

The long-term AI's societal implications vary based on the type, intention, and stakeholders involved. Where biases in datasets result in discrimination against certain groups affecting rapid unemployment cycles that are shown in rapid job losses which affect economies and societies on a global scale. Next is privacy threats as data security is compromised which misleads users from controlling data breaches or consequences faced. However, more patents and ethical frameworks have been established to enforce responsible considerations to ensure that decisions are unbiased stressing fairness and trust between users and businesses. This is applied to governmental bodies, multi-national entities, and private companies tailored for specific tasks or the general approach to using this technology company-wide (Verma, 2023).

The importance of public awareness lies in the mutual understanding of users and businesses regardless of the extent of these interactions and familiarity with the technology. Businesses are empowered to reduce their stress by having automated tasks that reduce overheads and stress and compete by having a distinctive vision based on the technology used. Additionally, institutions can transform their services offered while ensuring that redistributing the workforce is aligned with technological advancements, while selectively choosing jobs to be replaced by AI or the intellectual talent responsible for sustaining these improvements. Individuals with a high probability of being interested in technology should be aware of the positive outcomes of using AI through attending workshops, famous talks, intellectual conversations with experts, or even online courses. Even regular consumers should be aware of the features of their daily technology which helps them make accurate decisions, challenge new opportunities, and identify any negative threats.

8 Conclusion

As AI continues to reshape our world, its profound potential to address societal challenges is undeniable. From transforming healthcare with personalized medicine and revolutionizing climate solutions to making the world more accessible for people with disabilities, AI offers unprecedented opportunities. Yet, these advancements come with substantial ethical and societal responsibilities. Ensuring that AI development remains transparent, accountable, and ethical is paramount in safeguarding privacy, protecting individual freedoms, and preventing the misuse of surveillance technologies. The economic impact of AI cannot be overlooked. While it drives innovation, it also disrupts industries, leading to job displacement and deepening economic divides. Addressing this requires proactive efforts to retrain and adapt the workforce, ensuring that the benefits of AI are shared equitably and that individuals are not left behind in the digital transformation. Additionally, tackling algorithmic biases is critical, as AI systems can perpetuate discrimination against marginalized communities. By fostering inclusive design, using diverse datasets, and enhancing transparency, we can mitigate these risks and ensure AI systems are fair and just.

To harness AI's full potential responsibly, robust regulatory frameworks are needed. International cooperation, thoughtful governance, and policies that strike a balance between innovation and regulation will be essential in shaping AI's future trajectory. Looking forward, the role of public awareness and engagement will be crucial in guiding ethical AI development, ensuring that society remains an active participant in how these technologies evolve.

In the end, AI's future lies in our collective hands. By navigating its challenges with foresight, ethics, and collaboration, we can steer AI toward creating a more equitable, inclusive, and sustainable world.

References

Admin. (2024, May 23). *The Job Displacement Dilemma: How AI automation threatens traditional employment - Linvelo.* Linvelo. https://linvelo.com/the-job-displacement-dilemma/#blog-content-header-0

Akhilesh, K. P., & Aylin, Ç. (2020). *Iterative effect-size bias in Ridehailing: Measuring social bias in dynamic pricing of 100 million rides.*

Akter, S., Dwivedi, Y. K., Sajib, S., Biswas, K., Bandara, R. J., & Michael, K. (2022). Algorithmic bias in machine learning-based marketing models. *Journal of Business Research, 144*(144), 201–216. https://doi.org/10.1016/j.jbusres.2022.01.083

Alisha, S. (2023, February 16). *The rise of automation — how it is impacting the job market.* Medium. https://pub.towardsai.net/the-rise-of-automation-how-it-is-impacting-the-job-market-e8a6c7d5e6e3

An, K., Shan, Y., & Shi, S. (2022). Impact of industrial intelligence on total factor productivity. *Sustainability, 14*(21), 14535. https://doi.org/10.3390/su142114535

Arora, A. (2020). Conceptualising artificial intelligence as a digital healthcare innovation: an introductory review. *Medical Devices: Evidence and Research, 13*, 223–230. https://doi.org/10.2147/mder.s262590

Arora, A., Barrett, M., Lee, E., Oborn, E., & Prince, K. (2023). Risk and the future of AI: Algorithmic bias, data colonialism, and marginalization. *Information and Organization, 33*(3), 100478–100478. https://doi.org/10.1016/j.infoandorg.2023.100478

Barnes, A. J., Zhang, Y., & Valenzuela, A. (2024). AI and culture: Culturally dependent responses to AI systems. *Current Opinion in Psychology*, 101838. https://doi.org/10.1016/j.copsyc.2024.101838

Bartenschlager, C. C., Gassner, U. M., Römmele, C., Brunner, J. O., Schlögl-Flierl, K., & Ziethmann, P. (2024). The AI ethics of digital COVID-19 diagnosis and their legal, medical, technological, and operational managerial implications. *Artificial Intelligence in Medicine, 152*, 102873–102873. https://doi.org/10.1016/j.artmed.2024.102873

Bartlett, R. P., Morse, A., Stanton, R., & Wallace, N. (2017). Consumer lending discrimination in the FinTech Era. *SSRN Electronic Journal.* https://doi.org/10.2139/ssrn.3063448

Brown, P. (2023, November 3). *AI & sustainability: Artificial intelligence for tackling environmental challenges | FDM Group*. FDM Group. https://www.fdmgroup.com/news-insights/ai-and-sustainability/#:~:text=future%20with%20FDM-

Cecere, G., Jean, C., Le Guel, F., & Manant, M. (2024). Artificial intelligence and algorithmic bias? Field tests on social network with teens. *Technological Forecasting and Social Change, 201*, 123204. https://doi.org/10.1016/j.techfore.2023.123204

Clowes, R. (2014). Thinking in the cloud: The cognitive incorporation of cloud-based technology. *Philosophy & Technology, 28*(2), 261–296. https://doi.org/10.1007/s13347-014-0153-z

Corbett-Davies, S., Gaebler, J. D., Nilforoshan, H., Shroff, R., & Goel, S. (2023). *The measure and mismeasure of fairness*. https://doi.org/10.48550/arXiv.1808.00023

Costinhas, P. (2023, August 23). *AI's adverse effects on marginalized communities - Impakter*. Impakter. https://impakter.com/ai-adverse-effects-on-marginalized-communities/

Díaz-Rodríguez, N., Del Ser, J., Coeckelbergh, M., López de Prado, M., Herrera-Viedma, E., & Herrera, F. (2023). Connecting the dots in trustworthy Artificial Intelligence: From AI principles, ethics, and key requirements to responsible AI systems and regulation. *Information Fusion, 99*(101896), 101896. https://doi.org/10.1016/j.inffus.2023.101896

Esmaeilzadeh, P. (2024). Challenges and strategies for wide-scale artificial intelligence (AI) deployment in healthcare practices: A perspective for healthcare organizations. *Artificial Intelligence in Medicine (Print), 151*, 102861. https://doi.org/10.1016/j.artmed.2024.102861

Fontes, C., Hohma, E., Corrigan, C. C., & Lütge, C. (2022). AI-powered public surveillance systems: Why we (might) need them and how we want them. *Technology in Society, 71*(0160-791X), 102137. https://doi.org/10.1016/j.techsoc.2022.102137

Framework, S. A. (2023, October 17). *Unraveling the Impact of Automation: Separating Fact from Fiction on Job Loss | Service Automation Framework | Service Automation Framework Alliance*. https://www.serviceautomation.org/unraveling-the-impact-of-automation-separating-fact-from-fiction-on-job-loss/

Gavorník, A., Podroužek, J., Oreško, Š., Slosiarová, N., & Grmanová, G. (2024). Beyond privacy and security: Exploring ethical issues of smart metering and non-intrusive load monitoring. *Telematics and Informatics, 90*, 102132. https://doi.org/10.1016/j.tele.2024.102132

Google Scholar. (2017). Scholar.google.com. https://scholar.google.com/scholar_lookup?title=We%20Are%20Data%3A%20Algorithms%20and%20the%20Making%20of%20Our%20Digital%20Selves&author=J.%20Cheney-Lippold&publication_year=2017

Google Scholar. (2023). Scholar.google.com. http://refhub.elsevier.com/S0160-791X(24)00075-7/sref36

Google Scholar. (n.d.). Scholar.google.com. Retrieved July 17, 2024, from https://scholar.google.com/scholar?q=Tesla%27s%20

Kasperkevic, J. (2015, July 1). Google says sorry for racist auto-tag in photo app. . https://www.theguardian.com/technology/2015/jul/01/google-sorry-racist-auto-tag-photo-app

Kerry, C. F., Meltzer, J. P., Renda, A., Engler, A., & Fanni, R. (2021, October 25). *Strengthening international cooperation on AI*. Brookings. https://www.brookings.edu/articles/strengthening-international-cooperation-on-ai/

Keshta, I. (2022). AI-driven IoT for smart health care: Security and privacy issues. *Informatics in Medicine Unlocked, 30*, 100903. https://doi.org/10.1016/j.imu.2022.100903

Kinteh, L. D. (2024). *Adapting to technological unployment: Strategies for job displacement caused by AI*. http://www.ijrti.org/

Kordzadeh, N., & Ghasemaghaei, M. (2022). Algorithmic bias: Review, synthesis, and future research directions. *European Journal of Information Systems, 31*(3), 388–409. https://ideas.repec.org/a/taf/tjisxx/v31y2022i3p388-409.html

Lambrecht, A., Tucker, C., & Wiertz, C. (2018). Advertising to early trend propagators: Evidence from Twitter. *Marketing Science, 37*(2), 177–199. https://doi.org/10.1287/mksc.2017.1062

Lee, N. T., Resnick, P., & Barton, G. (2019, May 22). *Algorithmic bias detection and mitigation: Best practices and policies to reduce consumer harms*. Brookings. https://www.brookings.

edu/articles/algorithmic-bias-detection-and-mitigation-best-practices-and-policies-to-reduce-consumer-harms/

Legault, G.-A., Verchère, C., & Patenaude, J. (2017). Support for the development of technological innovations: Promoting responsible social uses. *Science and Engineering Ethics*. https://doi.org/10.1007/s11948-017-9911-5

Lin William, C., Gao, Y., Ta, N., Li, K., & Fu, H. (2023). Trapped in the search box: An examination of algorithmic bias in search engine autocomplete predictions. *Telematics and Informatics, 85*, 102068–102068. https://doi.org/10.1016/j.tele.2023.102068

Lorenzoni, G., Alencar, P., Nascimento, N., & Cowan, D. (2021). Machine learning model development from a software engineering perspective: A systematic literature review. *ArXiv:2102.07574 [Cs]*. https://arxiv.org/abs/2102.07574

McKinsey & Company. (2023, April 24). *What is AI?* Www.mckinsey.com; McKinsey & Company. https://www.mckinsey.com/featured-insights/mckinsey-explainers/what-is-ai

Nakanishi, J., Kuramoto, I., Baba, J., Ogawa, K., Yoshikawa, Y., & Ishiguro, H. (2019). Soliloquising social Robot in a Hotel Room. *Proceedings of the 31st Australian Conference on Human-Computer-Interaction*. https://doi.org/10.1145/3369457.3370913

Navarro, F. J. (2024, March 5). *In the era of data-driven decision-making, businesses are increasingly turning to Artificial Intelligence (AI) to gain insights, streamline processes, and enhance competitiveness. However, as AI systems become more complex and pervasive, the need for transparency and accountability in their decision*. Linkedin.com. https://www.linkedin.com/pulse/explainable-ai-gateway-transparent-decision-making-navarro-pnpjf/

Olesen, S. C., Butterworth, P., Leach, L. S., Kelaher, M., & Pirkis, J. (2013). Mental health affects future employment as job loss affects mental health: Findings from a longitudinal population study. *BMC Psychiatry, 13*(1). https://doi.org/10.1186/1471-244x-13-144

Potter, & Stilinski. (2024). https://www.researchgate.net/publication/381353270_The_Digital_Divide_and_its_Impact_on_Business_Opportunities_and_Economic_Inequality

Reed, J. (2024, April 10). *What should an AI ethics governance framework look like?* Security Intelligence; Security Intelligence. https://securityintelligence.com/articles/ai-governance-framework-ethics/

Ruairi O'Donnellan. (2020, February 24). *Disruption in financial services: Racist Robots? How AI bias may put financial firms at risk - intuition*. Intuition. https://www.intuition.com/disruption-in-financial-services-racist

Rubén, G.-S., Serrano, E., & Bajo, J. (2024). Mitigating bias in artificial intelligence: Fair data generation via causal models for transparent and explainable decision-making. *Future Generation Computer Systems*. https://doi.org/10.1016/j.future.2024.02.023

Silberg, J., & Manyika, J. (2019, June 6). *Tackling bias in artificial intelligence (and in humans)*. McKinsey & Company. https://www.mckinsey.com/featured-insights/artificial-intelligence/tackling-bias-in-artificial-intelligence-and-in-humans

Stankovich, M., Behrens, E., & Burchell, J. (2023). *Toward meaningful transparency and accountability of AI Algorithms in public service delivery*. DAI's Center for Digital Acceleration.

The Top Artificial Intelligence Trends | IBM. (2024, July 2). Ibm.com. https://www.ibm.com/think/insights/artificial-intelligence-trends

Top 12 Ways Artificial Intelligence Will Impact Healthcare | TechTarget. (n.d.). Healthtech Analytics. https://www.techtarget.com/healthtechanalytics/feature/Top-12-ways-artificial-intelligence-will-impact-healthcare#:~:text=AI%20tools%20can%20be%20used

Uzzi, B. (2020). A simple tactic that could help reduce bias in AI. *Harvard Business Review*. https://hbr.org/2020/11/a-simple-tactic-that-could-help-reduce-bias-in-ai

Verbeek, P.-P. (2017). In J. van den Hoven, S. Miller, & T. Pogge (Eds.), *Designing the morality of things: The ethics of behaviour-guiding technology*. Cambridge University Press. https://www.cambridge.org/core/books/designing-in-ethics/designing-the-morality-of-things-the-ethics-of-behaviourguiding-technology/03DBDBC44D06038FBB848C3B10EF02B9?utm_campaign=shareaholic&utm_medium=copy_link&utm_source=bookmark

Verma, D. (2023, February 28). *AI inventions – The ethical and societal implications*. MIP. https://www.managingip.com/article/2bc988k82fc0ho408vwu8/expert-analysis/ai-inventions-the-ethical-and-societal-implications

Vesnic-Alujevic, L., Nascimento, S., & Pólvora, A. (2020). Societal and ethical impacts of artificial intelligence: Critical notes on European policy frameworks. *Telecommunications Policy, 44*(6), 101961. https://doi.org/10.1016/j.telpol.2020.101961

Wei, X., Chu, X., Geng, J., Wang, Y., Wang, P., Wang, H., Wang, C., & Lei, L. (2024). Societal impacts of Chatbot and mitigation strategies for negative impacts: A large-scale qualitative survey of ChatGPT users. *Technology in Society, 77*, 102566. https://doi.org/10.1016/j.techsoc.2024.102566

Welker, Y. (2023, November 3). *Generative AI holds great potential for those with disabilities - But it needs policy to shape it*. World Economic Forum. https://www.weforum.org/agenda/2023/11/generative-ai-holds-potential-disabilities/

Why Is AI Hard to Define? | BCS. (2023, November 24). Www.bcs.org. https://www.bcs.org/articles-opinion-and-research/why-is-ai-hard-to-define/

Wren, H. (2024, January 18). *What is AI transparency? A comprehensive guide*. Zendesk. https://www.zendesk.com/blog/ai-transparency/

Yapo, A., & Weiss, J. (2018). Ethical implications of bias in machine learning. *Proceedings of the 51st Hawaii International Conference on System Sciences*. https://doi.org/10.24251/hicss.2018.668

Blockchain Technology in Supply Chain Management and Sustainability: Real-World Applications, Challenges, and Future Prospects

Pervez Akhtar, **Nora Azima Noordin**, **and Alyazya Abdulla Adam Mohamed Alraeesi**

Abstract The aim of this chapter is to explore the transformative capabilities of blockchain technology among various industries in supply chain management. Highlighting its real-world applications and the challenges it faces during the implementation stage. The decentralized and immutable nature of blockchain technology provides substantial benefits in improving security, traceability and transparency within the supply chains. This chapter offers a thorough review of contemporary advancements in the application of blockchain technology. As a result of through review this chapter finds that blockchain facilitates the improvements in data accuracy, enhances collaboration and frauds reduction among supply chain stakeholders. Moreover, this chapter critically explores the issues and challenges to integrate blockchain into existing systems, such as regulatory hurdles, high implementation cost and scalability. By incorporating the recent research and industry practices, this chapter highlights the role of blockchain in driving efficiency and enhancing sustainability in global supply chains.

1 Introduction

Blockchain is a cutting-edge technology that distributes decentralized encrypted ledgers over a network. It functions as a digital shared ledger. It is extremely safe for businesses to operate because once the records are added they cannot be changed without stakeholders' permission (Bogucharskov et al., 2018; O'Leary, 2017). Supply chain networks face complex situations that make risk management and information evaluation difficult due to the emergence of new markets, shifting laws, trade policies, cultures, and ultimately human behavior (Sarpong, 2014). An organization needs to undergo a corresponding structural transition to preserve end-user

P. Akhtar (✉) · N. A. Noordin · Alyazya Abdulla Adam Mohamed Alraeesi
Higher Colleges of Technology, Sharjah, UAE
e-mail: pakhtar@hct.ac.ae; nazima@hct.ac.ae

L. O. Yesufu, P. N. E. Nohuddin (eds.), *Technology for Societal Transformation*,
https://doi.org/10.1007/978-981-96-1721-0_10

support. One of the most important technological developments during the industry 4.0 revolution is blockchain technology. The overall blockchain focused on enhancing spheres. Data privacy, cost and time saving, etc. are things that ultimately help and support blockchain capabilities to be more precise. It is used to store data and generate an incorruptible distributed record that is also safer than the traditional database. It will help to secure IP as e-books. The whole payment system is encrypted through the blockchain. Blockchain is a storage technology that analyses data to make estimates which helps to solve problems. It also helps to make trade faster and more effective for new products. The results and payment from authenticated blockchain reduce human involvement. Blockchain is a vital partner in industry-related growth. This technology reduces risk and bribery and creates trust, and its encrypted nature makes it impossible to access. It eliminates the dependency on certain intermediaries (Ghafar et al., 2021), which decreases the chances of data entry errors and reduces processing fees. Blockchain automatically allows actions after the conditions are met. It will allow quicker and speed-up transactions. Inside blockchain intelligent agreements are rapidly becoming faster. The breakthrough of intelligent contracts will create trust-based ecosystems. One of blockchain's major advantages is that it enables stakeholders to make payments with a crypto wallet with a customized trustworthy experience. The integration of blockchain technology in supply chain management shows key components like manufacturers, suppliers, distributors, and retailers, connected through a blockchain network. It facilitates aspects such as real-time tracking, transparency, and smart contracts.

1.1 Industry 4.0 and Its Significant Advancements

Industry 4.0, also known as the fourth industrial revolution, has brought significant advancements to supply chain management (SCM) through the integration of smart technologies and digitalization. Noordin (2022) identifies nine technological pillars of Industry 4.0 as critical advancements that significantly enhance supply chain management, offering substantial benefits and improvements across various operational aspects. These includes the following:

The Internet of Things (IoT): Connects devices for real-time data exchange, enhancing production efficiency.

Cloud computing: Offers remote data management, accelerating product development and market entry.

Big Data analytics: Helps optimize processes and customize products through data-driven insights.

Cybersecurity: To ensure the protection of valuable information between collaborated parties in supply chain management.

Systems integration: To link various systems, promoting seamless communication across production lines.

Additive manufacturing: For instance, 3D printing enables lightweight, customized production.

Autonomous systems: Empower machines to operate independently, increasing productivity.

Augmented reality: Allows manufacturers to showcase virtual products without physical prototypes.

Simulations: To replicate real-world processes, enabling companies to refine operations in virtual environments before implementation.

More recently, blockchain technology has been increasingly added as an additional pillar that adds to the support of SCM, relative to Industry 4.0. Blockchain, with its decentralized and immutable ledger nature, adds much-needed transparency, traceability, and security for the efficient and sustainable functioning of supply chains. It aids in reducing fraud and delays, frequently enhancing the accuracy in the transactions that take place throughout supply chains, while allowing for real-time sharing of data among stakeholders. In addition, it provides a tamper-proof record of transactions that in many ways enhances operational efficiency and trust amongst partners in the supply chain ecosystem. Blockchain also helps in sustainability through enabling better resource tracking and promoting greener production practices. It also complements the Industry 4.0 elements like IoT and Big Data with a robust foundation of securely managing a large amount of supply chain data (Khan et al., 2022; Paliwal et al., 2020).

As a result, the integration of Industry 4.0 technologies has completely revolutionized the approach toward supply chain management; with such technologies, efficiency, safety, and innovation are guaranteed at all levels of operation. All nine technological pillars bring together improvements in process optimization, data management, and manufacturing. Besides, the recent addition of blockchain as a critical pillar adds greater value by increasing transparency, traceability, and confidence among supply chain ecosystems. These technologies will continue their development, which further means that in the future, they will play a more critical role in shaping the path of sustainable, efficient, and secure supply chain management.

1.2 Challenges of Industry 4.0 Undertaken by Blockchain

The adoption of Industry 4.0 technologies has introduced several transformative innovations, but with these advancements come significant challenges that blockchain technology seeks to address. One major issue in Industry 4.0 is data integrity and security, as the increased reliance on interconnected devices, sensors, and autonomous systems makes supply chains vulnerable to cyberattacks and data breaches. According to Saberi et al. (2019), blockchain, with its decentralized and immutable ledger system, offers a solution to this challenge by ensuring that data across the supply chain is encrypted, traceable, and tamper-proof. However, the widespread implementation of blockchain in such complex ecosystems presents its own technical and operational challenges. In particular, issues related to scalability, energy consumption, and interoperability among existing systems remain as significant obstacles (Yli-Huumo et al., 2016).

Another challenge is the transparency and accountability within multi-tiered supply chains. Industry 4.0 systems often rely on extensive collaborations across various stakeholders, ranging from manufacturers to logistics providers and retailers. These collaborations introduce complexities in maintaining trust and transparency, especially when dealing with global supply networks. Blockchain's distributed ledger technology can significantly enhance transparency by allowing real-time data sharing across all parties involved (Kouhizadeh & Sarkis, 2018). Despite this potential, the integration of blockchain into current supply chain infrastructures is hindered by the high costs of implementation, the steep learning curve for participants, and legal and regulatory uncertainties (Casino et al., 2019).

As a result of these challenges, organizations must navigate the technical, operational, and regulatory hurdles to fully realize the benefits of blockchain in Industry 4.0. Companies often struggle with the trade-offs between the costs of blockchain adoption and the security benefits it promises. Additionally, the lack of standardized blockchain protocols aggravates the issue of interoperability, making it difficult for firms to integrate blockchain seamlessly with other Industry 4.0 technologies. Overcoming these challenges will require collaborative efforts between industry players, policymakers, and blockchain developers to establish scalable solutions and regulatory frameworks that facilitate the effective deployment of blockchain in Industry 4.0 environments.

1.3 Traditional Supply Chains Versus Blockchain-Enabled Supply Chains

Blockchain is an organization and general management of supply chains. Blockchain plays a significant role in the organization and general management of supply chains. Its ability to guarantee the reliability, traceability, and authenticity of information makes it a valuable tool in supply chain operations. One of the interesting structures before a product is transferred to another actor is that both parties may sign a digital contract to authenticate the exchange. In this way, the blockchain removes the need for a trusted central organization. Customers can track product characteristics information which will increase trust (Tian, 2016). Its impact also extends to the supply chain interactions between different network parties (Hofmann et al., 2018). What will make trading processes among partners more efficient is the disintermediation of financial intermediaries, including payment networks (Tapscott & Tapscott, 2017). This fact lets us identify the effect of blockchain technology on sustainable supply chains. The centralized database causes bottlenecks and slowdowns to settle transactions. As it is expensive to provide insurance for transactions, these risks may ultimately result in lost productivity, delayed deadlines, and missed opportunities in the supply chain. These challenges will be solved through blockchain because they solve things such as counterfeit products, visibility, and traceability (Panetta 2018a, b). Key characteristics of blockchain technology are distribution, decentralization, encryption, immutability, and smart contracts. Figure 1 shows the traditional supply chains vs. blockchain-based supply chain.

1.4 Blockchain and Sustainable Supply Chains

Blockchains as distributed can also influence sustainable supply chain networks. A blockchain-based supply chain provides a better guarantee for human rights and work practices. Sustainable supply chains have gained interest among academics

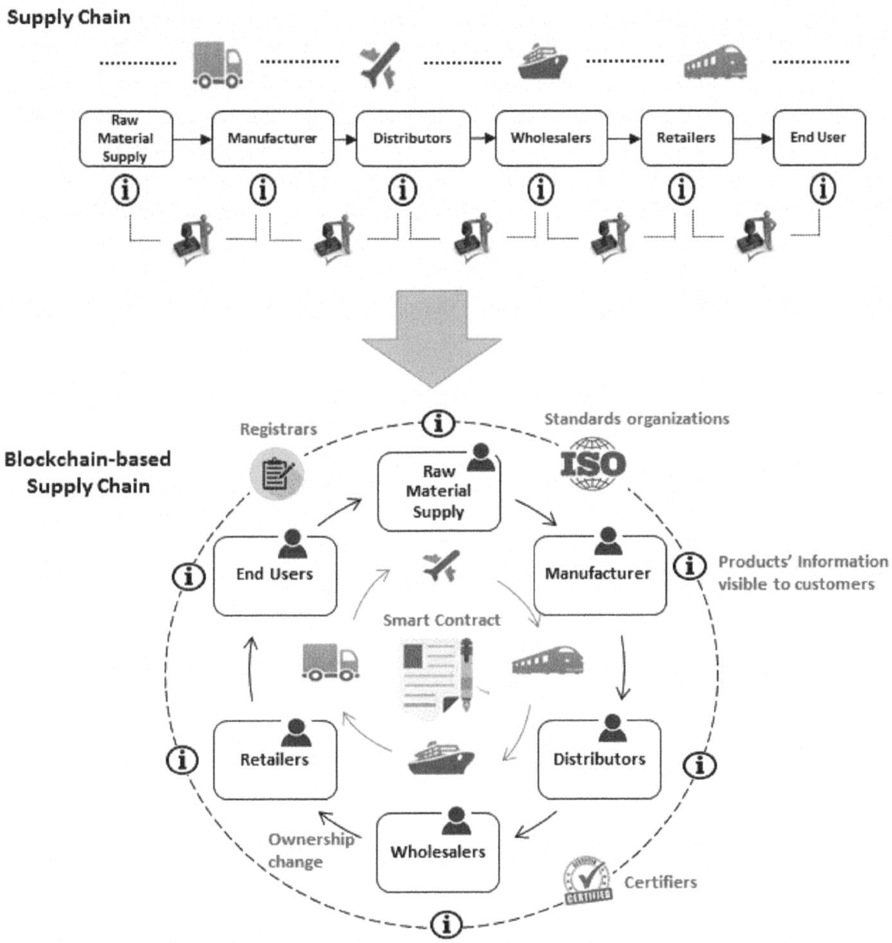

Fig. 1 Traditional supply chains vs. blockchain-based supply chain (Source: Saberi et al., 2019)

and practitioners (Fahimnia et al., 2015). Blockchain can support the collection and support important information about the product and supply chain. Blockchain can detect unethical suppliers and counterfeit products which can cause serious social harm. Economically, the benefit the blockchain can provide the dimensions of the business affecting their economic performance. Blockchain can result in a reduction in time and transactions which reduce business waste in the supply chain (Ward, 2017). It can share instantly every modification of the data which allows rapid deployment of products and processes. Also, it ensures the safety of data which reduces the costs from deliberate (Ivanov et al., 2018). The peer-to-peer networks based on blockchain technology for energy systems reduce electricity consumption. It will also reduce energy. Blockchain can be used to ensure that purportedly green products are environmentally friendly. Usually, the information is unavailable. If the manufacturing process is verified, the customer will be willing to purchase more green products. Ikea has a product made of wood cut; Ikea must follow the wood from the cut time till the final product to make sure it is made from wood. It is a complex process but it can be managed by Blockchain. IBM and Energy Blockchain Labs Inc. in China are developing a green asset. Blockchain can improve recycling. Blockchain technology has been used to motivate people through financial rewards through depositing recyclables like plastic or bottles. For example, there is a project called social plastic which turns plastic into money, it aims to reduce plastic waste. The use of blockchain supply chain governance. Disruptive technologies typically face challenges, whether in the short term or long term (Mendling et al., 2017). Participants in the supply chain should be prepared for it and use it as an opportunity rather than a threat as it might challenge the relationships through the supply chain

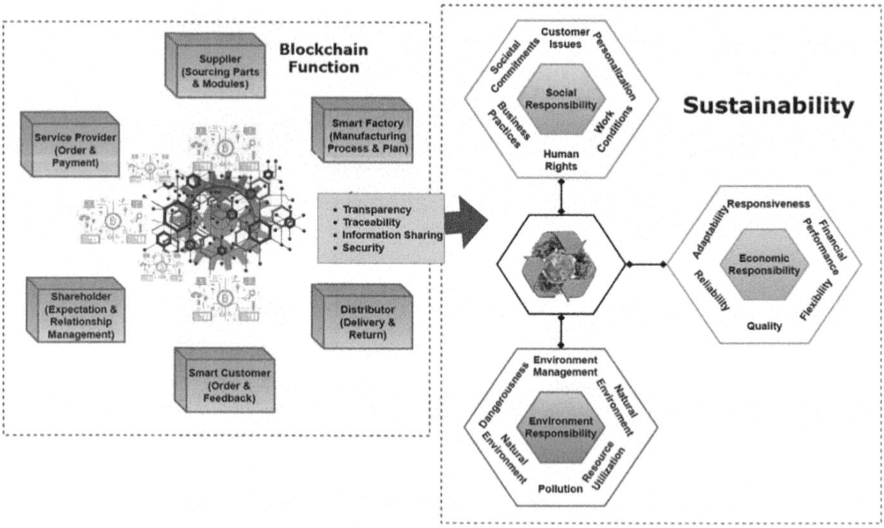

Fig. 2 Key benefits of using blockchain in supply chain management (Source: Uddin et al., 2023)

(Akhtar, 2023). Figure 2 shows the key benefits of using blockchain in supply chain management.

2 Challenges of Blockchain Adoption in Supply Chain Management

This part will explain the challenges in the adoption of blockchain technology in supply chain management. The immaturity of blockchain technology is in the developing stage. There are cases where companies face complex challenges due to the defects in the blockchain itself. As there are nodes that should be agreed for each transaction, it cannot be determined as efficient (Gervasi et al., 2018; Tian, 2016). Blockchain cannot store large amounts of data. Therefore, it is important to detect the amount of data on the chain (Tian, 2016). In addition, the privacy of the data is protected by asymmetric encryption, with the use of the key. However, if any of the keys get lost it will be hard to recover. So, the key itself is a prime challenge. The requirement of higher investment as it needs continuous financial support to incorporate the key function of the firm into the system (Menon, 2018). Another concern is that small suppliers may need to spend a large amount of time. It is crucial to ensure the quality of the data. To implement the blockchain, it is mandatory that all the stakeholders take part in it. It is a difficult task to have sensitive data on some products to balance confidentiality and transparency at the same time. Regulations and the global standard lack of legislation are another key challenge. Since blockchain is still in the developing process, there is still a lack of regulations, global standards, and other laws. In the twenty-first century, one product is produced and delivered by various suppliers, hence the supply chain is transformed into a global supply chain. The need for a global agreement increased as the supply chain became the nature of the global supply chain. A possible solution could be support from the government and the immediate incorporation of different systems. Below are the key challenges for the adoption of blockchain technology in supply chain management.

2.1 Scalability Issues

Block size and Throughput Limitations Blockchain network can handle limited number of transactions per second, which is not enough to accept high-volume demands of global supply chains, particularly those who use proof-of-work like Bitcoin. For example, Visa is a centralized system that can process tens of thousands of transactions per second (TPS) that is far more than Bitcoin, which processes only about 3–7 TPS (Narayanan et al., 2016).

Latency Blockchain can create delays in industries as it may take a few minutes to finalize which requires near-instantaneous updates (Wüst & Gervais, 2018).

2.2 *Integration with Existing Systems*

Legacy Systems Supply chains are usually built on established enterprise resource planning (ERP) systems which are complex and costly. It is a challenge due to differing data formats and transaction models (Dai & Vasarhelyi, 2017).

Data Format Compatibility The consistent data structure used in blockchain is clashed with the proprietary systems, complicating integration (Christidis & Devetsikiotis, 2016).

2.3 *Regulatory and Legal Challenges*

Lack of Legal Frameworks The uncertainty surrounding blockchain remains. According to PwC (2022), businesses are hesitant to adopt blockchain due to concerns about regulatory compliance, especially with data protection laws like general data protection regulation (GDPR) (Akhtar et al., 2021).

Data Privacy Concerns Privacy laws can conflict with blockchain's transparent nature, which requires individuals' personal data to have control over it, such as the general data protection regulation (GDPR).

2.4 *Cost of Implementation*

Initial investment Firms face significant upfront investment, and integration due to high initial costs of global supply chain.

Operational Costs The operational cost is added due to energy consumption, particularly the proof-of-work system. Blockchain in sustainability has raised concern, as bitcoin's network consumes more energy than some countries (Andresen, 2018).

2.5 Network Effect and Industry Adoption

Fragmented Adoption Wide adoption is relied on blockchain's effectiveness by supply chain stakeholder. Blockchain adoption is difficult in supply chains because of the absence of industry-wide standards and collaboration.

Coordination Among Parties The success of blockchain requires a cooperative environment to share data on a decentralized platform where all partners agree, to build trust across a diverse group of stakeholders to overcome the toughest barriers to blockchain adoption (Swan, 2015).

2.6 Trust Issues

Resistance to Change Stakeholders are reluctant to trust a decentralized system, especially in traditional industries. The unfamiliarity with its decentralized governance model makes blockchain adoption a trust barrier (Zohar & Rosenfeld, 2017).

Governance and Control The centralized entities are based on traditional supply chains for oversight. Many organizations may be unwilling to relinquish control due to blockchain's decentralized nature challenges.

2.7 Energy Consumption

Environmental Impact Bitcoin uses proof-of-work, which is used by the blockchain networks, this is highly energy-intensive. Energy consumption is a major barrier to adoption in eco-conscious industries. This has raised sustainability concerns in industries (Sedlmeir et al., 2020).

Proof of Stake Consensus mechanisms such as proof of stake offers more energy-efficient alternatives, transitioning to these mechanisms can be complex, that is why they are not yet adopted globally (Buterin, 2017).

2.8 Lack of Technical Expertise

Talent Gap Talent shortage is a well-known barrier in the blockchain. The demand on blockchain experts has outstripped supply. According to IBM's (2020) especially in industries like supply chain management which requires a unique combination of blockchain knowledge and supply chain experience.

Complexity in Development Blockchain supply chains often need solutions that demand deep technical knowledge to be tailored to the specific industry needs. It is difficult for companies to hire the necessary talent due to the complexity of designing scalable blockchain systems (Croman et al., 2016).

2.9 Security Concerns

Vulnerabilities Blockchain is not invulnerable to attacks, despite to its reputation for security, coding errors can lead to significant security risks, particularly in complex supply chain systems (Atzei et al., 2017).

Private vs. Public Blockchains The private blockchains offer more control over security, while it may lose some of the decentralization benefits that make blockchain appealing.

2.10 Cultural and Organizational Resistance

Change Management Shifting to blockchain-based supply chains will require a cultural shift within organizations. Many companies are struggling to adopt technologies like blockchain.

Stakeholder Trust It poses challenges for businesses that rely on third parties to verify transactions as blockchain seeks to eliminate intermediaries (Christidis & Devetsikiotis, 2016).

2.11 Maturity of Technology

Evolving Standards Businesses hesitate to adopt solutions that may become obsolete as blockchain technology is still developing.

Security Concerns Around New Features Smart contracts and decentralized applications (dApps) are still evolving features in blockchain. Smart contracts and decentralized applications (dApps) are still evolving features in blockchain, as there are still long-term concerns about the security and reliability of commercial applications (Crosby et al., 2016).

2.12 Environmental and Societal Impact

Sustainability Concerns Energy consumption of blockchains has sparked a debate on the environmental impacts. That will affect the environmental cost of mining cryptocurrencies (Sedlmeir et al., 2020).

Regulation of Crypto-Based Supply Chains There is increasing security concern over the use of cryptocurrencies in supply chains with the adoption of growth in blockchain. As blockchain solutions in supply chains are affected by the governments worldwide and governments are still developing policies to regulate cryptocurrency use (Hughes, 2020).

3 Key Applications of Block Chain Technology in Supply Chain Management

Blockchain technology is a turning point in supply chain management, and addressing the issues will be solved through long-standing issues like transparency, traceability, and efficiency. The Blockchain offers substantial benefits for industries that require verification systems and stringent tracking because an immutable ledger blockchain is decentralized and cannot be changed so based on that it can provide smooth operation and foster trust among stakeholders.

3.1 Improved Traceability and Transparency

The reason that it enhances transparency everywhere in the supply chain is that blockchain allows real-time tracking of products from the start till it reaches the final consumer. This is valuable, particularly in food and pharmaceuticals as all the transactions or movements of goods are recorded in blockchain which ensures that all parties can verify the product history. This is very important in these industries as it is crucial to safety and compliance to track the origin and handling of goods.

Example Walmart uses blockchain to trace food products, significantly reducing the time it takes to track the origin of contaminated goods—from days to mere seconds. This improves food safety and reduces the impact of recalls (Kamath, 2018).

3.2 Authenticity Verification and Fraud Reduction

Counterfeit products can lead to safety concerns and financial losses, especially for high-value goods such as luxury items, electronics, and pharmaceuticals can easily be counterfeited. Blockchain can provide tamper-proof records of products, which helps to verify their authenticity and reduce counterfeiting which will help these products.

Example VeChain, a blockchain platform, helps luxury brands verify product authenticity by tracking each item's origin and ownership, ensuring that consumers receive genuine products (Kim & Laskowski, 2018).

3.3 Real-Time Data and Efficiency

Blockchain can automatically execute transactions when the conditions are met through smart contracts, which enables real-time data exchange and automation. This will increase operational efficiency in such as inventory management and payment processing, it will reduce delays and eliminate manual paperwork.

Example Maersk and IBM's Trade Lens platform leverages blockchain to streamline global shipping operations, providing end-to-end visibility and reducing the time and cost of moving goods through the supply chain (Hackius & Petersen, 2017).

3.4 Sustainable and Ethical Sourcing

Blockchain can help to verify that the products meet the environmental criteria and are sourced responsibly and labor standards with the growing demand for sustainability and ethical business. With immutable record of the supply chain that is provided through the technology, will enable businesses to prove that their practices are sustainable.

Example Ever ledger uses blockchain to track the provenance of diamonds, ensuring they are ethically sourced and free from conflict, which helps meet the demands of consumers and regulators for ethical transparency (Iansiti & Lakhani, 2017).

3.5 *Collaboration and Trust Among Supply Chain Participants*

Blockchain enables all the participants in the supply chain, namely the suppliers, manufacturers, logistics providers, and retailers to collaborate by accessing and verifying the same data. This will cut costs and improve the speed of transactions by enhancing the trust among the partners and reducing the need for intermediaries.

Example IBM Food Trust uses blockchain to connect stakeholders across the food supply chain, allowing for real-time sharing of product data, reducing disputes, and improving response times in the event of product recalls (Carrefour, 2019).

4 Conclusion

The implementation of blockchain in the supply chain can reduce fraud, improve efficiency, and enhance transparency. Through robust solutions, blockchain can offer many benefits to the traditional supply chains. The stakeholders can verify the authenticity of the product to ensure ethical sourcing. However, issues such as standardization, cost, and scalability must be addressed for blockchain to achieve widespread adoption. As industries continue exploring and integrating blockchain technology it will impact global supply chains to drive new levels of both trust and efficiency.

References

Akhtar, P. (2023). Drivers and enablers of green purchasing adoption: An empirical investigation of retail hypermarkets in UAE. *International Journal of Management and Sustainability, 12*(2), 229–244.

Akhtar, P., Azima, N., & Ud Din, S. (2021). Barricades in the adoption of blockchain technology in supply chain management: Challenges and benefits. *Transnational Marketing Journal, 9*(1), 3–16.

Andresen, P. (2018). Blockchain's energy consumption and sustainability implications. *Journal of Sustainable Technology, 6*(3), 78–87. https://doi.org/10.1016/j.jst.2018.06.001

Atzei, N., Bartoletti, M., & Cimoli, T. (2017). A survey of attacks on Ethereum smart contracts. *Proceedings of the 2017 IEEE European Symposium on Security and Privacy*, 164–176. https://doi.org/10.1109/EuroSP.2017.49

Bogucharskov, V., Pokamestov, I., Korablev, V., & Kudryavtsev, D. (2018). Blockchain: A new accounting paradigm and its innovative potential. *European Research Studies Journal, 21*(1), 90–103. https://doi.org/10.35808/ersj/961

Buterin, V. (2017). Ethereum and the blockchain: How proof-of-stake provides energy-efficient consensus mechanisms. *Proceedings of the Ethereum Conference*, 12–19. https://doi.org/10.1109/ETHCONF.2017.00014

Carrefour. (2019). IBM Food Trust: Improving transparency in the food supply chain. *Carrefour Press Release*. https://www.carrefour.com/ibm-food-trust

Casino, F., Dasaklis, T. K., & Patsakis, C. (2019). A systematic literature review of blockchain-based applications: Status, classification and open issues. *Telematics and Informatics, 36*, 55–81.

Christidis, K., & Devetsikiotis, M. (2016). Blockchains and smart contracts for the internet of things. *IEEE Access, 4*, 2292–2303. https://doi.org/10.1109/ACCESS.2016.2566339

Croman, K., Decker, C., & Eyal, I. (2016). On scaling decentralized blockchains. *Proceedings of the 2016 ACM Symposium on Principles of Distributed Computing*, 106–115. https://doi.org/10.1145/2976749.2978358

Crosby, M., Pattanayak, P., Verma, S., & Kalyanaraman, V. (2016). Blockchain technology: Beyond bitcoin. *Applied Innovation Review, 2*, 6–19. https://doi.org/10.3310/air-2016-0002

Dai, J., & Vasarhelyi, M. A. (2017). Toward blockchain-based accounting and auditing. *Journal of Emerging Technologies in Accounting, 14*(1), 1–16. https://doi.org/10.2308/jeta-51895

Fahimnia, B., Sarkis, J., & Davarzani, H. (2015). Green supply chain management: A review and bibliometric analysis. *International Journal of Production Economics, 162*, 101–114. https://doi.org/10.1016/j.ijpe.2014.12.021

Gervasi, O., Milani, F., & Manzoli, M. (2018). Blockchain for supply chain management: A systematic review. In *Proceedings of the 12th International Conference on IT and Business Intelligence* (pp. 45–59). https://doi.org/10.1109/ITBI.2018.00015

Ghafar, A., Nair, M., & Akhtar, P. (2021). Innovation and lifestyle entrepreneurship: A study of Lifestyle enterprises in UAE. *International Journal of Entrepreneurship and Innovation, 25*, 1–14.

Hackius, N., & Petersen, A. (2017). Blockchain in supply chain management: The case of Maersk and IBM's TradeLens platform. *Springer Proceedings in Business and Economics*, 167–179. https://doi.org/10.1007/978-3-319-57078-3_12

Hofmann, E., Strewe, U. M., & Bosia, N. (2018). Supply chain finance and blockchain technology: The case of reverse securitisation. *Springer Proceedings in Business and Economics*, 97–116. https://doi.org/10.1007/978-3-319-62371-1_5

Hughes, P. (2020). The global regulation of blockchain in supply chains. *Supply Chain Law Journal, 14*(1), 12–22. https://doi.org/10.1109/SCLJ.2020.00012

Iansiti, M., & Lakhani, K. R. (2017). The truth about blockchain. *Harvard Business Review, 95*(1), 118–127. https://hbr.org/2017/01/the-truth-about-blockchain

IBM. (2020). IBM's blockchain talent gap in supply chain management. *IBM Blockchain Journal*. https://www.ibm.com/blockchain/talent-gap

Ivanov, D., Dolgui, A., & Sokolov, B. (2018). The impact of blockchain technology on the supply chain: A theory-based research agenda. *International Journal of Production Research, 56*(1-2), 110–129. https://doi.org/10.1080/00207543.2017.1389476

Kamath, A. (2018). Blockchain: The food traceability game changer. *International Journal of Supply Chain Management, 7*(3), 27–35. https://doi.org/10.1108/IJSCM-05-2018-0186

Khan, S. A., Mubarik, M. S., Kusi-Sarpong, S., Gupta, H., Zaman, S. I., & Mubarik, M. (2022). Blockchain technologies as enablers of supply chain mapping for sustainable supply chains. *Business strategy and the environment, 31*(8), 3742–3756.

Kim, H., & Laskowski, M. (2018). VeChain: Verifying authenticity with blockchain in luxury goods. *Blockchain Technology for Supply Chain Applications, 8*, 42–51. https://doi.org/10.1007/978-3-319-74728-0_5

Kouhizadeh, M., & Sarkis, J. (2018). Blockchain practices, potentials, and perspectives in greening supply chains. *Sustainability, 10*(10), 3652.

Mendling, J., Weber, I., van der Aalst, W. M., & Recker, J. (2017). Blockchain technology in supply chain management: A systematic literature review. *Business & Information Systems Engineering, 59*(6), 415–434. https://doi.org/10.1007/s12599-017-0502-y

Menon, J. (2018). Blockchain technology in supply chain management: Challenges and opportunities. *International Journal of Business Innovation and Research, 16*(1), 100–114. https://doi.org/10.1504/IJBIR.2018.088588

Narayanan, A., Bonneau, J., Felten, E., Miller, A., & Goldfeder, S. (2016). *Bitcoin and cryptocurrency technologies. Princeton University Press*. ISBN: 978-0-691-18314-7.

Noordin, N. A. (2022). Industry 4.0: Drivers and challenges in developing the smart supply chain management. In *Sustainable development through data analytics and innovation: Techniques, processes, models, tools, and practices* (pp. 97–111). Springer International Publishing.

O'Leary, D. E. (2017). Blockchain: Implications for the future of accounting. *Journal of Emerging Technologies in Accounting, 14*(2), 113–122. https://doi.org/10.2308/jeta-51911

Paliwal, V., Chandra, S., & Sharma, S. (2020). Blockchain technology for sustainable supply chain management: A systematic literature review and a classification framework. *Sustainability, 12*(18), 7638.

Panetta, K. (2018a). Blockchain: The digital ledger that's transforming business. *Forbes Technology Council*. https://www.forbes.com/sites/gartner/2018/05/15/blockchain-the-digital-ledger-thats-transforming-business/

Panetta, K. (2018b). The reality of blockchain. *Gartner Research*. Retrieved from https://www.gartner.com

PwC. (2022). The state of blockchain and cryptocurrencies in supply chain management. *Pricewaterhouse Coopers LLP*. https://www.pwc.com/crypto2022

Saberi, S., Kouhizadeh, M., Sarkis, J., & Shen, L. (2019). Blockchain technology and its relationships to sustainable supply chain management. *International Journal of Production Research, 57*(7), 2117–2135.

Sarpong, D. (2014). Strategizing risk management in supply chains: The rise of blockchain technology. *Supply Chain Management: An International Journal, 19*(4), 441–454. https://doi.org/10.1108/SCM-09-2013-0333

Sedlmeir, J., Krombholz, K., & Busch, C. (2020). Blockchain technology: The environmental costs. *Environmental and Sustainability Studies, 17*(2), 121–132. https://doi.org/10.1109/ESS.2020.00015

Swan, M. (2015). Blockchain: Blueprint for a new economy. *O'Reilly Media*. ISBN: 978-1-491-94958-6.

Tapscott, D., & Tapscott, A. (2017). How blockchain will change organizations. *MIT Sloan Management Review, 58*(2), 10–13.

Tian, F. (2016). An agri-food supply chain traceability system for China based on RFID & blockchain technology. In *13th International Conference on Service Systems and Service Management (ICSSSM)* (pp. 1–6). https://doi.org/10.1109/ICSSSM.2016.7538424

Ward, A. (2017). Blockchain in supply chain management: A new opportunity. *International Journal of Logistics Management, 28*(2), 467–484. https://doi.org/10.1108/IJLM-07-2016-0175

Wüst, K., & Gervais, A. (2018). Do you need a blockchain? *Proceedings of the 2018 Crypto Valley Conference on Blockchain Technology*, 45–57. https://doi.org/10.1109/CVCBT.2018.00012

Yli-Huumo, J., Ko, D., Choi, S., Park, S., & Smolander, K. (2016). Where is current research on blockchain technology? A systematic review. *PloS One, 11*(10), e0163477.

Zohar, A., & Rosenfeld, M. (2017). Decentralized trust: Blockchain technology and resistance to change. *Journal of Technology and Innovation Management, 2*(4), 235–245. https://doi.org/10.1007/s10916-017-0742-7

Blockchain for Social Good: Emerging Models of Crypto Philanthropy

Alessandro Lanteri and Belisa Marochi

Abstract This chapter examines how cryptocurrencies and blockchain technology are transforming philanthropy by enabling new decentralized models of fundraising and donation. Cryptocurrency and blockchain have given rise to innovative forms of charity and social impact projects that provide more transparency, efficiency, and accessibility than traditional giving.

This chapter first provides background on cryptocurrency philanthropy and its benefits, including lower fees, faster transfer of funds, and an immutable record of donations on the blockchain. It then reviews different models of crypto-based philanthropy: Direct crypto donations; NFT charity auctions; DAOs and crypto social impact funds; and "Giving" cryptocurrencies.

Each model is explained through real-world examples and case studies. The benefits and limitations are critically analyzed. This chapter concludes by reflecting on how these experiments in Web 3.0 philanthropy are making giving more open, equitable, and impactful. They present new opportunities for social innovation and financial inclusion using cryptocurrency's distinctive properties.

1 Introduction

After cryptocurrency was first introduced with the Bitcoin protocol in January 2009, it set off a type of modern-day gold rush, where users would "mine" for the eponymous digital token. In its first phases of development, the digital currency was relegated to more segmented corners of the internet and viewed as a decidedly non-mainstream asset and somewhat of a risky venture (Czervionke et al., 2022). Cryptocurrency has its risks, certainly, as seen with the breach of bitcoin exchange

A. Lanteri
ESCP Business School, Torino, TO, Italy

B. Marochi (✉)
Hult International Business School, Dubai, United Arab Emirates
e-mail: belisa.marochi@faculty.hult.edu

L. O. Yesufu, P. N. E. Nohuddin (eds.), *Technology for Societal Transformation*, https://doi.org/10.1007/978-981-96-1721-0_11

Mt. Gox in 2014, the collapse of the major cryptocurrency exchange FTX in 2022, and the resulting criminal trials that followed that exchange's collapse. However, other financial markets have had similar moments in their evolution and in the fifteen years since it was first introduced, cryptocurrency has expanded to hundreds of assets with a robust foundational industry.

Central to the cryptocurrency innovation is what's called the blockchain: A ledger that records in chronological order all the transactions that have ever been executed within a system. Most cryptocurrencies have a ledger that details every transaction ever completed since the creation of the currency. By using this ledger, someone can trace each individual unit of the associated digital currency back to the moment of its creation, through each and every transaction, across multiple owners and wallets.

The blockchain has evolved from a technology only used in cryptocurrency to becoming recognized as a general-purpose technology, considered equivalent to a new Internet (sometimes referred to as "Web 3.0"). The applications of the blockchain have potential to create a new technological infrastructure for big data, with very diverse features (e.g., private or public, permissioned or permissionless, tokenized or not, etc.)

Due to all of this, there is a growing understanding that the blockchain can be used as a general-purpose technology to increase efficiency and reduce transaction costs, including in financial services and particularly in emerging economies. For example, LendLedger is developing a blockchain-based system to facilitate P2P micro-loans, while disintermediating MFIs. Similar applications are applicable for the philanthropic sector.

Digital cryptocurrencies can be considered a social innovation (Lanteri, 2024), distinct from "real-world" currencies because they create a decentralized nature network of individual participants, who provide the computational power needed to operate the entire system (Ali et al., 2014; Feld et al., 2016; Maull et al., 2017; UK Government Chief Scientific Adviser, 2015). The main motivation for the development of bitcoin was making digital money transactions anonymous and therefore private, like cash transactions. This was not possible before, because the existing regulations require that financial intermediaries act as gatekeepers and track all digital money transactions. Early bitcoin users and crypto adopters used the currencies as a way to disrupt the traditional financial system, but as cryptocurrencies have grown in popularity, many traditional financial institutions have integrated them into their products and services, and consumers have relied on existing relationships and trust within these institutions to engage with the crypto market (Czervionke et al., 2022).

With this disruption, many nonprofits and philanthropies are taking notice and leveraging crypto and the blockchain to meet identified social outcomes—both in terms of raising funds and leveraging the unique technologies of Web 3.0 for innovative solutions to social problems. As crypto has gone more mainstream, the comfort and familiarity with the technology has allowed more and more organizations to experiment with the model and direct more resources by using the blockchain (Duffy & Wilson, 2024; Howson, 2021; Jayasinghe et al., 2018).

The acceleration of donations through cryptocurrencies has tracked with the growth of the industry overall. According to The Giving Block, which annually tracks trends in crypto philanthropy, over $2 billion has been donated using cryptocurrency as of January 2024. The organization has estimated that by 2032, over $10 billion will be donated using the blockchain (PwC, 2024).

With the expectation that cryptocurrencies and other blockchain technologies will only grow in their influence within philanthropy, nonprofits, international development, and other social good fields, this chapter will examine how this transformation is being driven through new decentralized models of fundraising and donation. Specifically, this chapter will cover four different areas:

- Direct crypto donations—Donors can now give bitcoin and other cryptocurrencies directly to nonprofits without any intermediary. This allows for pseudo-anonymous digital cash transfers anywhere in the world.
- NFT charity auctions—Nonfungible tokens (NFTs) are being leveraged by charities to create unique digital collectibles and artwork that are auctioned to raise money. The NFT space has funded various causes.
- DAOs and crypto social impact funds—Decentralized autonomous organizations (DAOs) are formed around crypto funds that pool capital for specific causes like climate change or gender lens investing. DAOs have decentralized governance.
- "Giving" cryptocurrencies—New cryptocurrencies have been developed specifically to fundraise for certain issues and nonprofits receive portions of the supply. They incentivize crypto holders to give.

This chapter will conclude with a broader analysis of Web 3.0 influence on philanthropy and social initiatives, making giving more open, equitable, and impactful.

1.1 Social Impact and the Dark Side of Innovation

Before going into the specific areas of the emerging models of crypto philanthropy, this section will first explore a definition of social impact and social innovation, as well as provide some consideration of the potential negative consequences of innovation.

This chapter discusses social impact and the potential of equitable financial inclusion; however, these terms are quite large in scope and can encompass many different aspects of social outcomes. In its most common uses, social innovation and the resulting social impact that comes from it refers to significant and lasting changes in a society or in its structures, regulations, norms, and values, such that the society's performance in satisfying the economic and social needs of its members is enhanced, at the individual, collective or system level (Hamalainen & Heiskala, 2007; Phills et al., 2008; The Young Foundation, 2012; Moulaert et al., 2014; Tepsie, 2014; Zollo et al., 2015). With the increasing complexity and interconnectedness of the globalized economy, social innovation is increasingly recognized as a driver of value creation for society and the economy (Krlev et al., 2023).

For this chapter, the impact resulting from the crypto innovations can be seen as leading to social impact if they facilitate some kind of beneficial outcome for society. Specifically, if they lead to increased resources (donations) toward organizations that are generally considered beneficial to society, such as NGOs or other charitable organizations.

Of course, this is a broad definition that does not lend itself to nuanced discussions of practical developments. Within the domain of innovative products such as cryptocurrencies, social impact can be subsumed by the pursuit of financial sustainability through earned income. For example, in a case study of the failure of a social enterprise, the Seedco Policy Center (2007, pp. 1–2) explored how a focus on financial innovations can lead to detrimental outcomes. It "found that nonprofits driven to meet a double bottom line [...] have far more typically led to frustration and failure, drawing attention and resources away from the organization's core work—and that even the oft-cited success stories are less cut-and-dried than they appear."

This focus on the double bottom line can cause negative social outcomes despite the promise of positive results. There is a longstanding debate, for example, around microfinance and its ability to effectively lift the unbanked out of poverty. One of the most celebrated microfinance institutions, Banco Compartamos of Mexico, achieved an astonishing growth by charging interests in excess of 100%, which eventually led to widespread backlash (Carrick-Cagna & Santos, 2009).

Each section in this chapter will acknowledge the relevant "dark sides" of the crypto innovations, including potential negative externalities and/or challenges with implementing the crypto methods.

2 Direct Crypto Donations

Nonprofits and community service organizations are typically regarded as behind the curve when it comes to innovation. Online giving of any type remains relatively low across the nonprofit sector, with only 12% of online donations globally given through online means in 2023. Even this was up a significant amount from the year previous: In 2022, only 8% of donations were given online (Blackbaud, 2024). Many nonprofits, particularly community-based nonprofits, remain anchored in donor cultivation behavior that was established years, if not decades ago. A lack of resources requires them to make use with what they have, rather than pursue new and different donation strategies.

Despite this, crypto donations are on the rise, particularly with larger organizations. Looking explicitly at the largest nonprofits in the USA, The Giving Block found that just over 50% have the ability to receive crypto donations. Of those that receive crypto donations, about two-thirds are not just accepting them but have an active strategy to directly appeal and fundraise for cryptocurrencies (Duffy & Wilson, 2024).

Crypto donations offer significant value for nonprofits. They allow for a broader reach in potential donors, as they are not constrained by currency exchange limitations. This extends globally, into new markets as well as crypto-inclined donors who may not have been on the nonprofit's radar previously. These crypto-donors are also more likely to give larger donations than the traditional "fiat donors" through their crypto giving (PwC, 2024).

The continued growth in the crypto market will likely only encourage greater donation amounts to nonprofits from crypto investors. There are currently 580 million crypto users worldwide, which offers nonprofit, particularly those working at a global level, a much larger base of potential users than more traditional, high-end donors. For example, the total number of crypto users is larger than the sum total of all enrollees in traditional brokerage funds (Duffy & Wilson, 2024). These brokerage funds, such as Schwab or Fidelity, are more traditional avenues for giving, through product offerings like a Donor Advised Fund.

Major charities that have leveraged crypto donations include organizations like the American Cancer Society, The Water Project, Orangutan Outreach, and Variety, a children's charity in Australia. All of these organizations have raised millions by embracing the crypto community and reaching out to crypto holders directly.

Example: Orangutan Outreach
Orangutan Outreach, which works to rehabilitate endangered Orangutans in Southeast Asia, found a natural partnership with an online crypto community, the "Bored Ape Yacht Club." Bored Ape is an NFT (or "non-fungible token") project that has morphed into a community of crypto enthusiasts. They found a natural pairing with Orangutan Outreach and have funneled a total of around $1 million to the charity. Much of this donation was given directly using the cryptocurrency Ethereum (Copeland, 2021).

The benefits from these donations are clear: The ability to tap into an engaged group of users with potentially a large amount of wealth to give. However, not every nonprofit has the capabilities to leverage or activate crypto donations (or even online giving), meaning that the benefits of crypto donations are open only to the nonprofits and charities who have the resources to successfully invest in crypto as a fundraising strategy. Many of these nonprofits are already large and have many streams of donations flowing in.

Additionally, because of the scale required to tap into crypto donations, many direct-service nonprofits may not be able to benefit from crypto donations. Most of these nonprofits tend to be community based, with limited resources, even though they are likely to have the most direct effect on individuals in need. As shown below, the blockchain can be leveraged through decentralized autonomous organizations (DAOs) for bottom-up community support, however; much of the crypto donation efforts remain top-down.

3 NFT Charity Auctions

In addition to direct donations to charities using cryptocurrency, nonprofits and philanthropies have been able to benefit from the development and sale of non fungible tokens, or "NFTs." NFTs are pieces of digital artwork that cannot be replicated because of their connection to the blockchain. Each one has its own unique signifier, making them "non fungible," or unable to be replicated. Essentially, NFTs operate as the fine art of the crypto world.

In the same way that fine art sales and donations have supported philanthropies and charities for years, NFTs have begun to be leveraged for charitable purposes. Whereas a charity might auction off a sculpture or a set of paintings from a famous artist, they can now do the same for NFTs.

The Bored Ape Yacht Club, in the example above, did not engage with their associated NFTs for direct donations; instead Orangutan Outreach leveraged the community around the NFT for direct crypto donations. Many other NFT communities have followed their lead, such as NodeMonkes NFT raising over $120,000 to fund the Pediatric Research Center (Duffy & Wilson, 2024). However, other charities have leveraged NFTs themselves to raise direct funds for their work (see box).

Example: Stella Artois and Water.org
Stella Artois, the European beverage company, partnered with digital art and NFT companies Art Blocks and Vayner3 to create a unique collection of NFT art for Water.org on "World Water Day" in 2022. This project created 1,024 unique NFTs inspired by Water.org's mission of delivering clean water to all. The sale of the collection raised over $200,000 for the international charity (Stewart, 2022). Art Blocks also worked with Cure Parkinson's and The ALS Association to create a charity auction of generative art pieces that has raised over $500,000 (Valeonti & Estorick, 2023).

Similar to the limitations described in the "direct crypto donations" section, above, NFT donations can be accessible to only the largest of nonprofits. The sale of NFTs is likely more fungible than direct crypto donations, as the sales of the NFTs themselves translate into real-world currency that any nonprofit could use to support their mission. NFT sales are likely to benefit more visible and "online" charities, however, and not more local charities that do not necessarily have a very visible digital presence.

4 DAOs and Crypto Social Impact Funds

Blockchain can also support the creation of more transparent and equitable organizational structures, through the creation of "decentralized autonomous organizations" or "DAOs." These are organizations that leverage blockchain technologies to distribute power through a voting process for decision making managed by a decentralized computer (Zwitter & Hazenberg, 2020).

Through DAOs, the blockchain has been proposed to help set agriculture prices and support contracts, typically a costly process, helping farmers and improving the quality of life (Xiong et al., 2020). DAOs, if implemented correctly, can support a complete restructuring of traditional organizations, creating more transparency and distributed power among staff and employees (Ahmed et al., 2024).

DAOs can be seen as analogous to the Donor Advised Funds of the traditional philanthropic industry. Donor Advised Funds (or "DAFs") are funds in which one or a few donors will put money into a fund and then make decisions on where to give that money. DAOs and other crypto social impact funds operate similarly, but instead of having just one or a few donors, the donors will make decisions more collaboratively or transparently about where and how to give.

To join a social impact DAO or similar, users typically must first purchase an NFT, the proceeds of which go into the DAO treasury. The purchaser then joins the community of the DAO, participating in meetings and other community channels, such as a Discord server or similar messaging platform. The DAO's transactions are tracked through a multisignature crypto wallet, and sometimes donations can be made automatically when terms and conditions are met.

Example: CowgirlDAO

CowgirlDAO is the philanthropic arm of the activist community Computer Cowgirls, which began with the sale of an NFT. The DAO is used by its members to vote on which organizations receive funds. Gitcoin is one of the more popular crypto social impact funds, in operation since 2017, and has distributed over $50 million with over 21,000 members backing the DAO (Dematteo, 2023).

Outside the normal confines of giving, DAOs can be leveraged for philanthropic aims, fundamentally altering the structure of philanthropy, allowing it to be bottom-up rather than top-down. In China, for example, the blockchain was used to help prevent bankruptcy from medical bills. Individuals with serious health conditions (such as cancer) were able to pay a small amount into a fund (around $1.50 USD equivalent), and then are eligible to receive up to around $44,000 USD to pay any associated medical bills (Wang & Desouze, 2019).

DAOs can counteract some of the issues highlighted above with the other blockchain related philanthropic efforts. By focusing on transparency and decentralization, DAOs and similar crypto social impact funds can help to create a more "bottom-up" approach to crypto donations, at least in theory. In practice, however, the promise of the decentralized nature of a DAO may not be realized: Research has found that many cryptocurrency exchanges and other platforms operated with a similar level of centralization as traditional financial institutions, which led to the ignoring of risk exposures and ultimately failure (Ecosystm, 2023).

5 "Giving" Cryptocurrencies

One of the benefits of cryptocurrencies is that anyone can create a currency for any purpose. As a virtual currency, they are inherently flexible and adaptable to user needs. Crypto currencies are what are called "bidirectional flow currencies" that are established currencies in their own right, with a set exchange rate with other currencies. In this way, crypto currencies have full interoperability with the real world, unlike other digital currencies such as Facebook credit or airline miles, which only have limited value in the real world, or video game currencies, which only have value within a digital world (ECB, 2012).

Individuals and organizations have leveraged the bidirectional nature of cryptocurrencies to create currencies that directly benefit nonprofits and philanthropies. These currencies are explicitly created by a nonprofit or by external partners in support of a nonprofit or series of nonprofits, to be used only for the benefit of those organizations. They are tied to the mission of the nonprofit or they raise funds through their sale for that nonprofit and are used for donor-related activities.

Example: RootProject
RootProject created a crowdfunding platform where a small amount of each donation goes to the purchase of what are called "Roots tokens." These Roots tokens are similar to bitcoin or other cryptocurrencies and work with the same properties. However, the value of the tokens are used to support low-skilled workers directly, rather than to the owner of the token or RootProject as an organization. Pinkcoin is another cryptocurrency that splits the value of the coin between the users who "mine" the tokens and charities. Around $1500 flows to participating charities in the USA and Canada each month from these Pinkcoin tokens (Blum, 2018).

Besides the limitations discussed above, which also apply in the case of giving cryptocurrencies, it is important to note that the process of mining cryptocurrencies requires massive amounts of energy. Essentially, a cryptocurrency network requires many different computers operating with very high computational levels, which uses a large amount of electric energy to maintain their operations. This causes a lot of power to keep computer servers running. The bitcoin network consumes as much energy annually as the entire country of the Netherlands and this is just one cryptocurrency of thousands (Lanteri & Rattalino, 2021). Nonprofits and philanthropies creating their own cryptocurrencies can have tremendous impacts on the environment at scale.

6 Conclusion: Web 3.0 for Social Good

This chapter illustrated four key areas in which the blockchain and advances in cryptocurrencies are supporting social development and social good. Specifically: Direct crypto donations; NFT charity auctions; DAOs and crypto social impact funds; and "giving" cryptocurrencies. These four areas have some drawbacks, including the potential "top-down," online nature of the giving, which limits the total number of nonprofits that can benefit from crypto philanthropy. Only around 12% of giving was done online (Blackbaud, 2024), which means most nonprofits cannot receive donations through cryptocurrencies.

However, despite these limitations the blockchain and cryptocurrencies offer tremendous opportunities for nonprofits, opening them to new potential donors and a vast amount of donated wealth. Web 3.0 philanthropic tools also offer nonprofits, philanthropies and community groups new opportunities to create collaborative and transparent giving options to drive various social outcomes. The inherently innovative nature of the blockchain will continue to spur new ideas and inspire new ways to make giving more open, equitable, and impactful for years to come.

References

Ahmed, I., Fumimoto, K., Nakano, T., & Tran, T. H. (2024). Blockchain-empowered decentralized philanthropic charity for social good. *Sustainability, 16*(1), 210. https://doi.org/10.3390/su16010210

Ali, R., Barrdear, J., Clews, R., & Southgate, J. (2014). Innovations in payment technologies and the emergence of digital currencies. *Bank of England Quarterly Bulletin, 54*(3), 262–275.

Blackbaud. (2024). *Spotlight: 2023 Trends in Giving*. https://institute.blackbaud.com/resources/2023-trends-in-giving-spotlight. Last accessed: 30th September 2024

Blum, D. (2018). Beyond donations: A sampling of efforts to use the blockchain for good. *Chronicle of Philanthropy*. https://www.philanthropy.com/article/beyond-donations-a-sampling-of-efforts-to-use-the-blockchain-for-good/. Last Accessed: 30th September 2024

Carrick-Cagna, A.-M., & Santos, F. (2009). *Kiva versus MYC4: Business model innovation in social lending*. INSEAD.

Copeland T (2021) NFT project Bored Ape Yacht Club has donated $850,000 to an orangutan charity. *The Block*. https://www.theblock.co/post/114030/nft-project-bored-ape-yacht-club-has-donated-850000-to-an-orangutan-charity. Last Accessed: 30th September 2024

Czervionke, C., Dienerowitz, N., Lamolo, W., Koyluoglu, U., Lai, K., Sizaret, L., & Wagner, M. (2022). *Navigating Crypto: How financial intermediaries can integrate cryptoassets*. Oliver Wyman.

Dematteo, M. (2023). Crypto philanthropy 101: What donors and organizations need to know. *CoinDesk*. https://www.coindesk.com/learn/crypto-philanthropy-101-what-donors-and-organizations-need-to-know/. Last Accessed: 30th September 2024

Duffy, P., & Wilson, A. (2024). *2024 Annual Report: Crypto philanthropy data, trends and predictions*. The Giving Block.

Ecosystm. (2023). *The degree of decentralisation in DeFi: Governance, management, processing, and economic measures across crypto networks*. Olivery Wyman.

European Central Bank. (2012). *Virtual currency schemes*. ECB.

Feld, S., Schönfeld, M., & Werner, M. (2016). Traversing Bitcoin's P2P network: Insights into the structure of a decentralised currency. *International Journal of Computational Science and Engineering, 13*(2), 122–131.

Hamalainen, T., & Heiskala, R. (Eds.). (2007). *Social innovations, institutional change and economic performance: Making sense of structural adjustment processes in industrial sectors, regions and societies*. SITRA: Edward Elgar.

Howson, P. (2021). Crypto-giving and surveillance philanthropy: Exploring the trade-offs in blockchain innovation for nonprofits. *Nonprofit Management and Leadership, 31*, 805–820. https://doi.org/10.1002/nml.21452

Jayasinghe, D., Cobourne, S., Markantonakis, K., Akram, R. N., & Mayes, K. (2018). Philanthropy on the Blockchain. In G. Hancke & E. Damiani (Eds.), *Information security theory and practice. WISTP 2017* (Lecture Notes in Computer Science) (Vol. 10741). Springer. https://doi.org/10.1007/978-3-319-93524-9_2

Krlev, G., Wruk, D., Pasi, G., & Bernhard, M. (Eds.). (2023). *Social economy science: Transforming the economy and making society more resilient*. Oxford University Press.

Lanteri, A. (2024). *Financial social innovations: A new framework to understand the social innovations disrupting the world of finance, from crowdfunding to Bitcoin*. Routledge.

Lanteri, A., & Rattalino, F. (2021). *Bitcoin must become more sustainable, for its own good (as well as the planet's)*. ESCP Impact Paper No 2021-38-EN.

Maull, R., Godsiff, P., Mulligan, C., Brown, A., & Kewell, B. (2017). Distributed ledger technology: Applications and implications. *Strategic Change: Briefings in Entrepreneurial Finance, 26*(5), 481–489.

Moulaert, F., MacCallum, D., Mehmood, A., & Hamdouch, A. (Eds.). (2014). *The international handbook on social innovation*. Edward Elgar.

Phills, J. R., Jr., Deiglmeier, K., & Miller, D. T. (2008). Rediscovering social innovation. *Stanford Social Innovation Review, 6*(4), 34–43.

PwC. (2024). *Redefining charitable giving in the digital age*. https://www.pwc.ch/en/insights/fs/crypto-contributions.html. Last Accessed: 30th September 2024

Seedco Policy Center. (2007). *The limits of social enterprise: A field study & case analysis*.

Stewart, R. (2022). Stella Artois Continues NFT Spree With Water.org Art Collection. *AdWeek*. https://www.adweek.com/brand-marketing/stella-artois-continues-nft-spree-with-water-org-art-collection/. Last Accessed: 30th September 2024

Tepsie. (2014). *Doing iocial Innovation: A guide for researchers, project: The theoretical, empirical and policy foundations for building social innovation in Europe (TEPSIE), European Commission – 7th Framework Programme*. European Commission, DG Research.

UK Government Chief Scientific Adviser. (2015). *Distributed ledger technology: Beyond Blockchain*. Government Office for Science.

Valeonti, F., & Estorick, A. (2023). reGEN | Generative Artists Fighting Degenerative Diseases. *Right Click Save*. https://www.rightclicksave.com/article/regen-generative-artists-fighting-degenerative-diseases-artist-interview-alzheimers. Last Accessed: 30th September 2024

Wang, X., & Desouze, K. (2019). China's new model of blockchain-driven philanthropy. *Stanford Social Innovation Review*. Summer 2019.

Xiong, H., Dalhaus, T., Wang, P., & Huang, J. (2020). Blockchain technology for agriculture: Applications and rationale. *Frontiers in Blockchain, 3*, 7. https://doi.org/10.3389/fbloc.2020.00007

Young Foundation. (2012). *Social innovation overview, project: The theoretical, empirical and policy foundations for building social innovation in Europe (TEPSIE), European Commission – 7th Framework Programme*. European Commission, DG Research.

Zollo, L., Marzi, G., Boccardi, A., & Surchi, M. (2015). How to match technological and social innovation: Insights from the biomedical 3D printing industry. *International Journal of Transitions and Innovation Systems, 4*(1/2), 80–95.

Zwitter, A., & Hazenberg, J. (2020). Decentralized network governance: Blockchain technology and the future of regulation. *Frontiers in Blockchain, 3*, 12. https://doi.org/10.3389/fbloc.2020.00012

The Role of Big Data in Transforming Communities and Shaping the Future

Amelia Ritahani Ismail and Zuraini Zainol

Abstract Big Data plays a central role in the progress and development of society, reshaping the ways in which societies function and determine the future across a variety of industries. Its value from the economic standpoint is evident from its capacity to improve decision-making, enhance economic growth, and raise living standards. Big Data encompasses numerous opportunities and challenges, centered on such points as optimizing project management, fostering socioeconomic development, and data privacy management. It allows better planning because it enables a much more understandable and quicker decision-making experience from which the response time can be reduced and risk management, operational resolutions straightforward. It takes less time for changes to be made and eliminates enterprise-related risks, thereby advancing risk management. The greatest contribution from an economic angle is made to social and economic development, encouraging sustainable development and shedding light on the new perspectives emerging indicators can offer. Nevertheless, successfully realizing the full transformative potential of Big Data implies overcoming certain obstacles and solving numerous ethical issues related to the extensive use of data. To overcome these challenges is critical to ensure that Big Data does make a difference in society and helps to improve the lives of people everywhere.

A. R. Ismail (✉)
Kulliyyah of Information and Communication Technology, International Islamic University Malaysia, Kuala Lumpur, Malaysia
e-mail: amelia@iium.edu.my

Z. Zainol
Department of Computer Science, Universiti Pertahanan Nasional Malaysia, Kuala Lumpur, Malaysia
e-mail: zuraini@upnm.edu.my

L. O. Yesufu, P. N. E. Nohuddin (eds.), *Technology for Societal Transformation*,
https://doi.org/10.1007/978-981-96-1721-0_12

1 Introduction

Big Data is a major driver for the ongoing progress and development of our societies. From helping us make informed choices and decisions to boosting the economy and our general quality of life, Big Data is shaping how we evolve as humans. Big Data also has an enormous influence on our societies and what life will be like for us in the future. That which assists us in forming and managing society should necessarily benefit that same society. Big Data is indeed a unique solution for society, in that it helps society function appropriately and leads to the ultimate economic development and progress of our communities. Due to the variety and amount of data now available both to the governments and to businesses, there is a way for them to create better systems and policies and manage projects. Data used to develop policies and management projects help get the most out of the Big Data's opportunities. Both the public and private entities increasingly effectively manage risks to their projects and improve planning. Overall, it appears to increase the odds of various projects' success developed by various industries and stakeholders. On a larger scale, data also leads to economic growth by smarter decisions made on trade by the governments of all sizes and shapes. Smart trade decisions boost the competitiveness of the various competitors and benefit the overall development that is sustainable and serves to protect the environment and raise living standards.

It is pertinent to emphasize that Big Data has huge implications for society. It enables us to do many things better, such as drive innovation and increase human efficiency in law, economics, and politics. Nevertheless, there is no denying that Big Data certainly has its disadvantages. These problems include various important issues, such as privacy, data security problems and the ethicality of using data. Moreover, the size of Big Data could have a significant effect on how it gets stored, analyzed, and understood. Factors like these could invariably contribute to high levels of inaccuracies and inconsistencies and subsequently lead to misjudgments and biases in the decision-making processes. For all its transformative promise, however, the challenges of Big Data must be addressed equally well. Resolving data privacy and other oversight issues will confirm that Big Data remains as a mechanism in fostering innovation and elevating the quality of life within communities on a global scale.

2 Understanding Big Data

Big Data has become one of the principal sources of modern knowledge, as it affects all industries in general. The data's specific nature is determined by the large quantities of information that are produced rapidly by different and numerous sources. It is necessary to point out that traditional data processing systems cannot effectively process big data. In other words, this type of data is largely characterized by being too big for ordinary systems (Gupta et al., 2014). Such changes in data management have made researchers and organizations innovate data analysis methodologies, thus opening up various opportunities in many industries. The main characteristic features of Big Data are usually referred to as the "three Vs": volume, velocity, and variety, which surpass the capacities of regular databases (Gupta et al., 2014). The data may be of a structured and unstructured form such as written text, video, or illustration taken from social media, smartphones, and the Internet of Things (Taylor-Sakyi, 2016). Big Data facilitates the representation of real-world phenomena through proxies, allowing for predictions based on discerned patterns within the data. Big Data analytics plays a fundamental role in decision-making as it helps a range of organizations, from business to engineering, to get a competitive advantage. Based on the analysis of large data samples, trends and patterns can be detected to provide a basis for implementing more rational decisions. In addition, Big Data is transforming the area of social sciences as large datasets enable researchers to employ new tools to study human behavior, patterns of movement, and a variety of social processes. Thereby, the understanding of events such as the spread of an epidemic has become more profound (Blazquez & Domenech, 2018). It also promotes innovation. Focusing on product development, as enterprises that invest in information technology capabilities and Big Data technologies are more likely to flourish in the creation of innovative products (Niebel et al., 2018).

Despite all the advantages, the adoption of Big Data also comes with a variety of disadvantages and needs to pay attention to. The management of the data lifecycle, the assurance of privacy and security, and the effective representation of Big Data are some of the important concerns of many organizations (Taylor-Sakyi, 2016). Moreover, the inherent complexity of Big Data systems requires specialized designs aimed at optimizing performance within data centers, thereby worsening its application challenges (Jia et al., 2017; Hofstee et al., 2013). The broad potential that Big Data has already been widely recognized in modern society and the technology is utilized in different contexts to improve the preciseness of predictions and analyses (Shiri, 2014). However, despite the numerous benefits associated with big data, it introduces ethical concerns and analytical challenges. Firstly, applications of this methodology require the detection of appropriate patterns and measurement of relevant variables, which becomes a sufficient obstacle in contexts where direct measurement and data collection are infeasible. Additionally, ethical concerns are very prominent in the context of big data; the technology produces a large array of information that allows making numerous informed decisions based on probability. However, Big Data could be a serious source of possible privacy concerns, which might result in the development of sophisticated governance systems that could work out the newly arising ethical problems. To conclude, it is ascertained that Big Data promises to be an enormous innovation; at the same time, however, it brings about many challenges and limitations of its extensive application that must be thoroughly discussed (Gupta et al., 2014).

The processing and analysis of extensive datasets depend on various fundamental technologies that are specifically engineered to reduce the challenges mentioned above. This technology features distributed computing models, intricate storage remedies, machine intelligence strategies, and cloud infrastructure solutions that can assists organization in solving the issues as well making decision as well as learning the future trends. In Big Data, distributed computing architectures serve as the cornerstone for managing extensive data such as Hadoop and MapReduce that provide a distributed storage and processing architecture. Hadoop facilitates the distribution of data across multiple servers, whereas MapReduce permits the parallel processing of extensive datasets through distributed algorithms executed across clusters of computational nodes (Singh & Singla, 2015). Another significant entity is Apache Spark, recognized for its rapidity and ease of use, which is the open-source processing framework that endorses real-time data processing, especially efficient for iterative algorithms and interactive data analytics (Singh & Singla, 2015). Storage Solutions are equally critical for applications involving Big Data as well as NoSQL databases, such as MongoDB and Cassandra, which are meticulously crafted to manage unstructured data, presenting flexible schema frameworks that are ideally suited for Big Data contexts (Warden, 2011). Furthermore, the Hadoop Ecosystem encompasses the Hadoop Distributed File System (HDFS), which delivers scalable storage solutions indispensable for the management of extensive data volumes (Singh & Singla, 2015). The application of MLlib in Spark has enhanced the adoption of machine learning in a Big Data process and provided a wide range of machine learning algorithms which are essential in the machine learning and analytics (Gupta et al., 2017). Hence, organizations are currently merging advance learning paradigms with Big Data technologies and platforms, to increase the productivity of predictive analysis and pattern detection. There are instances in which real-time data processing is required; hence real-time data stream processing tools are required. These tools are beneficial to organizations that require responding to data as it is produced. They present companies with necessary resources that can be used to process data at the source, thus reducing transfer costs and operational. Lastly, Cloud Computing platforms are key components of Big Data analytics as these platforms offer scalable resources that allow enterprises to process data where it resides, reducing data transfer costs and boosting efficiency. The cost-effectiveness and scalability of cloud platforms make them a popular choice for Big Data operations (Berisha et al., 2022).

3 Big Data's Impact on Key Sectors

Big Data is transforming a wide range of sectors by fostering innovation, increasing efficiency, and creating new business opportunities. Its influence spans economic development, healthcare, education, public policy, and environmental sustainability, demonstrating its powerful potential in each domain. In economic, the development of Big Data has become a key driver of business transformation, helping industries such as finance, retail, and manufacturing innovate by enabling better resource management and knowledge sharing. In the digital economy, Big Data is crucial for driving economic growth and fostering innovation. It helps improve competitiveness and resilience by providing the insights needed for informed decision-making and technological advancements (Elgendy & Elragal, 2016). Additionally, Big Data analytics optimize critical operational processes, including supply chain management and inventory control, resulting in cost reductions and greater efficiency (Saibabu et al., 2024).

Big Data has an enormous impact on the scope of healthcare making such things as disease prediction, personalized medicine, and the public health area management to become better than ever. Elaborate analysis of the health data gives a lot of new knowledge that doctors, and medical institutions can use to offer more efficient treatment to their patients (Adeleye et al., 2024). When it comes to the world of public health, it incorporates all the levels from individual measures of people to the global governmental policies that are shaped under the influence of the data analysis findings (Adeleye et al., 2024). In the field of education, Big Data is enhancing learning outcomes by providing data-driven insights that enable more personalized learning experiences. It aids in curriculum development, student performance tracking, and resource allocation, thereby improving both the efficiency and effectiveness of educational systems (Oancea, 2024). Schools and universities are using Big Data to better understand student needs and make informed decisions about teaching methods and educational resources. In the public policy and governance, governments are using it to plan cities more effectively, allocate resources more efficiently, and embark on public safety initiatives. In a bid to ensure that public decision-making and service delivery achieves great efficiency and effectiveness, internet of things will an increasingly important role. To ensures that officials have adaptive systems with which they are able to make quick, cost effective decisions that that will change the way governance has been conducted (Adeleye et al., 2024; Oancea, 2024). When it comes to environmental sustainability, Big Data is playing a critical role in monitoring ecological changes and promoting sustainable practices. It aids in efforts to mitigate climate change, conserve natural resources, and respond to disasters by offering real-time data and predictive analytics that help inform actions and policies (Oancea, 2024).

While Big Data offers many advantages, there are still significant challenges to address, including concerns around data privacy, security, and the digital divide. To fully unlock the potential of Big Data, collaborative efforts and strategic initiatives are essential in overcoming these barriers, ensuring inclusive and sustainable development across all sectors (Adeleye et al., 2024; Yan & Sviridova, 2024).

4 Big Data in Societal Development

Big Data is impacting societal development by improving decision-making, advancing sustainable urban growth, and fostering social engagement. It offers unique prospects to analyze socio-economic tendencies, fine-tune urban blueprints, and assist local agencies. Nevertheless, its inclusion into societal frameworks is not seamless and originates ethical and institutional changes.

4.1 Enhancing Socio-Economic

Big Data can be used as a digital tool for measuring and forecasting socio-economic phenomena in real time. For instance, researchers analyzed human mobility patterns according to mobile phone data and found a significant correlation of mobility diversity to socio-economic phenomena. According to this fact, Big Data can be used for nowcasting socioeconomic development (Pappalardo et al., 2015). Furthermore, by analyzing large-scale social data, such as mobile phone records, the user in society can generate reliable estimates of population density and better understand social structures, helping inform public policy and shape economic strategies.

Urban Systems and Big Data are now becoming a key players in improving urban systems by enhancing how the cities are planned, managed, and governed. It helps city officials make more informed decisions and creates tools to track economic and social activity, which supports goals like sustainability, transparency, and resilience in urban areas (Gupta et al., 2017). With Big Data, cities can gain a better understanding of their dynamics; like how resources are used and where inequalities exist, helping to drive smart city initiatives and address the challenges cities face today (Gupta et al., 2017). The rise of Big Data has revolutionized decision-making across various industries, offering quick insights that enhance efficiency. In sectors such as transportation, energy, and public health, data-driven decisions are leading to improved outcomes and streamlined processes (Golchha, 2015). The ability to process massive amounts of data quickly allows organizations to make real-time decisions, giving them a competitive advantage and fostering innovation (Golchha, 2015).

The role of Big Data in urban planning has led to the rise of "data-driven smart sustainable urbanism," which merges sustainable practices with smart city technology to improve urban performance. This model requires considerable institutional transformation to effectively balance sustainability with the use of data-driven solutions (Bibri, 2021). The existence of Big Data analytics (BDA) is also helpful for the local governments in smart city initiatives, helping them make decisions that improve the quality of life for residents. The success of these initiatives depends on a framework that emphasizes collaboration and information sharing to create public value (Cronemberger & Gil-Garcia, 2019) as well as empowering role for community-based organizations using data analytics (Olvera et al., 2024).

4.2 Challenges and Ethical Considerations

The rapid adoption of Big Data brings with it ethical and societal challenges, such as concerns over privacy and the risk of manipulative technologies. It is essential to uphold principles of human dignity and autonomous decision-making, ensuring that Big Data is used for societal benefit rather than harm (Helbing, 2019). To address these challenges, Europe has proposed a research roadmap aimed at optimizing the use of Big Data for societal good while mitigating risks such as privacy breaches (Cuquet & Fensel, 2018). Despite its potential, Big Data raises concerns about privacy, security, and the possibility of increased surveillance. The constant collection and analysis of data can lead to a form of societal self-control, where individuals are continuously monitored and influenced by data-driven feedback loops. As a result, it is crucial for data scientists and policymakers to collaborate on regulatory frameworks that encourage innovation while protecting individual rights. Such an approach will ensure that Big Data remains a force for positive societal development while addressing its ethical implications. The integration of Big Data into societal development brings both vast opportunities and significant challenges, especially when it comes to ethical concerns. As Big Data increasingly shapes sectors such as education, environmental management, and personal data handling, it raises critical issues around privacy, consent, transparency, and fairness.

Privacy and Consent The first ethical challenge is the very massive scale of data collection and analysis, which arises in the Big Data era. The most significant dilemmas here are the way how the data is mined and integrated, and how organizations show her approach to privacy information. This problem is aggravated by the rapid pace of technological changes since the development of clear rules and strategies has not kept pace with the pace of technological change. Despite the lack of comprehensive research about the ethical issues of each consent to be weighed, ethics frameworks in data science refer to information and privacy standards agreed to shape and maintain best practices (Okorie et al., 2024).

Transparency and Accountability Fostering trust in Big Data systems requires transparency in processing data. Innovations in decentralized data management and policies are being developed to enhance transparency and improve accountability in handling personal data (Asgarinia et al., 2023). Additionally, in such tools as software scraping, where the complexity of the ethics challenges that have arisen has been to ensure adequate consent to data collection or anonymization to protect participants.

Fairness and Bias The third challenge is that Big Data can reinforce fairness and bias. Thus, the most important factor here is that predictive analytics causes serious ethical problems that require a balanced approach to achieving satisfactorily fair outcomes in business and social interaction. One example is education, as the use of AI and Big Data can lead to inequality and scale, which must be avoided. An important conclusion that can be drawn here is that this requires an interconnected approach and a policy framework. The question remains as to why education will be different and what precise market or policy successes can protect any Big Data system (Zaman, 2024).

Regulatory and Ethical Frameworks As the complexities introduced by Big Data grow, the need for global regulatory and ethical frameworks becomes more pressing. These frameworks must guide researchers, policymakers, and practitioners in ethical data handling, while also promoting public involvement in discussions on data ethics (Okorie et al., 2024). Addressing the ethical dilemmas presented by Big Data requires a reevaluation of the ethics of science and technology, an improvement of institutional ethical practices, and the construction of an ethics of responsibility to balance rights and obligations.

Societal and Environmental Impact Big Data has the potential to drive sustainable development and tackle pressing social issues like poverty and inequality. However, issues such as privacy concerns and data quality must be carefully managed to ensure Big Data is used responsibly for social welfare and environmental management (Arumugam et al., 2024). While Big Data offers immense potential for societal growth, these ethical challenges must be addressed through comprehensive regulatory frameworks and ethical standards.

In conclusion, it can be noted that Big Data is a phenomenon that demands a balance between unlocking a vast number of benefits and maintaining its challenges. This balance needs to be continuously sought and considered through discussions and cooperation of all interested parties. As technology develops, so must the way it is assessed ethically in order to maintain Big Data's importance as a positive tool.

5 Conclusion

There is no doubt that Big Data has become one of the core elements of boosting societal progress, changing communities, and shaping the future in societal development. The influence of the idea under analysis is spread across a variety of areas, leading to the development of new means of recording decisions, predicting the consequences of certain strategies, and providing a substation improvement in the quality of life. At the same time, in order to launch the utilization of the idea, one will need to overcome a range of issues, including the problems related to the processes of data governance and privacy. By enabling more advanced decision-making and reducing risks, Big Data technology can significantly impact the future of governments. Private organizations will also gain the benefit of Big Data as it can help them manage risks and improve overall performance. As a result, Big Data will also have an essential value in terms of the advancements in economics and quality life of all people. In conclusion, Big Data is likely to become one of the core sources of competitiveness within the society. However, it is also clear that the wider implementation of Big Data-related technologies is likely to have a range of issues and problems. If not considered, these issues will compromise the overall advantages of Big Data. Thus, it is crucial to address the issue appropriately to ensure that the Big Data is utilized to enhance the overall quality of life within societies and communities on a global scale.

References

Adeleye, R. A., Awonuga, K. F., Ndubuisi, N. L., Oyeyemi, O. P., & Asuzu, O. F. (2024). Reviewing big data's role in the digital economy: USA and Africa focus. *World Journal of Advanced Research and Reviews*. https://doi.org/10.30574/wjarr.2024.21.2.0396

Arumugam, T., Ashifa, K. M., Vinayagalakshmi, V., Kiran, U., & Ramya, S. (2024). Big data in driving greener social welfare and sustainable environmental management. In S. Singh, S. Rajest, S. Hadoussa, A. Obaid, & R. Regin (Eds.), *Data-driven intelligent business sustainability* (pp. 328–343). IGI Global. https://doi.org/10.4018/979-8-3693-0049-7.ch022

Asgarinia, H., Chomczyk Penedo, A., Esteves, B., & Lewis, D. (2023). "Who Should I Trust with My Data?" ethical and legal challenges for innovation in new decentralized data management technologies. *Information, 14*. https://doi.org/10.3390/info14070351

Berisha, B., Mëziu, E., & Shabani, I. (2022). Big data analytics in cloud computing: An overview. *Journal of Cloud Computing, 11*, 24. https://doi.org/10.1186/s13677-022-00301-w

Bibri, S. E. (2021). A novel model for data-driven smart sustainable cities of the future: The institutional transformations required for balancing and advancing the three goals of sustainability. *Energy Informatics, 4*. https://doi.org/10.1186/S42162-021-00138-8

Blazquez, D., & Domenech, J. (2018). Big data sources and methods for social and economic analyses. *Technological Forecasting and Social Change, 130*, 99–113. https://doi.org/10.1016/j.techfore.2017.07.027

Cronemberger, F., & Gil-Garcia, J. R. (2019). Big data and analytics as strategies to generate public value in smart cities: Proposing an integrative framework. In M. P. Rodriguez Bolivar (Ed.), *Setting foundations for the creation of public value in smart cities*. Public Administration and Information Technology. Springer. https://doi.org/10.1007/978-3-319-98953-2_10

Cuquet, M., & Fensel, A. (2018). The societal impact of big data: A research roadmap for Europe. *Technology in Society, 54*, 74–86. https://doi.org/10.1016/j.techsoc.2018.03.005

Elgendy, N., & Elragal, A. (2016). Big data analytics in support of the decision making process. *Procedia Computer Science, 100*, 1071–1084. https://doi.org/10.1016/j.procs.2016.09.251

Golchha, N. (2015). Big data – The information revolution. *International Journal of Applied Research., 1*, 791–794.

Gupta, A., Thakur, H.K., Shrivastava, R., Kumar, P., & Nag, S. (2017). *A big data analysis framework using apache spark and deep learning*. arXiv: Databases.

Gupta, R., Gupta, S., & Singhal, A. (2014). Big data: Overview. *International Journal of Computer Trends and Technology, 9*(5).

Helbing, D. (2019). Societal, economic, ethical and legal challenges of the digital revolution: From big data to deep learning, artificial intelligence, and manipulative technologies. In D. Helbing (Ed.), *Towards digital enlightenment*. Springer. https://doi.org/10.1007/978-3-319-90869-4_6

Hofstee, H. P., Chen, G., Gebara, F. H., Hall, K., Herring, J., Jamsek, D. A., Li, J., Li, Y., Shi, J., & Wong, P. W. Y. (2013). Understanding system design for big data workloads. IBM Journal of Research and Development *57*, 3:1–3:10. https://doi.org/10.1147/JRD.2013.2242674.

Jia, Z., Zhan, J., Wang, L., Luo, C., Gao, W., Jin, Y., Han, R., & Zhang, L. (2017). Understanding big data analytics workloads on modern processors. *IEEE Transactions on Parallel and Distributed Systems, 28*, 1797–1810. https://doi.org/10.1109/TPDS.2016.2625244

Niebel, T., Rasel, F., & Viete, S. (2018). BIG data – BIG gains? Understanding the link between big data analytics and innovation. *Economics of Innovation and New Technology, 28*(3), 296–316. https://doi.org/10.1080/10438599.2018.1493075

Oancea, B. (2024). *Big data in economics*. https://doi.org/10.48550/arxiv.2406.11913

Okorie, G. N., Udeh, C. A., Adaga, E. M., Daraojimba, O. D., & Oriekhoe, O. I. (2024). Ethical considerations in data collection and analysis: A review: Investigating ethical practices and challenges in modern data collection and analysis. *International Journal of Applied Research in Social Sciences, 6*, 1–22. https://doi.org/10.51594/ijarss.v6i1.688

Olvera, R. G., Plagens, C., Ellison, S., Klingler, K., Kuntz, A. K., & Chase, R. P. (2024). Community-engaged data science (CEDS): A case study of working with communities to use data to inform change. *Journal of Community Health, 49*, 1062–1072. https://doi.org/10.1007/s10900-024-01377-y

Pappalardo, L., Pedreschi, D., Smoreda, Z., & Giannotti, F. (2015). Using big data to study the link between human mobility and socio-economic development. In *IEEE International Conference on Big Data (Big Data)* (pp. 871–878). IEEE. https://doi.org/10.1109/BIGDATA.2015.7363835

Saibabu, N., Chappa, M., Chaitanya, N., Das, S., Rao, A. L., & Mallam, M. (2024). Big data: An essential route for creating new business prospects. In *2024 International Conference on Advances in Modern Age Technologies for Health and Engineering Science (AMATHE)* (pp. 1–5). IEEE. https://doi.org/10.1109/AMATHE61652.2024.10582054

Shiri, A. (2014). Making sense of big data: A facet analysis approach. *Knowledge Organization, 41*, 357–367. https://doi.org/10.5771/0943-7444-2014-5-357

Singh, J., & Singla, V. (2015). Big data: Tools and technologies in big data. *International Journal of Computer Applications, 112*, 6–10.

Taylor-Sakyi, K. (2016). *Big data: Understanding big data*. arXiv: Distributed, Parallel, and Cluster Computing.

Warden, P. (2011). *Big data glossary*. O'Reilly Media.

Yan, C., & Sviridova, T. G. (2024). Research on the issues and effects of big data on business economic management. *American Journal of Economics and Business Innovation., 3*, 9–13. https://doi.org/10.54536/ajebi.v3i1.2371

Zaman, B. U. (2024). *Leveraging big data and ai for personalized learning opportunities, challenges, and ethical considerations*. Preprints (Basel). https://doi.org/10.20944/preprints202407.1211.v1.

The Role of Big Data in Societal Development

Rajeeshwaran Moorthy and Belisa Marochi

Abstract Big data has revolutionized various sectors by enabling significant advancements in healthcare, urban planning, and environmental conservation. In healthcare, big data drives predictive analytics, allowing for personalized care, improved disease prevention, and optimized operational efficiency. Notable examples include the Framingham Heart Study, which utilizes historical patient data to identify cardiovascular disease risk factors, and wearable health devices that personalize patient care by analyzing real-time data on physical activity and vital signs.

Urban planning has similarly benefited from big data, as seen in smart city initiatives like Singapore's Smart Nation. By leveraging IoT devices and sensors, cities can optimize traffic flow, manage resources sustainably, and make data-driven urban planning decisions. Such real-time data integration fosters more responsive and efficient city management.

Environmental conservation efforts are also bolstered by big data, which helps monitor climate change and promote sustainability. The World Bank's Climate Change Knowledge Portal exemplifies how aggregated climate data can guide policy-making and adaptation strategies. Precision agriculture, powered by big data, enables farmers to enhance crop yields and minimize environmental impact.

However, the widespread use of big data raises significant ethical and privacy concerns, including data ownership, consent, and bias. Addressing these challenges requires robust data governance frameworks and international collaboration. As big data continues to integrate with AI, machine learning, and blockchain technologies, its potential to drive societal development and achieve the UN Sustainable Development Goals (SDGs) becomes increasingly apparent.

R. Moorthy · B. Marochi (✉)
Hult International Business School, Dubai, UAE
e-mail: rajeeshwaran.moorthy@faculty.hult.edu; belisa.marochi@faculty.hult.edu

L. O. Yesufu, P. N. E. Nohuddin (eds.), *Technology for Societal Transformation*,
https://doi.org/10.1007/978-981-96-1721-0_13

1 Introduction

In recent years, big data has emerged as a cornerstone of innovation and progress, offering unprecedented opportunities to solve complex societal challenges. Defined by its sheer volume, variety, velocity, and veracity, big data refers to large, complex datasets that cannot be processed through traditional data-processing software. As digital transformation accelerates, the ability to capture and analyze massive amounts of information has become crucial for sectors such as healthcare, urban planning, environmental conservation, and beyond (Global Forest Watch, 2024).

The role of big data in societal development is multifaceted. It enables more informed decision-making, uncovers hidden patterns that improve policy-making, and supports efforts to create a more equitable and sustainable future. However, as promising as big data may be, it is also fraught with ethical and privacy concerns. Issues surrounding data ownership, consent, and bias have spurred global debates over how to harness big data responsibly. This chapter delves deeper into how big data is driving societal development, its applications across key sectors, the challenges it faces, and the ethical considerations it raises.

2 Applications of Big Data in Key Sectors

Big data has become a catalyst for innovation in healthcare. By aggregating and analyzing large volumes of data, healthcare providers can now offer more personalized care, improve disease prevention, and optimize operational efficiency (Framingham Heart Study, 2024). One of the most significant contributions of big data to healthcare is its ability to drive predictive analytics, enabling health professionals to anticipate trends and make better clinical decisions.

2.1 Wearables and Big Data: Personalizing Healthcare

The rise of wearable health devices—such as fitness trackers and smartwatches—has further fueled the integration of big data into healthcare. These devices generate massive amounts of data related to an individual's physical activity, heart rate, sleep patterns, and even stress levels. By aggregating data from millions of users, healthcare researchers can identify patterns that help improve general health recommendations and personalize patient care. For instance, Apple's HealthKit and Google Fit have revolutionized how users monitor their health, but the implications go far beyond individual well-being. These platforms aggregate data that public health institutions use to inform large-scale wellness initiatives and policies.

While big data's role in the COVID-19 pandemic management has been widely acknowledged, its use in chronic disease management is equally transformative. In countries like the United States, chronic diseases such as diabetes and heart disease are leading causes of death and impose significant financial burdens on healthcare systems. Through predictive analytics, healthcare providers can analyze historical patient data to identify at-risk populations before diseases manifest, thereby enabling early intervention.

For example, the Framingham Heart Study, one of the longest-running epidemiological studies, has relied heavily on big data to identify risk factors for cardiovascular disease. By collecting and analyzing patient data over decades, the study has provided invaluable insights into how lifestyle, genetics, and other factors contribute to heart disease. Healthcare providers now use such predictive models to target preventive care more effectively, reducing the incidence and severity of chronic diseases.

3 Urban Planning and Smart Cities

The potential of big data to reshape urban landscapes has materialized in the form of smart cities—urban environments that leverage data to enhance efficiency, improve quality of life, and optimize the use of resources. Through the use of sensors, cameras, and IoT devices, cities can now capture real-time data on everything from traffic flow to energy consumption, enabling data-driven urban planning.

3.1 IoT and Big Data for Real-Time Decision-Making

The integration of IoT and big data has led to the rise of real-time decision-making in cities. For example, in Los Angeles, the city's transportation department partnered with Google's Waze app to share data on road closures and traffic conditions. This collaborative effort allowed both the city and its residents to make data-driven decisions regarding traffic routes, reducing congestion during peak hours. Such systems represent a paradigm shift in how cities operate, enabling more responsive and adaptable governance.

Singapore, as an example, stands at the forefront of smart city development with its Smart Nation Initiative. The city-state has deployed a comprehensive network of sensors and data analytics platforms to tackle challenges such as traffic congestion, waste management, and public safety. By analyzing traffic patterns in real time, Singapore has been able to optimize its traffic light systems to reduce wait times and improve the flow of vehicles. Moreover, the city-state's use of IoT in its water management system has reduced water leakage and wastage, ensuring more sustainable use of resources (Government of Singapore, 2014).

Beyond traffic and water management, Singapore has integrated big data into its urban planning processes. By analyzing data from construction, land use, and housing trends, the government can predict the future demands for infrastructure, allowing for proactive development. This data-centric approach has enabled Singapore to maintain its status as a global leader in urban innovation.

4 Environmental Conservation and Sustainability

As the world grapples with climate change and environmental degradation, big data is playing an instrumental role in promoting sustainable development. From tracking wildlife populations to monitoring deforestation and reducing carbon footprints, big data has become a powerful tool for environmental conservation.

4.1 Precision Agriculture: Big Data for Sustainability

Big data is also revolutionizing agriculture by enabling farmers to optimize resource usage and minimize environmental impact. Through the use of precision agriculture, farmers can use big data to monitor soil conditions, crop health, and weather patterns, allowing them to apply water, fertilizer, and pesticides more efficiently. Platforms like Climate FieldView, which collects data from tractors, drones, and satellites, have enabled farmers to increase yields while reducing resource use. This data-driven approach to farming is critical as the global population grows, and the demand for food increases, placing pressure on land and water resources (The Climate Corporation, 2024).

In 2019, the World Bank launched its Climate Change Knowledge Portal (CCKP), a platform that aggregates climate-related data from various sources, including satellite imagery, national meteorological services, and international climate organizations. The portal provides governments, NGOs, and businesses with access to real-time climate data, allowing for more informed decision-making regarding adaptation and mitigation strategies. In particular, developing nations that lack the resources to conduct climate research can use the CCKP's data to shape policies and access funding for climate resilience projects.

5 Ethical Considerations and Data Privacy

The promise of big data to drive societal development is tempered by significant concerns about privacy, security, and ethics. As more data is collected and shared, particularly in sensitive sectors like healthcare and finance, the potential for misuse grows. Governments, businesses, and individuals must grapple with questions surrounding data ownership, consent, and bias.

5.1 Data Bias and Ethical Algorithms

One of the most pressing ethical concerns surrounding big data is the potential for bias in algorithms. Data analytics often rely on historical datasets that can reflect societal biases—such as racial, gender, or economic inequalities—leading to biased outcomes. For instance, AI-driven recruitment platforms have faced criticism for reinforcing gender and racial biases in hiring decisions due to biased historical data. To address these concerns, researchers and developers are working to create more transparent algorithms and diversify the datasets used in analytics.

Bias in healthcare algorithms has also drawn attention, particularly when it comes to predictive analytics. A well-known example involved an AI algorithm used to predict which patients would benefit from additional healthcare services. The algorithm favored wealthier, predominantly white patients over lower-income, predominantly minority patients because it used healthcare spending as a proxy for need, failing to account for socio-economic disparities in healthcare access. Addressing these biases is critical to ensuring that big data serves all sectors of society equitably.

5.2 Data Privacy and Security in the Age of Big Data

Another significant challenge is data privacy, particularly as big data analytics often involves processing sensitive personal information. In the European Union, the General Data Protection Regulation (GDPR) has set stringent rules on how data can be collected, stored, and used, particularly with respect to consent. However, not all countries have robust data protection laws, and even where regulations exist, enforcement can be difficult.

Anonymizing data is one way to address privacy concerns, but even anonymized datasets can be vulnerable to re-identification. For instance, researchers have shown that it is possible to re-identify individuals in anonymized healthcare datasets by cross-referencing them with other publicly available data sources. As more data becomes available online, the challenge of protecting individuals' privacy while enabling the beneficial use of big data becomes increasingly complex.

A central tension in the use of big data is the trade-off between maximizing the utility of data and protecting individual privacy. The more detailed the data, the greater its potential utility for societal development, but also the greater the risk to individual privacy. For example, detailed health data can enable groundbreaking medical research, but it also exposes individuals to privacy violations if not handled properly. Finding the right balance between these competing interests is critical for ensuring the ethical use of big data.

6 Challenges and Limitations in the Adoption of Big Data

While big data holds significant promise, its adoption is not without challenges. In many parts of the world, particularly in developing nations, the infrastructure necessary to collect, store, and analyze big data is lacking. The digital divide remains a major barrier to the widespread adoption of big data technologies.

The ability to generate and analyze big data requires advanced digital infrastructure, including high-speed internet, cloud computing platforms, and sophisticated data analytics tools. However, many developing nations lack these resources, limiting their capacity to fully engage with the potential of big data. For instance, while countries like the United States, Singapore, and China have invested heavily in smart cities, precision agriculture, and big data healthcare systems, nations in sub-Saharan Africa and parts of Southeast Asia are often constrained by poor internet connectivity, inadequate technological infrastructure, and limited access to data.

6.1 Data Quality and Standardization

Another challenge in the widespread adoption of big data is the issue of data quality. Data that is incomplete, outdated, or poorly formatted can lead to misleading analyses and erroneous conclusions. Inconsistent data standards between organizations and industries further complicate the effective sharing and analysis of data. For example, healthcare data in one country might be formatted differently from healthcare data in another, making it difficult to conduct large-scale, cross-border analyses.

To address these challenges, initiatives like Open Data Standards aim to create consistent frameworks for data collection, storage, and sharing across different sectors. Standardization efforts can improve data quality, enhance interoperability between systems, and increase the overall utility of big data for societal development. The International Organization for Standardization (ISO) has also introduced standards related to data management and big data to foster global collaboration and data-sharing practices.

In Kenya, for example, efforts have been made to bridge the digital divide through initiatives like the Konza Technopolis, a planned smart city aimed at fostering innovation, particularly in information and communication technology (ICT). The Konza project is designed to attract global tech companies and enhance Kenya's big data capabilities. However, it faces challenges, such as ensuring access to technology in rural areas where most Kenyans live. Addressing this rural–urban divide is crucial to ensuring that the benefits of big data reach all sectors of society (Konza Technopolis Development Authority, 2024).

Similarly, the M-Pesa mobile banking platform, launched in Kenya, leverages big data to provide financial services to millions of people who were previously unbanked. M-Pesa's success highlights the potential for big data to drive development in regions with limited infrastructure, but it also demonstrates the importance of building inclusive systems that are accessible to everyone (Safaricom, 2007).

6.2 Cost and Resource Intensity

Processing and analyzing big data requires substantial computational power and resources, which can be costly. Cloud computing platforms such as Amazon Web Services (AWS), Microsoft Azure, and Google Cloud have made it easier for organizations to access the resources needed to process big data, but these services are still out of reach for many smaller organizations, particularly in the non-profit and public sectors.

In addition to the cost of data storage and processing, there is the challenge of data security. Protecting sensitive data from cyberattacks, data breaches, and other forms of digital exploitation is a growing concern. Recent high-profile breaches in the healthcare and financial sectors underscore the need for stronger cybersecurity measures, which often come with significant costs.

6.3 Talent and Skill Shortage

Big data analytics requires specialized skills, including knowledge of data science, machine learning, and advanced statistical methods. The global shortage of data scientists and data engineers has made it difficult for many organizations to fully capitalize on big data. This skills gap is especially pronounced in developing nations, where education systems may not yet provide adequate training in data analytics and related fields.

6.4 Legal and Regulatory Hurdles

The legal landscape surrounding big data is evolving rapidly. Governments are struggling to keep pace with the rapid development of data technologies, leading to regulatory uncertainty. In many countries, existing laws around data privacy, intellectual property, and data ownership are outdated and inadequate to address the complexities of big data.

One of the most comprehensive international legal frameworks for data protection is the European Union's General Data Protection Regulation (GDPR), which imposes strict rules on how organizations can collect, store, and use personal data. While GDPR has set a global standard, many nations, particularly in the developing world, lack similar regulatory frameworks. In the absence of clear legal guidelines, organizations are left navigating a complex web of international regulations, which can slow down the adoption of big data technologies.

7 Future Prospects of Big Data in Societal Development

The future of big data in societal development is promising, particularly as new technologies such as artificial intelligence (AI), machine learning (ML), and blockchain become more integrated with data analytics. These technologies will enhance the power of big data, enabling more precise predictions, faster decision-making, and greater transparency (Knewton, 2024).

AI and ML technologies are already transforming the way big data is analyzed. By automating the data analysis process, AI allows for real-time insights into complex datasets. This is particularly useful in areas like predictive healthcare, where AI algorithms can quickly analyze patient data and recommend treatment plans based on patterns that may be invisible to human doctors.

In the realm of urban planning, AI-driven data analytics are being used to predict future population trends, enabling governments to plan infrastructure projects more efficiently. Machine learning algorithms are also improving the accuracy of climate models, helping policymakers craft more effective strategies to combat climate change.

Blockchain technology offers a potential solution to some of the security and privacy concerns surrounding big data. By creating decentralized, tamper-proof records of data transactions, blockchain can ensure that data remains secure and unaltered. This has significant implications for sectors like healthcare, where the integrity of patient data is crucial, and in finance, where blockchain is already being used to enhance the security of transactions.

Additionally, blockchain can help address the issue of data ownership. By creating transparent records of who owns and controls data, blockchain can give individuals more control over their personal information. In the future, this technology could be integrated with big data platforms to create more secure, decentralized data systems that protect individual privacy while enabling large-scale data analysis.

7.1 The Role of Big Data in UN Sustainable Development Goals

Big data will play a crucial role in achieving the United Nations Sustainable Development Goals (SDGs) by 2030. From eradicating poverty and hunger to promoting sustainable cities and combating climate change, data-driven insights are essential for making progress across the SDG agenda.

For example, the examples in this article show how big data can help governments track progress on SDG 3 (Good Health and Well-being) by providing real-time data on disease outbreaks and healthcare access. In the realm of SDG 11 (Sustainable Cities and Communities), big data is already being used to monitor air quality, manage waste, and optimize energy usage in cities. Similarly, for SDG 13 (Climate Action), big data plays a vital role in monitoring global emissions, predicting the impact of climate change, and assessing the effectiveness of mitigation efforts. These are only some of the goals that big data can contribute to in this development (World Bank, 2024).

As nations work toward these goals, the ability to collect and analyze data will become increasingly important. Big data offers the insights necessary to make informed decisions, allocate resources efficiently, and measure progress on a global scale.

8 Conclusion

Big data is poised to be one of the most transformative forces of the twenty-first century, offering unprecedented opportunities to improve healthcare, streamline urban planning, protect the environment, and foster economic growth. However, realizing the full potential of big data requires overcoming significant challenges related to infrastructure, data quality, privacy, and ethics (General Data Protection Regulation (GDPR), 2018).

As the use of big data expands, it is essential for governments, businesses, and civil society to collaborate on creating robust data governance frameworks that protect individual rights while enabling innovation. Addressing these challenges will allow societies to harness the power of big data to drive positive social change, reduce inequalities, and achieve the UN SDGs.

Looking forward, the integration of big data with emerging technologies like AI, machine learning, and blockchain will further enhance its potential, creating a future in which data-driven insights are central to solving the world's most pressing challenges. By fostering a global ecosystem of data sharing, transparency, and ethical responsibility, we can ensure that big data serves as a force for good in the years to come.

References

Global Forest Watch. (2024). Global Forest Watch. https://www.globalforestwatch.org

Framingham Heart Study. (2024). Framingham Heart Study. https://www.framinghamheartstudy.org

Government of Singapore. (2014). Smart Nation Singapore. https://www.smartnation.gov.sg

General Data Protection Regulation (GDPR). (2018). GDPR.eu. https://gdpr.eu

World Bank. (2024). Climate Change Knowledge Portal. https://climateknowledgeportal.worldbank.org
The Climate Corporation. (2024). Climate FieldView. https://climate.com/fieldview
Knewton. (2024). Adaptive Learning Technology. https://www.knewton.com
Safaricom. (2007). M-Pesa Mobile Banking. https://www.safaricom.co.ke/personal/m-pesa
Konza Technopolis Development Authority. (2024). Konza Technopolis. https://www.konzacity.go.ke

A Framework for Bridging the Digital Divide: Improving Connectivity and Opportunities in Rural Malaysia

Puteri Nor Ellyza Nohuddin, Zahidah AbdKadir, and Nora Azima Noordin

Abstract The digital divide between urban and rural Malaysia is a serious barrier in accessing core services, education, and economic opportunities for rural communities. This study addresses this challenge through the assessment of key national initiatives, such as the National Fiberisation and Connectivity Plan and Jalinan Digital Negara. These initiatives go a long way in trying to bridge this gap, but affordability, generally limited infrastructure, and a lack of digital literacy in the less privileged parts of the world are some problems that it may continue to encounter. This study, therefore, tries to explore how such programs have been effectively implemented to enhance digital connectivity and which ones still require further development. It identifies real-life examples and practical interventions aimed at the development of ways through which digital access can be widened, digital literacy enhanced, and community involvement developed. The solutions are to address the exact challenges that rural populations face, especially in those areas bounded by difficult topography. Hence, the study has called for collaborative efforts in investment targeted at policy reforms that ensure sustainable digital growth in rural Malaysia. It also calls for community-driven initiatives to make an inclusive digital ecosystem possible; here, rural residents would be at the heart of driving their full participation in the digital economy. It thus contributes to the ongoing efforts of bridging the digital divide with practical recommendations on infrastructure improvements, digital literacy, and inclusivity that are imperative for socio-economic development relevant to Malaysia and improvement in the quality of life in the rural settings.

P. N. E. Nohuddin (✉)
Institute of Visual Informatics, Universiti Kebangsaan Malaysia, Bangi, Malaysia

Higher Colleges of Technology, Sharjah, United Arab Emirates
e-mail: puteri.ivi@ukm.edu.my

Z. AbdKadir · N. A. Noordin
Higher Colleges of Technology, Sharjah, United Arab Emirates
e-mail: zabdkadir@hct.ac.ae; nazima@hct.ac.ae

L. O. Yesufu, P. N. E. Nohuddin (eds.), *Technology for Societal Transformation*,
https://doi.org/10.1007/978-981-96-1721-0_14

1 Introduction

In the digital economy, digital connectivity has been considered an important facilitator of economic progress, education, and social inclusion (Liu, 2021). However, rural communities continue to face high challenges in accessing digital access despite dwelling in Malaysia (Samsuddin et al., 2021a); this has created an apparent urban–rural divide in terms of its access disparity. This not only dampens the economic potential of the communities but also dampens their potential in accessing basic services and opportunities brought about by digital platforms (Dawood, 2019; Gao & Li, 2024). Closing this digital gap requires an improvement in infrastructure, along with addressing different aspects and factors related to technology, accessibility, and socio-economic inequities.

Improvement of rural connectivity has been identified by the Malaysian government, among other stakeholders, in terms of the comprehensive development of the country. Initiatives such as the National Fiberisation and Connectivity Plan (NFCP), which aims to provide high-speed broadband access to 98% of populated areas by 2023, and Jalinan Digital Negara (JENDELA), a national digital connectivity plan launched in 2020 to improve mobile broadband coverage and quality, have been proposed for better internet infrastructure and expanded services online (Gong, 2023). These services have been progressing gradually, however, most rural communities are still lag behind compared to metropolitan areas in terms of access to the internet, speed, and digital literacy (Gong, 2023). The Malaysian government has set ambitious goals to bridge the rural–urban digital gap, aiming to ensure that at least 50% of rural areas have 5G coverage by mid-2024, with a target of 85% by the end of 2023 (Tomás, 2023). However, achieving these targets will require coordinated efforts from various stakeholders, including the government, telecommunications companies, and local communities (Gong, 2023).

This would be bettered through an integrated approach to digital connectivity that will go beyond upgrading of infrastructure to technology adoption, digital literacy, and creation of local content. Through research, it is found that rural communities—even those with low literacy rates—read digitally mainly through smartphones. This underscores the need for digital literacy initiatives for developing a reading culture and self-development in citizens (Samsuddin et al., 2021b). Programs such as the National Reading Decade, 2021–2030, have been inspired to create such a reading culture considered critical in narrowing the digital gap (Samsuddin et al., 2021a). Digital literacy enables rural populations to contribute toward narrowing the gap by facilitating their access and participation in the use of information to live meaningfully in a digitized society (Samsuddin et al., 2021a, 2021b). Not only will the role of leading specific strategies help ensure that the digital initiatives are relevant and accessible, but by engaging local communities in their implementation, it catalyzes a more inclusive digital ecosystem: one that truly empowers rural residents to be integrated into the wide socio-economic framework.

This paper therefore seeks to inquire into the current state of digital connectivity in rural Malaysia with the view to assessing the effectiveness of active programs and making practical recommendations toward ensuring greater inclusivity. The paper will discuss the challenges and opportunities of the current situation for a deeper understanding of how certain interventions can narrow the gap in access to digital technologies and help contribute to long-term development in rural areas. With these key concerns addressed, Malaysia would go a long way in ascertaining how equal a digital future for all her populations would be.

The paper is structured as follows: In Sect. 2, the chapter discusses on the digital recourses and incentives for the rural digital development in Malaysia. Section 3 elaborates the framework and methodology of the framework development and validation. Section 4 presents the expected outcome from the proposed digital gap assessment framework. Lastly, Sect. 5 is a conclusion of the paper.

2 Literature Review

2.1 Historical Context and Current Landscape

The digital divide is the gap between individuals and communities who have the resources to access digital technologies and those who do not. This has been exacerbated by factors that include, but are not limited to, geography and socio-economic status. The development of the internet has almost always favored urban centers with superior infrastructure and greater economic investment, leaving rural areas far behind. Such inequality in access turns into unequal connectivity and technology use in which rural communities suffer from a lack of proper digital resources, further promoting disparities in educational opportunities, jobs, and social participation. Numerous studies have revealed certain observable consequences of the digital divide in rural populations. Specifically, this encompasses the consequences of limited access to online learning classes, obstacles in communication speed, and disparities in skills between various age groups, especially between young and old individuals (Dawood, 2019; Devisakti et al., 2023; Fang et al., 2022).

This gap is reflected in the data of recent studies. According to a publication by Malaysia Digital Economy Corporation, while 92% of urban households have access to the Internet, rural household connectivity stands at only 68%. This is particularly extreme for women, since a mere 58% of rural women are connected to the Internet, compared to 84% of urban women. For example, smartphone ownership is considerably low in rural areas, standing at only 62% of rural households having smartphones, compared to 92% in urban areas (Malaysia Digital Economy Corporation (MDEC), 2022). These statistics put into light a wider context where, generally, rural communities face significant barriers to accessing and benefiting from digital technologies.

Additionally, OpenSignal discovered a significant increase in long-term evolution (LTE) data use in Malaysia after the implementation of the COVID-19 lockdown. Increasingly, both urban and rural communities rely on LTE mobile coverage for broadband connectivity to facilitate their everyday activities. Considering this increasing dependence, the Malaysian Communications and Multimedia Commission (MCMC) has established an objective to attain complete LTE coverage in all densely populated regions by 2025, as specified in the national master plan, Jendela (Marzuki et al., 2023).

2.2 *Efforts to Improve Internet Access in Malaysia*

Efforts at improving internet access have been at the core of Malaysia's strategy in pursuit of increased digital inclusion and socio-economic development. The role that digital connectivity continues to play in fostering growth has thus seen both the government of Malaysia and other stakeholders initiating numerous projects toward expanding internet access. In particular, this involves extending internet access to many rural areas listed below. The Malaysian Communications Minister, Fahmi Fadzil, announced that, for Budget 2025, the focus of the ministry would be to improve Internet access at schools and higher learning institutions. He emphasized that the ministry was putting in place measures that would ensure students enjoy the best form of Internet connectivity. The increased effort aims at ensuring optimum Internet access within buildings and at compound areas of these institutions (Zailani, 2024).

2.2.1 National Fiberisation and Connectivity Plan (NFCP)

The earlier initiative to expand internet access in Malaysia is perhaps the National Fiberisation and Connectivity Plan that was launched in 2019. NFCP improves the quality and scope of internet infrastructure in the country. It places emphasis on the need to develop better broadband connectivity by expanding the fiber optic network to improve broadband in general. It includes ambitious targets to increase fiber coverage and reduce the costs of high-speed internet, especially in rural and underserved areas (Malaysian Communications and Multimedia Commission (MCMC), n.d.).

Based on the National Fiberisation and Connectivity Plan, their task objective is to decrease pricing for broadband services to 1% of gross national income in Malaysia by the year 2020. The target is to provide internet speeds of up to 500 Mbps to premises in state capitals, high-impact areas, and designated industrial zones. Most important, it promises broadband speeds of up to 500 Mbps for 20% of buildings in suburban and rural areas and fiber extension to 70% of schools, government offices, hospitals, and police stations by 2022. They take the ambition of achieving an average broadband speed of 30 Mbps in 98% of the most densely populated areas by the year 2023. The plan is funded by the USP budget and the capital expenditure of Malaysian telecommunications providers in the ratio of 50% contribution from the former. Therefore, the key objective of NFCP is to close the gap between rural and urban divides through investment in infrastructure and encouraging service providers to apply competition principles (Malaysian Communications and Multimedia Commission (MCMC), n.d.).

2.2.2 Jalinan Digital Negara (JENDELA)

Building on the NFCP, the Jalinan Digital Negara (JENDELA) initiative, introduced in 2020, further aims to accelerate the expansion of digital infrastructure. JENDELA is designed to improve the quality and reach of mobile and broadband services, with specific goals to enhance 4G coverage and prepare for 5G deployment. The initiative targets the upgrade of existing networks and the expansion of connectivity in remote areas. The implementation of the JENDELA project is structured into several stages, with the initial phase spanning from 2020 to 2022. The objectives of the project are to increase 4G coverage from 91.8% to 96.9% and to improve mobile broadband speeds from 25 Mbps to 35 Mbps. In addition, the program seeks to guarantee that 83% of properties in Malaysia have access to high-speed fixed broadband, through the implementation of measures to enhance 4G networks and extend fiber optic infrastructure. Phase 2 of the project would emphasize the complete implementation of 5G technology, in line with the objectives of the 12th Malaysia Plan, to further improve digital connectivity across the entire country (Malaysia Communications and Multimedia Commission (MCMC), n.d.; Malaysian Communications and Multimedia Commission (MCMC), 2022). By focusing on both infrastructure upgrades and technological advancements, JENDELA is a comprehensive approach to improving internet access and bridging the digital divide.

2.2.3 Rural Internet Connectivity Programs

In addition to national plans, various rural-specific programs have been implemented to address the unique challenges faced by remote communities. The irregular topography and dispersed population of rural and remote areas make the construction of highways, power lines, and data transmission lines hard to carry out. Similarly, providing internet connectivity to the underserved groups is challenging due to rugged landscapes and dense forests, which lead to high costs for laying fiber optic lines. The following are some of the initiatives taken to facilitate last-mile connectivity in countryside or remote areas. These include community internet centers, shared signal receivers for public wireless internet access, broadband over power lines, fixed wireless broadband solutions, satellite internet, and self-managed community networks. No one solution can erase the digital divide owing to variations in community needs and geography. What is required is a multi-point strategy underpinned by agile policy options and flexible regulation (Vassilakopoulou & Hustad, 2023).

According to research conducted by Khazanah Research Institute (Gong, 2023), three primary policy suggestions are put up in pursuit of this objective. Firstly, the

Universal Service Provision (USP) Fund will be expanded to enable non-profit organizations that operate in rural and remote areas to aid with last-mile connectivity projects. Furthermore, the advancement of community-led networks as a viable alternative for last-mile connectivity enables local groups to get control over their internet infrastructure. Furthermore, the incorporation of user-generated network evaluations into USP policies is crucial to guarantee the efficiency and flexibility of connection solutions. The objective of these strategies is to promote inclusiveness and fairness in reducing the digital gap.

2.2.4 Digital Literacy and Skills Development

Efforts to improve internet access are complemented by initiatives focused on digital literacy and skills development. This is further supported by the range of digital literacy and skill-building programs. A series of programs in place includes Digital Skills Training and multiple outreach projects to the community for bettering rural citizens' digital competencies. These programs would empower residents with knowledge and competencies needed for basic digital proficiency, safety online, and electronic commerce so that improved connectivity translates into tangible benefits for individuals and communities. It also means inherently that long-term digital inclusion provides rural populations with the skills needed to access and use various forms of digital technologies. In practice, community development projects in Malaysia are coordinated through the collaboration of various stakeholders, including the government, social organizations, the private sector, and non-governmental organizations. Many initiatives are jointly conducted by these parties to benefit local communities (Abiddin et al., 2022). In 2023, the Penang State Government, in collaboration with Maxis, introduced an initiative aimed at improving digital literacy through education and skill development among residents and students throughout the state. This initiative seeks to enhance educational experiences and prepare students with essential competencies for the digital era (Penang State Government and Maxis, 2024).

2.3 Innovative Technologies for Digital Transformation and Rural Communities in Malaysia

It is innovative technologies that play a critical role in helping to bridge the digital divide and further enable digital transformation in Malaysian rural communities by addressing unique challenges of remote areas and opening up new avenues of connectivity and digital engagement.

2.3.1 Satellite Internet

Till now, satellite internet is the most viable option that extends connectivity in these areas, as well as rural and isolated areas where building the infrastructure is extremely cumbersome. It makes use of satellite networks to provide high-speed access to the internet without depending on the large ground-based systems of traditional internet connections. Yet while early versions did suffer from extreme delays in the length of time it takes data to travel up and back from space, this has somewhat been overcome with newer technologies. A clear line of sight to the sky is still required in order to transmit data effectively—a potential problem for communities in heavy interior areas and on overcast weather. Satellite internet in Malaysia would open up connectivity options through geographical barriers, even to the most isolated communities in Malaysia. Such projects undertaken include the Malaysian government's deal with international satellite providers to deploy satellite internet solutions in underserved regions, therefore improving digital inclusion. Satellite internet services form part of a big government initiative to promote connectivity in Bawang Asan, a rural village in Sarawak, in collaboration with Measat Global Berhad, the Malaysian premier provider of satellite solutions—a proof that the government is determined to close the digital gap across the country's most remote communities (Asia Digital News, 2021). This deal has made high-speed internet possible even at the most unreachable areas, proving that satellite technology is crucially important in locations where conventional infrastructure can never be reasonably set up.

Additionally, MCMC also played its role in the extension of satellite connectivity to most parts of the country. It has called for the installation and provision of broadband access services via satellite, particularly for those remote areas in both Sabah and Sarawak. This includes the Orang Asli settlements in Peninsular Malaysia and also the more inaccessible areas of Sabah and Sarawak, where the deployment of public cellular services and mobile broadband is foreseen to be quite a while yet due to the relatively low population density and difficult geographical terrain. There are 178 locations or 21% in Peninsular Malaysia, 138 or 17% in Sabah, and 523 or 62% in Sarawak (MCMC, 2021).

2.3.2 Fixed Wireless Broadband

Fixed wireless broadband uses radio signals to provide high-speed internet access instead of physical cables. This can be more cost-effective, much faster to deploy, and especially useful in tricky areas of terrain. Fixed wireless broadband has been deployed in Malaysia as an alternate means of Internet access for rural communities by installing a base station that communicates with wireless receivers installed in homes and businesses (Hassan et al., 2021). This, in turn, expands coverage while reducing costs and minimizing the time required for laying physical infrastructure. For example, in Montana, people use fixed wireless access to reach the internet. This, in turn, allows for the conducting of a financial analysis of equipment costs and adoption rates against market share. With this analysis, the rural Wi-Fi networks can support themselves profitably. Based on this analysis, it appears this network would be able to cover its own costs and earn a profit and could be one feasible alternative for rural access to the internet (Zhang & Wolff, 2004). It also helped with the telemedicine aspect of medical access in rural areas. Fixed wireless access also made video conferencing possible between the hospitals and medical colleges in Hating, Vietnam. It furthered health and education. The fixed wireless technology also helped the developing countries narrow the digital gap (Rully et al., 2005). These above areas are a testament to the ways fixed wireless technology enhanced health and education in remote places and Internet access. Fixed wireless access contributes to narrowing the digital divide in the case of difficult terrains where it is impossible to have wired infrastructure by offering an affordable and quick-deployment solution. Its contribution includes, with this growing technology, helping the people of unserved communities with better living standards.

2.3.3 Community Networks

It is the grassroots initiative in digital connectivity developed by locals for the needs and aspirations of the community. They offer localized Internet services using mesh networking and Wi-Fi hotspots. Successful models of community networks in Malaysia point toward how local solutions could solve the issue of connectivity. Community-driven initiatives have played an important role in fostering affordable and reliable Internet Service Providers for underserved populations in remote areas. CoERI at Universiti Malaysia Sarawak pioneered an ambitious project offering access to the Internet for one of the most remote communities in Malaysia, the Kelabit Highlands in Borneo. Part of Malaysia's pilot program, the e-Bario project connected remote villages using wireless and mesh networking. This project gave an isolated community access to the Internet, improving communication, education, healthcare, and information. Satellite systems, Wi-Fi hotspots, and mesh networks have been deployed to bridge this rural divide. For addressing the power supply problem of rural equipment, solar power systems utilized the advantage of sunlight throughout the year in this region (Ab-Hamid et al., 2011). Another example, when the Salvadoran Ministry of Education could not afford to provide Internet access to schools in rural areas, the University of El Salvador Electrical Engineering Department began testing a number of communication technologies, including WiMax, satellite, and Wi-Fi, in order to improve internet access. They solved that with a low-cost Wi-Fi mesh network. First connection—using bamboo poles—allowed basic voice communication despite poor infrastructure. This community network project took part in solving the problem of rural connectivity (Eugenio, 2016).

Ideally, community networks address the digital divide in rural and underserved areas through low-cost, locally driven solutions. Community-driven projects demonstrate how to enhance internet access, communication, and basic services through mesh networking and Wi-Fi hotspots innovatively. Projects show how connectivity issues can be overcome by spearheading community efforts toward enabling digital inclusion even in the farthest areas.

2.3.4 Mobile Solutions and 5G Technology

This can be made possible through the deployment of 5G networks. Compared to the previous type, 5G has faster data speed and even lower latency, while network capacity is improved to handle a wide range of applications—from sophisticated telemedicine to smart agriculture. The launching of 5G in Malaysia forms part of a wider strategy aimed at increasing connectivity to allow the new set of digital services for the benefit of rural communities. In 2021, the Malaysian government established Digital Nasional Berhad to deploy a nationwide Single Wholesale Network for 5G coverage (Johan, 2023). The government has ascertained that a minimum of 85% of rural areas would be under 5G coverage by the end of 2024. However, the remaining 15%, comprising mountainous areas, is quite a challenge to achieve. More should be done in terms of bridging the divide between rural and urban areas, since infrastructure development in rural areas is still considerably behind those in urban centers. The government realizes this gap is important to them and sees substantial advantages of delivering healthcare opportunities through improved connectivity. With such capabilities of 5G, such as lightning-fast speed, ultra-low latency, and massive connectivity, applications of telemedicine, remote patient monitoring, and medical imaging can apply the usage efficiently. Telecommunication solutions and providers are ready to change the face of healthcare in Malaysia. Using the various 5G capabilities, healthcare providers will be able to provide quality medical services remotely while improving access to medical services mainly in under-resourced areas (Review, 2024).

Despite such challenges, the Malaysian government is committed to increasing coverage and co-ordination to advance connectivity (Tomás, 2023). Poor infrastructure development has led to generally very poor high-speed internet access in rural and remote areas of Malaysia. Such initiatives by the government and public–private partnerships do, however, hold great promise in expanding the 5G infrastructure and advancing digital inclusion as a guarantee that nobody is left behind in the revolution of digital healthcare. This is particularly critical in rural areas, where significant investment in broadband infrastructure development is needed, along with subsidized internet access for underserved communities and encouragement for telecommunication companies to ensure equitable and widespread deployment. With 5G infrastructure development, the door will swing wide open for rural communities to benefit from higher-order digital solutions and ultimately access connectivity. This indicates economic development, which spirals upward to mean social development. By integrating 5G infrastructure, rural communities can benefit from advanced digital solutions and greater connectivity, paving the way for economic and social development.

2.3.5 Digital Literacy and Skills Development Platforms

New technologies are also being utilized for the development of better digital literacy and skill development. E-learning platforms and mobile apps are serving as mediums for delivering training and resources to rural villages, thereby enabling the development of essential digital skills. Additionally, programs involving virtual reality and augmented reality introduce them to novel learning and, therefore, greater interest and acceptance in digital learning. The latter are implemented in Malaysia to provide training in basic digital skills, online safety, and e-commerce to equip rural residents in the use of new technologies for full engagement in the digital economy.

The Malaysian Government has targeted, through both the National Broadband Plan and the Rural Connectivity Program, an increase in the internet usage rate in rural areas, seeing that only 24.4% of rural households currently use the internet (Hashim et al., 2011). For instance, Sabah is the state with the lowest fixed broadband penetration rate in Malaysia, while Sarawak is relatively higher but low compared to most other states. This indicates a digital divide in the broad accessibility of rural areas and therefore may challenge the approach of digital literacy for social inclusion among rural communities.

The findings show that only 5.2% of the Semai tribe in Perak are computer literate (Ayob et al., 2022). This shows the huge digital divide in this minority within the rural settings. Policymakers therefore have an important role to play in developing technology and policies of social inclusion that avail opportunities for accessing digital resources and tools to develop citizens. Computer training, without formal education, should be emphasized whereby information literacy development will lead to the gradual rise in the usage of e-service. Improvement in information literacy competencies can make sure that more citizens of Malaysia become digitally competent.

With these programs, increasing rural ICT infrastructure and literacy aim at connecting all Malaysians to the broadband network. The objectives include access to the Internet and digital literacy among rural populations. As the programs began, there has been slow progress. Due to the lack of awareness and digital skills, the technology adoption is slow; the ICT users and professionals in the rural areas are lagging in digital awareness and skills. Some residents are uninformed about the benefits that come along with digital connectivity and hence further limiting the infrastructure improvements. Also, economic incentives for service providers to invest in these areas aren't motivating, and this slows progress. A study has also been conducted on the factors influencing ICT adoption among SMEs, utilizing a similar framework to address both internal and external barriers to enhancing digital connectivity and opportunities in rural Malaysia [47]. As a result of having no profitable business case, the less populated and more difficult areas are rarely served by telecommunications companies. It is these barriers that, if addressed, ensure successful government efforts in bridging the digital gap (Malaysia Digital Economy Blueprint, 2021).

Each technology helps rural Malaysians transform digitally: satellite internet, fixed wireless broadband, community networks, 5G, and digital literacy platforms. These technologies solve connectivity and access gaps that can bring scalable and effective digital divide solutions. Rural areas will benefit from continued investment in and deployment of these technologies by Malaysia through better connectivity, enhanced digital inclusion, and more development opportunities.

3 Framework of Digital Divide Assessment

In this study, it aims to develop an assessment framework to evaluate the effectiveness of strategies aimed at bridging the digital divide. Figure 1 illustrates the proposed framework's 4 components and approach, including (1) review of Government and Private Sector Programs, (2) Case Studies of Community-Based Solutions, (3) Assessment of Digital Literacy Programs, and (4) Analysis of Affordability Measures.

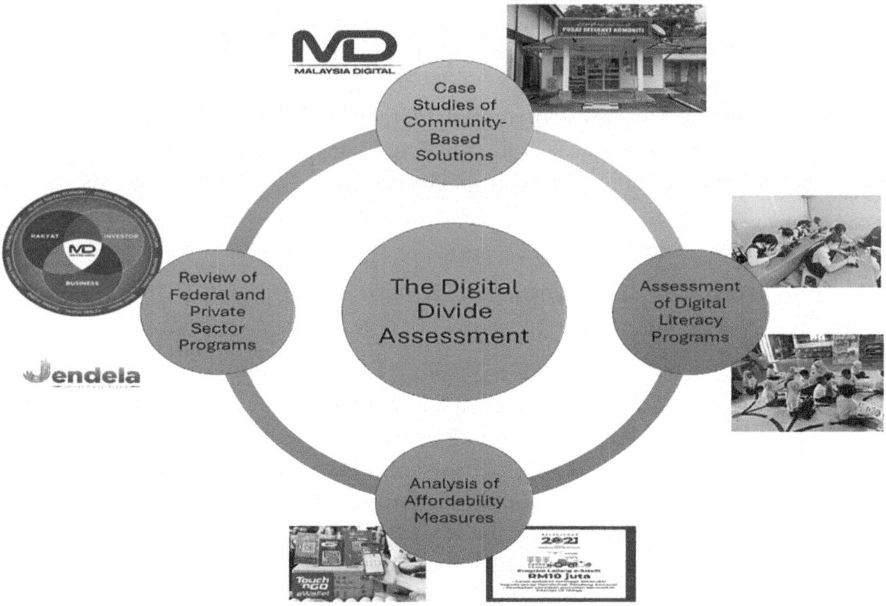

Fig. 1 Framework of digital divide assessment

3.1 Review of Government and Private Sector Programs

Most importantly, critical evaluation of programs offered by both the government and the private sector in the study of the digital divide in Malaysia's urban–rural development must be considered. In fact, the Malaysian government has instituted a series of initiatives that include the MyDIGITAL initiative, and the Malaysia Digital Economy Blueprint aimed at renovating or streamlining the digital infrastructure of most rural areas. These initiatives have ensured that no section of the population is left behind in the transition of a country to a digital economy (Bhandari, 2023; Lee, 2022).

The federal government has also promised to digitally empower low-income earners, including both youth and senior citizens, through various campaigns like the #SayaDigital Movement. Training sessions are specially designed for the three levels of digital familiarity to empower participants on how to use digital platforms to enhance their economic prospects (Bhandari, 2023). The government also promised to increase internet access—a very important factor in closing the digital gap that has prevailed between urban and rural areas so far (MDEC, 2024).

The involvement of the private sector in such gaps is of equal importance. It is also expected that these companies, while working in conjunction with the government, can devise innovative solutions to improve digital skills and infrastructure. Collaboration among its members is crucial in building an ecosystem where public and private entities together can work on creating a digitally inclusive information society. Further, its importance can be realized by analyzing federal and private sector programs.

A review of federal and private-sector programs in Malaysia suggests a conscious approach toward narrowing the gaps in digital divides between the rural and urban parts of Malaysia. In this case, Malaysia, through the development of infrastructure to improve the level of digital literacy and promotion of partnerships between the public and private sectors, is trying to ensure complete inclusiveness of its digital economy for all citizens irrespective of their geographic locations.

3.2 Case Studies of Community-Based Solutions

The assessment component extends to evaluate on community networks and digital hubs in order to consider their greater implications for local connectivity and digital inclusion within rural Malaysia. The classification of the different hubs, which would also include Malaysia Digital Hub and TEGAS Digital Innovation Hub, could give insight into how these kinds of platforms help in creating entrepreneurship and digital skills. For instance, the Malaysia Digital Hub, established in 2017, provides the necessary coworking space with high-speed Internet and opportunities for collaboration with technology and funding organizations for the successful rearing of startups that help in the growth of the local economy (Digital Sarawak, 2021).

Governance models around these hubs may also be researched further; often, a community ownership and management model prove to be more responsive to local needs. Hence, this becomes particularly important in sharing benefits related to digital inclusion among rural communities. For example, the TEGAS Digital Innovation Hub in Sarawak echoes the Sarawak Digital Economy Strategy by empowering local startups and social enterprises, and an emphasis on innovation and entrepreneurship is placed on digital arenas. In addition, these hubs will be sustained from funding sources such as government initiatives and private partnerships, including community contributions (BeEd World, 2024). Last-mile connectivity projects can also be funded through the USP Fund which is managed by the Malaysian Communications and Multimedia Commission (Malaysian Communications and Multimedia Commission (MCMC), n.d.).

This will incorporate qualitative and quantitative parameters, which include surveys and interviews with users to enhance digital literacy, access to the internet, and user satisfaction. These will act as centers where case studies of successful impacts, such as increased job opportunities and access to educational and government services, will be shared. Furthermore, taking a comparative case study from other countries will further implement the lessons that add to Malaysia's processes, positioning these community networks within the larger context of global digital inclusion.

3.3 Assessment of Digital Literacy Programs

Effective digital literacy programs in Malaysia address the effectiveness of reach, content, and impact brought forth by executed programs through educational institutions, government bodies, and technology companies. The Ministry of Education introduces the Digital Education Policy directed at equipping students with critical digital skills through integration into the learning environment, not only reaching school children but also educators and the community at large (The Star, 2023). The most recent notable initiatives include the Digital Literacy Empowerment Program for Persons with Disabilities, ensuring that the marginalized groups are included in the digital landscape (MDEC, 2021). It focuses on Internet awareness and digital entrepreneurship. The #SayaDigital Movement further enhances the digital literacy of low-income earners through basic technology use training, enabling participants to engage in the digital economy (Moises, 2024). These programs combined, shall bring about a digital-competent populace which can face modern realities.

These results of the digital literacy initiatives seem so promising, for they lead to empowering individuals for further economic growth. For instance, the introduction of training on digital skills in education prepares students for job markets in which this competency is highly sought after. The commitment by the government toward digital literacy development is shown by its ambition to equip 300,000 Malaysians with these skills by 2026 in collaboration with technology giants like Google (Digital News Asia, 2021). Therefore, the present study examines the coverage, content, and impacts of the initiatives with a description of inclusive digital literacy as imperative in empowering people to cope with rapid changes in technology and understand its respective implications for the advancement of society.

3.4 Analysis of Affordability Measures

The Malaysian government has been quite proactive, especially in ensuring that technology and internet access become more affordable, realizing very well that digital inclusion has a big role to play in the goal of ensuring economic growth coupled with social progress (Marzuki et al., 2023). Through a combination of government-led initiatives with support from nonprofits and private sector partners, it is ensured that digital devices and internet plans come with subsidies, discounts, and incentives so that they fall within the reach of every section.

To this end, one such initiative is the recently launched #MyDigitalWorkforce Work in Tech (MYWiT) by Malaysia Digital Economy Corporation, offering 1.3 million higher education students affordable package offers on devices and plans, hence giving them easy access to online learning resources and taking part in the digital economy (Ministry of Finance, 2021). The cost is subsidized by the government for both devices and internet plans to bridge the gap in digital divide and ensure equal opportunities among students of different socio-economic levels to develop their digital skills.

Moreover, special subsidies are given under the Jaringan Prihatin program to households with low incomes, senior citizens, and persons with disabilities. Beneficiaries can immediately enjoy the reduced price of internet plans, therefore making reasonably priced connectivity and necessary online services a reality (Whitacre, 2022). It has also joined hands with service providers in the private sector to extend these discounts and other incentives, thus giving an incentive to this arrangement of reducing financial burdens and additionally promoting digital inclusion.

As Malaysia soars further to become a high-income, technologically driven nation, it remains a key priority that all its citizens have access to ever-advancing digital technologies at affordable costs. In fact, through these collaborative efforts from the government, nonprofits, and private sector partners, Malaysia is at a strategic advantage to create an inclusive digital economy that works for all its people, irrespective of socio-economic status.

4 Discussion

4.1 Challenges and Barriers

The process of bridging the digital divide in Malaysia is slowed down with so many challenges (Malaysia Digital Economy Blueprint, 2021). For instance, technical and financial constraints hinder infrastructure development in the rural areas, as the expansion of a broadband network requires serious investment, and these rural areas may not be ready to handle high-speed internet access. Besides that, economic barriers are also very important to limit the access of people to technology. Rural families with low incomes, for example B40 communities, cannot afford the latest digital devices or internet plans (Monaghesh & Hajizadeh, 2020). Even with subsidized or discounted versions, the upfront costs of purchasing technology pose a major barrier.

Geographical and environmental considerations add an added problem in trying to develop better connectivity. In remote areas where the topography is hard to surmount, this may pose a challenge with regard to the installation and maintenance of infrastructures. Newer technologies like satellite internet and fixed wireless broadband promise greater outreach, but investment and further technological development are constantly needed.

4.2 Impact of Connectivity on Key Sectors

4.2.1 Education

The extended internet connectivity influences education in Malaysia by acquiring broadened e-learning resources and educational platforms, meaning rural students can participate in online classes and get a great deal of educational materials to successfully continue their studies. Rural school case studies indicate that improved access to the internet enhances student performance and level of engagement, thus enabling students to feel more connected with teachers and peers alike. However, challenges are still inconsistent internet quality and call for an increase in digital literacy training of students and teaching staff, especially in the state of Sabah, which is really very poor in infrastructure (Fang et al., 2022).

4.2.2 Healthcare

This, in turn, has brought revolutionary health care delivery to Malaysian communities, especially in rural areas. Telehealth services enable patients to consult with healthcare professionals remotely and thus reduce travel burdens, allowing improved access to specialist care. Successful telemedicine programs indeed show the effectiveness of digital technologies in improving health outcomes. For example, telehealth services initiated by governments realize better access to medical information and services where the same is crucial, especially in areas where health facilities are few. In the wake of the COVID-19 pandemic, telehealth had become a necessity where residents in the countryside depended on such services to keep healthy without the risk of exposure in crowded clinics (Rozmi et al., 2020).

4.2.3 Economic Opportunities

Furthermore, connectivity creates pathways toward economic improvement in villages. With better connectivity, there will be more opportunities to work from anywhere, to conduct online businesses, or to engage in e-commerce. The government's MyDIGITAL agenda also encourages digital entrepreneurship, in which online businesses are made easy to adopt into e-commerce (Lee, 2022). Digital financial services enhance financial inclusions through access to banking and payment systems that are so important in economic growth, especially in rural areas. However, there is also a need for disparity in access to technology and digital literacy for all communities to benefit from such opportunities.

This has indeed brought great benefits to Malaysia, in the form of improvement in education, health care, and economic sectors, yet it is further important that the gaps in the infrastructure are complemented by the development of digital literacy so that access and equity of opportunities to participate are available to all, especially in the rural areas.

5 Conclusion

Bridging the digital divide in Malaysia requires a coordinated and comprehensive approach, addressing various key areas such as connectivity, infrastructure, digital literacy, and affordability. The proposed evaluation framework offers direction based on which the impacts of initiatives taken up till now would be measured and determines what more needs to be done in this regard. In this connection, government and private sector programs seem to have considerably increased digital infrastructure and improved digital competency. However, there are still problems in rural areas because of very limited access to high-speed, low-cost internet, and technology. The contribution by the public and private sectors in the bridging of these gaps has been massive through the expansion of infrastructure and special support accorded to areas that have been underdeveloped.

Furthermore, wide access involves the addressing of technology affordability. Subsidies and collaboration toward the reduction of the cost of end digital devices and internet services are necessary steps toward all-inclusive technology access. Besides, the scaling of digital literacy across different populations, such as low-income families and the elderly, is required in order to foster digital inclusivity in society. Basically, continued investment in emerging technologies and innovative solutions should be effectively implemented to close the digital divide. Once these challenges are overcome, Malaysia can move toward an inclusive digital economy whereby every community, urban and rural, would be fully prepared to participate in and benefit from digital advancements.

References

Ab-Hamid, K., Tan, C. E., & Lau, S. P. (2011). Self-sustainable energy efficient long range WiFi network for rural communities. In *IEEE GLOBECOM Workshops, GC Workshops 2011, RuralComm* (pp. 1050–1055). https://doi.org/10.1109/GLOCOMW.2011.6162337.

Abiddin, A., Norhasni, N., Ibrahim, I., & Aziz, S. (2022). Advocating digital literacy: Community-based strategies and approaches. *Academic Journal of Interdisciplinary Studies, 11*, 198. https://doi.org/10.36941/ajis-2022-0018

Asia Digital News. (2021). *Measat 3d satellite launched to boost communications capabilities*. Retrieved September 16, 2024, from https://www.digitalnewsasia.com/business/measat-3d-satellite-launched-boost-communications-capabilities

Ayob, N. H., Aziz, M. A., & Ayob, N. A. (2022). Bridging the digital divide: Innovation policy and implementation in Malaysia. *International Journal of Academic Research in Business and Social Sciences, 12*(8), 1373–1389. https://doi.org/10.6007/ijarbss/v12-i8/14554

BeEd World. (2024). *Malaysian new education policy to foster digital-savvy students*. Retrieved September 16, 2024, from https://blog.beed.world/malaysian-new-education/

Bhandari, R. (2023). Bridging the skills gap: Fuelling careers and the economy in Asia-Pacific. *Economist Impact*. Retrieved September 16, 2024, from https://impact.economist.com/perspectives/talent-education/bridging-skills-gap-fuelling-careers-and-economy-asia-pacific

Dawood, S. (2019). Digital divide and poverty eradication in the rural region of northern peninsular Malaysia. *The Indonesian Journal of Geography, 51*, 172. https://doi.org/10.22146/ijg.37758

Devisakti, A., Muftahu, M., & Xiaoling, H. (2023). Digital divide among B40 students in Malaysian higher education institutions. *Education and Information Technologies, 29*, 1–27. https://doi.org/10.1007/s10639-023-11847-w

Digital News Asia. (2021). *MDEC rolls out US$24mil MyDigitalWorkForce work in tech initiative*. Retrieved September 16, 2024, from https://www.digitalnewsasia.com/digital-economy/mdec-rolls-out-us24mil-mydigitalworkforce-work-tech-initiative

Digital Sarawak. (2021). *Sarawak Digital Innovation & Entrepreneurship Ecosystem*. Retrieved September 16, 2024, from https://www.digital.tegas.org.my/_files/ugd/b6fbfb_17cc05acec924f3b82fb9291f08c265a.pdf

Eugenio, M. C. C. (2016). Low-cost internet mesh networks for public rural schools. In *2016 IEEE 36th Central American and Panama Convention, CONCAPAN 2016* (pp. 1–6). https://doi.org/10.1109/CONCAPAN.2016.7942363.

Fang, Y. X., Gill, S. S., Kunasekaran, P., Rosnon, M. R., Talib, A. T., & Abd Aziz, A. (2022). Digital divide: An inquiry on the native communities of Sabah. *Societies, 12*(6), 148.

Gao, X., & Li, M. S. (2024). The impact of the digital economy on the urban-rural income gap: Evidence from provincial panel data in China. *Applied Economics Letters, 31*, 2233–2236. https://doi.org/10.1080/13504851.2023.2212963

Gong, R. (2023). *Connecting the last mile: Solutions for rural and remote communities*. Khazanah Research Institute. License: Creative Commons Attribution CC BY 3.0.

Hashim, R., Baharud-Din, Z., Idris, K. S., & Ustadi, Y. A. (2011). Assessing digital literacy among the Semai tribe of Perak, Malaysia. In *ICCRD2011–2011 3rd International Conference on Computer Research and Development, 1* (pp. 9–12). https://doi.org/10.1109/ICCRD.2011.5763962.

Hassan, M., Mohd, S. M., Marzuki, A. S., Amiruddin, M., Bujang, S., Samingan, A., Salleh, M., Sulaiman, A., Nor, M., Ismail, M., Ishak, M., & Zainal Abidin, K. B. (2021). Bridging the digital divide in Malaysia using fixed wireless access. In *Proc. IEEE Asia-Pacific Conference on Communications (APCC)* (pp. 74–78). https://doi.org/10.1109/APCC49754.2021.9609825.

Johan, A. (2023). Unique deployment strategy utilizing a Single Wholesale Network. *GSM Association*. Retrieved September 16, 2024, from https://www.gsma.com/get-involved/gsma-membership/gsma_resources/5g-performance-shines-in-malaysia-but-there-is-room-for-greater-adoption/

Lee, C. (2022). *Strategic policies for digital economic transformation: The case of Malaysia*. ISEAS - Yusof Ishak Institute.

Liu, J. (2021). Bridging digital divide amidst educational change for socially inclusive learning during the COVID-19 pandemic. *SAGE Open, 11*(4). https://doi.org/10.1177/21582440211060810

Malaysia Communications and Multimedia Commission (MCMC). (n.d.). *JENDELA: Digital National Infrastructure Plan*. [Online]. Retrieved September 16, 2024, from https://myjendela.my

Malaysia Digital Economy Blueprint. (2021). *Economic Planning Unit, Prime Minister's Department*. Retrieved September 16, 2024, from https://www.ekonomi.gov.my/sites/default/files/2021-02/malaysia-digital-economy-blueprint.pdf

Malaysia Digital Economy Corporation (MDEC). (2022). Horizon: A perspective of Malaysia's digital economy. *MDEC*. [Online]. Retrieved September 16, 2024, from https://mdec.my/publications/horizon

Malaysian Communications and Multimedia Commission (MCMC). (2022). JENDELA Report Q1 2022. *Jendela.my*. [Online]. Retrieved September 16, 2024, from https://myjendela.my/Sitejendela/media/Doc/Jendela-Report-Q1-2022.pdf

Malaysian Communications and Multimedia Commission (MCMC). (n.d.). *USP Annual Report 2020*. [Online]. Retrieved September 16, 2024, from https://www.mcmc.gov.my/usp-annual-report/2020/page-nfcp

Marzuki, A. S. M., Hassan, S. M. M., Bujang, S., Sulaiman, A., Salleh, M. K., Nor, M. H. B. M., & Ismail, M. A. B. (2023). A case study of LTE coverage extension for rural Malaysia. In *2023 IEEE 13th Symposium on Computer Applications & Industrial Electronics (ISCAIE)* (pp. 151–156). IEEE.

MCMC. (2021). *MCMC looks to bring satellite broadband to remote parts of Malaysia*. Retrieved September 16, 2024, from https://www.satellitetoday.com/broadband/2021/03/15/mcmc-looks-to-bring-satellite-broadband-to-remote-parts-of-malaysia/

MDEC. (2021). *What is Saya digital?* Retrieved September 16, 2024, from https://mdec.my/sayadigital

MDEC. (2024). *What is Malaysia digital hub?* Retrieved September 16, 2024, from https://mdec.my/malaysia-digital-hub

Ministry of Finance. (2021). *Jaringan Prihatin: Digital access worth RM3.5 billion for B40 to Bridge Society's digital divide* [Press release]. Retrieved September 16, 2024, from https://www.mof.gov.my/portal/en/news/press-release/jaringan-prihatin-digital-access-worth-rm3-5-billion-for-b40-to-bridge-society-s-digital-divide

Moises, H. (2024). Malaysia and Google forge strategic partnership for digital growth and inclusive development. *W.media*: Clouds and Datacenter. Retrieved September 16, 2024, from https://w.media/malaysia-and-google-forge-strategic-partnership-for-digital-growth-and-inclusive-development/

Monaghesh, E., & Hajizadeh, A. (2020). The role of telehealth during COVID-19 outbreak: A systematic review based on current evidence. *BMC Public Health, 20*, 1193. https://doi.org/10.1186/s12889-020-09301-4

Penang State Government and Maxis. (2024, July 10). Maxis partners with Penang Government to advance digital skills. *Telecom Review Asia*. [Online]. Retrieved September 16, 2024, from https://www.telecomreviewasia.com/news/network-news/4388-maxis-partners-with-penang-government-to-advance-digital-skills/

Review, T. (2024). *Revolutionizing telemedicine and healthcare delivery in Malaysia with.* Retrieved September 16, 2024, from https://telecomreviewasia.com/news/featured-articles/4294-revolutionizing-telemedicine-and-healthcare-delivery-in-malaysia-with-5g/

Rozmi, A. N. A., Nohuddin, P. N. E., Abdul Hadi, A. R., Bakar, M. I. A., & Nordin, A. I. (2020). Factors affecting SME owners in adopting ICT in business using thematic analysis. *International Journal of Advanced Computer Science and Applications, 11*(7), 1–8. https://doi.org/10.14569/IJACSA.2020.0110727

Rully, A., Tan, T. N., Erkin, D., Urano, Y., Izumi, Y., Umezawa, Y., & Anh, P. X. (2005). Addressing digital divide: Experiment on tele-medicine applications using broadband wireless system in rural areas. In *2005 International Conference on Wireless and Optical Communications Networks* (pp. 98–101). https://doi.org/10.1109/wocn.2005.1435997

Samsuddin, S. F., Mohamed, N. A., & Bolong, J. (2021a). Understanding the digital capabilities of rural communities in low literacy rate areas in Malaysia towards digital society. *International Journal of Academic Research in Business and Social Sciences, 11*(15), 174–184.

Samsuddin, S. F., Mohamed Shaffril, H. A., Mohamed, N. A., & Bolong, J. (2021b). Into the unknown: Do people in low literacy rate areas practise digital reading? *Malaysian Journal of Library and Information Science, 26*(2), 23–36.

The Star. (2023). *Digital literacy to empower the disabled.* Retrieved September 16, 2024, from https://www.thestar.com.my/news/nation/2023/11/06/digital-literacy-to-empower-the-disabled

Tomás, J. P. (2023). Malaysia aims to cover 50% of rural areas with 5G by mid-2024. *RCR Wireless News.* https://www.rcrwireless.com/20231017/asia-pacific/malaysia-aims-50-of-rural-areas-to-have-5g-by-mid-2024

Vassilakopoulou, P., & Hustad, E. (2023). Bridging digital divides: A literature review and research agenda for information systems research. *Information Systems Frontiers, 25*, 955–969. https://doi.org/10.1007/s10796-020-10096-3

Whitacre, B. (2022). *Rural communities and digital device ownership: Barriers and opportunities* (Research Report).

Zailani, A. (2024, September 3). Enhancing internet access in schools, universities, and boosting creative economy top priorities for Budget 2025. *Malay Mail.* [Online]. https://www.malaymail.com/news/malaysia/2024/09/03/fahmi-enhancing-internet-access-in-schools-universities-and-boosting-creative-economy-top-priorities-for-budget-2025/149128

Zhang, M., & Wolff, R. S. (2004). Crossing the digital divide: Cost-effective broadband wireless access for rural and remote areas. *IEEE Communications Magazine, 42*(2), 99–105. https://doi.org/10.1109/MCOM.2003.1267107

Economic Disadvantage and Education for Youth Empowerment

Ahmed Aly Shaban Abdelmoteleb, Faisal Bin Badar, and Jon Mason

Abstract Education plays a pivotal role in empowering youths from economically disadvantaged backgrounds by providing the tools necessary for personal and professional growth. However, these young individuals often face significant challenges, including limited access to quality educational resources, inadequate infrastructure, and socio-economic barriers that hinder their academic success. Innovative strategies are essential to address these systemic issues and promote equitable access to education.

Effective interventions include scholarship programs that alleviate financial burdens, vocational training that equips students with practical skills, and mentorship initiatives that provide guidance and support. Tailored educational approaches are crucial, recognizing that each learner grows in their own unique way and requires personalized support to thrive.

Throughout the narrative the focus will be on strategies to empower youth living in economically disadvantaged contexts through education, providing insights into programs and initiatives aimed at developing skills and knowledge needed for participation in the digital economy.

The chapter provides successful case studies to illustrate how targeted initiatives can lead to significant improvements in academic achievement and overall well-being. By fostering collaboration among educators, policymakers, and community stakeholders, it is possible to create sustainable pathways that not only empower disadvantaged youths but also promote social mobility.

Through collective efforts, it is possible to transform the educational landscape for economically disadvantaged youths, enabling them to realize their full potential and contribute meaningfully to society.

A. A. S. Abdelmoteleb (✉)
Sharjah Private Education Authority, Sharjah, UAE

F. B. Badar · J. Mason
Charles Darwin University, Darwin, NT, Australia
e-mail: jon.mason@cdu.edu.au

L. O. Yesufu, P. N. E. Nohuddin (eds.), *Technology for Societal Transformation*,
https://doi.org/10.1007/978-981-96-1721-0_15

1 Section A

1.1 Contextualizing the Challenge

In today's rapidly evolving world, economic disadvantage continues to be one of the most persistent and widespread barriers to youth development. It has been a wicked problem for decades. Globally, one out of five young people, or 20.4% young people are classified as "NEET"—Not in Employment, Education, or Training—limiting their ability to break free from the cycle of poverty and unemployment (ILO, 2024). This glaring statistic represents more than just lost potential; it highlights the systemic inequities that create significant hurdles for youth from disadvantaged backgrounds, often leaving them with limited access to quality education, technology, and resources. Without meaningful interventions, these young people are trapped in a cycle where lack of education perpetuates economic exclusion, hindering social mobility.

1.2 Systemic Barriers and Their Consequences

Economically disadvantaged youth face significant systemic barriers that limit access to critical opportunities. These barriers include underfunded public education systems, a lack of digital infrastructure, inadequate teacher training, and insufficient resources for addressing the specific needs of underprivileged students. For instance, rural communities and inner-city schools tend to suffer from limited funding, outdated learning materials, and a lack of access to digital tools, creating a "digital divide" that is particularly challenging for students in underprivileged areas. In developing countries, the problem is amplified, with millions of children unable to attend school due to financial constraints, long distances to educational institutions, or the need to contribute to family incomes (Badar & Mason, 2020).

These barriers not only reduce the likelihood of academic success but also deprive young people of essential twenty-first-century skills needed to thrive in a digital economy (Alao & Brink, 2023). With fewer employment opportunities, reduced earning potential, and limited access to upward mobility, the long-term effects of economic disadvantage are often generational and deeply entrenched within families and communities.

1.3 A Human Face to the Challenge

Consider the story of Amina, a 14-year-old girl from rural Pakistan, who was forced to abandon her schooling to help her family make ends meet. With no local secondary school, her options for continuing her education were virtually non-existent.

Like millions of others, Amina faced the harsh reality of growing up in a community where education was a distant dream. She lacked access to both educational resources and the digital tools that many of her peers in more affluent regions took for granted. Her story exemplifies the struggles of countless youth who, through no fault of their own, are denied access to the education they need to thrive in an increasingly knowledge-based world.

Similarly, Aly's story exemplifies the struggles many young people face due to economic disadvantage. Living in a marginalized community, Aly attends a school that is underfunded and lacks basic resources. His classroom is equipped with outdated textbooks, teachers are teaching cross subjects since there is limited availability of specialized teachers, teachers also lack training and development, and the school has limited access to modern technology. Despite his dedication and potential, Aly's educational opportunities are constrained by systemic issues beyond his control. Despite the difficult situation, Aly was able to complete his primary education and the moment he moved to high school, he was not able to find a high school in his village, the nearest high school is 10 km away from his home with limited access to proper safe transportation. His experience is not unique but reflective of the broader challenges encountered by youths in similar economic situations. Aly's experience is not just contemporary, it reflects a personal experience that resonates with one of the author's fathers, where he did his best to secure the best educational opportunities despite challenging circumstances. Remarkably, Aly's two sons and one daughter have all since achieved their PhDs from prestigious universities around the world, including institutions in Malaysia, the UK, and Turkey.

Aly's and Amina's stories are not isolated. Across the globe, young people in economically disadvantaged communities face similar challenges—trapped in a cycle of poverty with little hope for escape. Addressing these challenges requires bold, innovative approaches to education that recognize and target the unique needs of these young individuals. By acknowledging the profound impact of economic disadvantage on youth and understanding the systemic barriers they face, we can better appreciate the critical need for targeted educational interventions. These interventions must be designed not only to bridge the education gap but also to empower youth with the skills and knowledge necessary to participate meaningfully in the digital economy and contribute to the broader development goals of their communities.

2 Section B: Importance of Education

2.1 Education as a Catalyst for Change

Education has long been recognized as one of the most powerful tools for breaking the cycle of poverty and creating pathways for economic empowerment. For economically disadvantaged youths, access to quality education is a game-changer, opening doors to opportunities that would otherwise remain closed. As the foundation for personal and societal growth, education not only equips young people with essential academic knowledge but also instills the skills, confidence, and critical thinking needed to navigate the complexities of today's rapidly changing global economy. The transformative potential of education is well-documented. For example, a UNESCO report estimates that each additional year of schooling can increase an individual's earnings by roughly 10% (UNESCO, 2011), underscoring the direct correlation between education and economic opportunity. This effect is even more pronounced in economically disadvantaged communities, where education often represents the only viable route out of poverty. Access to education helps bridge gaps in employment, reduces inequality, and fosters inclusive growth, which is critical for the sustainable development of underprivileged communities (Arsani et al., 2020).

However, the benefits of education extend far beyond the economic realm. Education empowers individuals to become active, informed citizens, able to contribute to the well-being and development of their communities. By fostering greater civic engagement and social cohesion, education serves as a cornerstone for the broader goals of the United Nations' Sustainable Development Goals (SDGs), particularly Goal 4: Quality Education, which aims to ensure inclusive and equitable education for all (Chankseliani & McCowan, 2020).

2.2 Current Gaps and Needs in the Education System

Despite the widely recognized importance of education, significant gaps remain in the availability, quality, and accessibility of education for economically disadvantaged youth. Many educational systems, particularly in low-income and rural areas, are ill-equipped to address the unique needs of underprivileged students. Schools in these areas often suffer from under-resourced infrastructure, outdated curricula, and a lack of trained educators. These challenges are compounded by socio-economic factors, including child labor, early marriage, and cultural barriers, which disproportionately affect girls and young women.

Furthermore, the digital divide—the gap between those who have access to digital technologies and those who do not—has exacerbated existing inequalities in education. The COVID-19 pandemic highlighted this divide starkly, as many schools shifted to online learning, leaving millions of students from economically disadvantaged backgrounds without access to the necessary tools or infrastructure to continue their education. According to UNICEF, at least 463 million students globally were unable to access remote learning during pandemic-related school closures, a problem particularly acute in regions where digital connectivity is sparse or unaffordable.

2.3 *The Need for Innovative Educational Interventions*

To address these gaps, there is an urgent need for innovative educational interventions tailored to the specific challenges faced by economically disadvantaged youths. These interventions must go beyond traditional schooling and focus on building digital literacy, fostering entrepreneurship, and developing practical skills that align with the demands of the modern economy (Dickson, 2024). This is where programs like EDLS (EDvantage Digital Learning System) play a crucial role. By integrating digital platforms, adaptive learning, and prioritizing local partnerships, EDLS provides a comprehensive educational model that not only addresses the academic needs of underprivileged students but also empowers them with the skills necessary for participation in the digital economy.

In addition to formal education, mentorship initiatives and community-based programs are essential in providing the guidance, resources, and support that economically disadvantaged youth need to succeed. Programs that focus on skill development, entrepreneurship, and vocational training offer young people the opportunity to build a sustainable livelihood and contribute to the economic growth of their communities. Innovative educational approaches like these are pivotal in closing the education gap and ensuring that all young people, regardless of their economic background, can reach their full potential.

3 Section C: Overview of Strategies and Initiatives

3.1 *Introduction: Context of Educational Interventions*

In response to the deep-rooted barriers faced by economically disadvantaged youth, various strategies and initiatives have been deployed worldwide to address gaps in education. Such initiatives, often driven by both public and private sector collaborations, seek to empower young people with the knowledge, skills, and confidence they need to thrive in a rapidly evolving world. However, one challenge remains persistent: how can educational initiatives be both scalable and adaptable while addressing the unique, context-specific needs of local communities?

To tackle this question, this section introduces some exemplar initiatives from all over the world that demonstrate different solutions and interventions, the Big Heart Foundation from Sharjah, the Digital School from the United Arab Emirates, and EDLS (EDvantage Digital Learning System).

EDLS and its pioneering model, DOORS (Digitally Operated One-Room Schoolhouses), exemplifies a holistic, community-based solution to empower underprivileged youth through innovative education strategies while also addressing broader community needs. With a strong foundation in Design-Based Implementation Research (DBIR), EDLS has demonstrated the ability to adapt to local contexts, leveraging global best practices, and ultimately transforming both education and communities.

3.2 Evolution of EDLS-DOORS: From Concept to Community Transformation

The EDLS-DOORS model began as a response to the overwhelming challenge of out-of-school children (OOSC) in marginalized communities in Pakistan. The initial goal was straightforward: to provide these children with access to basic education through a sustainable and scalable approach that could be replicated in other regions. However, the model has since evolved into something far greater.

EDLS's early days were characterized by the establishment of "one-room schoolhouses" using digital technologies to overcome barriers related to access, infrastructure, and teaching resources. Notably, one-room schoolhouses have symbolized local commitment to community development all around the world for centuries. The DOORS model extends the community focus and was designed to function in even the most resource-constrained environments, ensuring that education could reach the most marginalized populations. Over time, EDLS transitioned from a simple education provider to a platform for holistic community development.

The DOORS initiative expanded from basic educational provision to include targeted skills training for youth, local skills development for women, and programs designed to improve community health and well-being. Today, EDLS-DOORS is more than an educational platform; it's a proven solution for comprehensive community transformation that tackles the interrelated challenges of education, poverty, and social inclusion.

3.3 Design-Based Implementation Research (DBIR) in Action

A key feature that set EDLS apart from traditional educational models is its reliance on Design-Based Implementation Research (DBIR). This methodological approach enables the organization to not only co-design but also iteratively improve its educational programs by working closely with local communities and stakeholders. DBIR focuses on developing interventions that are both scalable and context-sensitive, and it emphasizes the importance of collaboration between researchers, practitioners, and community members (Penuel et al., 2022). EDLS's success lies in its adaptability—its ability to evolve based on real-world data, feedback from users, and the specific needs of the communities it serves.

For instance, the original DOORS centers faced significant challenges related to community trust, digital literacy, and gender norms, particularly in patriarchal societies where girls' education was not prioritized. Through ongoing DBIR cycles,

EDLS identified these challenges early on and worked with local leaders and families to create an environment that was conducive to girls' learning. Over time, DOORS became a space where girls felt safe to pursue their education, and gender parity in attendance dramatically improved. This iterative, research-driven approach to program design and implementation has allowed EDLS to expand and refine its model across various contexts—from urban slums in Pakistan to rural Tanzania—ensuring that the solutions provided are relevant and sustainable.

3.4 EDLS Curriculum: Covering Twenty-First Century Learning

Another distinctive feature of the EDLS-DOORS initiative is its forward-thinking curriculum, which is carefully designed to equip students with twenty-first-century skills that are critical for their success in the modern digital economy. The curriculum emphasizes core competencies such as critical thinking, collaboration, creativity, and communication, all integrated with a strong foundation in digital literacy and global awareness. Students are exposed to both academic subjects and skill-building activities that prepare them for the challenges and opportunities of the rapidly evolving job market.

EDLS leverages a blended learning model, incorporating both digital and traditional teaching methods to provide a holistic education experience. The curriculum is also aligned with the United Nations' Sustainable Development Goals (SDGs), particularly SDG 4 (Quality Education), ensuring that students are not only learning but are also being empowered to contribute to global challenges like climate change, inequality, and sustainable development.

3.5 The Pivotal Role of the Qualified and Experienced Central Team

A key factor behind the success and scalability of the EDLS-DOORS model is the strong leadership provided by the Central Team. Comprised of experienced educators, technology experts, and community development professionals, the Central Team plays an essential role in shaping the strategy, implementation, and continuous improvement of EDLS programs. This team brings decades of collective experience in educational innovation, digital transformation, and social impact, which allows EDLS to remain adaptable in diverse contexts.

The Central Team also drives the integration of Design-Based Implementation Research, ensuring that data-driven insights and community feedback inform ongoing program adjustments. Their expertise ensures that EDLS continues to operate with a high level of professionalism and efficiency, even in resource-constrained environments. Furthermore, the Central Team actively trains and supports local educators, ensuring that they are well-equipped to deliver high-quality instruction and sustain the program's long-term impact.

3.6 EDLS as a Low-Cost, High-Impact Model

Another standout feature of the EDLS-DOORS initiative is its cost-effectiveness. Designed to operate in some of the most economically disadvantaged communities, EDLS leverages low-cost technologies, local partnerships, and innovative resource-sharing models to minimize costs while maximizing impact. The use of solar-powered digital learning devices, open educational resources (OER), and volunteer-based teaching support ensures that operational costs are kept to a minimum.

Additionally, EDLS places a strong emphasis on local capacity-building, empowering communities to take ownership of the program, which further reduces long-term operational costs. Despite its low-cost structure, EDLS delivers high-impact educational outcomes, as evidenced by improved student retention rates, increased digital literacy, and the holistic development of students and their communities. This makes EDLS a sustainable and scalable solution that can be replicated in other regions facing similar educational challenges, positioning it as an effective model for both educational and community transformation globally.

3.7 Technological Integration: Bridging the Digital Divide

At the heart of EDLS-DOORS is the use of technology to overcome traditional barriers to education. The model leverages digital platforms to provide students with access to world-class educational resources that would otherwise be inaccessible. The Digitally Operated One-Room Schoolhouses are equipped with solar-powered devices, internet access (where available), and adaptive learning platforms that adjust to students' progress.

The incorporation of technology into the DOORS model has had multiple benefits:

(a) **Scalability**: The digital nature of the program allows for rapid scaling, as content can be replicated and shared across multiple locations without the need for physical textbooks or large-scale teacher training programs.
(b) **Adaptability**: The learning platform used by EDLS is highly adaptable, allowing for personalized learning experiences. Students who may have fallen behind in traditional educational settings can progress at their own pace, while more advanced students are continually challenged.

(c) **Teacher Empowerment**: While technology provides the foundation, teachers remain at the heart of the learning experience. The DOORS model emphasizes teacher empowerment by providing ongoing professional development through digital training modules and virtual mentorship programs.
(d) **Student Empowerment**: EDLS also focuses on bridging the digital divide by providing digital literacy programs to both students and their families. In communities where access to technology is limited, EDLS offers programs that introduce basic computing and digital skills, enabling students to better participate in the global economy. Moreover, these digital literacy programs often extend to women in the community, empowering them to take part in local entrepreneurship initiatives.

3.8 Empowering Communities Beyond Education: Global Skills for Youth, Local Skills for Women

As already highlighted, the holistic approach of EDLS foregrounds community empowerment. While the primary focus remains on education, the model recognizes that lasting change can only occur when sufficient members of a community are empowered to participate in the economy and in societal decision-making processes.

In response to this, EDLS developed two key initiatives: Global Skills for Youth and Local Skills for Women.

Global Skills for Youth focuses on equipping young people with the skills necessary to thrive in the global digital economy. This initiative goes beyond basic education to include training in areas such as coding, digital marketing, and entrepreneurship. By partnering with international organizations and corporations, EDLS ensures that the curriculum is aligned with the current demands of the job market. This helps economically disadvantaged youth access opportunities that were previously out of reach, allowing them to break free from the cycle of poverty.

Local Skills for Women addresses the specific challenges faced by women in marginalized communities. Many of these women are unable to participate in the formal economy due to a lack of education, skills, or social support. EDLS's initiative provides vocational training, financial literacy programs, and entrepreneurship support to help women create sustainable livelihoods. By fostering economic independence, EDLS not only empowers women but also strengthens the economic resilience of entire communities.

Additionally, EDLS has integrated **Community Health and Well-being Initiatives** into its model, recognizing the importance of a holistic approach to development. In many underprivileged areas, health issues such as malnutrition, waterborne diseases, and poor sanitation hinder educational progress. EDLS works with local healthcare providers and international NGOs to address these challenges, ensuring that students are not only educated but also healthy and able to learn effectively.

3.9 Measuring Success and Scaling Impact: Alignment with SDGs

EDLS's approach is deeply aligned with the United Nations' Sustainable Development Goals (SDGs), particularly those related to quality education (SDG 4), gender equality (SDG 5), decent work and economic growth (SDG 8), and reducing inequality (SDG 10). The program measures its success through a set of key performance indicators (KPIs) that assess both educational outcomes and broader community impact.

Some of the KPIs used by EDLS include:

- **Student Retention and Graduation Rates**: Monitoring how many students complete the DOORS program and move on to further education or employment.
- **Gender Parity**: Ensuring that girls have equal access to educational opportunities and that they are participating in programs at the same rate as boys.
- **Community Engagement**: Tracking the involvement of community members in educational initiatives and local development programs.
- **Health and Well-being Improvements**: Monitoring health outcomes as part of the integrated community health initiatives.

EDLS has demonstrated that its model is not only effective but also scalable. From its origins in Pakistan, the program has expanded to Tanzania and is poised for further growth in other regions. The adaptability of the DOORS model, combined with its focus on local partnerships and community involvement, makes it a powerful tool for addressing the educational needs of economically disadvantaged communities on a global scale.

3.10 Policy Impact and Collaboration

Another critical aspect of EDLS's success is its collaboration with local governments, NGOs, and international organizations to influence educational policy. By working directly with policymakers, EDLS advocates for the inclusion of digital education in national curricula and pushes for reforms that prioritize underserved communities.

One of the key policy impacts of EDLS has been its contribution to closing the digital divide. Through its partnerships with tech companies, EDLS has been able to demonstrate the effectiveness of digital learning tools in rural and underserved areas, leading to greater government investment in educational technology.

3.11 *Other Initiatives: Digital School UAE and Big Heart Foundation UAE*

In the United Arab Emirates, the Digital School initiative launched by the Al Maktoum Foundation aims to provide quality education to students in underserved regions through an online learning platform. It is considered the first integrated digitally enabled school that provides digital and hybrid learning smartly and flexibly. It provides learning models, processes, and materials that are compatible with national and international curricula. By engaging and interacting with licensed educators, as well as providing a smart evaluation mechanism, students will develop life-long autonomous learning skills.

The initial phase of the school started in November 2020 with 20,000 students. This phase aims to test the digital systems, content flow and suitability for each age group, as well as students' engagement and response to the curricula. The Digital School aims to reach one million students by the year 2026, the initiative primarily targets students in broader regions in the Middle East, North Africa, and parts of Asia where it has challenges in accessing education. The Digital School aims to bridge educational gaps by enabling and offering a flexible online learning environment that allows students to access high-quality educational resources regardless of their location.

The Digital School is designed to be accessible for students from low-income families, providing resources at no cost or minimal fees. The initiative also includes training for teachers to effectively utilize digital tools and engage students in a virtual learning environment.

Since its launch, the Digital School has served thousands of students, particularly during the COVID-19 pandemic, when remote learning became essential. The initiative has helped ensure continuity of education for students who might otherwise have limited access to traditional schooling.

Another prominent example from Sharjah, UAE, is The Big Heart Foundation (TBHF). Originally set up as a fundraising campaign in 2013, The Big Heart Foundation was developed into a full-fledged foundation, in 2015, proceeded by various initiatives and campaigns launched by Her Highness Sheikha Jawaher Bent Mohammed Al Qassimi, Wife of His Highness the Ruler of Sharjah and Chairperson of the Supreme Council for Family Affairs.

The Foundation's mandate is to protect and empower vulnerable children and their families in vulnerable situations across the world. Since then, TBHF has provided health, education, and emergency aid services—among others—to almost four million people in need in more than 25 countries.

In conclusion, the Big Heart Foundation, The Digital School and EDLS-DOORS represent contemporary case studies that demonstrate how a well-designed, research-informed educational initiative can transform not just individual lives but entire communities. Through its holistic approach, commitment to gender equality, and integration of technology, such great initiatives help to build a future where all young people—regardless of their background—have the opportunity to succeed.

4 Section D

4.1 In-Depth Exploration of Strategies and Initiatives

In this section, we reflect on key lessons learned from these three initiatives, by diving deeper into the strategies and initiatives discussed earlier and providing action points and key recommendations that can be replicated in similar solutions. Focusing on how these approaches empower economically disadvantaged youth, each lesson plays a critical role in ensuring that these students receive the education, resources, and support necessary to overcome systemic barriers and achieve long-term success. We also highlight how these strategies contribute to the broader mission of each organization in driving community transformation, aligned with the United Nations' Sustainable Development Goals (SDGs).

4.2 Design-Based Implementation Research (DBIR): A Data-Driven Approach

Design-Based Implementation Research serves as a foundational approach that provides a structured, iterative framework for organizations to adapt their programs based on real-world outcomes and community feedback. This methodology emphasizes collaboration among researchers, educators, and community stakeholders, ensuring that solutions are contextually relevant and scalable.

For economically disadvantaged youth, DBIR highlights that educational interventions must be dynamic, evolving in response to students' changing needs and emerging challenges. The data-driven nature of DBIR position organizations to measure the effectiveness of their curricula and teaching methods in real time. This approach is particularly valuable in innovative educational models where technology plays a key role in reaching remote or underserved populations.

Regular feedback from local educators, students, and program teams informs ongoing adjustments to both the curriculum and delivery methods. For instance, if students in a specific area face challenges in digital literacy, organizations can swiftly integrate additional resources and training into their programs to address these gaps. This agile methodology ensures that educational initiatives remain effective and responsive, maximizing their impact on economically disadvantaged youth.

Moreover, DBIR facilitates the collection of longitudinal data on student outcomes, enabling organizations to track progress over time. This data-driven insight supports informed decision-making and ensures that future strategies are evidence-based. Ultimately, DBIR helps organizations maintain sustainable programs that are continuously optimized for maximum impact (Hoadley & Campos, 2022).

4.3 Digital Literacy and Twenty-First-Century Skills Development

One of the most transformative challenges is equipping students with digital literacy and twenty-first-century skills. In today's rapidly evolving digital economy, such skills are essential for success. For economically disadvantaged youth, who often lack access to quality education and technological resources, this initiative is particularly critical. Through tailor-made programs and global curriculum, it is critical to introduce students to core digital competencies such as coding, digital communication, and online collaboration. Students also learn essential life skills like problem-solving, critical thinking, and adaptability, all of which are necessary to thrive in the twenty-first-century workforce. This holistic approach to education ensures that students are not just passive consumers of technology, but active participants in the digital world, capable of shaping their own futures.

By embedding digital literacy into the broader educational framework, organizations can close the digital divide and open up new opportunities for economic empowerment.

4.4 Community-Centric Approaches and Local Partnerships

A key element of success lies in a community-centric approach, which prioritizes the involvement of local stakeholders at every level of the program. From the design and implementation of curriculum to the selection of educators, community input is integral to ensuring that the solutions are both culturally relevant and effective. By establishing partnerships with local governments, businesses, and NGOs, organizations are able to leverage existing resources and infrastructures to scale its programs. These partnerships also ensure that the program is sustainable in the long term, as local communities are empowered to take ownership of the educational initiatives. In many cases, this can be depending on training local teachers and volunteers to manage the education model, creating employment opportunities and further embedding the program within the community.

One notable example of this community-centric approach is organization should leverage collaboration with local artisans and vocational trainers to offer skill-building workshops for youth and women. These workshops provide economically disadvantaged individuals with the skills necessary to pursue local employment opportunities or even launch their own entrepreneurial ventures. By aligning educational outcomes with local economic needs, accordingly organizations ensure that students can immediately apply what they have learned to improve their livelihoods.

4.5 Empowering Women: Gender-Responsive Education

While organizations primarily focus on empowering youth, it is also important to recognize the critical role of women in driving community transformation. Education has long been recognized as a powerful tool for empowering women and provides gender-responsive educational opportunities that address the unique challenges faced by women in economically disadvantaged communities. In many regions where such great initiatives operate, women have traditionally had limited access to education and economic opportunities. To address this gap, it is critical to offer tailored programs that focus on building both digital and practical skills, such as digital entrepreneurship and vocational training in locally relevant industries. These programs not only provide women with the skills they need to participate in the workforce but also foster a sense of self-reliance and confidence.

Additionally, mentorship programs can be implmented where successful women from local communities serve as role models and guides for younger female students. This intergenerational mentorship helps build a strong support network for women, encouraging them to pursue education and economic independence.

4.6 Financial Sustainability: Low-Cost, High-Impact Model

Another critical aspect and success factor is the ability to operate with a low-cost, high-impact model, making it financially sustainable even in the most resource-constrained environments. By using cost-effective technologies such as open-source educational materials and volunteer-based instruction, the initiative minimizes operational costs while maximizing its reach and impact. Further amplifying this approach, the organization is setting up learning centers in remote or underserved communities with minimal infrastructure. By leveraging locally available resources and utilizing partnerships with local governments, businesses, and NGOs, organizations ensure that its programs can be scaled without relying heavily on external funding.

This financial sustainability is crucial for maintaining long-term educational initiatives in economically disadvantaged communities, where resources are often scarce. By keeping operational costs low and focusing on high-impact outcomes, this ensures that it can continue to expand its reach, empowering more youth and communities with access to quality education.

4.7 *Leveraging Global Best Practices in Local Contexts (GLOCAL Approach)*

An important lesson learned from EDLS specifically and can be generalized in other solutions is attributing to its GLOCAL approach—leveraging global best practices while adapting them to meet local needs and challenges. This combination ensures that proposed educational programs are both innovative and contextually relevant. By studying successful educational models from around the world, organizations incorporate proven strategies such as blended learning, digital literacy programs, and community-led initiatives. However, these strategies are not simply replicated in local communities; they are adapted to fit the specific cultural, economic, and social contexts of each region. This approach ensures that students receive an education that is not only high-quality but also tailored to their unique circumstances.

For instance, in regions where internet access is limited, organizations implement offline-first learning platforms that allow students to access digital content without a continuous internet connection. Similarly, in areas where vocational training is more relevant than formal education, programs should be tailoring its curriculum to focus on locally applicable skills that can immediately contribute to economic development. This flexibility makes the GLOCAL approach highly effective, ensuring that proposed solutions remains both innovative and inclusive.

4.8 *Real-World Success Stories: Transforming Lives Through Education*

The impact of such great initiatives is best illustrated through the real-life success stories of students and communities who have benefited from the program. One such example is a group of young women in urban slums in Pakistan, who, through the EDLS digital entrepreneurship program, learned skills in coding, online marketing, and business management. With their new skills, they were able to launch a small e-commerce business selling handmade products to international markets, drastically improving their economic prospects.

Another example comes from a remote village in Pakistan, where a group of students from an EDLS-DOORS school used their newfound digital literacy skills to develop a community-led clean water initiative. By applying what they had learned in class, the students created a digital platform to raise awareness about the importance of clean water and to mobilize resources to install water filtration systems in their village. This project not only transformed their community but also empowered the students to see themselves as agents of change.

These stories underscore the power of education to transform lives and communities. Programs are not just about imparting knowledge—they are about empowering individuals to take control of their futures and drive positive change in their communities. These additional topics and success stories further illustrate how innovative and adaptable educational strategies are empowering economically disadvantaged youth and transforming communities around the world.

References

Alao, A., & Brink, R. (2023). Information and communication technology management for sustainable youth employability in underserved society: Technology use for skills development of youths. *International Journal of Sociotechnology and Knowledge Development (IJSKD), 15*(1), 1–19. https://doi.org/10.4018/IJSKD.322100

Arsani, A. M., Ario, B., & Ramadhan, A. F. (2020). Impact of education on poverty and health: Evidence from Indonesia. *Economics Development Analysis Journal, 9*(1), 87–96.

Badar, F. B., & Mason, J. (2020). Towards digital multigrade one-room schoolhouses for underprivileged communities in rural Pakistan. *Computer-Based Learning in Context, 2*(1), 21–39. https://doi.org/10.5281/zenodo.4057844

Chankseliani, M., & McCowan, T. (2020). Higher education and the sustainable development goals. *Higher Education, 81*, 1–8. https://doi.org/10.1007/s10734-020-00652-w

Dickson, C. O. (2024). Innovate education; bridging gaps; shaping futures. *International Journal of Learning Development and Innovation (IJLDI), 1*(1), 100–106.

Hoadley, C., & Campos, F. C. (2022). Design-based research: What it is and why it matters to studying online learning. *Educational Psychologist, 57*(3), 207–220. https://doi.org/10.1080/00461520.2022.2079128

ILO. (2024). https://www.ilo.org/sites/default/files/2024-06/Asia-pacific-employment-social-outlook-2024%20%28web%29.pdf

Penuel, W. R., Allen, C. D., Manz, E., & Heredia, S. C. (2022). Design-based implementation research as an approach to studying teacher learning in research-practice partnerships focused on equity. In A. C. Superfine, S. R. Goldman, & M.-L. M. Ko (Eds.), *Teacher learning in changing contexts* (pp. 217–237). Routledge. https://doi.org/10.4324/9781003097112-15

UNESCO. (2011). *Education counts: Towards the millennium development goals* (updated edition).

Bridging the Gap: Leveraging Online Higher Education for Displaced Persons

Amine Moussa, Clemens Wollny, and Carol Switzer

Abstract Online education holds significant potential for development cooperation, particularly in enhancing access to higher education for refugees and other vulnerable groups. Flexible learning pathways address the needs of individuals who cannot attend traditional in-person classes, such as women and adults. This contemporary case study focuses on refugees and explores the success factors and challenges of online education, considering region-specific factors like language and culture that can affect implementation. The research includes insights from a pilot project funded by Deutsche Gesellschaft für Internationale Zusammenarbeit (GIZ) and the University of the People, aimed at improving higher education access for Syrian refugees. The study evaluates whether this project's success can be applied to other refugee populations and offers policy recommendations for stakeholders. The study draws on a review of literature examining online higher education for Syrian refugees and identifying general success factors. Empirical evidence, particularly from the pilot project's mid-term review, provides specific examples, though data from other sources were limited due to challenges in accessing essential information. The pilot project successfully helped Syrian refugees gain skills, enhance employment prospects, and develop a new identity as students, improving their self-worth and mental health. Challenges include communication issues, feelings of loneliness, and unstable living conditions for refugees, such as unreliable electricity and internet. Additional barriers are negative perceptions of online education and limited recognition of online degrees by host country governments,

A. Moussa (✉)
Faculty of Business Administration and Economics, Notre Dame University – Louaize, Zouk Mosbeh, Lebanon
e-mail: amoussa@ndu.edu.lb

C. Wollny
Technical University Bingen, Bingen, Germany
e-mail: c.wollny@th-bingen.de

C. Switzer
Università della Svizzera italiana, Lugano, Switzerland
e-mail: carol.switzer@paeradigms.org

L. O. Yesufu, P. N. E. Nohuddin (eds.), *Technology for Societal Transformation*,
https://doi.org/10.1007/978-981-96-1721-0_16

which affects employment opportunities. To address these issues, development cooperation projects should support online education providers in overcoming negative perceptions through strategic, evidence-based communication, enhancing the image of online education and improving refugees' prospects.

1 Introduction

As the number of displaced persons continues to rise worldwide, host countries and governments face mounting economic, social, and security challenges. For instance, the Syrian refugee population, predominantly composed of youth and children, needs access to education as a critical asset for their empowerment, protection, and integration (Dereli, 2018). With many of these children now reaching university age due to the protracted Syrian civil war, higher education solutions have become urgent. This situation has compelled sponsors, development agencies, and education providers to devise innovative solutions to improve access and opportunities for these young refugees.

This case study examines a pilot project offering scholarships for online higher education to Syrian refugees in four neighbouring host countries in the Middle East and North Africa (MENA) region. The pilot was undertaken by the Deutsche Gesellschaft für Internationale Zusammenarbeit (GIZ) on behalf of the Federal Ministry for Economic Cooperation and Development (BMZ) through a grant agreement with University of the People (UoPeople), a global online higher education provider. The study investigates the potential for scaling and transferring the project to other regions and target groups within the framework of international development cooperation as a means of human capacity development.

1.1 Objectives of the Case Study

The pilot project aims to improve the employability of Syrian refugees in the MENA region by providing scholarships for online higher education to this disadvantaged group. A major goal is to ensure equitable scholarship distribution between men and women participants. The research study was commissioned by GIZ as an extension of the required mid-term review (MTR) of the pilot and addresses the following research questions:

1. Under which conditions is online higher education successful? What are the major success factors and challenges?
2. Are there any region-specific conditions (e.g., language, culture) that positively or negatively affect the successful implementation of online studies for selected target groups?

3. To which other vulnerable groups (e.g., socially disadvantaged youth, youth in rural communities, young women) can this approach be transferred? And how?

2 Brief Overview of Online Higher Education

This section addresses research question (1) Under which conditions is online higher education successful? What are the major success factors and challenges?

The field of online higher education is rapidly evolving, driven by technological advancements and widespread adoption due to the global pandemic. Terms like online learning, e-learning, distance education, flexible learning, and Massive Open Online Courses (MOOCs) are often used interchangeably. For this research, "online higher education" is predominantly used.

2.1 Online Education: Status Quo

While not new, online higher education has gained traction throughout the higher education landscape due to its flexibility and accessibility. Key aspects include:

- *Effectiveness and impact*. Online learning is regarded as one of the most effective methods for improving teaching and learning. Researchers studying higher education in Oman have concluded that online learning and solutions can significantly extend educational opportunities across the country (Encarnacion et al., 2021). Currently, experts like Yigal Rosen are incorporating artificial intelligence into online educational platforms to provide access to rigorous learning experiences (Cision, 2021). Organisations like the International Society for Technology in Education (ISTE) frequently highlight research and the practical applications of online education in achieving learning outcomes.
- *Student engagement and motivation*. A student's engagement and motivation influence their success in an online learning environment. It is not just the level of engagement that matters but also the emotional aspects of that engagement, as demonstrated in a study conducted at a state university in Turkey (Vezne et al., 2022).
- *Faculty perspectives and training*. Faculty need support and training for effective online teaching. Institutional policies should provide departmental support and mentoring (Quayson, 2022).
- *Hybrid and blended learning models*. Blended learning, combining online and face-to-face elements, has become common post-pandemic and produces outcomes equivalent to traditional learning (Müller & Mildenberger, 2021). This model is particularly useful for adult learning and continuing education (de Brito Lima et al., 2021).

- *Access and inclusivity*. Online higher education improves access for geographically constrained, disabled, or economically limited students and is suitable for marginalised populations, including refugees (Amy Lomellini et al., 2022; Yang et al., 2022).
- *Online collaboration and social learning*. Group-based online collaborative learning enhances individual outcomes but requires more effort than non-collaborative learning (Knopf et al., 2021).
- *Quality assurance and accreditation*. Ensuring quality and accreditation in online education is challenging due to the diversity of providers. Traditional quality assurance systems need to adapt to these new formats (UNESCO, 2020).

2.2 Online Higher Education Versus Face-to-Face Education

The choice between traditional and online education involves pedagogy, learner preferences, and readiness. Technological advancements and the COVID-19 pandemic have shifted many institutions towards online education. For refugees, face-to-face education is often impractical, making online education a viable option (El-Ghali & Al-Hawamdeh, 2017). Traditional instruction is evolving towards student-centred learning facilitated by digital technologies (Asghar et al., 2022). Online courses demand more effort from students but are rated lower in communication and interaction (Young & Duncan, 2014). Despite concerns about online learning quality, it can be a good substitute during exceptional times like the pandemic (Asaad Hamza Sheerah et al., 2022).

2.3 Formats, Delivery Methods, and Implications

Online learning includes synchronous, asynchronous, and blended approaches. Synchronous learning involves real-time interactions between students and instructors via voice, text, and video chats (Perveen, 2016). Asynchronous learning allows for flexibility with course completion, assignments, and exams by set deadlines, often using blogs and message boards (Perveen, 2016). Both methods commonly utilise learning management systems (LMS) like Moodle or Blackboard.

MOOCs represent a significant form of asynchronous learning, providing innovative educational opportunities to a global audience. They are popular for their revenue potential, expanded access, and new teaching methods but face challenges related to sustainability, quality, dropout rates, and credit transferability (Daniel et al., 2015; Yuan & Powell, 2013). MOOCs, such as those offered by Ecole Polytechnique Federale de Lausanne (EPFL) and Future Learn (FL), help widen access to education, particularly for non-traditional and underrepresented groups (Burd et al., 2015; Otoo, 2015). Kiron, an NGO, provides MOOCs and other online courses for refugees, aiming to support their transition to partner universities (Bajwa et al., 2017; Halkic & Arnold, 2019).

Blended learning (BL) combines face-to-face and online instruction and has been effective in fields like distance learning (Anthony Jnr, 2022). Syrian refugees found it beneficial for enhancing computer skills and academic success, though technical challenges persisted (Al-Husban & Shorman, 2020; Bajwa et al., 2017). A project between Germany and Morocco successfully implemented blended learning in bachelor programmes, incorporating practical tutorials and remote labs (Wollny et al., 2019).

Online learning has been found effective in areas such as time management and content clarity, sometimes surpassing face-to-face methods (Darius et al., 2021; Yu-Fong Chang et al., 2021). However, maintaining student engagement and interaction is challenging due to the lack of physical presence (Ren et al., 2021). Strategies like group chats, bulletin boards, and forum discussions can enhance engagement and learning outcomes (Jiang et al., 2022; Nasir, 2020). Despite these challenges, online education offers advantages like social egalitarianism and improved verbal and written skills (Arasaratnam-Smith & Northcote, 2017).

3 Online Higher Education for Refugees: Challenges and Opportunities

This section addresses research question (2) Are there any region-specific conditions (language, culture, etc.), which have a positive or negative effect on the possibility of successfully implementing online studies for selected target groups?

Online higher education for refugees addresses new integration challenges. Scholarships and online education expand access, but issues like accessibility, acceptability, and adaptability persist (Fincham, 2020). The perceptions and expectations that impact academic experiences, student satisfaction, and dropout rates include connectivity issues, limited internet resources, anxiety with digital tools, losing motivation, and the need for immediate feedback (Ren et al., 2021). External factors like geographical constraints and familial responsibilities are also significant (Nasir, 2020). The following analysis offers an overview of the benefits and obstacles of online education for refugee learners.

3.1 Challenging Nature of Online Higher Education

Life in refugee camps presents its own difficulties, with students needing to meet basic needs, before they can focus on education. Thus, refugee students have further complications, compared to other online learners.

- *Accessibility of online higher education for refugees.* Refugees face structural and cultural challenges in accessing online education, such as difficulty obtaining identification papers and educational documents (Anselme & Hands, 2010). Universities like UoPeople offer open access but require foundation programmes to prepare students, which can be daunting and limit accessibility (UoPeople, 2024).
- *Higher education in refugee camps.* These facilities not intended for long-term use significantly impact living conditions and educational performance. Refugees in camps have even worse living conditions than those in urban areas, including unstable electricity supply, slow internet connection, and difficulty accessing educational institutions (Duran, 2017). Some refugee households may have only one mobile device, which usually belongs to the patriarch, for socio-cultural and budgetary reasons. As a result, opportunities for a refugee to develop digital literacy may be restricted (Drolia et al., 2020).

MOOCs and blended learning initiatives are two examples of distance learning programmes that could help refugees who are physically or financially confined to remote camps. These initiatives provide access to higher education opportunities and open doors to better futures for the refugees and their communities (O'Keeffe, 2020).

An online survey of Syrian refugees participating in the pilot (April 2023) shows that 20% of respondents ($n = 15$) live in refugee camps and range in age from 20 to 39 years old, as shown in Fig. 1. Half of these individuals cited problems with connectivity, electricity, or computer devices as the key challenge they face in their

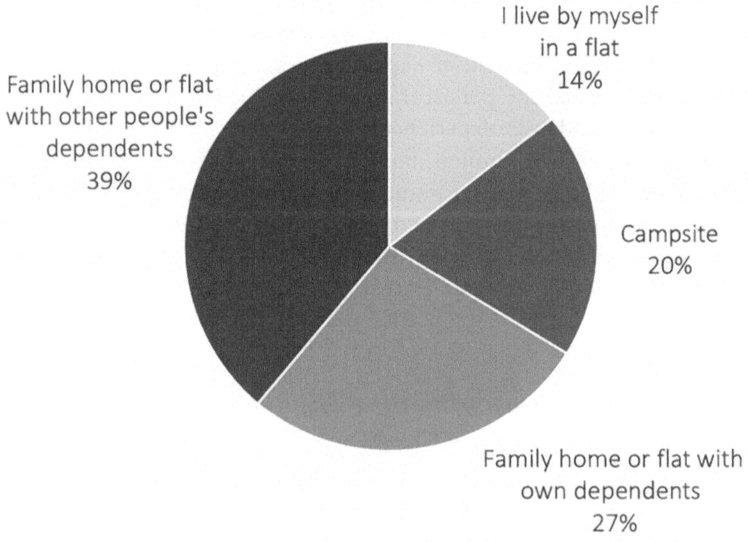

Fig. 1 Responses to where students live from an online survey of 77 students receiving a GIZ scholarship (campsite = refugee camp) (Paeradigms, 2023)

studies. Others cite financial struggles and their vulnerable status as their main challenge.

> [my main challenge] is to pursue my university studies in the difficult conditions we live in. Our camps suffer from the lack and weakness of the Internet and difficult living conditions especially that I am a head of family and in charge of my family.

Another describes the consequences of the lack of connectivity: "the weakness of the Internet caused me to interrupt a number of courses".

Although connectivity is a major issue for many, most students (53%) heard about UoPeople through social media, followed by recommendations from family members or friends (39%), which is considerably high. Only a small fraction (7%) indicated that their primary source of information was the university website (Paeradigms, 2023).

3.2 Student Perceptions and Expectations of Online Higher Education

Refugees often feel that higher education programmes lack sufficient challenge and that integration services fail to adequately recognise their educational progress, leading to frustration with poor communication and long waiting periods (Bucken-Knapp et al., 2019). Henry (2020) found that Australian students expected online courses to replicate on-campus education, with online delivery of materials and activities. Syrian refugee students viewed blended learning positively, valuing its convenience, adaptability, and the opportunity to enhance self-learning and computer skills (Al-Husban & Shorman, 2020). Conversely, Albanian students struggled with online learning, facing challenges in focus, subject comprehension, and test-related anxiety, with only a few finding it straightforward (Xhelili et al., 2021).

Expectations of online learning are shaped by the organisation of remote education, tools used, and uncertainty regarding government recognition of online degrees (Cicha et al., 2021). Clear advertising and detailed information about time commitments, contact levels, flexibility, technical needs, and skills required can help prospective students make informed decisions (Henry, 2020).

At the University of the People (UoPeople), the foundation programme aims to clarify connected learning expectations with information provided in manageable increments. Admissions advisors guide students through the foundation programme, with programme advisors assigned once students start their degree, addressing the significant growth in student numbers from 2019 to 2020 (Paeradigms, 2023).

3.3 Instructor and Public Perceptions of Online Degrees Around the World

A study by Rahayu and Wirza (2020) found that 49% of high school teachers in Bandung, Indonesia, perceived online education as beneficial for students and crucial for performance improvement. However, 51% perceived it as less effective due to lack of communication and interaction, along with difficulties using technology, creating engaging materials, and providing feedback. These issues led many teachers to prefer traditional instruction over online methods.

Perceptions of online higher education in host countries are influenced by government positions. In Lebanon, for example, higher education is not a priority due to other crises, and traditional parental views favour in-person learning, contributing to a negative stigma around online education (Paeradigms, 2023). Managing a connected learning environment and maintaining a positive public image can be challenging. Effective engagement with partners, such as international organisations and public institutions, requires a strategic approach beyond typical business growth models, focusing on changing mindsets and normalising online education.

3.4 Student Satisfaction and Dropout

Dropout rates in online learning are a significant concern, with high rates persisting despite efforts to minimise them (Mubarak et al., 2022). Key factors influencing student satisfaction and reducing dropout rates include course quality, clear course vocabulary, proper material illustration, reasonable module requirements, moderate course pace, easy-to-follow online directions, and passionate instructors (Ghaderizefreh & Hoover, 2018). Social presence and student age, particularly those between 22 and 35 years, also impact course satisfaction and success (Nasir, 2020).

UoPeople faces further challenges in retaining students, partly due to its non-selective admissions and low-cost model, which attract enrolments made without commitment. The flexible entry and exit points allow students to progress at their own pace, making it hard to determine if they have dropped out or temporarily suspended their studies (Paeradigms, 2023). Despite these issues, dropout rates can alert educators to problems, prompting them to intervene in real-time.

3.5 Student Success Factors

Reinhardt et al. (2021) examined 1024 refugee students using Kiron Open Higher Education and found that personal characteristics significantly impact success, as measured by grades and course completion. Key factors include academic English proficiency, cognitive functioning, autonomy, internet access, study motivation, and sociodemographic aspects. High English proficiency was associated with lower dropout rates, although cognitive functioning and motivation results were inconclusive due to potential biases. Women, despite lower overall participation, tended to start and complete more courses than men (Reinhardt et al., 2021).

The MTR also highlighted language proficiency as critical, with students who completed the foundation programme demonstrating higher retention rates and grades. Gender trends were similar, with fewer women participating but completing more courses (Paeradigms, 2023).

4 Employability of Online Higher Education Graduates

This section addresses employability, a key outcome of online higher education for refugees and, therefore, a common aim for all stakeholder groups (policymakers, donors, funders, implementing agencies, online education providers, and most importantly, students). Thus, it is an important aspect of both research questions (1) Under which conditions is online higher education successful? What are the major success factors and challenges? and (2) Are there any region-specific conditions (language, culture, etc.) that have a positive or negative effect on the possibility of successfully implementing online studies for selected target groups?

4.1 Job-Ready Curriculum Design

Kiron offers an online curriculum based on MOOCs for refugees worldwide. Halkic and Arnold (2019) analysed data from 1375 Kiron students, highlighting the challenges refugees encounter in accessing online higher education. The study questioned whether online education is a straightforward solution for integrating disadvantaged students, noting that reliance on MOOCs results in a lack of a cohesive curriculum and unrecognised coursework in host countries. The research stressed the importance of support structures for refugees, particularly in camps, to address technical, cultural, and language barriers. Most Kiron students used the platform as a stepping stone to traditional universities in host countries to obtain recognised degrees rather than to secure employment, as evidenced by high dropout rates due to transfers. The authors recommended refocusing the Kiron model to serve as a pathway to local universities, aligning better with student expectations (Halkic & Arnold, 2019). Additionally, an unpublished MTR report from the GIZ JOSY project found that Syrian and Jordanian postgraduate students and stakeholders considered Kiron courses too generic and not helpful for job placement (Wollny, 2018).

4.2 Learning Outcomes

Student motivation is fundamental for effective learning outcomes in both face-to-face and online settings. In online learning, where students are isolated from campus and peers, motivation becomes a key predictor of learning outcomes and satisfaction (Baber, 2020). Active participation in diverse learning activities, such as accessing academic databases, completing assignments, watching videos, and taking exams, can enhance these outcomes (Yu, 2021).

For refugee students, additional support is essential, particularly for those in camps (Paeradigms, 2023). Academic support, including adequate language proficiency, supports student integration into the online environment, which can improve retention. UoPeople addresses this through its foundation programme with eight levels of English-language courses. However, the lack of personal interaction makes language learning challenging. Refugee students also need non-academic support, such as study spaces, social interaction, and mentoring opportunities. For low-cost online universities, providing such support might be difficult. Therefore, partnerships with civil society organisations, international aid agencies, or public institutions are as important as scholarships in achieving targeted learning outcomes.

4.3 Accreditation of Online Higher Education in Countries of Residence

Higher education accreditation involves aligning institutions or systems with national or global performance standards, which enhances academic performance, educational quality, and research capabilities (Anaper et al., 2013). Accreditation improves the reputation of distance learning institutions and helps graduates secure jobs with multinational companies. It is essential for distance education programmes to adhere to national educational philosophies, admission requirements, and employment guarantees (Ertuğ, 2016).

Despite these benefits, many countries do not recognise or accredit online education. In Lebanon, for instance, online learning is not officially recognised, with only 40% of certification programmes allowed to be taught online due to a lack of legal framework for accreditation (El-Ghali & Ghosn, 2019). Additionally, the absence of uniform curriculum and accreditation for schools serving Syrian students presents a significant challenge in refugee education (Monk, 2021).

International online education providers like Kiron and UoPeople face difficulties navigating varying national regulations. The UNESCO Global Convention on the Recognition of Qualifications concerning Higher Education, effective from March 2023, aims to address these challenges by providing transparent principles for non-traditional learning models. This convention is particularly important for refugees, as it facilitates their continued education and qualification recognition across borders. However, economic crises often lead host country governments to deprioritise education, though there is a growing acknowledgment of online education's quality potential (Paeradigms, 2023).

4.4 Online Education for Improving the Employability of Refugees in Host Countries

Employability for youth in less developed contexts and refugees is a major challenge due to barriers like language, access to official documentation, immigration status, and unrecognised qualifications. Refugees often face limitations to low-skilled labour, and even highly qualified individuals may end up in underemployment. Access to online education can provide refugees with the skills needed for skilled jobs, but challenges such as degree recognition and accessibility persist (Paeradigms, 2023).

The case of Ukrainian refugees in Europe exemplifies these challenges. Despite having high skill levels, many Ukrainian refugees are relegated to low-skilled jobs due to difficulties in transferring qualifications and language barriers (OECD, 2023). This situation underscores that issues with degree recognition and employment are widespread among different refugee contexts.

To improve refugee employability through online education, qualification recognition must be addressed. The OECD (2023) advocates for host countries to promote skill-appropriate employment for refugees, including recognising credentials from online education.

5 Discussion

This section serves as a concluding discussion to the study by addressing research question (3) To which other vulnerable groups (e.g. socially disadvantaged youth, youth living in rural communities, young women) can this approach be transferred? And how?

5.1 Learning from Success

UoPeople proved to be an effective partner, offering courses that meet US Distance Education accreditation standards and quickly adapting to the needs of the students. This included developing full programmes in Arabic with corresponding advisory support and launching short certificate courses. The pilot project also identified specific areas for improvement that should be addressed in future iterations.

5.2 Strengths, Weaknesses, Opportunities, and Threats of the Pilot Project

Transferring the pilot project to other social and geographical contexts necessitates understanding its strengths and weaknesses and recognising its gaps.

- *Strengths*. The pilot project's strengths include its asynchronous model, which allows students to study at their own pace regardless of time zone, enhancing accessibility for women and increasing completion rates. The project's growing capacity is shown by rising enrolment numbers. UoPeople's programmes in Arabic cater to millions of native Arabic speakers, providing valuable educational opportunities. These strengths support knowledge acquisition, digital literacy, and language proficiency.
- *Weaknesses*. Key weaknesses include issues with degree recognition, low graduation rates, limited student services, and language limitations. Many countries do not recognise online degrees, impacting employability and further education. The low graduation rate raises concerns about the programme's effectiveness, especially for refugees who see higher education as an important path towards integration. Limited student support services and the need to expand language options to include languages like Spanish also pose challenges.
- *Opportunities*. The project has potential for adaptation to other refugee populations, addressing their high demand for relevant skills. Expanding into new contexts can bridge qualification gaps and empower displaced individuals. UoPeople's accredited online education, particularly in Arabic, could be scaled to other MENA regions. Aligning with local accreditation standards and forming partnerships with educational institutions and governments can enhance sustainability and employability.
- *Threats*. Negative perceptions of online education, reactive communication in crisis contexts, and challenges in monitoring and measuring progress pose significant threats. Overcoming these issues requires improving perceptions, establishing effective communication strategies, and refining monitoring techniques to ensure successful educational outcomes.

5.3 Identification of Groups that Can Benefit from Transferability

Online education significantly contributes to the massification of higher education, making it more inclusive and accessible to a broader range of students beyond traditional elite groups. The literature review and pilot project indicate that the challenges of online higher education are similar across diverse student populations. This suggests that the pilot project's success can be transferred to other vulnerable groups, particularly refugees and asylum seekers.

- *Venezuelan refugees*. With over 7.7 million refugees and migrants and one million asylum seekers from Venezuela seeking protection and a better life, primarily in Latin America and the Caribbean, this group represents a significant potential target for transferring the pilot project (UNHCR, 2023). The Venezuelan population's high level of English proficiency would facilitate quick progression through the Foundation programme into a degree programme. Expanding degree programmes to include Spanish, as UoPeople did with Arabic, would increase access to higher education for Venezuelan refugees and other Spanish-speaking individuals.
- *Ukrainian refugees*. Since the Russian invasion of Ukraine in February 2022, more than 6.5 million Ukrainian refugees have been recorded globally as of February 2024 (UNHCR, 2024). UoPeople currently serves Ukrainian refugees; expanding and strengthening this operation by translating programmes into Ukrainian could benefit a growing number of refugees impacted by the ongoing war.
- *South Sudanese refugees*. With 2.3 million displaced persons within and from South Sudan (Saifaddin, 2024), this group also presents a strong potential for the project's transferability.

In addition to displaced persons within or outside of the country or region, other disadvantaged groups could benefit from access to online higher education. These include individuals living with disabilities, those in rural communities, low-income individuals, individuals in recovery, and elderly learners. Scaling the project to these groups would require integrating student services, which has been repeatedly highlighted as an important success factor. The project's design should include mechanisms to measure, monitor, evaluate, and learn from efforts to ensure equal inclusion of women.

5.4 Conditions and Obstacles to Transferability Success

The scalability and transferability of online programmes to different refugee groups depend on various factors, including course design, content support, assessment, and teacher characteristics (Almaiah & Alyoussef, 2019). For Syrian refugees, additional factors such as language, culture, and accessibility also play significant roles (Arar, 2021).

- *Language and culture barriers*. Language is a significant barrier affecting the transferability of higher education systems. For instance, English poses a challenge for Middle Eastern and African refugees in Kakuma Camp Sudan, making online education difficult (Crea & Sparnon, 2017). Similarly, Turkish language barriers negatively impact Syrian refugees in Turkey, affecting their academic performance and social integration (Dereli, 2018). Venezuelan university students generally speak English as it is taught in schools, and it is the primary language in South Sudan. However, only 9% of Ukrainians feel confident using

English, which poses a challenge for UoPeople's English and Arabic courses (English Raven, 2023). Offering courses in Ukrainian, like the Arabic courses for Syrian refugees, might be necessary.

- *Access to online higher education.* Higher education in Ukraine has faced numerous challenges due to ongoing conflict. Distance learning has boosted student motivation and educational quality, using tools like Moodle and Kahoot to encourage interaction between teachers and students (Banyoi et al., 2023). However, challenges include interrupted internet access, inconvenient class schedules, unclear guidance, challenging material, prolonged screen time, and low self-motivation (Krylova-Grek & Shyshkina, 2021). Additional challenges include demanding accreditation requirements, lack of social interaction and immediate feedback, oral communication practice, technology access, and self-motivation (Voloshinov et al., 2020).
- *Accreditation of online higher education in other contexts.*
  - *In Ukraine*, distance education is recognised by the Ukrainian Ministry of Education and Science, making it convenient for Ukrainian students to join UoPeople (Ministry of Education and Science of Ukraine, 2019). The International European University is an active provider of online higher education for Ukrainians (IEU, 2023).
  - *In Venezuela*, the National Open University (Universidad Nacional Abierta UNA) is dedicated to distance education with 67 branches nationwide. However, it was not possible to confirm the recognition of UNA's online education due to an inoperative website and the absence of online governmental proof at the time of writing. The only available information is derived from third-party websites such as Counselor Corporation (National Open University, 2024).
  - *In Sudan*, there is no available information on the accreditation of online higher education, suggesting that refugee students from UoPeople may face similar recognition and employability obstacles as Syrian refugees.

References

Al-Husban, N., & Shorman, S. (2020). Perceptions of Syrian student refugees towards blended learning: Implications for higher education institutions. *International Journal of Emerging Technologies in Learning (iJET), 15*(1), 45–60. https://doi.org/10.3991/ijet.v15i01.11431

Almaiah, M. A., & Alyoussef, I. Y. (2019). Analysis of the effect of course design, course content support, course assessment and instructor characteristics on the actual use of E-learning system. *IEEE Access, 7*, 171907–171922. https://doi.org/10.1109/access.2019.2956349

Amy Lomellini, A., Lowenthal, P. R., Snelson, C., & Trespalacios, J. H. (2022). Higher education leaders' perspectives of accessible and inclusive online learning. *Distance Education, 43*(4), 574–595. https://doi.org/10.1080/01587919.2022.2141608

Anaper, S. N. Ç., Uluçay, M. T., & Çabuk, A. (2013). Accreditation of online and distance learning programs. *Turkish Online Journal of Distance Education, 14*(1), 231–244.

Anselme, M. L., & Hands, C. (2010). Access to secondary and tertiary education for all refugees: Steps and challenges to overcome. *Refuge, 27*, 89. https://doi.org/10.25071/1920-7336.34725

Anthony Jnr, B. (2022). An exploratory study on academic staff perception towards blended learning in higher education. *Education and Information Technologies, 27*(3), 3107–3133. https://doi.org/10.1007/s10639-021-10705-x

Arar, K. H. (2021). Research on refugees' pathways to higher education since 2010: A systematic review. *Review of Education, 9*(3), e3303. https://doi.org/10.1002/rev3.3303

Arasaratnam-Smith, L. A., & Northcote, M. T. (2017). Community in online higher education: Challenges and opportunities. *The Electronic Journal of E-Learning (Online), 15*(2), 188–198.

Asaad Hamza Sheerah, H., Sharma Yadav, M., Ali Elzein Fadl Allah, M., & Jalal Abdin, G. (2022). Exploring teachers and students' perceptions towards emergency online learning intensive English writing course during COVID-19 pandemic. *Arab World English Journal, 2*, 64–84. https://doi.org/10.24093/awej/covid2.5

Asghar, M. Z., Afzaal, M. N., Iqbal, J., & Sadia, H. A. (2022). Analyzing an appropriate blend of face-to-face, offline and online learning approaches for the in-service vocational teacher's training program. *International Journal of Environmental Research and Public Health, 19*(17), 10668. https://doi.org/10.3390/ijerph191710668

Baber, H. (2020). Determinants of students' perceived learning outcome and satisfaction in online learning during the pandemic of covid19. *Journal of Education and E-Learning Research, 7*(3), 285–292. https://doi.org/10.20448/journal.509.2020.73.285.292

Bajwa, J. K., Couto, S., Kidd, S., Markoulakis, R., Abai, M., & McKenzie, K. (2017). Refugees, higher education, and informational barriers. *Refuge, 33*(2), 56–65. https://doi.org/10.7202/1043063ar

Banyoi, V., Kharkivska, O., Shkurko, H., & Yatskiv, M. (2023). Tools for implementing distance learning during the war: Experience of Uzhhorod National University, Ukraine. *Arab World English Journal (AWEJ)*, Special Issue on Communication and Language in Virtual Spaces, 75–87. https://doi.org/10.24093/awej/comm1.6

Bucken-Knapp, G., Fakih, Z., & Spehar, A. (2019). Talking about integration: The voices of Syrian refugees taking part in introduction programmes for integration into Swedish society. *International Migration, 57*(2), 221–234. https://doi.org/10.1111/imig.12440

Burd, E. L., Smith, S. P., & Reisman, S. (2015). Exploring business models for MOOCs in higher education. *Innovative Higher Education, 40*, 37–49. https://doi.org/10.1007/s10755-014-9297-0

Cicha, K., Rizun, M., Rutecka, P., & Strzelecki, A. (2021). COVID-19 and higher education: First-year students' expectations toward distance learning. *Sustainability, 13*(4), 1889. https://doi.org/10.3390/su13041889

Cision. (2021). BrainPOP appoints renowned researcher and academic to lead assessment, efficacy, and data science efforts. *Cision*. Retrieved March 20, 2023, from https://www.prnewswire.com/news-releases/brainpop-appoints-renowned-researcher-and-academic-to-lead-assessment-efficacy-and-data-science-efforts-301211868.html

Crea, T. M., & Sparnon, N. (2017). Democratizing education at the margins: Faculty and practitioner perspectives on delivering online tertiary education for refugees. *International Journal of Educational Technology in Higher Education, 14*(1). https://doi.org/10.1186/s41239-017-0081-y

de Brito Lima, F., Lautert, S. L., & Gomes, A. S. (2021). Contrasting levels of student engagement in blended and non-blended learning scenarios. *Computer & Education, 172*, 104241. https://doi.org/10.1016/j.compedu.2021.104241

Daniel, J., Cano, E. V., & Cervera, M. G. (2015). The future of MOOCs: Adaptive learning or business model? *RUSC. Universities and Knowledge Society Journal, 12*(1), 64–73. https://doi.org/10.7238/rusc.v12i1.2475

Darius, P. S. H., Gundabattini, E., & Solomon, D. G. (2021). A survey on the effectiveness of online teaching–learning methods for university and college students. *Journal of The Institution of Engineers (India): Series B, 102*(6), 1325–1334. https://doi.org/10.1007/s40031-021-00581-x

Dereli, B. (2018). Refugee integration through higher education: Syrian refugees in Turkey. Policy Report, *UNU Institute on Globalization, Culture and Mobility (UNU-GCM)*. Retrieved March 20, 2023, from https://i.unu.edu/media/gcm.unu.edu/publication/4405/Final_Begu%CC%88m-Dereli_Policy-Report.pdf

Drolia, M., Sifaki, E., Papadakis, S., & Kalogiannakis, M. (2020). An overview of mobile learning for refugee students: Juxtaposing refugee needs with mobile applications' characteristics. *Challenges, 11*(2), 31. https://doi.org/10.3390/challe11020031

Duran, C. S. (2017). "you not die yet": Karenni refugee children's language socialization in a video gaming community. *Linguistics and Education, 42*, 1–9. https://doi.org/10.1016/j.linged.2017.09.002

El-Ghali, H., & Al-Hawamdeh, A. (2017). *Higher education and Syrian refugee students: The case of Jordan*. UNESCO. https://doi.org/10.13140/RG.2.2.19086.66884

El-Ghali, H. A., & Ghosn, E. (2019). *Towards connected learning in Lebanon*. Issam Fares Institute for Public Policy and International Affairs at American University of Beirut. Retrieved March 20, 2023, from https://www.aub.edu.lb/ifi/Documents/publications/research_reports/2018-2019/20190221_towards_connected_learning_in_lebanon.pdf

Encarnacion, R. E., Galang, A. D., & Hallar, B. A. (2021). The impact and effectiveness of e-learning on teaching and learning. *International Journal of Computing Sciences Research, 5*(1), 383–397. https://doi.org/10.25147/ijcsr.2017.001.1.47

English Raven. (2023). The importance of English in Ukraine. *English Raven*. Retrieved March 10, 2023, from https://www.englishraven.com/how-many-people-speak-english-in-ukraine/

Ertuğ, C. (2016). Open and distance education accreditation standards scale: Validity and reliability studies. *International Journal of Environmental & Science Education, 11*(14), 6444–6445.

Fincham, K. (2020). Rethinking higher education for Syrian refugees in Jordan, Lebanon and Turkey. *Research in Comparative and International Education, 15*(4), 329–356. https://doi.org/10.1177/1745499920926050

Ghaderizefreh, S., & Hoover, M. L. (2018). Student satisfaction with online learning in a blended course. *International Journal of Digital Society, 9*(3), 1393–1398.

Halkic, B., & Arnold, P. (2019). Refugees and online education: Student perspectives on need and support in the context of (online) higher education. *Learning, Media and Technology, 44*(3), 345–364. https://doi.org/10.1080/17439884.2019.1640739

Henry, M. (2020). Online student expectations: A multifaceted, student-centred understanding of online education. *Student Success, 11*(2), 91–98. https://doi.org/10.5204/ssj.1678

IEU. (2023). Join online classes. *International European University*. Retrieved January 12, 2024, from https://ieu.com.ua/join-online-classes

Jiang, X., Yi, X., Fang, J., & Lv, H. (2022). On-line and off-line teaching research based on BP neural network. In *2022 2nd International Conference on Computer Technology and Media Convergence Design (CTMCD 2022)* (pp. 40–49). Atlantis Press International BV. https://doi.org/10.2991/978-94-6463-046-6_6

Knopf, T., Stumpp, S., & Michelis, D.. (2021). How online collaborative learning leads to improved online learning experience in higher education. In *8th Eur. Conf. Soc. Media*, ECSM 2021, July (pp. 119–127).

Krylova-Grek, Y., & Shyshkina, M. (2021). Online learning at higher education institutions in Ukraine: Achievements, challenges, and horizons. *Information Technology and Learning Tools, 85*(5), 163–174. https://doi.org/10.33407/itlt.v85i5.4660

Ministry of Education and Science of Ukraine. (2019). Distance education. *Ministry of Education and Science of Ukraine*. Retrieved July 31, 2023, from https://mon.gov.ua/en/education/higher-education/distance-education

Monk, A. (2021). Futures under threat: Education policy and barriers to access for Syrian refugees in Jordan and Lebanon. *Global Islamic Studies Honors Papers*. Retrieved July 31, 2023, from https://digitalcommons.conncoll.edu/cgi/viewcontent.cgi?article=1001&context=islamichp

Mubarak, A. A., Cao, H., & Zhang, W. (2022). Prediction of students' early dropout based on their interaction logs in online learning environment. *Interactive Learning Environments, 30*(8), 1414–1433. https://doi.org/10.1080/10494820.2020.1727529

Müller, C., & Mildenberger, T. (2021). Facilitating flexible learning by replacing classroom time with an online learning environment: A systematic review of blended learning in higher education. *Educational Research Review, 34*, 100394. https://doi.org/10.1016/j.edurev.2021.100394

Nasir, M. K. M. (2020). The influence of social presence on students' satisfaction toward online course. *Open Praxis, 12*(4), 485. https://doi.org/10.5944/openpraxis.12.4.1141

National Open University. (2024). Courses: Fees. *Counselor Corporation*. Retrieved March 18, 2024, from https://counselorcorporation.com/national-open-university/

OECD. (2023). What we know about the skills and early labour market outcomes of refugees from Ukraine. *OECD Ukraine hub*. Retrieved March 19, 2024, from https://www.oecd.org/ukraine-hub/policy-responses/what-we-know-about-the-skills-and-early-labour-market-outcomes-of-refugees-from-ukraine-c7e694aa/

O'Keeffe, P. (2020). The case for engaging online tutors for supporting learners in higher education in refugee contexts. *Research in Learning Technology, 28*, 1–15. https://doi.org/10.25304/rlt.v28.2428

Otoo, H. (2015). Fast-track growth for social learning as The Open University builds on success of FutureLearn. *FutureLearn*. Retrieved April 24, 2023, from https://www.futurelearn.com/info/press-releases/fast-track-growth-for-social-learning-as-the-open-university-builds-on-success-of-futurelearn

Paeradigms. (2023). *Improving the participation of Syrian refugees in education through online study courses*. Deutsche Gesellschaft für Internationale Zusammenarbeit (GIZ) GmbH.

Perveen, A. (2016). Synchronous and asynchronous e-language learning: A case study of virtual University of Pakistan. *Open Praxis, 8*(1), 21. https://doi.org/10.5944/openpraxis.8.1.212

Quayson, F. O. (2022). Faculty perspectives on online teaching in higher education: A qualitative approach to understand faculty members' challenges and experiences. *Journal of Research Initiatives, 6*(2), 9.

Rahayu, R. P., & Wirza, Y. (2020). Teachers' perception of online learning during pandemic covid-19. *Jurnal penelitian pendidikan, 20*(3), 392–406. https://doi.org/10.17509/jpp.v20i3.29226

Reinhardt, F., Deribo, T., Zlatkin-Troitschanskaia, O., Happ, R., & Nell-Müller, S. (2021). The influence of refugee students' personal characteristics on study success in online education. *Journal of International Migration and Integration, 22*, 987–1008.

Ren, X., Zhang, Z., & Geng, X. (2021). Research and practice of online and offline blended teaching mode. In *6th Annual International Conference on Social Science and Contemporary Humanity Development (SSCHD 2020)* (pp. 425–428). Atlantis Press. https://doi.org/10.2991/assehr.k.210121.089

Saifaddin, G. (2024). Refugees from South Sudan 2024. *Statista*. Retrieved February 10, 2024, from https://www.statista.com/statistics/1241326/refugees-from-south-sudan-by-country/#:~:text=There%20are%20about%202.3%20million,displaced%20persons%20and%20asylum%20seekers

UNESCO. (2020). Quality assurance and recognition of distance higher education and TVET. *UNESCO*. Retrieved March 10, 2024, from https://unesdoc.unesco.org/ark:/48223/pf0000373754

UNHCR. (2023). Venezuela situation. *UNHCR*. Retrieved December 15, 2023 from https://reporting.unhcr.org/operational/situations/venezuela-situation#:~:text=As%20of%20the%20end%20of,Latin%20America%20and%20the%20Caribbean

UNHCR. (2024). Ukraine emergency. *UNHCR*. Retrieved February 10, 2024, from https://www.unrefugees.org/emergencies/ukraine/#:~:text=Nearly%206.5%20million%20refugees%20from,(as%20of%20February%202024)

University of People. (2024). Foundation courses. *UoPeople*. Retrieved February 11, 2024, from https://www.uopeople.edu/become-student/prepare-for-uopeople/foundation-courses/

Vezne, R., Yildiz Durak, H., & Atman Uslu, N. (2022). Online learning in higher education: Examining the predictors of students' online engagement. *Education and Information Technologies, 28*(2), 1865–1889. https://doi.org/10.1007/s10639-022-11171-9

Voloshinov, S., Kruglyk, V., Osadchyi, V., Osadcha, K., & Symonenko, S. (2020). Realities and prospects of distance learning at higher education institutions of Ukraine. *Ukrainian Journal of Educational Studies and Information Technology, 8*(1), 1–16. https://doi.org/10.32919/uesit.2020.01.01

Wollny, C. (2018). *New perspectives through academic education and training for young Syrians and Jordanians—Mid term evaluation report-draft*. Deutsche Gesellschaft für Internationale Zusammenarbeit (GIZ).

Wollny, C., Moeller, M., Weinmann, A., & Wegner, A. (2019). *Evaluation des Projekts Bachelor "Angewandte Mathematik und Informatik" und Bachelor "Biomedizinische Technik" der FH Aachen mit der Université Moulay Ismaïl (UMI), Meknès, Marokko*. Deutscher Akademischer Austauschdienst (DAAD).

Xhelili, P., Ibrahimi, E., Rruci, E., & Sheme, K. (2021). Adaptation and perception of online learning during COVID-19 pandemic by Albanian university students. *International Journal on Studies in Education (IJonSE), 3*(2). https://doi.org/10.46328/ijonse.49

Yang, D., Tang, Y. M., Hayashi, R., Ra, S., & Lim, C. P. (2022). Supporting inclusive online higher education in developing countries: Lessons learnt from Sri Lanka's university closure. *Education Sciences, 12*(7), 494. https://doi.org/10.3390/educsci12070494

Young, S., & Duncan, H. E. (2014). Online and face-to-face teaching: How do student ratings differ. *MERLOT Journal of Online Learning and Teaching, 10*(1), 70–79.

Yu, Z. (2021). The effects of gender, educational level, and personality on online learning outcomes during the COVID-19 pandemic. *International Journal of Educational Technology in Higher Education, 18*(1), 14. https://doi.org/10.1186/s41239-021-00252-3

Yuan, L., & Powell, S. J. (2013). MOOCs and open education: Implications for higher education: A white paper. *JISC cetis*, 1–21.

Yu-Fong Chang, J., Wang, L. H., Lin, T. C., Cheng, F. C., & Chiang, C. P. (2021). Comparison of learning effectiveness between physical classroom and online learning for dental education during the COVID-19 pandemic. *Journal of Dental Sciences, 16*(4), 1281–1289. https://doi.org/10.1016/j.jds.2021.07.016

Empowering Youths: Education for Economic Disadvantage in Sabah, Malaysia

Marja Azlima Omar

Abstract In Sabah, Malaysia, economic disadvantage has manifested in the educational opportunities afforded to the young, thereby influencing the population's skill development and future economic outlook. Indeed, the following paper deals with the imperative need for targeted education strategies to empower economically disadvantaged youths. The main objective of this study is to assess current programs and initiatives related to enhancing educational access and digital skills for financially disadvantaged youth in Sabah and to provide actionable recommendations on how such efforts could be further improved. In this vein, the methodology will combine quantitative data analysis on educational outcomes and program effectiveness with qualitative case studies of successful community-based and technology-driven initiatives. These will involve government reports, NGO records, and interviews with participants and stakeholders in the various programs. Considering the above, the impacts on educational attainment and economic empowerment in government initiatives, community-based programs, institutional partnerships, and technology-driven solutions will be varied. Whereas significant gains were registered in the study, infrastructural, resource allocation, and digital literacy challenges were also observed to persist. Successful programs include targeted scholarships and technology integration at schools, which have significant positive outcomes in improved education and employability outcomes. This paper adds to the debate of empowering education by highlighting effective strategies and areas that require improvement; it also gives policy recommendations to enhance access to education and utilize technology to leverage disadvantaged youths in Sabah. Its findings would be beneficial in offering valuable lessons drawn from addressing educational inequalities and promoting economic development through education to which many policymakers, educators, and community leaders are committed.

M. A. Omar (✉)
Universiti Malaysia Sabah, Kota Kinabalu, Malaysia
e-mail: mazlima@ums.edu.my

L. O. Yesufu, P. N. E. Nohuddin (eds.), *Technology for Societal Transformation*,
https://doi.org/10.1007/978-981-96-1721-0_17

1 Introduction

In Sabah, Malaysia, economic disadvantage is still one of the most substantial barriers to social mobility and economic development (Rahim, 2015). Special features of the state include a highly diversified geography and significant socio-economic disparities, making it even more difficult than elsewhere to ensure that young people have equal education opportunities. Most rural parts of Sabah lack infrastructure and educational resources, which is evident from their academic performance, and this creates a big divide between the urban and rural populations. For the youth in these economically deprived areas, education has the potential to help them break out of the poverty cycle and provide support for the better economic prospects that youths have in these areas.

Indeed, education provides a vital lever for youths to counteract the disadvantages wrought by their economic conditions by acquiring essential capabilities and skills that would pave the way for one's participation in and benefit from the increasingly digital and knowledge-based economy. However, youths from economically disadvantaged backgrounds in Sabah face many systemic barriers. These barriers include minimal exposure to modern technologies, a lack of access to digitized learning opportunities, and inadequate quality education. These challenges are essential to success in today's global economy (Jafar et al., 2022). This undoubtedly reduces the capacity of poor people to contribute fully both culturally and socioeconomically, not only to their personal development but also to the economic growth and social advancement of a state (Daily Express, 2024a; Fang et al., 2022).

The more Malaysia links to the digital economy, the more significant the gap in digital literacy and technological access among the less fortunate youth of Sabah. In light of the discussed challenges, this paper will strive to explore ways of developing better-empowered youth from economically disadvantaged backgrounds through education. This study evaluates the functionality of various programs and initiatives to establish better digital competencies and technical skills for improved educational outcomes, especially in marginalized communities.

This research aims to assess the effectiveness and efficiency of ongoing educational endeavors and highlight shortcomings. The paper has analyzed governmental and non-governmental programs, such as targeted scholarships and technology integration at schools, to develop appropriate policies to help provide equitable education. It also considers how targeted interventions, such as digital literacy initiatives and technological resource allocation, can be better addressed to meet the specific needs of Sabah's youth.

This paper offers practical recommendations that could help improve the educational outcomes of Sabah's disadvantaged youth. Given modern economic imperatives, particularly the increasing demand for digitally competent workers, this study also aims to contribute to the broader discussion of youth empowerment and economic development in Malaysia (Krauss et al., 2022).

2 Literature Review

2.1 Economic Disadvantage in Sabah

Sabah is one of Malaysia's most economically diverse states, comprising affluent urban areas besides poor rural communities. Various economic disparities are reflected in every aspect of the state, even in the income distribution, which largely falls below the poverty line. As per the statistics provided by the government, Sabah still tops the poverty chart in Malaysia, and it is affecting rural areas disproportionately because of economic disadvantage (Sang et al., 2022).

These are some of the causes of Sabah's economic problems. Geographical isolation is a substantial contributing factor because many rural communities are inaccessible, making constructing much-needed roads and health and educational facilities difficult (Samat & Elhadary, 2016). Inadequate infrastructure adds to the economic disparity between the towns and the countryside because, with limited access, job opportunities, markets, and social services become restricted to such areas.

Additionally, a large fraction of the population living in rural areas relies on subsistence farming, which is highly vulnerable to economic fluctuations, shifting weather patterns, and lack of access to improved agricultural technology (Snodgrass, 1999). Since there is no economic diversification in these areas, this perpetuates poverty and reduces social mobility.

This has led to impacts on education access and quality. Most rural schools need more basic resources like accredited teachers, facilities, and learning materials. Therefore, such schools need better educational attainment among their students. This discontinuity between economic and educational realms perpetuates poverty since the less educated find it hard to get well-paid work in the formal economy (Loganathan et al., 2023).

2.2 Educational Disparities

While resources and infrastructures are highly unequal, the level of educational attainment in Sabah may be highly polarized between the city and the countryside. Facilities in rural schools are often inadequate, such as outdated and/or insufficient classrooms, a lack of technological equipment, and poorly maintained infrastructures. These challenges hinder the delivery of quality education and contribute to the disparity in educational outcomes. Added to this, schools are also frequently short of qualified teachers because so few are willing to work in remote areas due to issues of professional development and living conditions in isolated areas (Perman, 2021).

This disparity is further compounded by limited access to higher education. Rural Sabahan youths faced difficulties pursuing post-secondary education due to geographic distances and financial barriers. Most rural families needed help to afford the tuition fees and transportation costs, among other additional costs, leading to continued low enrollments in colleges and universities (Sawai et al., 2023). This situation is always emotionally debilitating and further cripples the youths of rural areas by demoralizing them in their pursuit of attaining the essential skills and qualifications for better, more stable, and higher-paying employment. The psychological toll of these challenges cannot be overstated, as it affects the motivation and self-esteem of these youths.

In this respect, educational gaps for young people with an economically disadvantaged background mean limited skill development and economic growth chances. Without quality schooling and vocational training, too many are barred from contributing meaningfully to today's economy and gaining the skills needed to navigate it—perhaps most urgently in the technology and digital industries. Because the global economy is ever-increasingly reliant on acquiring digital competencies, there is an uphill fight for youth to realize employable opportunities (MIDA, 2023).

Addressing these disparities calls for specific, targeted interventions beyond providing basic infrastructure. Efforts should include improving the quality of education and access to digital resources. This would provide opportunities for rural schools to embrace digital literacy, better equip teachers, and thereby make scholarships or financial support toward higher education available, eventually bridging the educational divide and leading to economic empowerment for the disadvantaged youths of Sabah (The Edge Malaysia, 2010).

3 Strategies for Empowering Youths Through Education

3.1 Government Initiatives and Policies

The government of Malaysia has also embarked on several initiatives to improve learning outcomes, with reduced income inequalities among people with low incomes. Regarding improving this status, one of the most significant initiatives implemented by the government is the Bantuan Prihatin Rakyat, which covers financial assistance to poor-income families; special assistance in educational expenses was provided to cover school needs, tuition fees, and transportation costs. It will relieve the financial burden on the families, increase enrollment, and reduce dropout rates, particularly in the rural areas of Sabah (The Star, 2022).

Some of the government initiatives within Sabah specifically aim to meet the needs of the rural communities. These interventions include infrastructural development in constructing and upgrading rural schools and providing better learning facilities to provide a conducive environment for student learning. Pre-service and in-service teacher training programs have been designed to enhance qualifications and skill levels among teachers, particularly in remote areas where attracting and retaining qualified and competent teachers is challenging. This policy was meant to ensure that this rural group of students received an education paralleled to the urban groups amidst all the odds in geography and economy these children often faced (Marwan et al., 2012).

The National Education Policy further supplements this, as it carries forward the recommendations of the NEP concerning the need for all students to have digital skills for proper response in the global economic environment. The policy embeds technology in the national curriculum, so learners and school leavers from rural and economically disadvantaged backgrounds have the digital competencies needed to compete in the modern workforce. In Sabah, this has translated into initiatives such as the 1BestariNet project, where schools are equipped with high-speed internet access and digital tools to supplement students' learning and better equip them for the digital economy (Daily Express, 2014).

These government initiatives illustrate a more general approach to empowering youths through education by acting on infrastructural barriers that affect access to good quality education and economic ones. Hence, The Malaysian government primarily focuses on equity in education through rural education, teacher quality, and integration of digital skills into the school curriculum to improve opportunities for disadvantaged youths regarding social mobility and economic advancement in Sabah (Tan et al., 2016).

3.2 Community-Based Programs and NGOs

Local NGOs and community-based organizations complement the government's efforts to address issues that militate against the educational outcomes of these disadvantaged youths in Sabah. Organizations at this level often have a better grasp of specific problems affecting the communities in which they operate. Thus, they can formulate targeted interventions that precisely address the unique needs of students from economically challenged regions. Perhaps among the most highly publicized in this space are the scholarships of the Sabah Education Foundation, given out to poor-income families so that their students can pursue higher education or vocational training (Daily Express, 2024b).

Besides financial assistance, community-based programs address skill and vocational training. The significance of vocational programs can be realized when such youths have probably lost their chance to attend traditional academic routes. Such initiatives would equip the students with practical skills applicable to local industries such as agriculture, tourism, and small business management, improving their employability and economic prospects accordingly (Noor et al., 2023).

Other successful community-based programs include after-school and technology workshops to develop digital literacy among underprivileged youth. This type of program intends to close the digital divide for the students through access to computers, internet resources, and digital training. For example, technology workshops often focus on basic computer skills, coding, and digital tools, which are crucial in one's attempts to participate in the current economy. These after-school programs give students extra help with their academics to improve their overall educational performance and, at the same time, build further knowledge of technology (Statti & Torres, 2022).

These involve many programs that require partnerships with local industries and academic institutions through the availability of resources like funding, expertise, and infrastructure. The partnership will help secure stable programs not only to improve current immediate needs in education but also to ensure that the community's long-term growth is achieved. By leveraging community resources, these programs can better address issues like digital illiteracy, limited access to education, and a lack of career opportunities among Sabah's underprivileged youth (Basir, 2024).

3.3 Educational Institutions and Partnerships

Educational institutions in Sabah are playing an increasingly proactive role in collaborating with the private sector to enhance their educational offerings and address the skills gap prevalent in economically disadvantaged communities. These partnerships ensure that educational programs equip students with academic knowledge and practical skills to succeed in the modern workforce. Vocational training centers and polytechnics are at the forefront of these efforts, offering specialized programs that align with industry needs. By focusing on practical, job-oriented training, these institutions provide students with the skills necessary for manufacturing, tourism, and agriculture employment (Wee, 2019).

Partnerships with technology companies have become particularly valuable in recent years, especially as the global economy becomes increasingly digital. These collaborations facilitate access to crucial digital tools and resources, such as computers, software, and high-speed internet, often out of reach for students from disadvantaged backgrounds. Through such partnerships, schools and training centers can integrate technology more fully into their curriculums, enhancing students' digital literacy and preparing them for roles in the digital economy (Muhammad et al., 2024). For instance, collaborations with companies like Microsoft and Google provide schools with the latest educational software and cloud computing platforms, enabling students to engage in more interactive and advanced learning experiences.

Mentorship programs represent another critical aspect of these partnerships. By connecting students with professionals from various industries, these programs offer guidance, career advice, and exposure to real-world work environments. Mentorship helps students understand the pathways to different careers and fosters essential soft skills such as communication, teamwork, and problem-solving, which are highly valued in the workforce (McDonald & Lambert, 2014). These programs often include internships, apprenticeships, and job placement opportunities, providing students with practical experience and a smoother transition into the workforce.

These collaborations between educational institutions and the private sector ensure that the education provided in Sabah is relevant and effective in preparing youths for the demands of the digital workforce. By bridging the skills gap and aligning educational programs with industry needs, these partnerships empower disadvantaged youths with the tools and opportunities necessary for economic advancement and social mobility (Braun et al., 2024).

3.4 Technology-Driven Solutions

Technology-driven solutions will be increasingly adopted to improve education access and outcomes for students in Sabah, especially those who are rural and economically disadvantaged. The use of technology-enhanced solutions to help overcome the failures of the traditional educational system leverages innovative means of offering flexible and remote learning opportunities that can transcend barriers due to geographical constraints and a lack of infrastructure. The Sabah state government's major initiatives include developing the Sabah Smart School project, emphasizing digital tools in enhancing classroom learning and offering students more comprehensive access to educational resources. More specifically, this project assists schools with computers, tablets, and other devices for accessing digital learning tools through interactive learning platforms, allowing teachers and learners to engage with the content more dynamically and meaningfully (The Malay Mail, 2024).

E-learning platforms and mobile applications are also widely adopted to allow students to learn remotely. This is a critical advantage for those living in rural areas far from schools or with inadequate resources. Such platforms offer varied learning modules, video lessons, and interactive quizzes for students to pursue education outside the classroom. Similarly, students in remote parts of Sabah can be equated to enjoy studying at their own pace and time through such platforms as a mitigating factor against the challenges associated with transportation, infrastructure, and teacher shortages (Vanar, 2020).

Apart from conventional forms of digital platforms, advanced technologies using Virtual Reality and Augmented Reality are being tried out in the development of learning experiences that can raise the level of engagement and understanding among students for diverse subjects (Nguyen & Dang, 2017). For instance, VR can simulate scientific experiments or historical events; students can study them interactively in three dimensions. AR makes learning materials more interactive by overlaying digital information in the real world, thus enhancing lessons in subjects like biology, geography, and engineering. These technologies bring about possibilities that might be taught to students, especially rural ones, that would otherwise require special equipment or field trips (Muzyleva et al., 2021).

This will enhance learning and create a way to bridge the digital divide for the future, where students must have some level of digital literacy and technical skills. Through this presentation of technology-enhanced learning, the education system in Sabah can better equip its students to handle the demands of a modern economy and promote inclusiveness whereby even the most disadvantaged students can access quality education and opportunities for growth (Said et al., 2013).

4 Impact Assessment

4.1 Measuring Success

It requires an integrated approach to assessing effectiveness through quantitative and qualitative analysis. The quantitative indicators that can be used in performance measurement for a program include graduation rates, acquisition of skills, and job placement. These indicate whether students attain the required knowledge and skills to uplift their socio-economic status. For instance, employment rates upon program completion directly measure how well the students have been prepared for the job market through educational interventions. Indeed, studies have recorded that programs on digital skills development in Sabah have paid dividends in the form of enhanced employability, economic empowerment, and even entrepreneurship, in some cases among beneficiaries (Chan, 2024).

Qualitative evaluation is another significant aspect of monitoring the far-reaching benefits accrued from the program. Student feedback, teacher evaluations, and case studies can be employed to assess personal and social changes occurring as part of these programs. These measurements often reflect how education programs introduce individual changes, such as differences in confidence, aspirations, and economic independence. By incorporating quantitative and qualitative data, educators and policymakers can fully understand program results and make informed modifications to enhance overall effectiveness (Outhwaite et al., 2019).

4.2 Success Stories and Case Studies

Success stories abounded, from basic to the numerous educational programs in Sabah, demonstrating the tangible benefits of targeted interventions. A particularly successful example was the Sabah Youth Empowerment Program, which equipped hundreds of young people with computer skills training that improved employability and stirred entrepreneurial passions. Courses include coding, graphic design, and digital marketing skills, which are very much in demand in the modern economy. The program participants go on to find work in local businesses, establish their digital startups, or freelance in the global digital marketplace (Daily Express, 2023a).

Among other factors, participant testimonials show the transformative impact these programs can have. Most students report an astonishingly increased level of confidence and independence, emphasizing how digital literacy has previously opened new career paths beyond their reach. These success stories prove the effectiveness of such programs and motivating examples for other youths in similar circumstances. For this reason, technology integration in education has been a critical differentiator in empowering disadvantaged youths to overcome economic challenges and contribute toward Sabah's growing digital economy (Daily Express, 2023b).

4.3 Challenges and Lessons Learned

While there have been marked successes, areas still need attention to ensure that relevant educational programs are effectively implemented, particularly in rural areas. The main challenges include a general lack of funds, which automatically cuts down the scale and reach of programs (Busst, n.d.). An example is that while technological resources and infrastructure may be provided, maintenance costs become prohibitive, especially in remote communities (Mohamad & Ali, 2017). The logistical barriers to accessing these areas add to the challenge of delivering educational services to students since these children are regularly inaccessible due to poor transportation and communication (Yakin et al., 2023).

Besides, technological adoption differs in terms of depth among students and educators. Some far-off area teachers and students might need more exposure or acquaintance to use digital tools, which would otherwise remain confined to limited benefits only. This calls for more significant interventions in training and support so that educators and students can reap maximum benefits from the availability of resources at hand (Muslihudin et al., 2023).

Conclusions that can be drawn from these key lessons relate to the success of such programs: community involvement allows a program to be accepted at the grassroots level, ensuring continuity. In addition, when community leaders and local stakeholders are actively involved, programs are more effective and closer to citizens' needs. Another crucially important lesson is that one has to evaluate and adapt continuously. Programs should be flexible and responsive to changed circumstances and emerging challenges. They have to make adjustments in their approach through regular feedback and assessment. Finally, programs in partnerships among stakeholders are government agencies, NGOs, and the private sector, pooling resources and expertise in various ways.

5 Policy Recommendations

5.1 Enhancing Access to Education

Improvement in access to education in Sabah should be affected by the disbursement of policies that consider the difference in challenges presented by rural and economically less privileged populations. Infrastructure expansion is needed in rural areas for equal opportunity in education. These include building new schools, improving transport systems, and access to basic amenities, including libraries, technology labs, and clean water. Additionally, through scholarships, grants, and subsidies, financial assistance to low-income families will offset the cost of education for the populace and have more children regularly attending school.

Equitable resource distribution between rural and urban areas should also ensure that students in the most economically underprivileged locations receive the same level of education as their urban counterparts. This will be realized by strengthening efforts in rural schools by providing textbooks, learning materials, and technological equipment to bridge the education gap. Salary bonuses, house allowances, and professional development offered to teachers working in disadvantaged and rural areas act as an incentive to bridge the gap between qualified teachers and improve educational standards.

5.2 Strengthening Community and Institutional Support

Success will include developing stronger partnerships among community-based organizations, educational institutions, and the private sector to increase educational programs. A collective impact will result in more effective programs, improved resource use, and more sustainable results. These partnerships will allow them to pool resources and expertise effectively to meet local challenges.

This would also involve supporting local NGOs and community groups in their educative work, maximizing the effects of the many programs already assisted. These organizations generally have intensive roots at the grassroots levels of the areas they operate within, where they are optimally placed to carry out educative programs that target underprivileged youths. Government policies should promote such partnerships through finance, logistical backup, and policies that allow cooperation between learning institutions, NGOs, and companies.

5.3 Leveraging Technology for Educational Advancement

Expanding the use of technology in education is one important strategy that could lead to better educational outcomes in the State of Sabah, especially for rural and disadvantaged groups. However, to achieve this end, the digital divide must be addressed in several places by ensuring all students have computers, internet connectivity, and other devices needed to access digital learning platforms.

Besides, the investment in developing digital infrastructure should be used for its bridging, including expanding access to broadband in rural areas and equipping schools with state-of-the-art technological tools. An early-age promotion of digital literacy will be important to prepare the student for navigating and succeeding in a more and more digital economy. Besides, integrating technology into all levels of education will provide a unique learning experience for learners, enabling them to have hands-on, interactive experiences in developing the skills required in the future workforce.

Implementing the above policy recommendations allows Sabah to empower its disadvantaged youths more through education, providing them with various tools and abilities that will enable them to rise beyond economic barriers and succeed in the new era.

6 Conclusion

This paper has explored various possibilities through which empowerment through education could be provided to economically disadvantaged youths in Sabah. It has highlighted government initiatives, community-based programs, institutional partnerships, and technology-driven solutions as some of the most important interventions to address educational inequity and promote digital inclusion to bridge the gap between rural and urban education prospects toward the success of youths from economically challenged backgrounds.

These strategies will improve educational outcomes and increase opportunities for disadvantaged youth in Sabah. The next stage involves assessing the educational programs' longer term impacts and examining emerging technologies and new approaches to improving digital literacy. This will further refine existing interventions and identify other areas where support is needed.

The developing phase needs more investment in education and technology, and much community and institutional support is required for its lasting empowerment and economic benefits. Education is a vital tool to help overcome economic disadvantages, create social mobility, and provide an equitably balanced society. Suppose comprehensive strategies are implemented in the design of emerging trends. In that case, Sabah has every potential to create a more inclusive educational environment that would equip the state's youths with what they need to be beneficially competitive in the digital economy. With continuous commitment and collaboration by the government, educational institutions, NGOs, and the private sector, Sabah can empower its youths to contribute toward a more prosperous and resilient future. These coming-together acts of improving education will uplift not just individual lives but broader socio-economic developments of the state.

References

Basir, E. K. (2024, September 24). Championing education for marginalised children in Sabah. *Bernama* [online]. Retrieved October 10, 2024, from https://www.bernama.com/en/bfokus/news.php?id=2343669

Braun, G., Rikala, P., Järvinen, M., Hämäläinen, R., & Stahre, J. (2024). Bridging skill gaps–A systematic literature review of strategies for industry. In *Sustainable production through advanced manufacturing, intelligent automation and work integrated learning* (pp. 687–696).

Busst, N. (n.d.). Not enough development funds for East Malaysia says activists. Retrieved September 21, 2024, from https://www.freemalaysiatoday.com/category/nation/2024/10/19/not-enough-development-funds-for-east-malaysia-say-activists/

Chan, J. (2024, August 6). Hajiji: Sabah set to become technology hub as it targets tech driven economy. *The Malay Mail* [online]. Retrieved September 21, 2024, from https://www.malaymail.com/news/malaysia/2024/08/06/hajiji-sabah-set-to-become-technology-hub-as-it-targets-tech-driven-economy/146198

Daily Express. (2014, April 30). 1Bestari net bridges education gap in Sabah. *Daily Express*. Retrieved September 21, 2024, from https://www.dailyexpress.com.my/news/89428/1bestarinet-bridges-edu-gap-in-sabah-jame/

Daily Express. (2023a, March 7). RM16.4 million for youth development programme. *Daily Express*. Retrieved September 21, 2024, from https://www.dailyexpress.com.my/news/208805/rm16-4-million-for-youth-development-programme

Daily Express. (2023b, February 17). Three focus areas to boost Sabah education. *Borneo Post Online* [online]. Retrieved September 21, 2024, from https://www.dailyexpress.com.my/news/208805/rm16-4-million-for-youth-development-programme/

Daily Express. (2024a, February 4). Education struggle for poor Sabah natives. *Daily Express* [Online]. https://www.dailyexpress.com.my/read/5454/education-struggle-for-poor-sabah-natives/

Daily Express. (2024b, September 12). State education fund increased to RM113 million. *Daily Express* [online]. Retrieved September 21, 2024, from https://www.dailyexpress.com.my/news/241766/state-education-scholarship-fund-increased-to-rm113-million-/

Fang, Y. X., Gill, S. S., Kunasekaran, P., Rosnon, M. R., Talib, A. T., & Abd Aziz, A. (2022). Digital divide: An inquiry on the native communities of Sabah. *Societies, 12*(6), 148.

Jafar, A., Dollah, R., Sakke, N., Mapa, M. T., Hua, A. K., Eboy, O. V., Joko, E. P., Hassan, D., & Hung, C. V. (2022). Assessing the challenges of E-learning in Malaysia during the pandemic of covid-19 using the geo-spatial approach. *Scientific Reports, 12*(1), 17316.

Krauss, S. E., Zeldin, S., Abdullah, H., Ortega, A., Ali, Z., Ismail, I. A., & Ariffin, Z. (2022). Malaysian youth associations as places for empowerment and engagement. *Children and Youth Services Review, 112*, 104939.

Loganathan, T., Ong, Z. L., Hassan, F., Chan, Z. X., & Majid, H. A. (2023). Barriers and facilitators to education access for marginalised non-citizen children in Malaysia: A qualitative study. *PLoS One, 18*(6), e0286793.

Marwan, A., Sumintono, B., & Mislan, N. (2012). Revitalizing rural schools: A challenge for Malaysia. *Educational Issues, Research and Policies, 1*(1), 172–188.

McDonald, S., & Lambert, J. (2014). The long arm of mentoring: A counterfactual analysis of natural youth mentoring and employment outcomes in early careers. *American Journal of Community Psychology, 54*, 262–273.

MIDA. (2023). Sabah ramping up digitalisation efforts to maximise digital economy potential. Retrieved September 20, 2024, from https://www.mida.gov.my/mida-news/sabah-ramping-up-digitalisation-efforts-to-maximise-digital-economy-potential/

Mohamad, M., & Ali, M. M. (2017). Inequality in education: Experience of critical pedagogy and community engagement with orang Sungai in Paitan, Sabah. *ASEAN Journal of Community Engagement, 1*(2), 1–24.

Muhammad, I., Reskiawan, B., & Arsyad, M. (2024). Technology integration in education curriculum. *Journal of Education Global, 2*(1), 1–9.

Muslihudin, M., Hussin, R., Wulan, T. R., & Santoso, J. (2023). The role of non-government organizations in the education of migrant workers' children in Sabah Malaysia. *KnE Social Sciences*, 363–373.

Muzyleva, I., Yazykova, L., Gorlach, A., & Gorlach, Y. (2021). Augmented and virtual reality technologies in education. In *2021 1st International Conference on Technology Enhanced Learning in Higher Education (TELE)*, June (pp. 99–103). IEEE.

Nguyen, V. T., & Dang, T. (2017). Setting up virtual reality and augmented reality learning environment in unity. In *2017 IEEE International Symposium on Mixed and Augmented Reality (ISMAR-Adjunct)* (pp. 315–320). IEEE.

Noor, M. S. M., Mohamad, M., & Paimin, A. N. (2023). Implementation of skilled training programs at vocational college: A view of the instructors' perspectives. *Online Journal for TVET Practitioners, 8*(3), 125–131.

Outhwaite, L. A., Gulliford, A., & Pitchford, N. J. (2019). A new methodological approach for evaluating the impact of educational intervention implementation on learning outcomes. *International Journal of Research & Method in Education, 43*(3), 225–242. https://doi.org/10.1080/1743727X.2019.1657081

Perman, A. A.. (2021). *Teaching science and mathematics in a rural area: A case study of Sk Sabur, Sabah, Malaysia.*
Rahim, S. B. A. (2015). Economic inequality in Malaysia: The enemy within. In *Proceedings of International Conference on Development and Socio Spatial Inequalities* (pp. 82–101).
Said, M. N. H. M., Hassan, J., Idris, A. R., Zahiri, M. A., Forret, M., & Eames, C. (2013). Technology-enhanced classroom learning community for promoting tertiary ICT education learning in Malaysia. In *PBL across cultures* (p. 326).
Samat, N., & Elhadary, Y. A. (2016). *Tackling poverty issues in Malaysia: A spatial dimensional approach.*
Sang, L. T., Qi, C. J., Beatrice, L. F. Y., & Idris, R. (2022). Income differentials in Sabah, Malaysia. In *Demographic and socioeconomic changes in Sabah* (p. 115).
Sawai, J. P., Ibrahim, H., Nawi, N. H. M., Latif, R., Moi, S. N., Abdullah, S., & Sofian, F. A. (2023). The readiness of B40 Sabah rural students to enter university: A preliminary overview. *Journal of Southeast Asia Psychology (SAPJ), 11*(2), 22–22.
Snodgrass, D. R. (1999). Income inequality and poverty in Malaysia. *Pacific Affairs, 72*(3), 462.
Statti, A., & Torres, K. M. (2022). Digital literacy: The need for technology integration and its impact on learning and engagement in community school environments. *Peabody Journal of Education, 95*(1), 90–100.
Tan, S. C., Ho, C. M., & Pang, V. (2016). Why has education inequality widened in Sabah, Malaysia? *Economics Bulletin, AccessEcon, 36*(1), 569–575.
The Edge Malaysia. (2010, September 15). Malaysia Day focus: Education key to bridging east-west gap. *The Edge Malaysia*. [Online]. Retrieved September 21, 2024, from https://theedgemalaysia.com/article/malaysia-day-focus-education-key-bridging-east-west-gap
The Malay Mail. (2024, June 14). Education D-G: Five primary schools in Sabah chosen for digital school pilot project. *The Malay Mail* [online]. Retrieved September 21, 2024, from https://www.malaymail.com/news/malaysia/2024/06/14/education-d-g-five-primary-schools-in-sabah-chosen-for-digital-school-pilot-project/139811
The Star. (2022, November 15). Govt cash aid to ease people's financial burden. *The Star* [online]. Retrieved September 22, 2024, from https://www.thestar.com.my/news/nation/2022/11/15/govt-cash-aid-to-ease-peoples-financial-burden
Vanar, M. (2020). Better IT facilities needed in rural areas to meet E-learning needs says Joanna Rampas. *The Star.* Retrieved September 21, 2024, from https://www.thestar.com.my/news/nation/2020/05/19/better-it-facilities-needed-in-rural-areas-to-meet-e-learning-needs-says-joanna-rampas
Wee, T. C. (2019). *Examining the mediating role of employee job engagement on employee retention among gen Y in Malaysian manufacturing sectors* [Doctoral dissertation, Universiti Utara Malaysia].
Yakin, H. S. M., Jawing, E., & Januin, J. (2023). Digital poverty in the endemic era: A case study of the Bajau-Sama Community in Sabah of East Malaysia. *Journal of Namibian Studies: History Politics Culture, 35*, 4650–4664.

Smart Cities and Sustainability Awareness: Using Animated Infographics to Drive Sustainable Development

Zahidah Abd Kadir and Safurah Abdul Jalil

Abstract As smart cities increasingly rely on information technology to foster sustainable development, innovative communication tools become crucial in engaging citizens and promoting environmentally conscious behavior. This chapter explores how animated infographics, widely disseminated on social media platforms, can contribute to sustainability awareness in smart cities. Drawing upon the National Environmental Education and Awareness Strategy launched by the UAE, the study showcases the potential of visual media to educate the public on energy consumption and conservation, leveraging the SUCCES framework for effective communication. The Green Home Mission case study illustrates how infographics simplify complex information, making it accessible and engaging through digital media channels. By integrating such media within the broader context of smart cities, this chapter demonstrates how targeted campaigns using animated infographics can enhance citizen engagement and foster sustainable urban development. The effectiveness of these tools is supported by survey data, highlighting their role in spreading "sticky" messages that drive behavior change.

1 Background

Smart cities are at the forefront of leveraging information technology to enhance urban living and foster sustainable development. By integrating digital solutions and advanced communication tools, these cities aim to create more efficient, livable, and environmentally friendly urban environments. Research indicates that the successful development of smart and sustainable cities requires an inclusive approach

Z. A. Kadir (✉)
Higher Colleges of Technology, Sharjah, UAE
e-mail: zabdkadir@hct.ac.ae

S. A. Jalil
Higher Colleges of Technology, Ras Al Khaimah, UAE
e-mail: sabduljalil@hct.ac.ae

L. O. Yesufu, P. N. E. Nohuddin (eds.), *Technology for Societal Transformation*,
https://doi.org/10.1007/978-981-96-1721-0_18

that integrates smart people, effective policies, and advanced technologies, emphasizing the importance of public awareness and engagement (Yigitcanlar et al., 2019). Effective communication tools play a crucial role in engaging citizens and promoting environmentally conscious behavior. One powerful tool in this context is digital media content, particularly animated infographics. Animated infographics can help simplify complex information using visual formats like graphs, diagrams, and statistics, making it much easier to understand and remember. Their ability to use concise text, along with icons, images, illustrations, and multimedia elements makes them ideal for distributing information across various digital platforms. The widespread use of social media, which has now become an integral part of everyday life, further supports the rapid dissemination of digital content to target audiences. Organizations, including governments and NGOs, have effectively used social media as a platform to spread information and raise public awareness (Osatuyi, 2013; Rapada et al., 2021).

The UAE State of Energy Report 2015 projected that energy demand would rise by 9% annually due to rapid economic and population growth. In 2013, residents consumed about 20–30 kilowatt-hours of electricity daily, resulting in a total demand of 105 billion kilowatt-hours, making the UAE one of the highest per capita electricity consumers globally (UAE Government, 2018). In line with the UAE government's National Environmental Education and Awareness strategy, which seeks to enhance community commitment to sustainability and environmental protection, it is essential to foster active engagement and accountability for positive change. To address these challenges, the study aims to: (1) create an effective animated infographic to raise awareness about energy saving and sustainability, (2) develop engaging social media content to communicate energy-saving practices, and (3) assess the effectiveness of the animated infographic and social media posts in influencing energy-saving behaviors. The expected outcome of the animated infographic is to promote sustainability awareness within the community.

2 Literature Review

2.1 Animated Infographics for Enhance Engagement

The digital media content, presented as a video explainer, combines infographics by integrating information or data displayed through text, motion, and graphics, accompanied by audio narration and sound. Formally, Infographics are visual representations of data and ideas, designed to simplify complex content for easy communication and quick comprehension (Smiciklas, 2012). As a result, infographics offer numerous benefits as a medium for conveying messages, simplifying scientific information when visually appealing data is effectively designed. They play a crucial role in raising awareness and providing knowledge to the target audience in the digital age. According to Coates and Ellisson (2014) presenting information in a clear, graphical format captivates users, as the engaging visuals make it more appealing to view. Furthermore, Bateman et al. (2010) suggest that when well-designed visuals are presented, they enable the brain to process the information upon first exposure, allowing the content to be understood even before reading any text. As a result, visual learning can provide more engaging content and offer a distinctive approach to enhancing comprehension and learning (Lankow et al., 2012).

Infographics can be classified into three formats: static infographics, interactive infographics, and animated infographics, each presenting various multimedia components (Lankow et al., 2012). Animated infographics, which incorporate motion graphics, combine text, motion, and graphics, often enhanced with sound and narration (Freeman, 2018). Unlike static infographics, animated infographics provide the advantage of offering additional and unique engagement for the audience. Their dynamic nature can improve audience comprehension and learning (Liao & Lonsdale, 2018).

2.2 *Design Guidelines for Effective Animated Infographics*

Multimedia learning, grounded in the theory named cognitive load allowed to process information when two channels of auditory and visual are involved (Clark & Mayer, 2011; Mayer & Moreno, 1998). Key criteria for multimedia content include well-organized visuals, effective use of color, interactivity, high-quality graphics, and effective visual compositions. The design of this animated infographics is crucial because poor design can result in less engaging and less appealing messages. According to Clarke (2001) multimedia products must adhere to specific design guidelines to ensure effective content delivery. Infographics, by utilizing concise text and incorporating elements such as vector images and video that employ creative approach can be adapted into various digital formats to reach a broader audience. Previous research on design guidelines for infographics is limited, primarily focusing on the presentation of numerical data and the use of text in conveying information. Additionally, there is a lack of empirical studies exploring the design of animated infographics to assist in information recall and understanding complex contexts. However, dos Santos Lonsdale et al. (2019) have compiled a set of principles for infographics that can guide the visual composition, particularly for organizing information in the online platform. Table 1 describes the design principles used as a framework for designing such communication.

3 Methodology

This study conducted a mixed-method approach that involved: (a) planning the conceptual storytelling by utilizing the literature for a sustainability focus called "Green Home Mission," inspired by viral marketing principles; (b) producing creative

Table 1 Design guidelines for animated infographic (dos Santos Lonsdale et al., 2019)

Elements	Key points
Animated infographics	Readable text should be minimal
	San-serif style can ensure legibility with no more than two font types
	Use different sizes, contrast, and spacing to differentiate titles from body text Use an average of three to five colors when choosing a color palette and ensure the mood and tone reflect the message and purpose
	Music and narration can assist auditory viewers
	Apply the principles of motion design
Online information for social media post	Limit to two typefaces with different scales and weights for titles and body content
	Reading speed can be improved if characters range between 75 and 100 per line
	Highlight important information with bold text for emphasis
	Align text to the left
	Consistently use color contrast for text and images in a logical manner to ensure user satisfaction and trust
	Provide white space to increase clarity and reduce cluttered information

animated infographics with a focus on energy efficiency and conservation; and (c) evaluating the video. This study aims to enhance the creative approach in designing animated infographics as tools for raising awareness about sustainability.

3.1 The SUCCES Framework

The literature review focused on the viral marketing framework to identify effective strategies for making sustainability awareness messages "sticky" through animated infographics. This framework, known as SUCCES, stands for Simple, Unexpected, Credible, Concrete, Emotion, and Story. It serves as a guideline for developing content that is engaging and memorable.

3.2 The Creative Production

A three-minute animated infographic was thoroughly developed and aims to raise awareness about energy efficiency and conservation. The video titled *Green Home Mission* was uploaded to the YouTube platform. The video URL can be viewed at: https://www.youtube.com/watch?v=Twhm6BYTS3E. Interviews with four experts in sustainability fields and data gathered from media resources published online by the Sharjah Electricity, Water, and Gas Authority (SEWA) were used to inform the creative production. To ensure that the main idea sticks and is easy to remember, this infographic's content also considers the framework suggested by viral marketing literature.

3.3 *Evaluation*

The methods used to evaluate the creative production were based on data gathered from an online survey, with questions that were developed and reviewed based on existing literature.

4 Findings

The following sections explain the implementation of the creative production stages undertaken in this research project.

4.1 *Development of the Animated Infographics Video*

In the development of creative production for the animated infographics, the content design employed the SUCCES framework from viral marketing strategies. This framework is believed to make ideas memorable and sticky (Heath & Heath, 2007). The acronym SUCCES stands for Simple, Unexpected, Concrete, Credible, Emotion, and Story. Moreover, according to Berger and Milkman (2012) when six key attributes—namely, social currency, triggers, emotion, public, and story—are used, they can make the presented idea both compelling and contagious. Therefore, by integrating the SUCCES elements from viral marketing communication, the development of creative production is believed to ensure the content is compelling in raising public awareness. Heath and Heath (2007) highlight that when SUCCES elements are integrated, they lead to understandable and memorable information. As a result, this can influence the audience by using social currency, triggering them, touching their emotions, providing practical value, and increasing public visibility. Fries et al. (2020) found that when content resonates with individuals, it increases the chances of sharing the post and discuss issues within their social network circle. Thus, the sticky idea can engage the target audience, capture attention, and make them understand and remember the message, resulting in a call to action for the viewer.

4.1.1 Simple

To effectively communicate a message, it is essential to keep the idea focused, simple, and clear, following key design principles for compelling content (Picazo-Vela et al., 2013). To avoid confusion, the core message must be simple and clear, narrowed down to its essential point. This allows the audience to easily understand it without confusion, enabling them to discuss its implications on sustainability. For example, the main idea of sustainability awareness is to demonstrate how the cause and effect of excessive energy consumption can impact the global environment. By encouraging individuals to change their habits at home and raising awareness, they can contribute to sustainability efforts.

4.1.2 Unexpected

To capture the audience's attention, content must incorporate an element of surprise and stimulate curiosity, encouraging them to pause and seek more information from the message (Heath & Heath, 2008). To grab the audience's attention and spark curiosity, the unexpected principle presents surprising elements by showing the severe consequences that can impact and pose threats to other issues, such as climate change, pollution, and declining personal health (Chun-sheng et al., 2012). This unexpected revelation sparks curiosity, prompting viewers to compare their existing knowledge with new information they have yet to learn. As a result, it effectively grabs their attention and motivates them to watch the video until the end to gather more information.

4.1.3 Concrete

An effective communication strategy requires delivering a concrete message to facilitate audience learning (Andrews & Shimp, 2017). By employing specific and tangible details, rather than abstract or complex concepts, and by connecting to sensory experiences, the core idea becomes more understandable and easier to remember. In this study, concrete visuals were used to highlight everyday routines, illustrating how energy consumption often goes unnoticed. These visuals, accompanied by text captions, reflect common activities people perform at home. According to Clark and Mayer (2011) words paired with visuals are more likely to be remembered, as the combination allows the audience to process both visual demonstrations and textual information, aiding in memory retention.

4.1.4 Credible

Credibility is key to persuading people to agree with and believe in the communicated idea, particularly regarding energy consumption and conservation for a better environment through sustainability awareness. As Andrews and Shimp (2017) emphasized, effective communication must be believable, either by conveying the message with authority or by providing support to influence the audience in accepting the presented facts. In this study's exemplar work, the researcher ensured the animated infographic was based on reliable sources, enhancing the trustworthiness of the information provided (Nurse et al., 2015).

4.1.5 Emotion

Credibility is linked to the trustworthiness of a message when it reflects real-life situations, allowing people to relate to the content. The creative content of this animated infographic evokes emotions by highlighting the significance of using energy adequately, which can contribute to a healthier environment. The idea becomes easy to remember, making the audience care about the importance of energy saving and leading them to take action. Heath and Heath (2008) pointed out that when the context appeals to a person's interest, it can become a powerful motivator. By offering practical tips as guidelines on what to do and what not to do to reduce monthly electric bills, the content appeals to individuals' rational self-interest, encouraging them to make informed decisions.

4.1.6 Story

The story element involves using simulations or demonstrations to motivate people to take action, as stories inspire individuals to consider how they would respond in similar situations (Heath & Heath, 2008). Mckee (2016), in his book, outlined the classic three-act storytelling structure, which consists of a beginning, middle, and end. In this study's example, the animated infographic follows this storytelling approach, focusing on the crucial use of energy for a better environment. The narrative highlights the goal of reducing electricity bills by 30% in the Sharjah emirate, an initiative led by an authoritative government organization. Practical tips are presented through the animated infographic, helping people connect the message to their daily routines and understand how to take action. To improve the environment, individuals must start by making responsible choices at home.

Table 2 The SUCCES framework applied to the animated infographic video

SUCCES Framework	Energy consumption and conservation context
Simple	Core idea: Excessive energy consumption negatively affects the global environment. Solution: Encourage individuals to modify their household habits, increasing awareness and contributing to sustainability efforts
Unexpected	Highlighting the impact of energy consumption, which poses significant threats to climate change, environmental pollution, and human health (Chun-sheng et al., 2012)
Concrete	Use clear and vivid language with easily digestible details to help the audience understand the message, avoiding abstract or complex terms. The video illustrates everyday activities that many people don't realize consume energy, raising awareness about the importance of energy conservation (Heath & Heath, 2008)
Credible	The animated infographic video effectively presents convincing details by illustrating the cause and effect of energy consumption and conservation (Heath & Heath, 2008)
Emotion	The video clips showcasing the efforts of the UAE and SEWA in promoting energy consumption and conservation evoke a sense of responsibility in the audience. By highlighting practical tips to reduce utility bills, the video taps into basic emotions, encouraging viewers to avoid wasting energy and potentially achieve a 30% reduction in their actual bills (Heath & Heath, 2008)
Story	The animated infographic guides viewers on how to take action by presenting situations that help them respond effectively when faced with similar scenarios in real life. For instance, one clip provides tips on how to conserve water while showering, offering practical advice that can be easily applied in everyday situations (Think Insights, n.d.)

4.2 The Adaptation of SUCCES Principles into Animated Infographics Video

Table 2 describes the method used to incorporate the principles of SUCCES in the animated infographic. The keyframes outline the content analysis from the video to ensure that it integrates SUCCES elements, thereby demonstrating the purpose of each shot created in the video. Keyframe analysis is a valuable method for gaining insight and understanding into the video creation process. Herbert (2016) presents a summary of the keyframe analysis, showcasing how the concepts of sustainability awareness were blended with the SUCCES framework during the creative content production.

Table 3 presents the keyframe analysis, demonstrating how each individual shot aligns with and reinforces the SUCCES framework to make the ideas memorable. A design guideline for the infographic was also incorporated to guide the design solution, as referenced in dos Santos Lonsdale et al. (2019).

Table 3 Keyframe analysis of animated infographics video

<table>
<tr><th>Illustration</th><th>Description</th></tr>
<tr><td>
</td><td>Shot #1
Framework: Simple
Focus to the main issue</td></tr>
<tr><td colspan="2">Description: The shot opens with the title “the green home Mission,” capturing the viewer’s attention and emphasizing the key theme of energy consumption and conservation. A sans-serif font with contrasting colors ensures readability on screen. The shot is accompanied by motivational background music to set the tone and engage auditory learners.
Purpose: To establish the core idea and main focus of the animated infographic right at the start of the video</td></tr>
<tr><td>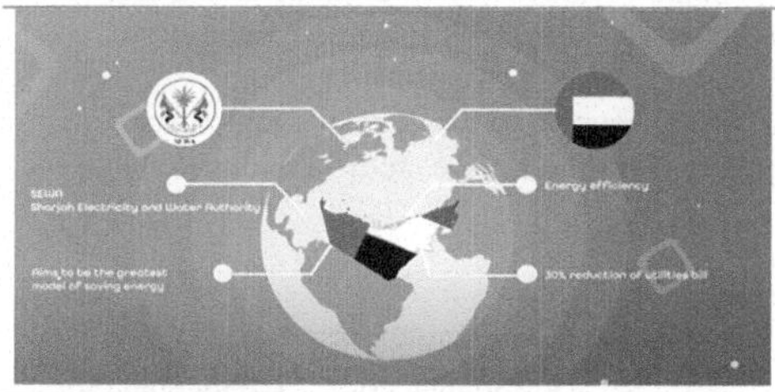
</td><td>Shot #2
Framework: Unexpected and emotion
Create a curiosity for engagement and pay attention</td></tr>
<tr><td colspan="2">Description: The shot transitions to an animation with a narrator explaining the importance of sustainability awareness and the UAE’s efforts in energy consumption and conservation. Practical tips are provided to help reduce utility bills by 30%, aligning with the goals of the Sharjah emirate. This evokes basic emotions in the audience, motivating them to avoid wasting energy and to support the authorities’ goals for energy conservation and a better environment.
Purpose: To spark curiosity in the audience, encouraging them to stay engaged, pause, and absorb the information presented in the video</td></tr>
<tr><td></td><td>Shot #3
Framework: Concrete
Show visual to inform and make audience understand and remember</td></tr>
</table>

(continued)

Table 3 (continued)

Illustration	Description
Description: The video provides an explanation of tips to reduce electricity bills, using visuals paired with short text captions and an audio narrator to convey the message clearly *Purpose*: To offer a concrete element by presenting visuals with easily digestible details, directly relating to the audience's daily routines in energy consumption and conservation.	
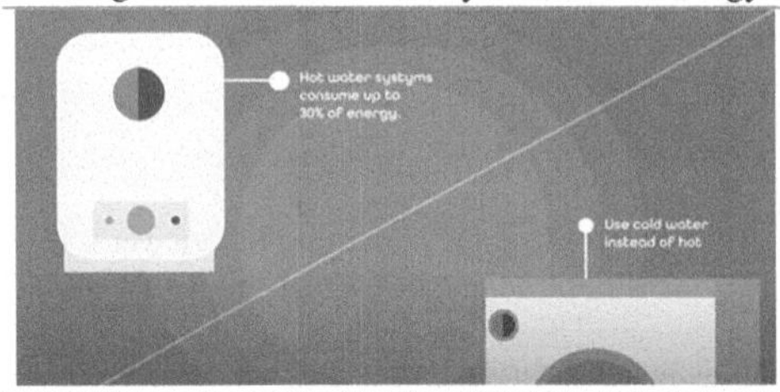	Shot #3 Framework: Credible story people agree and believe
Description: The video demonstrates common household energy usage and explains how small changes in behavior can significantly impact sustainability. By reflecting familiar, real-world situations, the content helps viewers relate and encourages them to take action when they encounter similar scenarios in their own lives. *Purpose*: To build agreement and trust by showing the cause-and-effect relationship between energy consumption and conservation, making the information more credible and actionable for the audience.	

Table 4 Respondents' demographics data

Demography		Frequency (*f*)	Percentage (%)
Gender	Male	5	8.2
	Female	56	91.8
Age	19–22	45	73.8
	23–26	12	19.7
	27–30	3	4.9
	31–34	1	1.6
	>35	0	0
Location	Sharjah	34	55.7
	Ajman	8	13.1
	Umm Al-Quwain	1	1.6
	Dubai	10	16.4
	Ras Al Khaimah	0	0
	Abu Dhabi	6	9.8
	Outside UAE	1	1.6
Knowledge about sustainability	School/university	29	47.5
	Social media	14	23
	News	2	3.3
	Friends and family	13	21.3
	Others	3	4.9

Table 5 Respondents feedback

Item	Frequency (*f*) Percentage (%)								
After watching the video, you will likely to...	1	2	3	4	5	Mean	SD	Mode	Median
Tell someone else about this video	2 3.3	0 0	7 11.5	9 14.8	43 70.5	4.49	0.94	5	5
Share this video with friends on social media (e.g., Facebook)	1 1.6	2 3.3	11 18	7 11.5	40 65.6	4.36	1.00	5	5
Find out more about energy efficiency and consumption	2 3.3	2 3.3	5 8.2	12 19.7	40 65.6	4.40	1.00	5	5
Follow the tips to save light and electricity to reduce 30% of electricity bills	2 3.3	0 0	6 9.8	8 13.1	45 73.8	4.54	0.92	5	5

Note: 1 = Very unlikely, 2 = Unlikely, 3 = Neutral, 4 = Likely, 5 = Very likely

4.3 Evaluation

Table 4 shows that 61 respondents participated in the study, comprising 5 males (8.2%) and 56 females (91.8%). Most participants are aged 19–22 (45 respondents, 73.8%), followed by 23–26 (12 respondents, 19.7%), 27–30 (3 respondents, 4.9%), and 31–34 (1 respondent, 1.6%). In terms of location, 34 respondents (55.7%) are from Sharjah, 10 from Dubai (16.4%), 8 from Ajman (13.1%), 6 from Abu Dhabi (9.8%), 1 from Umm Al-Quwain (1.6%), and 1 from outside UAE (1.6%). Regarding knowledge sources on sustainability, 29 respondents (47.5%) gained their understanding from school or university, 14 respondents (23%) from social media, 13 respondents (21.3%) from friends and family, 2 respondents (3.3%) from the news and 3 respondents (4.9%) from other sources. Overall, the majority of respondents were female and from Sharjah. However, only 23% of respondents obtained knowledge about sustainability from social media.

Table 5 illustrates that after watching the video, respondents reported being most likely to follow the tips for saving on lighting and electricity, aiming to reduce their bills by 30% (M = 4.54, SD = 0.92, Mod = 5, Med = 5). This was followed by respondents expressing a high likelihood of telling others about the video (M = 4.49, SD = 0.94, Mod = 5, Med = 5). The third item shows respondents' intention to further explore energy efficiency and consumption (M = 4.40, SD = 1.00, Mod = 5, Med = 5). Lastly, respondents indicated they would likely share the video with friends on social media (M = 4.36, SD = 1.00, Mod = 5, Med = 5). Notably, the median and mode for all items were 5, indicating that respondents strongly agreed with the actions suggested after watching the animated infographic. This demonstrates that the video had a positive impact on raising sustainability awareness, particularly in the areas of energy consumption and conservation.

Participants were presented with eleven adjectives to describe the video, with three response options: disagree (1), undecided (2), or agree (3). Findings from Table 6 indicate that none of the respondents disagreed with the statements, and

Table 6 Description of the animated infographics video

Item	Frequency (*f*) Percentage (%)						
If you were to describe the video, would you say the video is:	1	2	3	Mean	SD	Mode	Median
Believable	0	11	50	2.81	0.38	3	3
	0	18	82				
Informative	0	8	53	2.86	0.34	3	3
	0	13.1	86.9				
Engaging	0	14	47	2.77	0.42	3	3
	0	23	77				
Motivational	0	13	48	2.78	0.41	3	3
	0	21.3	78.7				
Agree with the importance of sustainability awareness	0	9	52	2.85	0.35	3	3
	0	14.8	85.2				
Memorable	0	17	44	2.72	0.45	3	3
Raise awareness	0	27.9	72.1	2.85	0.35	3	3
Telling information in graphic (infographic)	0	9	52	2.85	0.35	3	3
	0	14.8	85.2				
Concerning/care about reducing electric usage	0	12	49	2.80	0.40	3	3
	0	19.7	80.3				
Trusted information	0	13	48	2.78	0.41	3	3
	0	21.3	78.7				
Agree with the saving electricity to reduce bills	0	10	51	2.83	0.37	3	3
	0	16.4	83.6				

there was a very strong agreement (>80%) that the video was believable, informative, highlighted the importance of sustainability awareness, conveyed information effectively through graphics, emphasized the importance of reducing electricity usage, and promoted agreement to save electricity to lower utility bills. Approximately 78% of viewers found the video to be motivational and to provide trustworthy information. Additionally, 77% reported that the video was engaging, while 72% agreed that it raised awareness about sustainability, particularly in the context of energy consumption and conservation.

5 Conclusion

This study demonstrates that animated infographic videos can contribute to sustainability awareness in smart cities. Designed using the SUCCES framework (Heath & Heath, 2007) these videos can attract attention, trigger emotions, and motivate information sharing. In this study, an animated infographic video was designed using this SUCCES framework as an exemplar and evaluated. The findings indicate a very strong agreement whereby over 80% of the respondents found the video believable, informative, and engaging, while 72% agreed it increased their awareness of sustainability. Moreover, 78% of respondents felt motivated to share the video on social media, further contributing to wider community engagement. This finding is consistent with Fries et al. (2020), who noted that viewers are highly likely to share animated infographics through their social networks using social media platforms. This is crucial for smart cities, where effective communication and citizen participation are key to achieving sustainable development goals. The study also underscores the need for using simple, credible, and visually appealing content, along with a clear storyline, to make sustainability messages resonate and drive behavior change. Providing concrete language that is vivid and incorporates digestible details helps the audience better understand the message, compared to using abstract or complicated terms. Design elements like appropriate fonts and background music were also found to play a crucial role in creating impactful videos for awareness campaigns. Integrating such strategies into smart city initiatives can amplify the impact of public awareness campaigns, fostering a more informed and engaged community that supports sustainable urban development.

References

Andrews, C. J., & Shimp, T. A. (2017). *Advertising, promotion, and other aspects of integrated marketing communications* (10th ed.). Cengage Learning.

Bateman, S., Mandryk, R. L., Gutwin, C., Genest, A., McDine, D., & Brooks, C. (2010). Useful junk? The effects of visual embellishment on comprehension and memorability of charts. *Conference on Human Factors in Computing Systems - Proceedings, 4*, 2573–2582. https://doi.org/10.1145/1753326.1753716

Berger, J., & Milkman, K. L. (2012). What makes online content viral? *Journal of Marketing Research, 49*(2), 192–205. https://doi.org/10.1509/jmr.10.0353

Chun-sheng, Z., Shu-wen, N., & Xin, Z. (2012). Effects of household energy consumption on environment and its influence factors in rural and urban areas. *Energy Procedia, 14*, 805–811. https://doi.org/10.1016/j.egypro.2011.12.1015

Clark, R. C., & Mayer, R. E. (2011). *E-learning and the science of instruction: Proven guidelines for consumers and designers of multimedia learning* (3rd ed.). Pfeiffer.

Clarke, A. (2001). *Designing computer-based learning materials*. Routledge.

Coates, K., & Ellisson, A. (2014). *An introduction to information design*. Laurence King Publishing.

dos Santos Lonsdale, M., et al. (2019). Visualizing the terror threat: The impact of communicating security information to the general public using infographics and motion graphics. *Visible Lang, 53*(2), 37–71. [Online].

Freeman, H. D. (2018). *The moving image workshop*. https://doi.org/10.5040/9781474222471

Fries, S., Cook, J., & Lynes, J. K. (2020). Community-based social marketing in theory and practice: Five case studies of water efficiency programs in Canada. *Social Marketing Quarterly, 26*(4), 325–344. https://doi.org/10.1177/1524500420971170

Heath, C., & Heath, D. (2007). *Made to stick, 336*. https://doi.org/10.1108/07363760810858882

Heath, C., & Heath, D. (2008). Made to stick: Teacher's guide.

Herbert, Z. (2016). *Sight, sound, motion: Applied media aesthetics* (Vol. 40, 8th ed., p. 6). Cengage Learning.

Lankow, J., Ritchie, J., & Crooks, R. (2012). *Infographics: The power of visual storytelling* (p. 272).

Liao, H., & Lonsdale, M. D. S. (2018). Improving obesity prevention among university students through a tailored information design approach. *Information Design Journal, 24*(1), 3–25. https://doi.org/10.1075/idj.24.1.02lon

Mayer, R. E., & Moreno, R. (1998). A cognitive theory of multimedia learning: Implications for design principles. *Annual meeting of the ACM SIGCHI ...* (pp. 1–10).

Mckee, R. (2016). *Dialogue: The art of verbal action for page, stage, and screen*. Hachette.

Nurse, J. R. C., Agrafiotis, I., Goldsmith, M., Creese, S., Price, D., & Jones, G. (2015). Information trustworthiness as a solution to the misinformation problems in social media. *International Conference on Cyber Security for Sustainable Society* (pp. 28–35).

Osatuyi, B. (2013). Information sharing on social media sites. *Computers in Human Behavior, 29*(6), 2622–2631. https://doi.org/10.1016/j.chb.2013.07.001

Picazo-Vela, S., Fernandez-Haddad, M., & Luna-Reyes, L. F. (2013). IT's alive!! Social media to promote public health. *ACM International Conference Proceeding Series* (pp. 111–119) https://doi.org/10.1145/2479724.2479743

Rapada, M. Z., Yu, D. E., & Yu, K. D. (2021). Do social media posts influence consumption behavior towards plastic pollution? *Sustainability (Switzerland), 13*(22), 1–19. https://doi.org/10.3390/su132212334

Smiciklas, M. (2012). The power of infographics: Using pictures to communicate and connect with your audience. In *The power of infographics* (pp. 1–17).

Think Insights. (n.d.). *SUCCESS - How to design messages that stick?* [Online]. https://thinkinsights.net/consulting/success-messages-that-stick/

UAE Government. (2018). *Electricity - The Official Portal of the UAE Government*. [Online]. https://u.ae/en/information-and-services/environment-and-energy/electricity

Yigitcanlar, T., Kamruzzaman, M., Foth, M., Sabatini-Marques, J., da Costa, E., & Ioppolo, G. (2019). *Can cities become smart without being sustainable? A systematic review of the literature*. Elsevier Ltd. https://doi.org/10.1016/j.scs.2018.11.033

The manufacturer's authorised representative in the EU is Springer Nature Customer Service Centre GmbH, Europaplatz 3, 69115 Heidelberg, Germany. If you have any concerns regarding our products, please contact ProductSafety@springernature.com

Printed and bound by CPI Group (UK) Ltd, Croydon, CR0 4YY
01/10/2026
02225925-0015